AMERICAN ECONOMIC DEVELOPMENT SINCE 1945

D0064327

AMERICAN ECONOMIC DEVELOPMENT SINCE 1945

AMERICAN ECONOMIC DEVELOPMENT SINCE 1945: GROWTH, DECLINE AND REJUVENATION

Samuel Rosenberg

First published 2003 by
PALGRAVE MACMILLAN
Houndmills, Basingstoke, Hampshire RG21 6XS and
175 Fifth Avenue, New York, N.Y. 10010
Companies and representatives throughout the world

PALGRAVE MACMILLAN is the global academic imprint of the Palgrave Macmillan division of St. Martin's Press, LLC and of Palgrave Macmillan Ltd. Macmillan® is a registered trademark in the United States, United Kingdom and other countries. Palgrave is a registered trademark in the European Union and other countries.

ISBN 0–333–34533–9 hardback
ISBN 0–333–34534–7 paperback

This book is printed on paper suitable for recycling and made from fully managed and sustained forest sources.

A catalogue record for this book is available from the British Library.

A catalog record for this book is available from the Library of Congress.

10   9   8   7   6   5   4   3   2   1
12   11   10   09   08   07   06   05   04   03

Printed and bound in Great Britain by
Creative Print & Design (Wales), Ebbw Vale

To Monique, Stephanie and Sophie

Contents

Preface

This book provides a historical analysis of the economic development of the United States since 1945. It addresses key issues such as macroeconomic trends and policies, the development of business–labor relations, the evolution of social and labor policies, and the changing role of the United States in the world economy. Three post Second World War phases are examined. The first is the creation of an institutional framework which set the stage for prosperity in the United States after the Second World War. It was based on a limited, though growing, governmental role in stabilizing and fostering the growth of the economy and protecting individuals from market competition, a limited conflict between business and labor, and the country's international economic and political dominance. The second is the undermining of this framework at the end of the 1960s and the resulting stagflation of the 1970s. The stagflation reflected the decline of the US dominance of the world economy and the economic and political stalemate over who would bear the burden of this decline. The third is the recreation of a new institutional structure in the 1980s, based on free market conservatism and the restoration of American international hegemony, which paved the way for the economic expansion of the 1990s.

This book was essentially completed in April 2001. I have not tried to revise it by integrating more recent developments such as the end of the economic expansion, the bursting of the stock market "bubble," the corporate scandals and bankruptcies at Enron and WorldCom among others, and the events of September 11, 2001. The economy went into a recession in early 2001 but the downturn appears to have been short and shallow. As I write this, the recession seems to be over and the economy is showing signs of a fragile recovery. Neither the sharp drop in equity prices nor the likely criminal behavior amidst the collapse of such corporate giants as Enron and WorldCom seems to have significantly influenced overall economic performance.

These were not the first scandals to hit corporate America nor will they be the last.

On September 11, 2001, two airplanes were flown into the twin towers of the World Trade Center in New York City, destroying both buildings and killing approximately 3000 people. A third airplane crashed into the Pentagon, outside of Washington DC, killing approximately 200 people. These actions, while significant in many respects, do not seem to have had much long-lasting impact on the macroeconomy.

I had always wanted to write a compact, readable history of the US economic development since the Second World War. However, other research and writing projects always seem to have taken precedence. I would like to thank Bill Issel for providing me with the opportunity to do so. His encouragement, patience and comments on drafts of the manuscript helped me complete this project and enabled me to write a better book than I otherwise would have. This book has taken longer to finish than anticipated. I would like to thank my editors at Palgrave Macmillan for their understanding and willingness to extend deadlines more than once. I am particularly grateful to Terka Acton, my current editor, who firmly informed me that the complete manuscript needed to be delivered and gave excellent editorial advice.

I would like to thank Roosevelt University for awarding me several research leaves and summer grants over the life of this project. They provided crucial time and resources for researching and writing. I did most of my research at five Chicago-area university libraries – Roosevelt University, DePaul University, University of Illinois-Chicago, Northeastern Illinois University and Northwestern University. Their collections complemented each other very well. What one library did not have, another one often did.

I have had the opportunity to try out my ideas in a variety of forums. I would like to thank members of the Roosevelt University Political Economy seminar for their careful reading of chapter drafts and their insightful comments. I have also benefited from the comments of participants at several seminars and conferences at Notre Dame University and several meetings of the International Working Party on Labor Market Segmentation, an international network of researchers on labor markets and labor policies based in Europe. My students at Roosevelt University were also crucial to the book's development. Their questions and requests for clarification reminded me that the communication of ideas is just as important as the ideas themselves.

Jack Metzgar took time away from his own busy schedule of research and writing to read and comment on chapter drafts. I am very grateful for our many conversations on postwar America over the life of this work.

Most importantly, I would like to thank my family for their support. My two daughters, Stephanie and Sophie, have patiently awaited the end of this project. My wife, Monique Tranchevent, has been very patient and supportive even in light of the many missed deadlines I set for myself for the completion of this book.

Chicago, August 7, 2002   SAMUEL ROSENBERG

Editors' Preface

Mention the United States and few people respond with feelings of neutrality. Discussions about the role of the United States in the contemporary world typically evoke a sense of admiration or a shudder of dislike. Pundits and politicians alike make sweeping references to attributes of modern society deemed "characteristically American". Yet qualifications are in order, especially regarding the distinctiveness of American society and the uniqueness of American culture. True, American society has been shaped by the size of the country, the migratory habits of the people and the federal system of government. Certainly, American culture cannot be understood apart from its multi-cultural character, its irreverence for tradition and its worship of technological imagery. It is equally true, however, that life in the United States has been profoundly shaped by the dynamics of American capitalism and by the penetration of capitalist market imperatives into all aspects of daily life.

The series is designed to take advantage of the growth of specialised research about post-war America in order to foster understanding of the period as a whole as well as to offer a critical assessment of the leading developments of the post-war years. Coming to terms with the United States since 1945 requires a willingness to accept complexity and ambiguity, for the history encompasses conflict as well as consensus, hope as well as despair, progress as well as stagnation. Each book in the series offers an interpretation designed to spark discussion rather than a definite account intended to close debate. The series as a whole is meant to offer students, teachers and the general public fresh perspectives and new insights about the contemporary United States.

CHRISTOPHER BROOKEMAN
WILLIAM ISSEL

PART I: INTRODUCTION

Introduction

The US economy was prosperous for much of the 1920s. However, toward the end of the decade, in August 1929, the economy began to contract. It was not the start of a mild recession. Rather, it was the beginning of the most serious economic depression experienced in the United States. Worldwide in scope, the Great Depression, lasted from 1929 to 1939. This economic catastrophe was the catalyst for the New Deal. While the New Deal federal governmental economic, social and labor policies represented significant new directions in federal policy-making, they did not lead to the end of the Great Depression. Rather, it was not until the country mobilized for war in 1940 that the economy emerged from the Great Depression.

No one single factor led to the Great Depression. A confluence of causes help to explain why the economy slowed in the second half of 1929, prior to the stock market crash in October 1929, and why the depression was so deep and long-lasting.

Overinvestment in new plant and equipment, resulting in overcapacity in many industries, led to the initial contraction in economic activity. Inventories were rising sharply as growth in industrial output was outpacing the consumer demand for goods. Seeing excess inventories, firms curtailed production and the economy began to slow.

Strong profits and new products had stimulated investment in new plant and equipment and new residential construction. Throughout the 1920s, production and labor productivity (output per worker hour) were increasing rapidly. However wages and salaries were only rising slowly. Unions were very weak and under attack by employers. The unionization rate fell from 12.1 percent in 1920 to 7.2 percent in 1929 and the number of strikes fell steadily throughout the 1920s (Devine, 1983, p. 14). Given that labor productivity increases were outpacing growth in wages and salaries, costs of production were falling. At the same time, prices were relatively stable. As a result, profit rates were high and rising.

Furthermore, the development of the automobile had a strong effect on investment. Though invented earlier, the full impact of the automobile on the US economy was not felt until the 1920s. Car production increased three-fold during this decade. This generated strong demand for investment in the automobile industry as well as in other industries dependent on car production such as tires, auto parts, plate glass and steel. Roads and traffic lights needed to be built and gas stations soon followed. The automobile fostered the growth of the suburb. With suburbanization came increased spending on new housing. Many of the new homes would be electrified and have telephones and radios. Thus, investment spending in the electric power, telephone and communications industries took off.

However, toward the end of the 1920s, overcapacity emerged in many industries, such as automobiles and textiles. Residential construction was also facing an overbuilt situation. Eventually, business expectations turned negative. There were cutbacks in consumer durable and capital equipment production and, somewhat earlier, housing construction. The economy turned down in August 1929. Initially, at least, the downturn was not particularly severe, not obviously different from earlier contractions in production in 1923–24 and 1926–27. Yet, this would not turn out to be a short, mild recession. Rather, it was the beginning of the Great Depression.

In hindsight it is clear the economy was fundamentally unsound in 1929. First, consumer demand was constrained by a highly unequal income distribution. A small share of the population had reaped the bulk of the benefits of the prosperous economy. The top 5 percent of the population had seen their share of income increase from 24 percent in 1920 to 34 percent in 1929 (DuBoff, 1989, p. 87). As a result, the economy became overly dependent on the spending of the rich on luxury items or on investment in new plant and equipment.

Second, to foster mass market purchases of major consumer durables, more and more items were purchased on credit. Approximately 75 percent of all cars were sold on credit. There was a rapid growth of personal debt, both installment debt and home mortgages. The total personal debt, including home mortgages, grew much faster than disposable income after 1922, rising to 30 percent of disposable income by 1929 (DuBoff, 1989, p. 88). With the increasing importance of consumer debt, the economy was becoming more vulnerable to problems emerging from debt-deflation.

Third, rampant speculation was fostered by the growing concentration of personal savings. More than two-thirds of all personal savings were accounted for by only slightly more than 2 percent of all families (DuBoff, 1989, p. 87). Many with savings to play with wanted to get even richer quickly and with as little effort as possible. The mood of the country in the 1920s, one of unbridled optimism, fostered the belief that it would be easy to do so. Many were convinced that fortunes could be made, literally overnight, in real estate or in the stock market.

A prime example of real estate speculation occurred in Florida. Land values boomed in the mid-1920s as people believed that the warm climate of Florida would lure millions of people to the "Sunshine State", people with the economic means to vacation there or even to relocate there. Yet, two severe hurricanes in 1926 made it clear that the Florida climate was not as hospitable as promoters claimed and spelled the end of the land boom. Prices collapsed by 1928; the speculative bubble burst.

Yet, the collapse of the Florida real estate market did little to tone down the euphoria on the stock market. Share prices had begun rising in the second half of 1924. Until the beginning of 1928, rising share prices seemingly reflected strong profitability and expectations of continued healthy corporate earnings in the near future. Yet, in early 1928 the situation changed. Now, stock prices moved rapidly higher and the price gains could not, realistically, be rationalized by economic events. A full-blown speculative frenzy had begun. Of course, there were times when share prices declined. But these moments were not viewed as harbingers of problems to come. Rather they were seen as buying opportunities and share prices would move upward again. The following examples demonstrate the extent of the speculative bubble in share prices. The stock market peaked on September 3, 1929. Adjusted for stock splits, shares of Radio went from $94½ a share on March 3, 1928 to $505 a share on September 3, 1929; shares of General Electric from $128¾ to $396¼; shares of Montgomery Ward from $132¾ to $466½; shares of Union Carbide from $145 to $413⅝; and, finally, shares of American Telephone and Telegraph from $179½ to $335⅝ (Campagna, 1987, p. 68). With the rapid runup in stock prices, the economy was becoming more vulnerable to a stock market crash.

Fourth, when the stock market would collapse, it would bring into full view the underlying fragility of the banking system. The US financial system was characterized by many small, independent banks. Some of the banks were quite weak and bank failures were not unknown. In fact, approximately 2–3 percent of all banks in operation failed in each year of the 1920s (Bernanke, 1983, p. 259). While there were no serious "runs" on the banks during the 1920s, the potential for one was always there. And bank deposits were not governmentally insured.

While the economy was fundamentally unsound, it did not necessarily mean that it was ripe for a severe depression. However, the stock market crash provided the catalyst for the start of the Great Depression. After peaking on September 3, 1929, the stock market began its descent. In late October, share prices dropped sharply. On Monday, October 28 and Tuesday, October 29 the stock market went into a free fall. By the end of Tuesday, the stock market crash had erased 22 percent of the value of all stocks. While the hopes and dreams of those who chose to sell were shattered, those holding on to shares of stock saw the value of their holdings decline even further. The stock market continued to drop until July 8, 1932. By that time, stocks on average were 89 percent below the heights reached in September 1929 (DuBoff, 1989, p. 89).

After the stock market crashed, the economy declined precipitously. The depth of the depression was reached in 1932–33. The real Gross National Product (GNP), a measure of economic output, fell by about 30 percent from 1929 to 1932–33. There was virtually no investment in new plant and equipment or residential construction. Overall, investment expenditures fell by nearly 90 percent. Many people were thrown out of work. The unemployment rate rose from 3.2 percent in 1929 to 24.9 percent in 1932–33. Prices fell sharply. On average, in 1932–33, prices were just 60 percent of their 1929 peak (Gordon, 1974, p. 47).

The economic collapse was the result of the interaction of the underlying sources of economic instability with misguided government domestic and international economic policy. First, even though the stock market had become firmly embedded in the heart of the nation's culture and mentality, the highly unequal income distribution and the highly concentrated distribution of savings meant that relatively few actually participated in it. Only 1.5 million people out of a population of approximately 120 million and of between 29 and 30 million families had any connection with the stock market (Galbraith, 1997, p. 78). Nevertheless, for those who did the crash had a devastating effect on the value of their wealth.

Consumption expenditures of wealthier individuals dropped by more than could be explained by the fall in disposable income. As share values continued to decline, household net worth continued to erode and consumption fell even further. Industries particularly vulnerable to the cutback in the consumption spending of the wealthy, such as those producing durable goods and luxury items, experienced sharp declines in demand for their products. They reduced production and many lost their jobs.

Second, as unemployment rose many workers saw their disposable income decline. Now, consumption expenditures fell throughout the society. Excess capacity became more widespread and production was cutback even further. With the decline in consumer demand and the growth of excess capacity, firms reduced spending in investment in new plant and equipment. The reduction in investment spending led to a further slowdown in the economy.

Third, given the excess inventories and the overall decline in economic activity, firms reduced prices to attempt to stimulate demand for their products. There had been a rapid growth of personal debt and the price deflation made it more difficult for individuals to pay off their debts. As prices declined, there was a fall in money incomes. However, the price declines did not lead to a decline in interest rates or principals on previously issued loans or mortgages. Thus, people found it more difficult to pay off their debts. Overall, the ratio of payments for debt service to national income rose from 9 percent in 1929 to 19.8 percent in 1932–33 (Bernanke, 1983, p. 260). As the debt burden became heavier, more and more people found themselves in default on their loans. The "debt crisis" caused problems for both borrowers and lenders. Those borrowers delinquent in their loan payments were forced to reduce their consumption spending in order to attempt to generate the funds for repayment of their loans. This led to a further decline in demand for goods and services.

Fourth, lenders had to write down the value of their assets as borrowers went into partial or total default on their loans. Banks with large amounts of nonperforming loans in their portfolios were vulnerable to bank "runs" as depositors feeling insecure about their deposits demanded their funds. In 1930, banks began failing in larger numbers than in the previous decades. The severity of the banking crisis continued to worsen. The percentage of operating banks which failed in each year from 1930 to 1933 inclusive were 5.6, 10.5, 7.8 and 12.9. Overall, the number of banks operating at the end of 1933 were just over half of the number in operation in 1929 (Bernanke, 1983, p. 239). Those banks which did survive experienced heavy losses. The "debt crisis" and the "financial crisis" forced banks to reduce their lending activities and raise the cost of loans. This credit crunch put a further damper on overall economic activity.

Fifth, not only did firms find it harder to raise capital from banks, the stock market collapse cut off another source of funds for corporations. Firms had found it relatively cheap to raise funds by issuing new shares of stock on the stock market. Now this source of financing was virtually eliminated. The difficulty in raising funds combined with the decline in product demand, the growth of excess capacity and the poor prognosis for the future led to a sharp decline in investment spending.

Thus, consumption and investment expenditures were being reduced. Sixth, while increasing government spending (or decreasing taxes) and increasing exports can potentially counterbalance declines in consumption and investment, misguided government domestic and international economic policy served to worsen the situation. The notion that the federal government budget should always be balanced strongly influenced government macroeconomic policy and led to perverse policies being implemented. Both the Democratic and Republican parties held this view. In November 1929, with the federal budget in surplus and projected to be in surplus in 1930, a small and temporary reduction in tax rates was implemented. In 1930, as the economy worsened and tax revenues declined, the budget surplus disappeared. The tax cut was restored and by the end of 1931, President Herbert Hoover proposed a large tax increase to try to eliminate the federal budget deficit. The tax increase went into effect in June 1932, close to the trough of the Great Depression. As taxes are increased, individuals have less disposable income and with less disposable income, consumption is reduced thereby lowering the demand for goods and services. Such a policy was contrary to what was needed at the time.

Thus, fiscal policy was contractionary at the bottom of the Great Depression. Monetary policy, as well, did not serve to improve the economic situation. The Federal Reserve did little to stimulate the economy as the contraction worsened. From the end of 1929 to mid-1931, Federal Reserve policy was just designed to lower short-term interest rates. Long-term interest rates remained stable. Lower short-term interest rates had little effect on the economy. Similarly, the Federal Reserve stood by passively as banks began failing in large numbers. Rather than supply monetary reserves to the banking system so as to lessen the number of banks likely to close, the Federal Reserve allowed the liquidation of the banking system to run its course. Treasury Secretary Andrew Mellon advised President Hoover to "Liquidate labor, liquidate stocks, liquidate the farmers, liquidate real estate ... purge the rottenness out of the system" (Eichengreen, 1995, p. 251). The Federal Reserve's policies were consistent with this approach to the economy.

However, in September 1931, the Federal Reserve ceased its passive stance. Its policies now turned from passive to totally perverse, though understandable. An international financial crisis was brewing and gold was flowing out of the United States. To stem the outflow of gold and restore European faith in the dollar, the Federal Reserve raised interest rates. Higher interest rates in the midst of an economic downturn, or even a depression, further slow the economy. However, the Federal Reserve feared the United States would soon reach a point when the gold stock in the country would be inadequate to support the amount of currency in circulation. Protection of the gold standard was the dominant objective of monetary policy regardless of the effect policy would have on the domestic economy. The United States was trying to protect the gold standard at a time when more than 40 countries, including Great Britain, were being forced off the gold standard.

Fiscal and monetary policies were not the only government policies which increased the severity of the economic downturn. International trade policy did as well. In June 1930, the US Congress passed the Smoot–Hawley Tariff Act which raised duties on a wide variety of agricultural and manufactured products. Other countries soon followed suit with their own protectionist measures. World trade declined and the potential for increased exports to ameliorate the US economy was closed off.

With the economy in depression, Franklin Delano Roosevelt, the Democratic Party candidate for President, trounced incumbent Republican Herbert Hoover in the 1932 Presidential election. The voters rejected Hoover's laissez-faire approach to the domestic economy. In the electoral campaign, Roosevelt promised a "new deal" for the American people. His policy program, which would come to be known as the New Deal, included more direct government intervention into the economy and more direct government concern with the economic well-being of the population. Though representing a significant new direction in federal governmental policymaking, the New Deal did not succeed in pulling the economy out of the Great Depression.

The economy began to recover from the depths of the depression in the second quarter of 1933, shortly after Roosevelt took office. Business confidence improved amidst the hope that the government policy would succeed in reversing the ongoing price deflation. The expansion, lasting until 1937, though long was weak. At its peak in 1937, real GNP had just recovered to its 1929 level. Many were still jobless and the unemployment rate exceeded 14 percent. There was a minor downturn and then the economy began to recover in 1938. By the end of 1939, the economy was still weak and unemployment was still very high. The unemployment rate was now 17.2 percent and the real GNP was about the same as a decade earlier. The economy was still in the Great Depression.

The anemic nature of the economic recovery was due to the unwillingness of business to make long-term investments in new plant and equipment and the inadequate federal government response to the depressed economic conditions. Roosevelt, like Hoover, believed in balancing the federal budget. While the federal budget was in deficit in each year from 1933 to 1939, this was not the outcome of conscious government policy. Rather, it was the result of reduced tax revenues flowing from reduced incomes rather than significantly increased government expenditures. The deficits, however, were too small to increase aggregate demand enough to counteract the sluggishness in the overall demand for goods and services. Monetary policy was essentially passive throughout this period. Furthermore, with substantial excess capacity and little expectation of increased future demand for goods and services, business was unwilling to risk funds in building new plants and buying new equipment.

While the fiscal and monetary policies of the Roosevelt administration did not have much of an impact on the overall demand for goods and services, the New Deal program did positively effect the economy and the society. First, the Roosevelt administration helped to stabilize the banking system. When Roosevelt took office in March 1933, the banking system was on the brink of a total collapse. The "bank holiday" proclaimed by President Roosevelt closed all banks and froze all deposits. Some banks were closed permanently but most were allowed to reopen. Many bank loans were renegotiated to effectively scale down the debt so as to increase the likelihood of repayment.

The Emergency Banking Act of 1933 allowed the federal government to provide direct financial aid to banks. The Banking Act of 1933 created the Federal Deposit Insurance Corporation (FDIC) which insured bank deposits thereby raising people's confidence in the banking system. Bank "runs" ceased to be a major issue and the number of bank failures were substantially reduced.

Second, the Roosevelt administration effectively took the dollar off the gold standard by suspending the convertibility of the dollar for gold at the existing official price of $20.67 per ounce of gold. Unlike the Hoover administration, the Roosevelt administration considered reviving the economy more crucial than defending the gold standard. To do so, they believed that prices had to rise in the United States and that devaluing the dollar relative to gold would help in this regard. The government began purchasing gold and paying prices above the official price. Eventually under the terms of the Gold Reserve Act of 1934, President Roosevelt set an official price of gold at $35 per ounce. Limited convertibility was reestablished. The sharp rise in the dollar price of gold was equivalent to a sharp depreciation of the value of the dollar relative to currencies of countries still on the gold standard. Eventually the gold standard would be abandoned by all.

Third, if the economy were to recover, the economic conditions of the unemployed would improve. However, the vast numbers of jobless and their dire straits made direct relief of their condition a major priority of the government. A Federal Emergency Relief Administration was established early in the Roosevelt administration. It provided grants to the states to distribute to the needy. The funds were not sufficient and eventually the administration decided to substitute public works employment opportunities for direct relief. The Works Progress Administration, created in 1935, employed over 8 000 000 different individuals at some point over the six years it was in operation (Ratner *et al.*, 1993, p. 462). Many highways, roads, bridges, public buildings, parks and stadiums were constructed. The income gained from direct relief or public works employment raised disposable income thereby improving people's ability to purchase goods and services and providing some level of support for the overall demand for goods and services in the economy.

Fourth, eventually the Roosevelt administration developed a more systematic approach to income security. The Social Security Act of 1935 included provisions for unemployment insurance, means-tested social assistance, and old-age and survivors benefits. While these programs have gone through many changes over the past 65 years, they remain in operation to this day. The federal unemployment insurance system was designed to provide some support to individuals with a history of stable employment who were out of work. With this program, the federal government recognized that it had a responsibility for assisting the unemployed in times other than just a depression since many individuals became unemployed through no fault of their own. The means-tested social assistance program was known as Aid to Dependent Children (ADC). It provided cash assistance to low-income families with dependent children. Initially ADC was viewed as primarily for "deserving widows," most of whom were white, and their children. Eventually this program would become more controversial as more and more recipients would be black and an increasing proportion of cases would involve families with divorced or unmarried mothers. Old age and survivors insurance provided retirement benefits to individuals over the age of 65. Payments were somewhat related to contributions based on prior employment earnings. These retirement benefits were widely supported since people perceived this program as equivalent to a private insurance plan they had purchased rather than a welfare payment.

Fifth, the passage of the National Labor Relations Act (NLRA), also known as the Wagner Act, in 1935, gave workers the right to join unions, provided for the creation of the National Labor Relations Board (NLRB) to oversee labor–management relations and proscribed "unfair labor practices" of employers. This law remains the basis for labor relations today. Many employers ignored the law until the US Supreme Court declared it constitutional in 1937 in the NLRB v. Jones and Laughlin Steel Corporation case. Even after this ruling, many were unwilling to come to terms with the legislation. In fact, in 1939, a *Fortune* magazine poll of business executives found that only 3.7 percent were satisfied with the NLRA. Repeal of the legislation was supported by 40.9 percent and an additional 41.9 percent wanted to see it modified (Harris, 1982, p. 40). Nevertheless, the enabling legal framework together with a labor militancy born out of the pain of the Great Depression and facilitated by the Committee for (later the Congress of) Industrial Organization(s) (CIO) resulted in an upsurge of unionism. The share of the labor force unionized jumped from 6.7 percent in 1935 to 15.8 percent in 1939 (Campagna, 1987, p. 83). Unions negotiated for higher pay for workers. From 1934 to 1939, average hourly earnings in manufacturing rose faster than prices and real wages at the end of the 1930s were significantly higher than in 1929 (Campagna, 1987, p. 85).

Proponents of the NLRA hoped this would occur. Senator Wagner argued that the only way to secure "the fair distribution of purchasing power upon which permanent prosperity must rest" was by strengthening collective bargaining (Renshaw, 1991, p. 21). In other words, higher wages by raising worker incomes would be good for everyone since they would be crucial for raising aggregate demand throughout the economy.

Sixth, a similar concern with worker pay lay behind the passage of the Fair Labor Standards Act (FLSA) of 1938. This law set a minimum wage and a standard workweek of 44 hours, to drop to 40 hours by 1941. Wage workers working longer than the standard workweek were to receive overtime pay. The FLSA established very minimal standards and many workers were excluded from the protection of the law. Nevertheless, the FLSA set a floor under the wage structure, thus helping to push up the pay of many workers. It represented an important advance for workers and would be reformed over time further improving conditions of workers.

The New Deal labor and social policies did somewhat mitigate the impact of the depression on workers and nonworkers alike. Furthermore, many of the labor and income security arrangements developed during the New Deal ended up serving as the basis for future governmental social and labor policy initiatives. The New Deal macroeconomic and international economic policies were much less successful. They failed to end the depression.

It was only with the mobilization for the Second World War in 1940 that the economy emerged from the Great Depression, and in the years following the end of the war the economy never experienced another depression. It is here where the story begins. This book surveys aspects of the US economy since 1940 focusing, for the most part, on aggregate economic performance. The main themes include macroeconomic policy, industrial relations, the role of the United States in the world economy, social and labor policy, and the structure of the labor force and the distribution of income by race and gender.

The premise of the book is that after the ending of the Second World War an institutional framework gradually evolved setting the stage for postwar economic prosperity in the United States. Domestically, this structure included two important elements. First, the federal government played a more important role in stabilizing and fostering the growth of the macroeconomy and in protecting, to a degree, individuals and businesses from competitive forces in the economy. Second, while labor and management continued to be in competitive conflict, there was a shared set of understandings about the nature of the conflict with "management's rights" and labor's role becoming more clearly defined. Internationally, the postwar institutional structure was characterized by the economic and political dominance of the United States. This was manifested in the creation of an international monetary system which, while providing the basis for international economic relations beneficial for more than a few countries, was particularly advantageous for a time to the United States.

From 1948 to 1959, the average rate of growth of real GNP exceeded 3 percent per year. The business cycles were milder in intensity than those of earlier periods. Reflecting this, the unemployment rate fluctuated around lower levels than in earlier periods. With rare exception, inflation rates were generally low. The longest cyclical upswing on record to that time, running for eight years, began in 1961. In the first half of the 1960s, economic growth occurred with minimal inflation and unemployment fell. However, by the end of the 1960s, the situation changed dramatically.

Serious economic problems began to emerge and the institutional framework began to unravel. The federal government utilizing Keynesian macroeconomic policies was unable to adequately deal with the simultaneous occurrence of inflation, unemployment and balance of payments difficulties. Furthermore, increasing demands were placed on the federal government by diverse social movements: the civil rights movement, the welfare rights movement, the women's movement and the organized elderly. The process of distributing income became more politicized and the federal government could not satisfy all of the claimants, especially given the slowdown in economic growth. Labor–management relations became more conflictual. Profit rates fell and struggle increased over compensation, work rules and the introduction of new technology. Employers, both unionized and nonunion, became more resistant to unions. Previously accepted notions of "management's rights" and labor's place came to be questioned. Internationally, the US political and economic hegemony began to decline. The competitive position of Western Europe and Japan improved. In 1971, the Nixon administration dismantled the international monetary system which had been created by the United States in the period of its maximum relative power. That such a step needed to be taken was a measure of the relative decline in the international standing of the US economy.

The strains in the institutional structure continued in the 1970s. Stagflation, the simultaneous occurrence of high rates of inflation and high rates of unemployment, was the outward manifestation of a more fundamental problem, the decline of US dominance of the world economy. At the same time as the rate of economic growth was slowing, foreigners were, in effect, increasing their claims on real output produced in the United States. Western European and Japanese firms became more formidable competitors on the world scene. Oil producing countries were demanding a larger share of world output. If the increased claims of foreigners were to be satisfied in the context of a slowly growing economy, a noninflationary environment required the claims of those living in the United States to be scaled back.

But business was attempting to rebuild profits after the profit squeeze of the late 1960s. And workers were not willing to voluntarily accept a decline in the rate of improvement of their real income, let alone an actual decline in their standard of living. Furthermore, beneficiaries of government programs wished to see the real value of their benefits grow as well. A political–economic stalemate emerged as each group had the necessary economic or political power to press their claims in terms of higher prices, higher negotiated wages and higher government-provided benefits. But given that the level of output was inadequate to satisfy the claims and monetary growth validated the claims, inflation was the result.

Double-digit inflation and substantial unemployment characterized the US economy in 1980. The rate of inflation was 13.5 percent and the rate of unemployment was 7.1 percent. Ultimately for there to be a way out of stagflation, the economy would need to grow more rapidly and the claims being placed on economic output would need to be brought more in line with the available goods and services. Yet, in 1980 it was not totally apparent how this would occur. Whose claims should bear the brunt of the adjustment? While not explicitly discussed in these terms, the Reagan administration attempted to create a new institutional framework to guarantee economic prosperity in the 1980s and beyond. This conservative Republican administration pursued a policy agenda designed to restructure the domestic economy by freeing up market forces. Ideologically, the federal government was attacked as the most important cause of the economic problems faced by the United States. The government would no longer have the main responsibility for maintaining employment and economic security. Programmatically, this attack on the state, on the one hand, translated into policies reducing the tax and regulatory burdens faced by business along with the taxes of the wealthy. On the other hand, it also led to a weakening of the minimal social protection policies benefiting workers, in general, and the poor in particular. Union power was reduced through high aggregate levels of unemployment, increased labor market competition and the reinterpretation of existing industrial relations legislation in a pro-business manner. The market-based conservative strategy was closely aligned with an on-going corporate restructuring. Facing growing domestic and international competition, US-based corporations were trying to become more low-cost producers. This often meant reducing labor costs. Federal governmental policy weakening the bargaining power of organized and unorganized workers alike was just what employers desired. Wishing to dominate labor, employers became more adversarial in their relations with their workers. More often than not employers gained wage and work rule concessions from their employees. Aggressive anti-union management behavior led to a sharp trade union decline. Internationally, the Reagan administration wished to restore the US political and economic supremacy. The Reagan program together with the employer offensive did not lead to a more well-functioning economy. The rate of economic growth did not accelerate in the 1980s. What the conservative economic agenda did lead to was growing income inequality, reversing the trend toward less income inequality over the post Second World War period into the 1970s.

The market-based conservative strategy for restructuring the economy reached its limits during the Reagan years. Nevertheless, the Reagan legacy strongly influenced the Clinton administration policy program and the nature of the economic expansion in the 1990s. Clinton's macroeconomic policy was constrained by the large federal budget deficits of the previous decade. Clinton's social policy carried out the Reagan attack on welfare benefits to its conclusion. Clinton's labor policy was the least pro-union of any Democratic administration in the post Second World War period, perhaps reflecting the decline in the economic and political strength of labor, a legacy of the Reagan era. Collective bargaining relationships remained conflictual and even in long-term collective bargaining relationships unions were often on the defensive.

Driven by rising investment spending, particularly on information technology, and rising consumption spending arising out of increased household wealth due to the spectacular stock market boom, the economic expansion of the 1990s was the longest in the history of the United States. The US economy was strong in the face of world financial tremors. The US worldwide political and economic dominance continued to strengthen. However, the lengthy expansion was marked by increased economic inequality and high poverty rates, continuing the pattern of the 1980s.

As the twentieth century drew to a close, the US economy seemed to be looked on with a measure of envy and fear. There did not seem to be any end in sight to the economic expansion. Yet, all economic booms eventually come to an end.

This book is structured chronologically and thematically over the period from 1940. Chapter 1 analyzes the dramatic transformation of the US economy from a depressed peace-time economy to a full-employed war-time economy during the Second World War. All the changes caused by the war were not permanent and many of the war-time institutions were consciously dismantled. However, crucial aspects of the postwar institutional framework evolved during this time. Chapters 2–4 describe central elements of the postwar institutional framework upon which economic prosperity from 1945 to 1960 was based. Chapter 2 demonstrates that macroeconomic policy played a more important role in the economy than prior to the war and that the postwar federal government was more committed to economic stabilization and growth and maintaining high employment levels. While most employers had not accepted the existence of unions or their legal responsibilities to them prior to the war, this would change during the war. Chapter 3 shows that in the years following the war labor and management, while continuing to be in competitive conflict, were able to reach a shared set of understandings about the nature of the conflict. While Chapters 2 and 3 analyze domestic aspects of the postwar institutional framework, Chapter 4 investigates its international elements. Postwar economic prosperity was facilitated by an international monetary system centered around the dollar which was particularly advantageous, at least for a time, for the United States and by the US dominance of the world economy.

While there was a lengthy economic expansion in the 1960s, by the end of this decade strains were clearly developing in this postwar institutional framework. Chapters 5–8 document the strains emerging in government macroeconomic policy, labor–management relations, government social policy and the international arena. Chapter 5 shows that the conservative form of Keynesianism dominating macroeconomic policymaking in the 1960s was not suitable for handling the stagflation characterizing the domestic economy in the early 1970s. Economic controls were imposed in 1971. The accelerating inflation in the late 1960s reflected a growing imbalance between the claims being placed on the US economy and the economic output it could deliver. Chapter 6 demonstrates that within the collective bargaining context there were heightened tensions over the relative claims of employers and employees. Chapter 7 analyzes the increased demands being placed on the government by those benefiting minimally, if at all, from collective bargaining. Chapter 8 shows that the growing economic and social conflict within the United States was being played out against the backdrop of a relative decline in the international standing of the US economy, a decline leading to a crisis of confidence in the dollar.

Chapters 9–12 document the unmaking of the postwar institutional framework and the creation of another. The 1970s stagflation in the United States analyzed in Chapter 9 was the outward manifestation of unresolved conflicts over the production and distribution of goods and services in the United States and throughout the world. Chapter 10 discusses the economic and political stalemate which arose over which groups would bear the burden for the decline in the relative strength of the United States in the world economy. Chapter 11 demonstrates the Reagan administration's approach to resolving stagflation by restructuring the economy utilizing a market-based conservative strategy and attempting to restore US international economic dominance. The longest economic expansion in the US economic history took place in the 1990s and Chapter 12 shows the reinvigoration of the US economy.

1. Economic Mobilization for Survival, 1940–45

Rapidly increasing military spending during the Second World War pulled the United States out of the Great Depression. The dramatic transformation from a peace-time to war-time economy required a massive mobilization of factors of production.

Many of those previously unemployed were quickly hired. New sources of labor, including women leaving the home and blacks migrating from rural to urban areas, were found to replace those going to war and to fill new positions in the expanding industrial economy. Higher wages, patriotism, and government directives and indirect compulsion served to mobilize workers and influence them to migrate to where they were most needed. Questions of race and sex discrimination arose as black males and white and black women moved into new spheres of production.

Relatively peaceful relations between organized labor and employers evolved. The American Federation of Labor (AFL) and Congress of Industrial Organizations (CIO) gave "no-strike" pledges to the federal government and the National War Labor Board (NWLB) pushed the introduction of "maintenance of membership" clauses in collective bargaining agreements. Though a "no-strike" pledge was in effect, many strikes, mostly of short duration, occurred.

The federal government used financial incentives and rules and regulations to mobilize the necessary war production. The manufacture of consumer items was restricted so that industrialists focused on military goods. As the expansion of private sector manufacturing capacity was inadequate, the government constructed many new war plants which were operated by private companies.

Macroeconomic policies shaped the overall economic environment. They included monetary and fiscal policy and wage and price controls. The monetary policy was subordinated to the goals of fiscal

19

policy. The war-time fiscal policy, characterized by huge federal budget deficits, provided striking evidence of the ability of properly developed policy to foster an economic expansion. Wage and price controls, complementing the fiscal policy, slowed the inflationary spiral guaranteed to emerge in a war economy.

Overall, the domestic economy performed relatively well. Important transformations occurred in the economy and society during the Second World War. All the changes caused by the war were not permanent and many of the war-time institutions were consciously dismantled. But crucial aspects of the postwar institutional framework evolved during this time. The impact of the war would be felt for many years to come.

ECONOMIC GROWTH

The defense buildup began in June 1940 after the Germans invaded France. At that time, the central problem facing the economy was a lack of effective demand for goods and services. There was substantial unused capacity and many were out of work. Approximately two years later, there were high employment levels and labor shortages were developing in some areas and occupations. By 1944, the unemployment rate had fallen to a low of 1.2 percent, a level never again achieved in the postwar period.

The total output of the economy in constant prices – the real Gross National Product (GNP) – increased from $319.8 billion (in 1972 dollars) in 1939, the last year unaffected by the war or the prospect of war, to a peak of $561.9 billion (in 1972 dollars) in 1944. The GNP is composed of personal consumption expenditures, investment expenditures, government (federal, state and local) purchases of goods and services, and net exports of goods and services. Federal government purchases of goods and services, mainly military related, grew from $22.8 billion in 1939 to $269.7 billion in 1944. This increase is virtually identical to the overall increase in real GNP. Consumption expenditures rose moderately though not as fast as disposable income as people were "forced" to save a larger proportion of their income. There was a decline in real private investment, mainly due to a fall in residential investment (*Economic Report of the President*, 1985, pp. 234–235).

Thus, the output of armaments came from expanded production. As the war progressed, the main economic problem was no longer a lack of effective demand. The government provided the demand for goods and services. Rather, it was increasing the nation's ability to produce the necessary output. Herein lay the importance of effectively mobilizing labor and capital for war production.

THE LABOR MOBILIZATION

The economic expansion was facilitated by a substantial increase in the number of people employed. Between 1939 and 1944, total civilian employment rose from 45.8 million to 54.0 million, a gain of 8.2 million. Membership in the Armed Forces increased to 11.4 million from 0.4 million. Thus, approximately 19.2 million additional people were either working or in the Armed Forces. Of these 8.8 million came from the ranks of the unemployed as there were 9.4 million unemployed in 1939 and only 0.6 million without work in 1944. The additional 10.4 million were people who had been out of the labor force in 1939, over one-half of whom were civilian women (Wool, 1947).

The dynamism of the labor force is clearly reflected in the changing status of blacks and women. At this time, both black males and white and black women could be viewed as important components of the labor reserve, available to be "mobilized for service" in the expanding sectors of the economy. Initially, the new jobs arising from the defense buildup were filled by prime-aged white males, most of whom were previously unemployed or holding less desirable positions. Black males and white and black women were trained for the war industries only after the supply of prime-aged white men was exhausted.

The employment of blacks in civilian jobs increased by almost one million from April 1940 to April 1944, with the number of employed black men rising from 2.9 to 3.2 million and the number of employed black women from 1.5 to 2.1 million. In addition, almost three-quarters of a million entered the Armed Forces. There was a vast shift of blacks from the farms to the factories. The proportion of employed black men on farms declined from 41 to 28 percent and the proportion of employed black women in agriculture fell from 16 to 8 percent. Close to 30 percent of black men were craftsmen or operatives – mainly industrial workers – in 1944 as compared to only 17 percent in 1940. The proportion of employed black women in these occupational groups grew from 6.5 percent in 1940 to 18 percent in 1944. Also, a substantial number of black women left extremely badly paid positions as domestic servants to take better-paying jobs in the industrial and service sectors (Wolfbein, 1945).

The most important factor explaining this occupational upgrading was the general increased demand for labor in the war industries and the shortage of white male workers. Though the military buildup had been on for two years, blacks composed only 3 percent of the war-production work force in the summer of 1942. By the fall of 1944, they were more than 8 percent, slightly less than the overall proportion of blacks in the labor force (Weaver, 1946, p. 79).

With the development of labor shortages in the latter part of 1942, traditional behavior patterns of employers, unions, training institutions and government agencies limiting the labor market options of blacks were forced to change. Initially, many employers refused to hire blacks for positions other than menial work deemed suitable for them. A Bureau of Employment Security survey in September 1941 found that over half of the anticipated openings in the defense industries would be explicitly closed to black applicants. Firms in the aircraft and ordnance industries only considered black workers for janitorial positions (Kryder, 2000, pp. 39, 103). The President of North American Aviation frankly stated:

> While we are in complete sympathy for the Negro, it is against company policy to employ them as aircraft workers or mechanics ... regardless of their training .... There will be some jobs as janitors for Negroes. (Quoted in Foner, 1982, p. 238)

However, given labor shortages, employers reluctant to employ blacks in other than traditional positions would eventually be unable to profitably utilize their plant and equipment.

Initially, some unions organizing workers in defense industries excluded blacks from membership either by provisions in their constitutions or unwritten policy. Others, while accepting them implicitly, provided them with a second-class status by organizing them in segregated auxiliary locals having no say in overall union affairs and discriminated against these black locals in referring people to jobs (Northrup, 1944). Where a closed shop agreement existed, employers were only allowed to hire union members. In this situation, if blacks were unable to join the union they were unable to be hired (Weaver, 1946). In most instances closed shop arrangements were not in effect and employers were able to hire anyone they wished. Here, the racism of the employers combined with the racism of the workers and the practices of the unions to restrict black opportunities. Eventually, the necessities of war production forced the upgrading and entrance of blacks into many new occupations and plants. Furthermore, government litigation broke down color bars in some of the unions which still had them. Under pressure from the black community, President Roosevelt issued an executive order banning racial discrimination in defense industries and set up the Fair Employment Practices Committee which began functioning on July 18, 1941. Its objectives were to gain war industry positions for blacks and individuals from other minority groups and raise the morale of victims of discrimination.

Initially, many government-funded schools training workers for the defense industries would not accept blacks either because blacks could not join unions or because they could not get job offers. In addition, the policies of the US Employment Service served to reinforce the labor market discrimination experienced by blacks. For example, from October 1940 to March 1941, blacks were only 4 percent of the placements made by the US Employment Service in 20 main defense industries. And the vast majority of those placed were given unskilled work (Weaver, 1946, p. 20).

Even in areas where blacks lived and had the necessary skills or were willing to be trained, they were rejected while whites, even without training, were recruited from other parts of the country. The depletion of the white male labor supply caused this pattern to change. By 1942, most northern areas where labor shortages existed made training more available to blacks. In the South, progress was slower but eventually training opportunities opened for them. Furthermore, these labor market developments resulted in substantially more blacks being placed in a wider range of occupations by the US Employment Service.

As the racial bars began to bend, blacks responded to their new-found opportunities. Their migration rates significantly increased, surpassing those of whites. Most blacks migrants left the South and went to areas in the North and West having defense jobs to fill. They were more likely than whites to be found in areas classified as experiencing acute labor shortage (Kryder, 2000, p. 111). Here, the relative proportion of blacks in skilled and semi-skilled occupations significantly grew.

The entrance of blacks in occupations and industries from which they had previously been excluded did not always progress smoothly.

There were instances where white males went on strike over the hiring and promotion of blacks. While they occurred in the early part of mobilization, they became more prevalent in 1943 and 1944 as more blacks were hired or promoted in defense industries. In addition, there were strikes by blacks against racial discrimination. Overall, there were 50 strikes in 1943 and 57 strikes in 1944 over racial questions (Crowther and Cole, 1944, p. 938, 1945, p. 968).

In addition to black males, white and black women had expanded job opportunities as labor shortages emerged. The number of women in the civilian labor force increased from some 14 or 15 million in mid-1940 to some 19 or 20 million in mid-1945. The labor force participation rate of women rose from 27 percent in April 1940 to 37 percent in April 1945 (Pidgeon, 1947, pp. 666, 670). Under normal circumstances some of these new women workers would have been expected to enter the labor force from 1940 to 1945. Kessler-Harris estimates that 3.5 million women workers who might not otherwise have entered the labor force did so during the war years. Seventy-five percent of these new female workers were married and many were over the age of 35 (Kessler-Harris, 1982, p. 277).

Work commonly thought of as "men's work", actually white men's work, was opened to women during the war. The most dramatic increase took place in war-related industries. While women had always been an important segment of the work force in nondurable manufacturing industries such as the making of apparel, textiles, shoes and food products, they had generally played a small role in the manufacture of durable goods. During the war, the proportion of production workers in durable manufacturing who were women rose from 8.6 percent in late 1939 to a wartime record of nearly 25 percent by late 1944. The number of women production workers in the transportation equipment industry (exclusive of automobiles) rose from less than 2000 in October 1939 to over half a million by July 1943. Similarly, their number increased by about a quarter of a million in the iron and steel, machinery and electrical machinery industries and by 150 000 in the automobile sector. Overall, while there were only 340 000 women production workers in durable goods industries in 1939, there were more than 2 million of them four years later (Pidgeon, 1947, pp. 666–667).

Not only did vast numbers of women enter manufacturing, a second place where women went to work was in offices. There was an increase of over 2 million women clerical workers. Almost half of the increase was accounted for by the federal government. By the end of the war, women were 38 percent of all federal workers, more than twice the percentage of the last prewar year (Chafe, 1972, p. 141).

Just as with black men, the most important factor explaining the wide availability of work for women was the shortage of white male workers. In the early phase of the defense buildup very few women were hired by the defense industries, primarily due to the large backlog of unemployed white men on which the munitions industries could draw. In addition, many employers felt hiring women would increase their cost of production. Women were viewed as lacking mechanical ability. New bathrooms would have to be built. Employers were also unwilling to risk costly conflict with their white male workers over employing women in traditionally male occupations. Furthermore, some employers who might have been interested in hiring women were restricted from doing so due to closed shop arrangements with unions. As with blacks, several unions representing workers in the defense industries initially barred women from their membership. A survey of 12 000 factories in early 1942 showed that employers in war industries were willing to employ women in only one-third of the jobs available.

In addition to facing difficulties finding work, women had problems gaining entrance into training programs. Women comprised only 1 percent of the 700 000 workers who received training in industrial skills in government financed training programs in the second half of 1941. The policy of the Office of Education operating these programs was that since women were not being hired by the defense industries they should not be trained for positions in them.

Barriers faced by women began to fall in 1942. Employers became more willing to hire them. According to Mary Anderson, the director of the US Women's Bureau, "almost overnight women were reclassified by industrialists from a marginal to a basic labor supply for munitions making" (Chafe, 1972, p. 137). Virtually all union bars against women as members disappeared by the end of 1942. As employment opportunities increased, so did access to government sponsored training programs.

As the sexual bars began to bend, women responded to their newfound opportunities. Many holding low-paid "women's jobs" quit for higher paying positions in the defense industries. Wages in munitions plants and aircraft factories averaged 40 percent higher than in factories producing consumer goods. While there was a conscious campaign to induce women to seek a job, the attractive wage and job opportunities and the suspension of overt animosity increased the willingness of women to work. Many women whose husbands went off to war needed a job to supplement the money received from the government, taken from their husbands' wages. Though the child-care programs funded by the government or provided by employers were unsatisfactory, their existence made it easier for some women raising families to also hold jobs.

Women ran into difficulties as they entered occupations and industries from which they had previously been excluded. Questions of sex discrimination were raised throughout the war period. Some male unionists struck to prevent women from being hired. For example, in November 1941, members of the United Auto Workers (UAW) struck a machine gun plant owned by the Kelsey-Hayes Wheel Co. when the firm hired women at 85 cents an hour which was 15 cents an hour less than the rate the men received. While the strikers might have demanded that women receive the same pay as men, instead they asked the company to remove women from all machine jobs in the plant (Milkman, 1980, p. 131). Eventually the UAW and other unions realized that women would be an important part of the industrial work force, at least for the duration of the war. Paying less to women than to men for equal work threatened the wage rates of their male members and thus they championed the notion of "equal pay for equal work". But discriminatory job classifications by sex still remained limiting the area of applicability of this notion. Also, many unions maintained separate seniority lists for men and women. This would have major implications when the demobilization occurred at the end of the war.

Black women faced even more difficulties than white women. They suffered from both sexism and racism. Employers running war plants willing to hire black men and white women were often unwilling to hire black women, or if they did employ them it was often for the worst, most poorly paid jobs. In Detroit, for example, in 1943 the Fair Employment Practices Commission estimated that 25 000 black women were available to work in defense plants but were unable to get hired. Employers argued that they were unwilling to hire black women at all or unwilling to hire them for better paying positions since they feared a backlash from their white workers, both men and women. And, in Detroit there were instances of hate strikes where white men and women staged job actions to protest the hiring or upgrading of black women (Anderson, 1981, p. 37).

In addition to increasing the number of available workers, the mobilization of labor included inducing people to work where they were needed. Initially, a "free" labor market operated with people being free to choose where they wished to work, that is assuming they were able to find an employer willing to hire them. By the middle of 1943, there were few unemployed and many of them were in the process of moving from one job to another. As it was easy to find work, many were quitting jobs for better opportunities elsewhere. The quit rate rose from "a peacetime normal of 1 or 2 percent per month to a war time level of 6 or 8 percent" and "many firms found it necessary to hire and train 1000 workers in order to bring about a net increase of 100 in the work force" (Haber, 1945, p. 227). As insurance against such high labor turnover, many firms hoarded labor, hiring more people than were currently needed. In addition, it became more difficult to induce those remaining workers in nondefense industries to transfer to those areas most needed for war production.

As a result, some controls were placed on the operation of the "free" labor market. To limit hoarding, ceilings were placed on employment levels in particular war plants located in areas of the country experiencing the most severe labor shortages. To reduce labor turnover, restrictions were placed on employers to prevent their "pirating" of workers from other war production facilities and on the freedom of workers engaged in essential activities to change jobs. The policies of the Selective Service System also helped to channel workers. Those engaged in essential war work were given draft deferments. Others not engaged in such activities but having the necessary skills were given time to find such work before being inducted into the Armed Forces.

The distinction between a "free" labor market and a wartime "controlled" one should not be exaggerated. For many, the freedoms of the "free" labor market during the Great Depression amounted to little more than the unrestricted right to "pound the pavement" in an unsuccessful search for work. Most did not object to the war-time system of labor channeling which freed them from the burden of unemployment and induced them into war jobs. In a sense, "the war substituted a different and more elaborate set of controls for those that had existed all along" (Polenberg, 1972, p. 36).

THE STABILIZATION OF LABOR–MANAGEMENT RELATIONS

An increased supply of labor was important for the growing war economy. But the needed weapons would not have been made without relatively peaceful relations between employers and workers.

Substantial labor–management strife would delay production and likely increase its cost. Thus, a central goal of the Roosevelt administration was to create an environment in which relatively stable industrial relations would evolve.

As of 1940, some firms such as General Motors (GM), US Steel and General Electric (GE) had accepted the labor movement. However, many large and small firms were still avoiding unions and their legal responsibilities toward them. Even where workers had labor representation, unions often had great difficulties reaching agreement with employers on the terms of the first contract. Reflecting this situation, half of the strikes in 1940 and 1941 were over matters concerning union recognition or union organization. Had employers more readily accepted unions, the vast majority of strikes would have been over questions of compensation and working conditions rather than union recognition and organization. Eventually, some of the large employers capitulated. By the end of 1941, first contracts were finally being signed by such companies as Goodyear, Armour and Westinghouse. Workers for Ford and the Little Steel companies (Republic, Bethlehem, Youngstown and Inland) had their unions recognized by their employers. (These steel companies were called "Little Steel" to distinguish them from US Steel, the major steel producer in the United States at the time.)

Several serious strikes occurred in war-related industries in 1940 and 1941, and President Roosevelt threatened to seize the plants to maintain production. Finally, on June 9, 1941, he ordered the Army to reopen and operate a struck North American Aviation plant in Inglewood, California.

With the bombing of Pearl Harbor by the Japanese on December 7, 1941, production for the war effort took on added urgency. On December 17, 1941, President Roosevelt convened a conference of representatives of labor, management and the government to lay the basis for peaceful industrial relations in defense industries. Though substantial differences remained, from this conference emerged a no-strike pledge on the part of labor and a no-lockout pledge on the part of management and the creation of an NWLB.

The NWLB, a tripartite board with 12 members, four of them to represent labor, four to represent employers and four to represent the public, became the arena where labor–management disputes were often settled. Unsettled industrial disputes brought to the NWLB were those certified by the Secretary of Labor as likely to "interrupt work which contributes to the effective prosecution of the war" (Seidman, 1953, p. 81). The three major topics of concern faced by the NWLB were union security, worker compensation and day-to-day contract administration. Labor, in giving up the right to strike, surrendered its most powerful weapon at a time of low unemployment when its bargaining power would have been strongest. Union leaders wished a strong union security provision in return. This would protect them from anti-union employers trying to convince workers that unions were unnecessary, as unions had given up their major weapon and the NWLB was regulating wage increases. It would also protect them from other unions trying to "raid" their membership. Affiliates of the AFL and CIO often competed for the same workers.

Employer representatives felt that there was no need for any union security arrangements other than the protections afforded by the Wagner Act and the National Labor Relations Board (NLRB). Their preferred situation was the open shop, where employers are free to hire anyone and employees are not required to join a union to maintain their jobs. They feared that any union security clause would unduly strengthen labor after the war, when free collective bargaining would, hopefully, return. Union representatives had no interest in the open shop. Rather, they preferred the union shop, where a person must join a union shortly after being hired to retain the job.

The compromise reached by the NWLB on disputes brought to it concerning union security issues was the following: (1) closed shop arrangements would not be approved; (2) where an established union shop existed, it would be maintained; and (3) where a union shop did not exist but was desired by a union, maintenance of membership would often be provided. Under a maintenance of membership clause, union members who did not resign from a union during a "15 day escape period", usually at the beginning of a collective bargaining agreement, would have to retain their membership over the life of the contract. Those who did not maintain their union standing could lose their job. But no one, not already a union member, would be required to join a union in order to be hired for a job. Basically, the maintenance of membership arrangement prevented employers from eliminating unions from their firms and reduced jurisdictional conflict between unions by requiring union members to stay put in their unions.

By 1945, approximately one-third of workers under collective bargaining contracts were covered by maintenance of membership provisions. And extremely few workers chose to leave their unions during the "escape period". Overall union membership increased from 9 million in 1939 to 14.8 million in 1945. Unions were particularly prevalent in the manufacturing, mining and transportation sectors. By 1945–46, more than 80 percent of workers in the transportation and mining sectors worked in unionized plants and almost 70 percent of workers in manufacturing were covered by collective bargaining agreements (Harris, 1982, p. 43).

The second major question taken up by the NWLB was labor compensation. This issue is crucial for peaceful industrial relations during a war-time emergency as many strikes are likely to occur over this matter. In addition, trends in labor compensation have implications for price stability. Regulation of such payments is often one component of an anti-inflation strategy.

Initially, the NWLB ruled on wage and fringe benefit questions only in those disputes referred to it. Its rulings did not directly apply to situations where labor and management were able to come to an agreement by themselves. Wage increases were based on a formula developed in the Little Steel companies case decided by the NWLB on July 16, 1942. As the Consumer Price Index (CPI) had risen by 15 percent from January 1, 1941 to May 1, 1942, the NWLB sanctioned wage improvements to increase wage rates for particular occupations by no more than 15 percent from January 1, 1941 to May 1, 1942. The NWLB used this 15 percent measure in cases following Little Steel. Yet, the logic of this figure could only be maintained if prices remained stable after May 1, 1942. If not, increases in occupational wage rates would be outstripped by increases in the cost of living and severe strains would develop in labor relations.

Prices did not remain stable. Also, the fact that many wage negotiations were settled outside the purview of the NWLB proved problematic. As the defense buildup rapidly expanded and labor shortages emerged, employers became more concerned with maintaining an available work force than in keeping wage costs down. Also, the government contracted for war products on a cost-plus-fixed-fee basis. Thus, increases in labor costs could eventually be passed on to the government. Conditions were ripe for wage increases exceeding the NWLB guidelines.

As the threat of inflation became more serious, on October 2, 1942 the US Congress passed the Economic Stabilization Act which directed President Roosevelt to stabilize all wages and salaries, as far as practicable, on the basis of their levels as of September 15, 1942.

With this legislation, the NWLB became responsible for stabilizing wages throughout the society, not just in situations where labor disputes existed. Stiff penalties were provided for violations of the wage stabilization program.

The Little Steel formula continued as the basis on which general wage increases were determined. As this was a wage stabilization program and not a wage freeze, wage increases would be allowed if they were needed to "correct maladjustments or inequalities, to eliminate substandards of living, to correct gross inequities, or to aid in the effective prosecution of the war" (Taylor, 1948). Employers and unions used great ingenuity in gaining increases in hourly earnings based on inter-plant and intra-plant wage inequities, incentive systems, merit increases and the like. In addition, bargaining over fringe benefits, such as travel time allowances, night-shift differentials, and vacations and other holidays with pay, became prevalent. They were deemed noninflationary and thus more likely to be approved.

Due to the rulings of the NWLB, wage rate increases were probably less than they would have otherwise been, especially given the general shortage of labor. The basic wage rate in manufacturing rose by 24 percent from January 1941 to July 1945 while the cost of living increased by about one-third. But the weekly earnings of manufacturing employees rose by 70 percent from $26.64 to $45.45 (Seidman, 1953, p. 129). This was due to the abundant opportunities for overtime and to the fact that while wage rates were stabilized, the wages received by workers were not, given opportunities for upgrading, merit increases and the reclassification of jobs. Despite higher taxes, the take-home pay of the average factory worker rose more than did the cost of living.

In addition to the issues of union security and worker compensation, the NWLB dealt with matters regarding day-to-day contract administration and dispute settlement. Many employers had little experience in union–management relations and little interest in dealing with unions beyond the absolute minimum required by law. Realizing that peaceful labor relations required a means for handling day-to-day disputes between labor and management, the NWLB attempted to strengthen the grievance procedures in mass production industries. Broad procedures were set up to speed dispute settlement. When a settlement of a grievance could not be reached, an arbitrator was to be brought in to resolve the dispute. In its rulings on day-to-day contract disputes, the NWLB defended management's right to manage the enterprise. The union was left to police the contract and challenge management in instances where it felt management was violating the agreement. Overall, the NWLB codified the notion that management acts and the union grieves (Harris, 1982).

While the NWLB was stabilizing labor–management relations, conflicts did not disappear. Though labor leaders gave a no-strike pledge, there were 14 731 strikes from December 8, 1941, the day after Pearl Harbor to August 14, 1945, VJ day, when the Japanese surrendered ending the war. The vast majority were short "wildcats", occurring within the term of the contract. As such, only a very small amount of labor time was lost due to strikes (Crowther, 1946, p. 723). In most cases union leadership quickly forced workers back to work. Many local union leaders paid for this behavior as they were defeated in union elections in 1944–45.

The major question in the disputes was labor compensation as workers felt their wage rates were being unfairly stabilized while prices were rising. While some union leaders called for prices to be rolled back, the best the government would offer was a price freeze. Labor's frustration with the Little Steel formula came to a head in the large coal strikes of 1943. Four hundred thousand bituminous coal miners struck on three separate occasions in May and June for wage increases which could not be reconciled with the Little Steel formula. The government seized the mines stating that the strikes interfered with the war effort and threatened to end the draft deferments of the miners.

Congress reacted to these strikes by passing the War Labor Disputes Act (also known as the Smith–Connolly Act) over the President's veto. Designed to weaken the bargaining strength of labor, it increased the power of the President to seize plants useful in the war and made it a crime to encourage strikes in such plants. It required a 30-day "cooling off" period and a strike vote conducted by the NLRB before a strike could be called in a defense plant. Supplementing the War Labor Disputes Act were many state laws passed in 1943 restricting the activities of unions. Most disputes were eventually settled peacefully by the NWLB. But governmental seizure of struck plants was used in cases due to labor intransigence and cases due to management's unwillingness to abide by NWLB rulings.

THE MOBILIZATION OF PRODUCTION

Developing a labor force and stabilizing industrial relations were two important preconditions for armament manufacture. In addition, as the government was not going to undertake all such production in government-owned and operated plants, it needed to gain the cooperation of private industrialists. Such behavior could be induced by providing monetary incentives to them. For as Henry L. Stimson, the Secretary of War from 1940 to 1945, clearly stated:

> If you are going to try to go to war, or to prepare for war, in a capitalist country, you have got to let business make money out of the process or business won't work. (Quoted in Polenberg, 1972, p. 12)

And the war was highly profitable for business. Corporate profits after taxes rose from $5.8 billion in 1940 to $10.7 billion in 1944 (*Economic Report of the President*, 1985, p. 328).

Yet, the responses of business people to market incentives are not totally predictable. Thus, such incentives were supported by rules and regulations concerning what was to be produced and what was forbidden to be made. The Second World War led to the most extensive set of governmental economic controls ever experienced in the United States. Overall, excluding military agencies, there were about 165 economic and noneconomic emergency war agencies (Vatter, 1985, p. 87).

Prior to Pearl Harbor, major industries were reluctant to prepare for defense. Some industrialists felt that American intervention would not occur and most were unwilling to convert from profitable peacetime work. It was feared that those who shifted into defense production would lose a large share of the domestic market to competitors who continued to produce for that sector. In addition to being against the conversion of existing capacity, they were unwilling to consider an expansion of capacity. Remembering the depressed conditions of the 1930s, many business people were concerned that they would be left with excess capacity when the war ended. There were even those firms such as Standard Oil of New Jersey, Dow-Chemical, US Steel, DuPont, General Motors and the Aluminum Company of America which were assisting the growth of Nazi industry and delaying America's preparation for war (Bernstein, 1968, p. 291).

In mid-1940, the US Congress gave President Roosevelt the authority to decide in which instances the production of military supplies should take precedence over civilian production. A year later, as shortages were developing in inputs used for both armaments and consumer items, the President was allowed to authorize priorities for essential civilian goods. Some goods would be forbidden to be produced, quantities of others would be limited and restrictions would be placed on the use of essential inputs in the making of nonessential civilian items. In January 1942, President Roosevelt created the War Production Board (WPB), whose job was to exercise general responsibility over the economy. The Second War Powers Act of March 1942 permitted the WPB to allocate materials or facilities in any manner it thought necessary for defense. Basically, it had the right to force industrialists to convert their plants to military production. Those who did not comply with its directives could be prosecuted.

As it is impossible to summarize all the resource allocation decisions of the WPB, a few examples will suffice. Most civilian construction and most investment for nonmilitary purposes were forbidden. The last car was produced on February 10, 1942. After that, the automobile companies produced more than 50 percent of all aircraft engines, 33 percent of all machine guns, 80 percent of all tanks and tank parts and 100 percent of all Army trucks. Car companies also produced about 20 percent of all airplanes made for the war effort (Gropman, 1996, pp. 59–60). Nonmilitary, nonessential use of steel, copper, other metals and rubber was prohibited. As a result by September 1942, the production of the following items for civilian use had been prohibited: electric refrigerators, vacuum cleaners, sewing machines, electric ranges, washing machines, radios, phonographs, metal household furniture and many other household appliances. There was a reduction and simplification of styles of many consumer goods (Webb, 1942, 1943).

The conversion of existing facilities was not adequate to meet defense needs. The WPB developed procedures to induce owners of business to expand. Most military contracts were issued on a cost-plus-fixed-fee basis providing manufacturers with a guaranteed profit. Those who increased capacity were allowed to amortize the cost of expansion over only five years even if the facilities had a productive life of more than five years. This lowered their taxable income and expanded their earnings ability.

Expansion of private sector manufacturing capacity remained inadequate. The government was forced to construct many new war plants which it then leased to private companies for a nominal fee. These plants were mainly in the following industries: (1) transportation equipment, except automobiles, which includes the building of ships, airplanes, railroad equipment, tanks and combat vehicles;

(2) chemicals and allied products which includes the small-arms ammunition industry; (3) iron and steel and other products; and (4) nonferrous metals and other products. In September 1943, approximately 20 percent of all workers in the munitions industries were working in government-owned, privately operated plants (Schloss, 1944, pp. 40–41).

MACROECONOMIC STABILITY

Macroeconomic policy shaped the overall economic environment in which the mobilization of labor and capital occurred. The central macroeconomic problem was to guarantee that adequate resources were made available for war production with minimal disruption to the economy and society. Macroeconomic policies included fiscal and monetary policies and wage–price regulations. In addition, the rationing of consumer goods and the rules and regulations governing the allocation of capital and labor complemented those policies more normally thought of as comprising a macroeconomic strategy.

Three possible means of financing the war and gaining the needed war materials are the following:

(1) Taxes paid by individuals and businesses to the federal government could be raised by an amount equal to the additional military expenditures. Due to the increase in taxation, consumer demand would be less than it would have otherwise been at the new level of GNP, freeing up factors of production for use in defense industries rather than in consumer goods production.

(2) Rather than totally financing the war through increased taxation, a second alternative would be to partially pay for the war in this manner and raise the rest of the necessary money through increasing the annual federal budget deficit. Bonds would be sold by the US Treasury to fund the deficit. The output of armaments would mainly come from expanded production. If the economy operated at close to full capacity, an inflationary situation would develop. The government would be able to pay whatever price it needed to for military output. Those unable to maintain their standard of living in the face of inflation would be indirectly paying for the war by cutting back on their demand for goods and services.

(3) To lessen the likelihood of inflation, lower the prices of military goods and guarantee that the desired weapons would be produced, the federal government could institute a set of controls on the economy. Such controls might include wage–price controls, rationing of consumer goods, prohibitions on the production of consumer goods, directives on the production of military goods by the private sector and the development of government-owned and perhaps operated weapons facilities. Wage–price controls would deal with inflation. Rationing would allocate consumer goods and services in an equitable manner. Restricting the production of nonessential goods would free up factors of production for the defense sector and increase the willingness of private sector firms to become defense contractors. Government facilities would guarantee the needed output. In this strategy, "compulsion" replaces "voluntary" market incentives as the primary resource allocation mechanism.

The strategy ultimately utilized by the federal government combined elements of options (2) and (3). Government expenditures rose substantially during the war. Taxes were raised and tax revenue dramatically increased. But, less than half of federal government expenditures were funded by tax revenues (Murphy, 1950, p. 251). Substantial federal budget deficits were run every year during the war. The funds to cover the deficits were raised through the sale of government bonds by the US Treasury.

Slightly more than half of the bonds were sold to individuals, corporations, insurance companies, and state and local governments. The rest were purchased by commercial banks and the Federal Reserve system (Chandler, 1951, p. 133). The government's goal was to place most of its war bonds in the hands of individuals and non-financial corporations. Media campaigns were designed to induce people to save more and purchase government securities. Payroll savings plans were implemented at work where, with the worker's approval, deductions were automatically taken from paychecks and used for war bonds. Due to war-time regulations which reduced the supply of consumer goods, personal savings as a percentage of disposable income rose from 5.5 percent in 1940 to 25.2 percent in 1944 (Freeman, 1960, p. 56). Approximately 40 percent of the value of personal savings and 25 percent of corporate business savings went into government bonds (Chandler, 1951, p. 135).

As the US Treasury was unable to secure adequate funds from individuals and nonbank entities, it was forced to borrow heavily from commercial banks and the Federal Reserve system. The Federal Reserve played the role of lender of last resort. It was committed to purchasing as large a volume of bonds as necessary to enable the government to raise its funds at low and stable rates of interest. Low rates of interest lowered the cost of financing the war effort. Fixed rates of interest reflected stability in the bond market and made it impossible for bond speculators to profit off the war effort.

Yet, this action by the Federal Reserve meant that monetary policy was totally subservient to fiscal policy. The money supply was strongly determined by the government's need for funds from the Federal Reserve. Whenever the Federal Reserve would purchase government bonds from the US Treasury, it would write a check. As this money was spent, the supply of money in the economy would expand. This increase in the supply of money in a war economy was inflationary.

Fiscal policy was supplemented by direct controls over prices, wages, and the production and use of goods and services. Price controls, along with the previously discussed wage controls, were used to lessen the likelihood of inflation. During 1941, price controls were placed only on a small number of particularly scarce commodities since inflation was thought to be a problem affecting only a small segment of the market. By the spring of 1942, the problem of inflation was seen to be more systemic in nature. On April 28, 1942, the General Maximum Price Regulation was issued, placing a ceiling over most prices, excluding many farm prices, at the highest levels reached the month before. Prices of most agricultural commodities were not really controlled until 1943. These price controls were fairly effective. The annual rate of inflation slowed from 10.7 percent in 1942 to 6.1 percent in 1943 to 1.7 percent in 1944 and 2.3 percent in 1945. The relatively high rate of inflation in 1943 was totally due to trends in food prices (*Economic Report of the President*, 1985, p. 296).

As prices were regulated and consumer goods were in short supply, there was an excess demand for particular commodities. Without an explicit system of rationing, those most likely to be able to purchase necessary items would be those who were most friendly with the local shopkeeper or who arrived earliest in a morning or who were most able to stand in lines. A formal system of rationing was implemented to more equitably distribute consumer goods. Shoes, gasoline, coffee, canned food and sugar were some of the goods rationed. Ration

coupons were issued to individuals and families giving them the right
to purchase a particular amount of the relevant items. They would
present these coupons to the local shopkeeper when making a purchase. In order to replenish the inventory, the dealer would have to
present these coupons to the suppliers. Eventually the ration coupons
would end up in the hands of the government.

Rationing lowered the demand for particular products by limiting
the freedom of people to purchase all they desired. By helping to
adjust the demand to the limited supply, rationing complemented the
price controls in the fight against inflation. It also provided the majority of the society with access to consumer goods. In this way, it made
the restrictions on consumer goods production seem less onerous. But,
those unable to afford necessary items were still shut out of the market as they would have been without an explicit system of rationing.

IMPLICATIONS OF THE WAR MOBILIZATION

The war-time economy evolved during an emergency. Decisions
were taken, not because their long-run implications had been
thought out but, because the situation seemed to offer no other
choice. These decisions, however, had implications for the economy
in the years to come.

The labor force was permanently changed by the war-time experience. Women would be more likely than men to lose their jobs in
war industries during the demobilization and many would leave the
labor force. However, the decline in female labor force participation
would quickly cease and the participation rate would begin to rise,
eventually surpassing its war-time high. Black men would not return
to the farms but would remain an important component of the
industrial work force.

The war-time growth in union membership solidified the presence
of unions in the economy. The war-time regulation of industrial relations forced employers to recognize and deal with unions in a reasonable manner. While the NWLB and its rules would quickly
disappear from the scene at the end of the war, its decisions would
continue to influence the overall direction of labor–management
relations in the postwar period. Unions would not disappear nor
would collective bargaining. However, with the end of the war, the
nature of collective bargaining and with it the proper roles of labor
and management would be in dispute.

By the end of the 1946, most of the administrative controls would be removed from the economy and many of the war-time agencies would be dismantled. There would be a quick, substantial conversion, at least temporarily, to a peace-time economy. But the federal government would not shrink to its prewar size. It would have an important role to play in the postwar economy and would increasingly come to be seen as being responsible for the overall performance of the economy. However, its policy agenda and policy tools would be in dispute.

The domestic political economy would develop in a postwar world shaped by an international monetary system created at Bretton Woods, New Hampshire in 1944. These monetary arrangements would be particularly advantageous to the United States. The United States would dominate the world economy, at least for a short while.

PART II: THE MAKING OF AN INSTITUTIONAL FRAMEWORK, 1945–60

2. Macroeconomic Policy, Economic Instability and Economic Growth

With the ending of the Second World War, many economists predicted, and many people feared, that the economy would plunge into a depression. Production for war would cease; the federal government would cut back its demand for goods and services. No other source of demand would replace it and overall production levels would decline. This prediction was incorrect. There was a great demand for consumer goods and investment goods, including plant and equipment for replacement, modernization, and expansion, and housing and exports.

Yet, the expectation of economic decline colored the policy discussions of the day. The role of the federal government in the postwar economy was being debated. The war had demonstrated the positive effect the federal government could have on the economy. It was assumed that the government had a responsibility to maintain a healthy, growing economy. The government's commitment to stabilizing the economy and maintaining high employment levels was formalized in the Whittington–Taft Employment Act of 1946. It stated that the aim of economic policy was to "promote maximum employment, production and purchasing power." While the goals were vague, it was clear this was not a full employment bill.

In addition, the legislation was extremely vague on how the goals were to be attained. There were several directions government policy could take. One was to continue the war-time planning and resource mobilization in a peace-time setting. Another was a return to a more laissez-faire economy, minimizing the role of the state. Neither of these two paths were taken. Rather, a third path was forged, somewhere between the two. After the demobilization, government macroeconomic policy played a more important role in the economy than prior to the war. Also, the government did not shrink to its prewar size. But explicit planning of economic activity or control over resource allocation was, for the most part, shunned.

The Truman and Eisenhower administrations had different macroeconomic policy goals, with Truman emphasizing economic growth and Eisenhower focusing on stabilizing the business cycle. While their goals were different, they both pursued, but not always systematically, a "passive" form of Keynesianism. While economic instability and unemployment continued to characterize the economy, economic growth did occur. From 1948 to 1959, the average rate of growth of real Gross National Product (GNP) exceeded 3 percent per year. The pronounced upward trend in federal expenditures on goods and services after the Second World War demobilization fostered a growing economy over the period as a whole (Hickman, 1960, p. 237). High levels of government military spending helped to maintain aggregate demand but fluctuations in such spending were important destabilizing elements in the economy. There were four business cycles during the Truman and Eisenhower administrations. They were milder in intensity than those of earlier periods. Reflecting this, the unemployment rate fluctuated around lower levels than in earlier times.

Serious economic problems emerged toward the end of the Eisenhower years. High levels of unemployment and high levels of inflation, by the standards of the period, occurred simultaneously. In addition, there was a large deficit in the balance of payments. The Eisenhower policies were unable to handle the situation and perhaps even made matters worse.

FROM A "FULL EMPLOYMENT BILL" TO AN "EMPLOYMENT ACT"

Remembering the Great Depression, the public feared that peace would be accompanied by high levels of unemployment. Public opinion favored the federal government assuring jobs for all. The Murray–Wagner Full Employment Bill of 1945 was drafted.

The initial version stated that every American able and willing to work had the right to a job. The government was to guarantee this right. Annually it would present to the US Congress a National

Production and Employment Budget. This would show the number of jobs needed for full employment, the nominal level of GNP that would provide these jobs, and the nominal value of GNP expected to be produced if no specific government actions were taken. If expected GNP fell short of full employment GNP, the President would be required to submit a policy program designed to increase the GNP to its full employment level. The bill provided the appropriations needed to carry out the program (Stein, 1969, p. 198).

To improve its chances for passage, the bill was watered down. Rather than beginning with every American able and willing to work having the right to a job, the legislation started off with it being the policy of the US government to foster "free competitive enterprise." Also, the right to useful, paid full-time employment was only for those who had finished their schooling or did not have full-time housekeeping responsibilities. In effect, many youth were being sent back to school and many women back to the kitchen.

The initial version listed a variety of actions the federal government could undertake to guarantee full employment. They included the provision of increased public services in the areas of health and education, slum clearance and urban rehabilitation, conservation and development of natural resources, rural electrification, as well as programs designed to foster small business and increased investment by private enterprises. The implicit message was that the private sector did not adequately provide for social needs and needed to be complemented by specific public programs.

This implication was eliminated when, in referring to federal expenditures to guarantee full employment, the new version merely stated they should be used to stimulate additional non-federal investment and expenditures. In addition, a new clause was added directing the President to include with the National Production and Employment Budget a general program for preventing inflationary dislocations if the economic conditions warrant it. Thus, the goal of fighting inflation was beginning to be mentioned in the same breath as the goal of providing employment. Finally, no money was appropriated for carrying out federal job creation initiatives. New laws would need to be passed authorizing any new programs (Bailey, 1950, pp. 57–58).

This Full Employment Bill proved too radical for Congress. The business community sent many representatives to testify against it. A few business people criticized the proposed legislation because it would eliminate the unemployed willing to work at low wages.

But most representatives of the business community claimed to support the notion of full employment, but not this particular bill. (Even if they were concerned about the drying up of the pool of the unemployed, it would have been impolitic to be explicit about it.) Some feared a return to the high unemployment levels of the 1930s and the resulting social and political turmoil.

The faults the business community found with the legislation ran the gamut. Of course, everyone did not endorse all of the objections. The bill's conception of full employment was not consistent with the free enterprise system. First, the government would stifle individual initiative if it provided work for everyone. Second, inflation would emerge before full employment would be reached. Price controls, which restrict individual freedom, would then be imposed. Third, business confidence would be undermined by the likely reliance on federal deficit spending for achieving the goals of the bill. Fourth, public job creation would drain away the labor force from the private sector making it more difficult for firms to remain in business (Bailey, 1950, pp. 129–133; Currie, 1977, p. 99).

The business community claimed that the proper path to full employment should be through the private sector. The proper role for the government should be to improve business confidence. A healthy business environment will, it was argued, result in economic growth and improved employment opportunities for all. In this light, rather than developing public employment programs, the government should cut corporate capital gains and income taxes, and increase the mobility of the labor force. If, after these policies were implemented, adequate job creation did not occur and unemployment remained, the government should strengthen and expand the unemployment insurance system (Currie, 1977, p. 99).

The business community effectively scuttled the Murray–Wagner Full Employment Bill. The US Congress eventually enacted the Whittington–Taft Employment Act of 1946. The US Chamber of Commerce played an influential role in developing this legislation (Collins, 1981, pp. 105–108). Full employment was gone from the title and from the bill. The act stated that it was the continuing policy and responsibility of the government to "foster and promote free competitive enterprise" and in so doing create conditions "under which there will be afforded useful employment for those able, willing and seeking work." In addition, the government should "promote maximum employment, production and purchasing power."

Thus, the relevant population was narrowed even further. The government was only to be concerned with those able, willing and seeking to work and not those who are able to work but have given up seeking work since they feel they cannot find a job. In addition, the goal of maximum employment, not full employment, was not to override the other goals of maximum production and purchasing power.

The goals were vague as were the means for attaining them. The legislation set up the Council of Economic Advisers and the Joint Economic Committee of the Congress. It required that an annual Economic Report of the President be prepared. The National Production and Employment Budget was eliminated. No money was appropriated for specific federal job creation programs, nor was there any mention of such policies. In effect, all the government had to do to increase employment was to stimulate the private sector.

The business community had enough political clout to have legislation passed furthering their objectives. This was not a full employment bill. At best, it was a codification of the expectation that the government had an important responsibility for maintaining a healthy economy and some responsibility for employment levels.

THE OVERALL DIRECTION OF ECONOMIC POLICY

The controversy surrounding the employment legislation reflected an ongoing debate over the general direction of government economic policy. To what extent and how would the government intervene in the postwar economy? Gold (1977) argues that three distinct coalitions – which he characterizes as left, right and center – representing three distinct policy positions participated in this debate.

The left coalition, which included the Congress of Industrial Organizations (CIO) unions and many liberal organizations, supported the outlook of the initial version of the full employment legislation. It wanted the state to play a substantial role in the economy to guarantee full employment and lessen economic inequality. State social spending should grow and economic planning should occur.

On the contrary, the right coalition, reflecting a conservative business perspective, argued that the role of the state should diminish and the competitive market should play a greater role in organizing economic activity. Full employment was not a desired goal; in fact, occasional bouts of unemployment served a therapeutic purpose by limiting the bargaining power of unions and keeping wages down. Government intervention into the economy, more often than not, worsened conditions. It interfered with private capital accumulation. Also, attempts at income redistribution increased the likelihood of political instability by explicitly politicizing the distribution of income. To restrain the growth of the state, they proposed keeping taxes on high incomes low thereby leading to low levels of investment and keeping the federal budget balanced at this low level of revenue.

The center coalition, quite heterogeneous in nature, included elements of the business community as well as many who would consider themselves politically liberal. It emerged the dominant coalition in the policy debate. It favored a strong government whose goal in economic policy would be to stabilize the economy and foster economic growth. Such growth, it was argued, would limit the need for the redistribution pushed by the left coalition. High employment would replace the left coalition's goal of full employment. Conscious economic planning would not occur, nor would there be a conscious mobilization of resources. Rather economic growth and stability would be achieved by the use of aggregate policy tools, such as monetary and fiscal policy. Focusing on growth rather than redistribution and emphasizing aggregate measures rather than conscious planning increase the likelihood that the income distribution will be perceived as deriving from the impersonal workings of the economy. As such the chances of politicizing the income distribution, a fear of the right coalition, would be lessened. In addition, the aggregate policy tools would be tailored to reinforce rather than undermine the forces of the market. The market would still determine specific economic results, such as what would be produced and how it would be produced.

In short, the position of the center coalition was quite in line with the Whittington–Taft Employment Act. While its entire program was not immediately adopted, the evolution of macroeconomic policy during the Truman and Eisenhower years demonstrated the extent to which the center coalition left its imprint on government policy.

MACROECONOMIC DEVELOPMENTS FOLLOWING THE SECOND WORLD WAR

As the war came to a close, economic reconversion took on added importance. There were two central macroeconomic policy concerns.

First, which, if any, war-time controls should remain? Second, what measures should be taken to attempt to stave off the predicted recession or, perhaps even, depression? The controls were eliminated rather quickly. The anticipated serious economic slowdown did not materialize due to the existence of tremendous pent-up demand for consumer and investment goods, and foreign demand for American exports to help in the rebuilding of countries devastated by the war.

The most influential segment of the business community – big business – actively supported the ending of production controls. Most small business groups took no position on this matter. Government restraints limited the freedom of business. "Industrialists did not want the reconversion process guided by professors and planners" (Bernstein, 1965, p. 244). In general, there was little effective opposition to the removal of controls. By the end of 1945, very few production controls remained.

The decontrol began in earnest shortly after VE day – May 8, 1945 – when Germany surrendered. The War Production Board (WPB) lifted more than 130 orders prohibiting the use of materials for civilian production. Right after VJ day – August 16, 1945 – when Japan surrendered, the War Manpower Commission ended all labor controls. On August 18, President Truman issued Executive Order 9599 telling all government agencies to "continue stabilization of the economy." But they were also to "move as rapidly as possible without endangering the economy toward the removal of price, wage, production, and other controls" (Bernstein, 1965, p. 252). Shortly thereafter on August 20, 210 WPB orders concerning consumer goods production were revoked. When the WPB was replaced by the Civilian Production Administration on November 3, 1945, only 55 control orders remained of the nearly 650 which it had enforced at the peak of its activity. Within a relatively short period of time, these, too, were eliminated. With the ending of restrictions on consumer goods production and the expected increase in output, little need was seen for a system of rationing and it, too, was eventually stopped.

The philosophy behind the decontrol was that business would lead the way to a successful peace-time economy. Though a system for planning economic activity had been in place and had worked reasonably well during the war, it was rapidly dismantled. The government would not actively direct resource allocation.

Controls on prices remained for a longer time than did production controls, but they, too, were eventually ended. Except for the business community, there was strong support for maintaining price controls after VJ day. The National Association of Manufacturers and the US Chamber of Commerce conducted a massive lobbying campaign against the price controls, claiming they represented a "socialistic" program that was inhibiting production and employment. The labor settlements in the steel industry in 1946 (discussed in the following chapter) marked the beginning of the abandonment of the price control program. Following this agreement, new regulations were issued increasing the freedom of business to raise prices. In June 1946, the US Congress renewed the Emergency Price Control Act but attached amendments to it further weakening the program. Fearing its effect on inflation, President Truman vetoed the legislation. The sustaining of the veto meant that all prices were decontrolled as the Emergency Price Control Act was no longer in effect.

In one month, prices rose by 5.4 percent, an annual rate of inflation of 67.4 percent. By the end of July, the Price Control Extension Act introduced weak price controls. A three person board was set up to oversee the Office of Price Administration and foster decontrol. The prices of a variety of products, including meat, were decontrolled by the legislation and could only be recontrolled by an act of the board. In September, it rolled back meat prices to their June 30 levels. Angry meat producers withheld meat from the market and serious shortages developed. Public support for continued price control sharply declined. In October, Truman lifted controls on meat prices to end the shortage. On November 9, he ordered the removal of all remaining price ceilings, except those for rents, sugar and rice. For all practical purposes, the war-time price controls were no longer in operation. At the same time, wages and salaries were totally decontrolled (Rockoff, 1984, pp. 103–108).

Prices increased as controls were in the process of being lifted. From February 1946 to June 1946, the annual rate of inflation was 8.4 percent. From June 1946 to March 1947, prices rose at an annual rate of 21.4 percent (Rockoff, 1984, p. 109). Had the predicted post-war recession or depression materialized, it is likely that the rate of inflation in the reconversion period would have been distinctly lower. There would have been less of an imbalance between the effective demand for and supply of goods and services at the existing prices. The pent-up demand kept the economy in relatively high gear.

People wished to buy the consumer goods denied them during the war. Returning veterans, understandably, were interested in going on a spending spree. The high marriage rate made many purchases necessary for the establishment of new households. People wanted better housing and there was a serious housing shortage at the end of the war. Nonresidential investment complemented the demand for consumer items and housing. Consumer goods industries needed to undertake projects postponed during the war. Facilities converted to war production had to be reconverted to consumer goods production. The government had constructed billions of dollars of new plant during the war. These were often sold to their original war-time lessees at a price of less than one-quarter of the original cost. Many of them needed to be transformed to be suitable for nonmilitary production.

Enough individuals were in decent financial condition to spark a vast increase in expenditures on consumer goods and housing. The savings rate had been abnormally high during the war and people had an unprecedented amount of liquid assets. Returning veterans had accumulated savings and demobilization benefits. The Revenue Act of 1945 reduced individual income taxes, thus providing people with more money to spend.

This legislation also repealed the excess profits tax and lowered corporate income tax rates. Firms were awash in funds at the end of the war. New working capital – the difference between current assets and current liabilities – more than doubled during the war as did the ratio of corporate holdings of cash and government securities to current liabilities (Hickman, 1960, p. 42). The liquid assets of individuals and businesses were supplemented by easy access to credit at low rates of interest. To facilitate borrowing by the US Treasury, the Federal Reserve was still following a monetary policy designed to ensure low interest rates.

The high foreign demand for American exports complemented the demand for consumer and investment goods. War-ravaged countries needed food for their people, raw materials for their industries, and new and rebuilt production facilities. A variety of federal grants and loans helped to finance these purchases. (Foreign economic relations will be discussed in Chapter 4.)

The increased consumer, investment, and foreign demand for goods and services counterbalanced the scaling back of government military purchases. A postwar expansion ensued. But, it took some time for it to develop. Initially, there was a sharp drop in production. Real GNP (measured in 1958 dollars) fell from an annual rate of $361.7 billion in the second quarter of 1945 to $297.4 billion in the first quarter of

1946. Total government military purchases fell from an annual rate of
$163.8 billion to $37.2 billion. Real GNP declined by an amount
approximately half the drop in government defense purchases because
consumption expenditures increased from $162.9 billion to $185.9 billion, gross private domestic investment increased from $21.1 billion to
$45.1 billion and net exports grew from −$6.0 billion to $7.8 billion.
It is quite unusual for consumption and investment expenditures to rise
when the overall level of economic activity is falling. However, this was
due to the pent-up demand (Blyth, 1969, p. 212).

The decline in government military purchases continued but at a
much slower pace. The pent-up demand pushed real GNP higher
but it still remained well below its war-time peak. The expansion continued, though not steadily, into 1948. The economic rebound made
it easier for the economy to absorb many of the returning veterans.
From May 1945 to December 1946, the number of people in the
Armed Forces fell from 12.1 million to 1.9 million while civilian
employment rose from 53.8 million to 56.6 million. The official
unemployment rate rose from 1 percent to 4 percent, still a relatively
low rate for the American economy (Blyth, 1969, p. 67).

The unemployment rate remained low because many women left
the labor force. The labor force participation rate of women fell from
37 percent in April 1945 to 30 percent in April 1947 (Pidgeon, 1947,
p. 668). Some women voluntarily left the labor force and returned to
the home, perhaps, to start families. Many others, laid off from well-
paying jobs in the war industries and unable to find equivalent work
elsewhere, stopped seeking work and left the labor force.

Prices continued to rise through 1948 with the rate of inflation
being 7.8 percent in that year. This postwar inflation, as do all
inflations, represented an imbalance between the claims placed on
the economy and the economic output available to satisfy them.
Government claims on economic output were dramatically reduced
and nonmilitary production was increasing though not at an
adequate rate. A small portion of this nonmilitary production – the
excess of exports over imports – can be thought of as the claims of
the foreign sector. The remaining civilian production was unable to
satisfy the claims of workers and owners of businesses. At the end of
the war, both workers and business people were unsatisfied with
their income positions. Workers demanded higher money wages in
hopes of, at least, maintaining or perhaps increasing their real
income. Employers placed their claims by raising prices in hopes of

increasing their profit margins. A price–wage spiral or wage–price spiral developed. In this instance, the spiral was facilitated by individuals and corporations drawing upon their large idle money balances built up during the war.

A restrictive monetary policy is one possible means of partially restraining an inflationary spiral. The Federal Reserve would refuse to provide the growing supply of money required to finance economic transactions at ever higher prices. But during the postwar inflation, monetary policy was focused on maintaining low interest rates, not restraining inflation.

An agreement among the various groups of claimants to economic output is another means for slowing an inflationary spiral. Such an agreement might take the form of wage–price controls. Yet, this was a period of decontrol. The inflationary process was allowed to run its course.

Inflationary pressures subsided toward the end of 1948 amid signs of an impending economic downturn. Consumer demand and private investment began to level off and the export surplus declined. A large federal budget surplus in 1947, arising from the effect of inflation on tax revenues, contributed to the economic downturn.

ACCEPTING A FEDERAL BUDGET DEFICIT

The Truman administration under the guidance of Leon Keyserling, Chairman of the Council of Economic Advisers, emphasized the importance of economic growth as a primary goal of economic policy. Economic growth should supersede efforts to redistribute income since a growing economy can generate the resources to improve the conditions of poorer members of society. How such economic growth was to be achieved was not particularly clear. Keyserling favored increasing government expenditures rather than reducing taxes, a policy he considered generally regressive and to be avoided (Collins, 2000; Hargrove and Morley, 1984). The response of the Truman administration to the impending recession is a useful gauge of the nature of macroeconomic policy at this time. In retrospect it is apparent that one of several proper policies – a tax cut – was undertaken helping to make the recession a mild one. Yet, the Revenue Act of 1948 was passed by the US Congress over President Truman's veto and fostering economic growth was not its primary goal.

The legislation lowered marginal tax rates, especially for the wealthy. Its supporters claimed this would increase managers' incentives to work and investors' willingness to provide venture capital. Furthermore, they argued that lower government revenues would forestall further increases in government expenditures and perhaps force the government to retrench and begin to reverse the New Deal. This would not be the last time such arguments would be made in favor of tax relief for the rich. John Hanes, a former Assistant Secretary of the Treasury, and a supporter of the legislation, saw the issue as "whether you are going to encourage the free enterprise system to go ahead, and stay with the capitalistic system, or whether we are going to a socialist economy" (Holmans, 1961, p. 69).

President Truman vetoed the bill on the grounds that it was inequitable, inflationary and an example of poor finance. Not realizing that a recession was on the way, the Truman administration saw the tax plan providing people with more disposable income, most of which would go toward additional consumption. Believing there were labor and material shortages, the administration felt this increased demand would result in price increases rather than additional production. (They did not believe the undocumented assertions concerning an increase in work effort and venture capital.) In addition, the Truman administration argued that sound finance required that taxes not be reduced but rather that the federal budget be in surplus and that the surplus be used to reduce the national debt.

Several months after the tax plan was passed the economy began to contract. Though the Truman administration did not actively use macroeconomic policy to counter the recession, its actions at this time were quite significant. It did not try to eliminate the federal budget deficit that was developing. The President's mid-year economic report stated:

> if we tried to avoid a budget deficit by cutting essential expenditures, we would contribute to lower national output and lower employment. Federal receipts would fall further, and the burden upon Federal expenditures would increase. We cannot expect to achieve a budget surplus in a declining national economy. (Quoted in Holmans, 1961, p. 113)

This was an important break with past notions that the federal budget must never be in deficit, except perhaps during war time.

The President further elaborated on his approach to fiscal policy in a special message to the US Congress on January 23, 1950. He argued:

> Our general objective should be a tax system which will yield sufficient revenue in times of high employment, production, and national income to meet the necessary expenditures of the Government and have some surplus for debt reduction. (Quoted in Lewis, 1962, p. 123)

In short, there should be a high employment budget surplus. Thus, even though the Truman administration placed an emphasis on economic growth, its approach to macroeconomic policymaking could be characterized as merely a "passive" form of Keynesianism. Active "discretionary" macroeconomic policy was not pursued.

THE CED AND MACROECONOMIC POLICY

Nevertheless, the Truman administration's position on the federal budget marked an important step in the development of macroeconomic policy. It was similar to some of the notions being advanced by the Committee for Economic Development (CED). The CED program represented the ideas of the liberal wing of the business community. Its significance lay in the fact that macroeconomic policy would develop along many of its lines as time went on.

The major statements of the CED on fiscal and monetary policy were issued between 1944 and 1948. It opposed discretionary fiscal policy. It did not believe that accurate nonpolitical forecasts of economic developments, necessary for such a policy, could be made. Also, the CED felt that the budgetary process was so politicized that it would be impossible to change taxes and expenditures in a timely, efficient fashion. Furthermore, the business people of the CED did not feel represented in the budget-making process. Rather than discretionary fiscal policy, they proposed, in effect, a fixed-rule fiscal policy.

Under the fixed-rule fiscal policy, once a level of expenditures had been decided upon, tax rates should be set to yield a small budget surplus if the economy would be producing the high employment level of output. The CED quite arbitrarily defined high employment as a 4 percent rate of unemployment. Though there was minimal basis in fact for this figure and while it was the CED's representation of high employment, not full employment, it became the conventional measure of full employment for the next two decades. The CED was not interested in full employment, though it was concerned with the employment problem. Full employment might be accompanied by serious inflation and to achieve it would require too much government intervention in the free market.

Not only was the unemployment level set for high employment crucial, but the notion of measuring the budget at a high employment level was also very significant. This allowed for budget deficits to occur if the economy was producing at a level of output well below the high employment level. Such a deficit would arise from the operation of automatic stabilizers – the automatic response of taxes and government expenditures to fluctuations in economic activity. For example, everything else equal, as economic activity declines tax revenues fall and expenditures on government transfer payments, for example, unemployment compensation and social welfare expenditures, rise. This lessens the severity of the economic downturn. Being against discretionary fiscal policy, the CED did not wish such deficits to emerge from conscious government actions – such as raising expenditures and cutting taxes – to increase aggregate demand and, thus, real GNP.

In fact, the CED argued that tax rates should generally remain constant and discipline should be exercised over government expenditures. Stable tax rates were necessary for business planning. Over time, with a growing economy, normal increases in expenditures and stable tax rates, the CED argued that government tax revenues would be more than enough to enable the government to consider lowering tax rates in the future. Also, in times of severe economic instability, when discretionary fiscal policy changes would be required, tax changes rather than expenditure changes should be used. The CED did not wish to see the government play an expanded role in the economy and tried to shift the policy discussion away from the use of government expenditures as the primary fiscal policy tool to the use of tax rates.

While the CED was opposed to discretionary fiscal policy, it was in favor of discretionary monetary policy implemented by the Federal Reserve. This was at a time when the Federal Reserve was, in effect, following a fixed rule monetary policy – pursuing a monetary policy which guaranteed low interest rates. Many members of the CED were bankers and some were directors of Federal Reserve banks. All were friends of directors. They felt their views were consistent with those making monetary policy and did not wish to have monetary policy-maker's hands tied by fixed rules (Stein, 1969, pp. 220–232).

Also, monetary policy is more congenial to corporate values than is fiscal policy. While manipulating monetary aggregates influences the general economic environment, decisions concerning what will be produced still remain totally in the hands of the private sector. But with fiscal policy, especially government expenditures, the potential is there for the public sector to make some of those decisions.

In short, the CED developed a macroeconomic policy program fully consistent with corporate values. As CED chair Ralph Flanders put it, the CED's program would allow "natural adjustments under the laws of supply and demand and under the incentives of the profit system, rather than efforts by direct regimentation" (Collins, 1981, p. 139).

The CED's vision of monetary policy became a reality with the Treasury–Federal Reserve Accord of March 3, 1951. The Federal Reserve would no longer feel obligated to base its monetary policy on the needs of the US Treasury. It would no longer be committed to buying government bonds so as to maintain stable, low interest rates. It would be free to sell government securities to reduce the money supply and tighten credit if the need should arise. Interest rates might then rise.

THE KOREAN WAR

A few months after the Treasury–Federal Reserve Accord the Korean War broke out. Remembering the shortage of goods during the Second World War, consumers and business people went on a buying binge. In response, production was increased and inventories rebuilt. Capital budgets were expanded to provide for new investment in plant and equipment. The military build-up had not yet occurred but serious inflation had already emerged. In the last six months of 1950, the Consumer Price Index (CPI) rose by 5 percent and the index of wholesale prices of manufactured goods rose by 10 percent (Holmans, 1961, pp. 133–134). With a substantial military mobilization still to come, restraining inflation took on high priority.

The Second World War provided lessons for managing a war economy. The Truman administration was well aware of them. But the Korean War was of a much smaller magnitude. The economy would not need to be fully mobilized for war.

The Truman administration raised income and corporate taxes in September 1950 and enacted an excess profits tax in January 1951 to both fight inflation and finance the war. Government tax revenues increased faster than did expenditures and a federal budget surplus was run in the last half of 1950 and the first quarter of 1951. A federal budget surplus during a war period is most unusual.

Higher taxes alone proved inadequate for fighting inflation and fighting the war. To further curb the demand for goods and services, controls were placed on installment credit and mortgage credit. In addition in January 1951, an Office of Price Stabilization was created similar to the Office of Price Administration in the Second World War. It was to enforce the newly created wage and price controls. Most wages were frozen at their existing level and most prices were frozen at levels based on their maximum level during the period December 19, 1950 to January 25, 1951. The ensuing wage and price stabilization program was much less restrictive than during the Second World War. But public support for the program quickly diminished as the US Congress restricted the ability of the Office of Price Stabilization to control prices.

Military rearmament outraced tax revenues. The federal budget surplus turned into a substantial deficit. Expenditures on national security programs increased from $13 billion in 1950 to $22.3 billion in 1951, to $44 billion in 1952 and to $50.4 billion in 1953. Only a part of the dramatic increase in military expenditures was to pay for the Korean War (Block, 1977, p. 108). This was the beginning of a permanent expanded military presence in the federal budget.

Prior to the Korean War, the Truman administration asked representatives of several government agencies to analyze US military strategy and capabilities. Their report – National Security Council Document Sixty-Eight (NSC-68) – written under the guidance of Secretary of State Dean Acheson and Chair of the State Department Policy Planning Staff Paul Nitze – remained classified until 1975. Their key recommendation was that the military budget should be substantially increased immediately.

Containing the spread of communism was a primary concern. And the Soviet Union had recently exploded an atomic bomb ending the US monopoly on nuclear weapons. But the policymakers also saw military spending having positive economic effects. A large military budget would provide a floor under the economy, limiting the risk of another depression. Increasing military expenditures would stimulate the economy along Keynesian lines.

While it would seem that military leaders and business leaders would support this new policy direction, opposition was initially expressed by both groups. The Chairman of the Joint Chiefs of Staff General Omar Bradley argued that such lavish military spending would threaten the nation's economic system and constitute as great a threat as the Soviet Union (Koistinen, 1980, p. 13). Business leaders were worried about the costs, both their costs and the costs to the economy. They feared higher taxes or a rising national debt if tax revenues were inadequate. They were concerned by the growing role to be played by the government in determining what was to be produced. They feared a loss of efficiency, given the expected waste and duplication in military procurement. Excessive military expenditures might cause an economic boom resulting in wage and price controls (Lo, 1982). Business leaders did not accept the notion of a potential need for government stimulation of the economy. Their misgivings about military spending were borne out by their experiences during the Korean War. The federal budget was in deficit, wage and price controls were implemented, and after-tax profits fell strongly from the second quarter of 1951 on. Business opposition slowed somewhat the accelerated increase in defense spending during the Truman years. (Eventually, military leaders and business leaders would become more comfortable with bloated defense budgets.)

AFTER KOREA

The Korean War ground to a stalemate. An armistice was signed on July 26, 1953. In his first year in office, Dwight Eisenhower grappled with the questions of decontrol and demobilization. All wage and price controls were ended by March 1953.

Defense orders began to decline prior to Eisenhower taking office. A more rapid fall occurred after the armistice was signed. Defense purchases declined from an annual rate of $50.5 billion in the second quarter of 1953 to $38.4 billion in the fourth quarter of 1954. Almost simultaneously, a recession set in with the unemployment rate rising from 2.6 percent in August 1953 to 6.2 percent in September 1954 (Holmans, 1961, pp. 211–213).

In the face of the economic downturn, the Eisenhower administration did not substantially increase government spending on goods and services, one possible anti-recessionary strategy. The administration was not interested in increasing the role of the federal government in the economy. Rather it wished to lower federal spending, balance the federal budget and generally reduce the role of the government in economic affairs. It believed that excessive government intervention would negatively effect private enterprise. Furthermore, it felt that inflation, as well, was inimical to long-term economic growth. With this perspective, it argued that the main goal of the government should be to foster price stability, a prerequisite for private enterprise led growth. As such the Eisenhower administration was willing to accept a slower rate of economic growth in the short term in the interest of price stability. Overall, it interpreted its responsibilities under the Employment Act of 1946 somewhat differently than did the Truman administration. While accepting federal responsibility for the economy, it interpreted its main responsibility under the Employment Act of 1946 to be to "foster and promote free competitive enterprise." The Truman administration, being more focused on economic growth, wished to emphasize promoting "maximum employment, production and purchasing power" (Hargrove and Morley, 1984, p. 92; Collins, 2000).

While the economic perspectives of the Truman and Eisenhower administrations differed, their responses to unfolding recessions were similar. The Eisenhower administration also practiced a "passive" form of Keynesianism. It accelerated some previously authorized spending programs. It allowed a previously scheduled reduction in personal income taxes and the expiration of the war-time excess profits tax to take effect in January 1954. The Eisenhower administration's passive policy was particularly distinctive in one respect. As did the Truman administration, it did not heed the call to balance the federal budget. During the contraction, it accepted a federal budget deficit, mainly arising from the operation of the automatic stabilizers. Thus, a federal budget deficit was acceptable, at least during a recession.

The downturn was mild and short-lived, lasting only 13 months. By 1955, the economy had fully recovered from the recession. Between 1955 and 1957, real GNP advanced. Though not the only factor responsible for the expansion, it is important to note that federal military expenditures rose as well. While the amount of spending was still below Korean War levels, a more permanent armaments industry was being created.

There were two more recessions during Eisenhower's time in office. A short but very rapid economic contraction occurred during 1957–58 and a brief but mild downturn took place toward the end of 1960. Contrary to earlier recessions, prices did not fall during these downswings. The rate of inflation was relatively low but concern was expressed about "creeping inflation."

The government was more worried about inflation than unemployment. Between 1954, the first year after the ending of the Korean War and 1960, the last year of the Eisenhower administration, the unemployment rate averaged somewhat higher than 5 percent. This was considered a high rate of unemployment. The government fostered a high level of unemployment in order to increase the likelihood of price stability. With high unemployment, workers are less able to place their claims for higher wages, thus lowering the rate of increase of costs of production. In addition, firms are less able to continually raise prices.

The government viewed "creeping inflation" as inimical to long-term economic growth. Since inflation erodes the value of money, there is less of an incentive to save. Thus, the real value of savings falls and there are fewer funds available to be used for investment in new plant and equipment. The amount of new investment will decline and the growth of additional productive capacity will slow. (This view of investment relied on the controversial notion that the volume of real savings is the primary determinant of investment. However, even if the funds are available, business people may be less likely to increase investment expenditures if there is weak demand for goods and services.) In addition, the government feared that "creeping inflation," if not halted, would turn into "rampant inflation" with very dire economic consequences (Holmans, 1961, p. 314).

To combat inflation, as well as increase economic growth and protect the international position of the dollar, the government focused on generating a large federal budget surplus in 1959–60. When there is a federal budget surplus, tax revenues exceed expenditures on goods and services and transfer payments. As the government withdraws more funds from the economy than it returns to the economy, the demand for goods and services, especially consumer goods, declines. The weakening of overall conditions of demand limits the ability of businesses to raise prices, thus lowering the rate of inflation.

While in the short term the government saw a budget surplus leading to a lower rate of inflation, over the long term the Eisenhower administration believed it would foster economic growth. In their view, the surplus represented funds not spent for current consumption, or by the government. The surplus would be used to retire outstanding government bonds, thus providing bondholders with money that could potentially be used to finance investment in new plant and equipment. Assuming that the surplus was generated in a manner that did not reduce private savings by an equivalent amount, then the total amount of funds available to finance private investment would increase. Investment would rise leading to an expansion and modernization of productive capacity. Strong economic growth would follow (Stein, 1969, pp. 350–351).

The connection which the Eisenhower administration tried to draw between running a federal budget surplus and protecting the international position of the dollar was extremely tenuous, at best. The underlying issue was the balance of payments deficits being run by the United States every year since the ending of the Second World War. The United States payments to the rest of the world were exceeding the US receipts from the rest of the world. Foreigners were accumulating dollars. The United States had pledged to redeem those dollars for gold, if desired. In 1958 and 1959, gold was draining out of the United States, as large quantities of dollars were being redeemed for gold.

International confidence in the dollar needed to be restored. However, there is little connection between running a federal budget surplus and being able to redeem the dollars for gold or goods and services. To the extent that a budget surplus is anti-inflationary, the international competitiveness of products made in the United States would increase. But international competitiveness was not what the Eisenhower administration had in mind. Rather according to Stein (1969, p. 355), the government believed that "our creditors – mainly foreign bankers – thought that a balanced budget was a good thing; and as long as they thought that, it really was a good thing." And if a balanced budget was viewed in a positive light, a budget surplus would be viewed even more positively.

The economy did not respond as the government anticipated. The rate of inflation did slow to 0.8 percent in 1959 and 1.6 percent in 1960 from 3.6 percent in 1957 and 2.7 percent in 1958. But, the economy grew at a slower than expected rate. The rate of unemployment remained high. And by the end of 1960 the economy was in a recession once again. Striving for a budget surplus led to a more restrictive fiscal policy than would otherwise have been the case. The tight fiscal policy restricted the demand for goods and services and helped cause the failure of the economy to recover fully from the 1958 recession.

CONCLUSION

During the 1940s and 1950s, Keynesian demand management policies were not systematically applied toward economic stimulation. Nevertheless, growing federal expenditures on goods and services helped to maintain aggregate demand and economic growth. Military expenditures were an important component of federal expenditures and fluctuations in such spending, reflecting changes in overseas military activity, did destabilize the economy at times.

Labor–management relations were played out against the backdrop of a growing economy. Right after the Second World War, unions attempted to redistribute income from employers to employees. However, they were not particularly successful. By the end of the 1950s, labor and management had created a mode of operating whereby both workers and employers shared, to an important degree, the benefits of economic growth. The evolution of labor–management relations during the second half of the 1940s and the 1950s is the subject of the next chapter.

3. Business–Labor Relations: Conflict Amidst Stability

With the ending of Second World War, great uncertainty surrounded labor–management relations. Both parties wanted to move from the regulated environment of the war period to a more unregulated "free collective bargaining." Unions felt wage increases were long overdue, especially given their perception of high levels of corporate profits earned during the war. Management, on the other hand, felt profit margins were too low due to unfair price controls. While both labor and management desired free collective bargaining, the terrain over which bargaining was to occur and the tactics to be used were in dispute. A government convened Labor–Management Conference ended in failure. Agreement could not be reached on the dividing line between labor prerogatives and management rights.

While the conference was on, a strike wave was engulfing the country. The conflicts appeared to center on wages, prices and profits. But lying behind them was a more central issue, that being the relative power of management and organized labor. Employers wanted to regain what they considered to be their proper sovereignty in the workplace. Unions, in most cases, wanted to extend more deeply into areas thought, by some, to be management's domain.

The strike wave led to the passage of the Taft–Hartley Act in 1947. This law limited the ability of unions to press their demands and provided the legal basis for the purge of radicals from the labor movement. This law, along with the Wagner Act and the rulings of the National Labor Relations Board (NLRB) and the courts, set the legal boundaries within which collective bargaining would take place.

Employers chose to live with unions where they existed. But nonunion firms fought strongly to keep unions out and unionized firms often opposed union organizing drives in new facilities. The initial collective bargaining settlements foreshadowed the types of agreements entered into in the following decades. A typical contract would include provisions for a union shop, a grievance procedure ending in binding arbitration, a no-strike clause and a residual management rights clause. The result was a management guarantee that the union was safe as an institution and a union guarantee that production would not be interrupted except possibly during a contract renegotiation. In addition, workers received increased compensation and a share of the benefits from increased productivity.

Some have argued that an accord developed between business and unions (Bowles *et al.*, 1983). This was not the case. A truce was not signed, an accord was not reached. Rather labor and management continued to be in competitive conflict. There was a shared set of understandings about the nature of the conflict. But the rules of the conflict continually evolved reflecting the relative power of business and labor.

LABOR–MANAGEMENT CONFERENCE ON INDUSTRIAL RELATIONS

Against a background of labor strife, President Truman's National Labor–Management Conference met from November 5 to November 30, 1945. Representatives from the leading groups of organized labor (American Federation of Labor (AFL), Congress of Industrial Organizations (CIO), United Mine Workers and Railroad Brotherhoods) and business (National Association of Manufacturers and the US Chamber of Commerce) and several nonvoting delegates representing the public attended.

Agreement was reached on several issues though some important areas of dispute remained. They agreed that once a union was certified as the duly chosen bargaining agent for the employees, an employer should promptly bargain in good faith with it. During the bargaining for the first contract, strikes should be postponed until all peaceful procedures had been utilized. Grievances under the terms of an existing contract should be settled by an effective grievance procedure ending in voluntary arbitration rather than in strikes or lockouts. There should be no discrimination in hiring or union membership on the basis of race, sex, color, age or creed. But many issues remained unsolved. The delegates were unable to agree upon a means for avoiding or minimizing strikes in the reconversion period. Management rights were another stumbling block. The labor representatives were unwilling to create a special list of management functions, off-limits to workers. They argued that "the responsibilities of one of the parties today may well become the joint responsibilities of both parties tomorrow" (Chamberlain, 1948, p. 8). For management that was akin to saying that the terrain of collective bargaining might continue to expand, perhaps going as far as joint management of the enterprise. Employers found this prospect totally unacceptable.

The conference reflected the mood of the time. By this point, most employers with unionized workers had come around to the view that unions would be a permanent part of the American landscape and that collective bargaining would be an activity they would be forced to participate in. Grievances would arise and would need to be adjudicated in a legitimate fashion. Unions would place some limits on their freedom of action. But what would those limits be? That was to be struggled over.

Given that the conference could not agree on how to minimize strikes, it was fitting that the participants could not use public transportation on the second day of the conference. A transit strike was in progress. More importantly, on November 21, while the conference was still in progress, a nation-wide work stoppage by the United Auto Workers (UAW) against General Motors began. It was to prove to be one of the most important strikes of the Great Strike Wave of 1945–46.

THE GREAT STRIKE WAVE OF 1945–46

The Japanese surrendered on August 14, 1945, ending the Second World War. Organized labor's no-strike pledge ended on that day as well. The 12-month period following the cessation of hostilities was characterized by a wave of strikes. The US Bureau of Labor Statistics described the first six months of 1946 as "the most concentrated period of labor–management strife in the country's history" (Crowther, 1947, p. 788). During a ten-day period, from January 13 to January 23, 1946, over a million workers in the steel, electrical-manufacturing, meat-packing, and farm equipment industries struck their employers. During this time, workers involved in strikes tripled in number, rising from slightly less than a half-million to approximately 1.5 million (US Department of Labor, 1946, p. 877). The country has never experienced anything like this since.

Overall, from August 15, 1945 to August 14, 1946, there were 4630 strikes, directly involving about 5 million workers. The number of strikes, while high for the time, had been exceeded in 1944 and was exceeded several times thereafter. But the number of workers involved in strikes has never been matched. About 14.5 percent of employed workers were on strike at some point in 1946 (Crowther, 1947, p. 782).

About one out of every 100 stoppages were sympathy strikes to support walk-outs of other unions or to protest actions of government agencies or employers, other than one's own (Crowther, 1947, p. 796). Several of these sympathy actions were general strikes. These occurred in Stamford, Connecticut, Lancaster, Pennsylvania, Rochester, New York, Pittsburgh, Pennsylvania and Oakland, California. In Rochester, both AFL and CIO unions stopped work for one day to protest the city's refusal to recognize or bargain collectively with the AFL Federation of State, County and Municipal Employees and the firing of approximately 500 employees in the Department of Public Works trying to unionize. The two-day Oakland general strike was a protest against a police escort of nonunion truckers making deliveries to two major department stores being struck by the AFL Department Store and Specialty Clerks Union (Lipsitz, 1982).

On the surface, most strikes were over labor compensation. Unlike the situation prior to the war, relatively few stoppages were over union recognition or union security, reflecting the fact that many employers had accepted the right of unions to exist. In addition to desiring higher wages for their own sake, the labor movement argued that a general increase in hourly wage rates was required to prevent an economic collapse and the massive unemployment that would accompany it. With the ending of the war, government purchases of military products would decline. To maintain the overall demand for goods and sevices, private consumption demand, which is strongly affected by the level of disposable income of workers, needed to rise. Thus, maintaining prosperity required that wage rates be increased so that workers would have adequate amounts of money to spend.

The Truman administration supported the overall logic of labor's position. On October 30, 1945, in a radio broadcast, President Truman said:

It had been estimated that, unless checked, the annual wage and salary bill in private industry will shrink by over twenty billions of dollars. That is not going to do anybody any good – labor, business, agriculture or the general public .... Wage increases are therefore imperative – to cushion the shock to our workers, to sustain adequate purchasing power and to raise the national income. (Quoted in Seidman, 1953, p. 220)

On the basis of estimates by the Office of War Mobilization and Reconversion, the government felt that business in general could increase wages by 24 percent while holding prices steady and still earn profits at the prewar levels. The government allowed employers and workers to negotiate wage increases, without government approval, as long as they did not result in price rises. As this was a governmental policy, it should come as no surprise that some leaders of CIO unions, such as Walter Reuther of the UAW, would ask for wage increases without price increases. This demand was totally in line with the governmental policy.

But many employers were aghast at the thought of improving wages while at the same time, keeping prices constant. While some felt they could not afford it, most believed that price setting was their own prerogative, and not something to be discussed jointly with their workers. They were in no mood to surrender any more of their "rights." In fact, they wanted to restore many of those they had lost to the unions in the past decade. Clark Kerr, an industrial relations expert, succinctly summarized the situation:

The basic conflict during 1945 to 1947 was over relative power of management and organized labor ....
Efforts to alter the location of economic and political power in the union–management relationship were the prime source of the bitterest controversies. (Kerr, 1949, pp. 46–47)

The stage was set for bitter labor strife. The time was ripe for workers to press their demands. Right after the war, unemployment levels were still low though there was a strong fear that they would rise in the near future. Employers were financially able to resist labor if they so desired, and they did. War-time profits had been extremely high and substantial retained earnings remained, even after the payment of "excess profits" taxes. Also, during the demobilization period, firms able to show losses due to the costs of reconverting to peacetime production received refunds of portions of their paid excess profits taxes. As the costs of reconversion were particularly hard to define, firms suffering losses due to strikes were compensated under this program. These refunds lowered the cost to employers of taking a strike, that being the lost profit due to shutdown, thus strengthening their will at the bargaining table.

Workers made their demands, employers resisted and strikes ensued. Though it was legal to do so, employers did not attempt to break the strikes by running the plants with nonunion labor. As many workers struck at some point during this time, and unemployment was low, it would have been difficult to recruit adequate numbers of strikebreakers. Also, many employers, though forced by governmental pressure, had learned to live with unions during the Second World War. But they would not do so on labor's terms.

When the strike wave began, war-time labor regulations were still in effect. But the National War Labor Board (NWLB), in the process of shutting down by the end of 1945, was not effectively functioning. President Truman appointed fact-finding boards to help mediate the major disputes. While fact-finding was not always successful, the solution advanced by the fact-finding board in the steel strike of 1946 set the pattern for many other settlements in major industries. The steel workers initially demanded a wage increase of $2 per day. According to the companies, wage improvements would require a lifting of the war-time price ceilings. Negotiations were unsuccessful and a strike occurred in January 1946. On February 15, 1946, an agreement was reached with the workers accepting an $18\frac{1}{2}$ cent per hour wage boost and the steel industry being granted price relief averaging $5 per ton. The government's price control program was in the process of being abandoned.

The $18\frac{1}{2}$ cent per hour increase served as the basis for settling some other significant disputes, though often after long strikes. For example, the UAW requested that General Motors open its books and prove that it was financially unable to meet the union's demand of a 30 percent wage increase without a price increase. The fact-finding board agreed with the UAW that the company's ability to grant a wage increase without raising prices should be investigated in the fact-finding process. The company refused to participate in the hearings as long as its ability to pay was at issue. With the steel settlement, the UAW could no longer demand that General Motors raise the compensation of its members without increasing prices. The fact-finding board recommended a wage increase of $19\frac{1}{2}$ cents per hour which the union accepted. Rather than settling on that basis, General Motors held out for one more month until the UAW accepted an

18½ cents an hour increase, the same granted to the steel workers and to autoworkers at Ford and Chrysler. General Motors refused to "open its books" and its power to set prices was completely protected. Furthermore, the company received permission from the government to raise prices. The company maintained its management prerogatives and ended up with an agreement, basically on its own terms.

By the end of 1946, the first wave of strikes was over. With minimal exception, management prerogatives survived relatively unscathed. While the United Mine Workers won an unprecedented health and pension fund financed by the mine operators, on the whole settlements concerned the narrow questions of wages. Furthermore, the rise in the cost of living exceeded the rise in weekly earnings, as prices exploded with the general price decontrol of June 1946. Those working in industries with the largest declines in weekly hours due to the curtailment of military production, such as steel, electrical equipment, machine tools and automobiles, saw their nominal weekly earnings fall from April 1945 to February 1947. Their real weekly earnings dropped by more than 20 percent. Workers in most other industries, though receiving higher nominal weekly incomes, suffered losses in real weekly income (Derber and Netreba, 1947). The stage was set for another round of wage negotiations. This would take place under the specter of the Labor–Management Relations Act of 1947, more commonly known as the Taft–Hartley Act.

THE TAFT–HARTLEY ACT

The Taft–Hartley Act, passed on June 23, 1947 over President Truman's veto, was designed to reduce the power of labor. Several factors account for its passage. The US Congress elected in 1946 was quite conservative in orientation. Many members of the US Congress ran on platforms opposing state regulation of the economy, a reaction to the war-time economic controls. Yet that would not stop them from voting for the Taft–Hartley Act which placed strong restrictions on the operation of unions.

The election of a conservative Congress reflected a shift in the overall political climate. The status of business was rising in the public eye. Business took credit and was credited by the public for the superior performance of the economy during the war. While business was gaining political standing, organized labor was in the process of losing some public support. However, the business community was still concerned with the support labor retained due to its war-time patriotic activities and the lingering distrust of business, and how labor's influence had spread since the New Deal. Even though the public was inconvenienced by the strikes after the war, labor still received community support during these disputes. The mayors of Pittsburgh and Cleveland publicly spoke in support of organized labor in their battle with Westinghouse Corporation. General Electric was shocked by the hostility it faced from the community during the postwar strike wave. In Three Rivers, Michigan more than 100 businessmen and professionals signed advertisements supporting workers in their dispute with Fairbanks Morse Company (Fones-Wolf, 1994, pp. 138–139). Nevertheless, well-publicized abuses of some unions made all unions vulnerable to attack.

The business community led by the National Association of Manufacturers (NAM), an organization of mainly small and medium-sized manufacturers, though with big-business support, felt conditions were ripe for a legislative attack on labor. The NAM had fought the passage of the Wagner Act. Once passed and declared constitutional, its policy became one of accepting collective bargaining but attempting to curb union power. One way to do so would be to amend the Wagner Act. While it wished decreased government regulation over the affairs of industry, it pushed for increased government control of the activities of organized labor. It made a series of recommendations to the US Congress and virtually all of them were incorporated into the Taft–Hartley Act (Kerr, 1949, pp. 58–59).

The business community threw its full support behind the Taft–Hartley Act. The NAM alone spent over $3 000 000 on full-page ads in 287 daily newspapers in 193 key industrial centers (Fones-Wolf, 1994, p. 43). Its positions were put forward, not in terms of interest of employers, which they were, but in terms of the interests of the general public and of individual workers. The NAM used "typical propaganda methods of appealing slogans, half-truths, misrepresentation and possibly known misrepresentation, as well as failure to disclose real motives" (Millis and Brown, 1950, pp. 290–291). Though this was the case, the viewpoints of organized labor, opposing the Taft–Hartley Act, did not receive the same exposure. Unions did not have the financial resources to purchase extensive newspaper advertising. Furthermore, the trade union public relations effort lacked the sophistication of the business community's campaign.

72 AMERICAN ECONOMIC DEVELOPMENT

Labor's lobbying effort in the US Congress failed and the Taft–Hartley legislation was passed.

Overall, the Taft–Hartley Act, an amendment to the Wagner Act, weakened organized labor by making it more difficult for union membership to grow and curbing its strike power. Closed shops were declared illegal; union shops were allowed to exist if the majority of workers voted for them. But states could override federal law and pass "right-to-work" laws outlawing the union shop. In an open shop environment, where workers are organized, newly hired workers are not required to join the union though they receive the benefits of union representation and union members are free to cease paying dues at any time and still retain their jobs.

Employers were given more freedom to express their views during a union organizing campaign. On company time, they could address their workers and try to convince them not to vote for a union. Employers could not threaten workers if they chose to join a union or promise benefits if they did not. Yet, there is a fine line between a threat and a "statement of fact." The National Labor Relations Board (NLRB) would have to determine the limits of appropriate employer behavior.

Once organized, unions were restricted in the tactics they could use in labor disputes. Sympathy strikes, secondary boycotts and mass picketing were outlawed. These tactics had been successfully used by unions in the very recent past. Forbidding sympathy strikes lessened effective worker solidarity as workers were restricted in what they could do to help their "brothers and sisters" involved in labor disputes. Secondary boycotts were deemed illegal to protect the "neutral employer" not involved in a given labor dispute. In this situation, a union tries to encourage workers in other firms to cease using, handling or dealing in the products of the producer with whom it is having a dispute. Mass picketing was not allowed if it barred nonstrikers from entering struck plants. Here, the right of the struck employer to continue operating superseded the right of workers on strike to attempt to shut down operations.

Not only were labor's tactics limited, strikes at the end of the contract were regulated and strikes during the term of the contract – wildcat strikes – were made more costly. Sixty days prior to the expiration of a contract, a union needed to inform an employer in writing if it wished to modify or terminate the collective bargaining agreement. The unions must be willing to meet and negotiate with the employer and if an agreement is not reached must inform the federal and state mediation and conciliation services. Regarding wildcat strikes, unions became liable for damages if their members violated the contract and could be sued by employers in Federal district courts. Thus, even if the union leadership condemned such actions, the union was still vulnerable to a court suit. And union officers could be fined and imprisoned if they did not oppose wildcat strikes.

In short, under the Taft–Hartley Act the only allowable union activity was that occurring in direct bargaining between a union – the "duly certified bargaining agent" – and the employers of the workers it represented. Worker solidarity and actions taken outside of the contract were not protected by law. Allowable strikes would only be those which fell within the confines of governmental rules and regulations. By making it more difficult for unions to grow and by carefully demarcating allowable union activities, the Taft–Hartley Act was designed to weaken organized labor, limit worker militancy and lessen the disruptive impact of strikes.

In addition, by providing a conducive environment for the weakening of communist-led unions and the elimination of communists from the labor movement as a whole, the law may have helped to stifle labor militancy. While anti-communists argued that the communists were exploiting workers and were dupes of the Soviet Union, many of the communists were effective labor leaders committed to civil rights and civil liberties (Renshaw, 1991; Zieger, 1995). Unions which failed to file affidavits stating that their union officers were not members of the Communist Party lost the protection of the Wagner and Taft–Hartley Acts on matters concerning worker representation and unfair labor practices.

Overall, the Taft–Hartley Act represented a defeat for organized labor and for workers as a whole and was a sign that the conservatism of American business was once again dominant in national policy-making. Yet, some of its elements designed to correct certain union abuses were likely positive for individual workers and perhaps, in the long run, for the labor movement. In a union shop situation, unions could not charge excessive initiation fees. Nor could they force an employer to fire or refuse to hire anyone refused admission to the union for reasons other than the nonpayment of initiation fees or dues. A union could not induce workers to strike to force their employer to recognize it as the bargaining agent when another union had been duly certified. Procedures were set up whereby workers could petition the NLRB to hold a decertification election in the event they became dissatisfied with their union. But employers, too, were given the right to petition for such elections as well as for union representation elections. Thus, they could potentially interfere with the unionization of their workers.

AFTER TAFT–HARTLEY

With the passage of the Taft–Hartley Act, the legal framework for the development of labor–management relations in the postwar era was essentially in place. Collective bargaining was institutionalized in a series of rules and regulations derived from rulings of the NLRB, judicial interpretations of law, and the laws themselves. Also, labor and management created procedures to regulate their day-to-day interactions. The broad framework which evolved was essentially accepted by the labor movement and large segments of the business community though both parties would try to use it and change it to advance their own interests. While there was a sense of stability in the collective bargaining relationship, serious conflict did not disappear. And it is probably fair to say that "if American management, upon retiring for the night, was assured that by the next morning the unions with which they dealt would have disappeared, more management people than not would experience the happiest sleep of their lives" (Brown and Myers, 1956, p. 92).

Unions would not disappear though they would not be particularly successful in organizing the growing nonagricultural work force. Union membership as a percentage of employees in nonagricultural establishments peaked at the end of the Second World War at 35.5 percent and steadily fell to 31.5 percent in 1950. Unions grew during the Korean War reaching 34.7 percent of nonagricultural workers in 1954. A steady decline in relative union membership then set in. By the end of the 1950s, it would fall to 32.1 percent of nonagricultural workers and continue to drop in the decades to follow (Blum, 1968, p. 45).

During the 1950s, structural changes were occurring in the economy making it more difficult for the labor movement to grow. Job growth was faster in white-collar and service positions where unions were less likely to be than in blue-collar areas, the heart of organized labor. In addition employment gains in the South, the least organized region, outpaced those in the rest of the country. Yet, too much should not be made of these structural changes. To do so would be to assume that the relative importance of unions in particular occupations or regions is fixed and should not change. They may change the difficulty of unionization but they do not determine the extent of unionization. Rather, public policy, management behavior and union organizing efforts are crucial in this regard.

By the middle of the 1950s, management seemed to be developing a stiffer attitude toward unions. The Taft–Hartley Act provided employers with the legal means to resist union organizing drives if they wished to do so. The NLRB gave wide scope to allowable management "free speech" during union organizing drives. The following employer statements were found legal in the Silverknot Hosiery Mills, Inc. case (1952). In talking about the likelihood of a strike if workers unionized, company representatives stated:

everybody "knows that strikes mean trouble, misery, lost work and lost pay" if everybody's wages were raised "with the result that the cost of producing hose would be so high that we could not obtain any orders, the mill would then be forced to close."

"I am not saying that if the Union came in here that this thing would necessarily happen. I certainly hope it wouldn't." (Klein and Wanger, 1985, p. 82)

Legal managerial opposition was complemented by illegal managerial tactics. From 1955 to 1960, there was a doubling in the number of cases brought to the NLRB claiming that workers had been illegally fired for union activity. Such activity most often took place during the organizing drives. The number of workers ordered reinstated by the NLRB rose by about 50 percent. Such legal and illegal campaign tactics were bound to influence workers and make it more difficult for unions to win representational elections.

It was not that all employers became rabidly anti-union, attempting to stop every organizing drive, for they did not. Even in some industries in the South, branch plants of unionized firms were at times organized without a struggle. But, this was not true of all industries. For example, many textile and apparel manufacturing firms, with unionized work forces in northern states, opened new plants in the South and fought hard to remain nonunion. A US Senate study on labor relations in the southern textile industry concluded:

> ... for all practical purposes self-organization and collective bar-
> gaining are steadily losing ground. The retreat of union organiza-
> tion is being compelled by employer campaigns on an area-wide
> front. Much of this campaign is conducted in violation of the
> Labor-Management Relations Act and the National Labor
> Relations Board appears powerless to cope with the situation.
> (Quoted in Troy, 1958, p. 418)

On balance, Troy argues that for the South as a whole, employer
opposition was the most serious obstacle to the growth of union
organization.

The passage of state "right-to-work" laws complemented employer
opposition and further stifled union growth. By 1955, 17 states,
largely in the South and Far West, had such laws. And conservative
business interests tried to have them passed in some of the more
heavily industrialized states. The labor movement was able to defeat
most of these attempts.

In the face of anti-labor public policies and stiffening employer
resistance, the labor movement needed to devote substantial resources
to organizing efforts to maintain its relative membership. It did not do
so. Union organizing expenditures did not keep pace with the growth
of the work force. And some of the money went toward raiding other
unions' memberships rather than organizing the unorganized.

Serious divisions emerged around the issue of communists in the
union movement. The United Electrical Workers did not sign the
noncommunist affidavit until the autumn of 1949. From the summer
of 1947 until the autumn of 1949, this union experienced more than
500 raids on its locals (Schatz, 1983, pp. 179–180). At its annual convention in 1949, the CIO revised its constitution to provide for expul-
sion by a two-thirds vote of any affiliate following the "Communist
line." Within a year, 11 unions, only two of which were large – the
United Electrical Workers and the Mine, Mill and Smelter Workers –
had been expelled. The purged unions accounted for one-fifth of
total CIO membership (Renshaw, 1991, p. 120). The CIO was
unable to recruit enough new members to replace them.

With the purging of "communist-dominated" unions from the
CIO and the prevalence of destructive raiding, the AFL and CIO
signed a no-raiding agreement in 1953 applying to raids on currently

existing union members but not to disputes over organizing the unorganized. The number of raid elections substantially declined. With the merger of the AFL and CIO in 1955, and the lessening of destructive interunion competition, some thought that a new era in union organizing was to begin, with substantial growth of organized labor. That was not to be.

While in 1950, unions organized 2.0 percent of the private wage and salary work force in new elections, that figure fell to 0.7 percent by 1960. Many representation elections were held. But there was an increase in the proportion of workers voting against union representation and a decrease in the percentage of elections won by unions. To a degree, this reflected the increased ability of management to influence workers' votes. Yet, the decline in the proportion of representation elections won by unions began toward the end of the Second World War, prior to the passage of the Taft–Hartley Act. Thus, it also seems that there was a decline in the popularity of unions. Overall, workers won by unions in organizing drives as a percentage of workers eligible to vote in union representation elections fell from 84 percent in 1950 to 59 percent in 1960 (Freeman, 1985, p. 46).

Not only was there labor–management conflict over the unionization of workers, serious disputes still remained once employers accommodated themselves to their unionized work forces. Accommodation, manifested by a relatively stable collective bargaining relationship, does not imply consensus. Workers were quite likely to engage in strikes in the 1950s, particularly during the late 1950s. In 1958 and 1959, over 30 percent of the workers in manufacturing, under contracts covering bargaining units of 1000 or more workers each whose contracts expired went on strike. These figures were never reached in later years (Kaufman, 1978, p. 423).

This strike activity during the late 1950s coincided with a change in management behavior in the major manufacturing industries. Contemporary observers claimed that employers were following a "harder line" in their dealings with unions. Mass production union leaders were convinced that management "at the very least looks to a drastic cutting down of union power and, at the most, offers a challenge to union existence" (Barbash, 1961, p. 25). In retrospect, there was not a challenge to union existence though employers did try to cut down union power.

The evolution of the typical postwar collective bargaining agreement can serve as a basis for understanding management's tougher line.

Long-term contracts became the rule rather than the exception. Multi-year contracts accounted for only 25 percent of the agreements negotiated in 1948 but for 87 percent of those negotiated in 1960 (Garbarino, 1962, p. 75). These agreements provided a measure of certainty and stability in labor–management relations as they were negotiated at lengthier intervals. Full-scale industrial conflict was less likely to occur during the term of a contract than at its expiration.

Not only were contracts longer, they were more inclusive. In the late 1940s, rulings of the NLRB, subsequently upheld by the courts, widened the definition of wages to include pensions and health and welfare funds. Thus, employers were forced to bargain over these issues if so requested by the unions. Workers covered by private pension plans increased from 3.8 million in 1940 to 15.2 million in 1956. While some workers receiving pensions were not covered by collective bargaining agreements, most of the postwar growth in coverage was due to trade unionism (Ulman, 1961, p. 437).

In addition, there was a vast growth in the number of workers receiving health and welfare benefits. Estimated coverage of workers under health and welfare plans under collective bargaining in 1945 was ½ million, in 1948 it was 3 million, and in 1954 about 11 million. By 1954, approximately 70 percent of all workers covered by collective bargaining agreements had such benefits (Slichter et al., 1960, p. 403).

Some workers were even able to gain a measure of protection from the financial distress of unemployment. In the early 1950s, the UAW and the United Steel Workers of America (USWA) pushed the notion of a guaranteed annual wage for their members. Employers were unwilling to accept this possibility. But they were convinced to set up programs providing for supplemental unemployment benefits, funded by company contributions. Laid-off eligible workers would receive limited payments, in addition to their unemployment insurance. The automobile companies set up the first plans in 1955 and they soon spread to firms in the steel, can, rubber and glass industries.

Beyond the general issue of compensation, unions were able to gain a modicum of say over personnel decisions and work rules. Employers often had to follow specific procedures for layoffs, transfers, promotions, retirements and assigning overtime. Though situations varied, seniority considerations were often important in this regard. Union input into work rules provided workers with some control over the work process as management often had to negotiate over production standards and rates. Workers would need to be consulted, in some cases, when new equipment was being introduced or when jobs were being changed. Elaborate grievance procedures were set up, often ending in arbitration if an agreement could not be reached.

Management's freedom of action was somewhat limited and operating costs perhaps increased. But management still retained control over the operations of the firm. Many important areas such as pricing and investment lay outside the realm of subjects on which employers were legally required to bargain. Of course, employers would have preferred no restrictions on their decision-making powers. Yet, employers benefited from these arrangements. Personnel and work rules collectively determined by labor and management helped reduce the sources of industrial conflict. Grievance procedures and arbitration resolved disputes while maintaining stability. In effect, they allowed for the continued operation of the plant while determining solutions to the problem. In a generally healthy economic climate, maintaining production is an extremely important consideration for management. In a wide-ranging survey of postwar industrial relations, Slichter *et al.* (1960, p. 946) conclude: "The pressure for concessions (from management) was increased by the war and by large profits of the postwar boom, which made managements extremely reluctant to lose production."

It was this desire for stability which led to an important innovation in wage payments – automatic wage adjustments over the life of the contract. General Motors led the way in its negotiations with the UAW in 1948. A two-year contract was signed calling for 8 cents an hour to cover recent price increases, a cost-of-living adjustment every three months (the "escalator clause") and an additional 3 cents an hour each year as labor's share of expected productivity increases (the "annual improvement factor"). The escalator clause protected workers' real wages. Their nominal wages would rise with inflation, but would fall if prices declined. The annual improvement factor would guarantee that the standard of living of workers would improve.

The company did not want another lengthy strike as there was a tremendous demand for automobiles. It would have signed a five-year contract if the union would have been willing. General Motors would gain two years of, hopefully, uninterrupted car production. The workers would not have to struggle to maintain their living standards in the face of inflation, and would receive benefits from economic growth, resulting from technological advance and general increased productivity.

The company saw the annual improvement factor as an implied acknowledgment by the union that productivity increase was the only basis for increases in real wages. In effect the company was saying that economic growth should be the only means for improving the living standards of workers. The redistribution of income from owners to workers should no longer be on the union's agenda. Needless to say the UAW did not see it that way. It argued that the contract was only a beginning. At its expiration, labor would still fight for improvements in wage and nonwage aspects of the contract.

There were few followers of this contract. In fact, the cost-of-living declined during 1948–49 and workers lost a total of 5 cents an hour in wages. The 1950 agreement would be more a model contract for negotiators in other industries. The duration of the contract was extended to five years. To gain union acceptance, the company improved on the annual improvement factor and granted a modified union shop, requiring new employees to join the union but allowing withdrawals after one year.

In the early 1950s, it was rare for workers not organized by the UAW to have both cost-of-living escalators and annual improvement factors in their contracts. As the rate of inflation accelerated during the Korean War, many had cost-of-living escalators at that time. But many of these were dropped in the ensuing period of price stability. The typical contract, though long term, had provisions for annual wage reopenings where bargaining would take place over the wages to be paid in the following year.

After 1955, automatic wage adjustments along the lines of the UAW–General Motors (GM) agreement began to take hold. Railroads, steel, aluminum and meat-packing negotiated this type of agreement in 1956. By the end of the decade, it became the most common form of contract. Employers had seen the success of this arrangement in the automobile industry, as no major company had a company-wide strike since adopting this approach to wage payment. Nor had wages increased at an unacceptably fast rate. In addition, employers were relatively confident of continued economic growth. Though there had been two minor recessions in 1949 and 1953–54, by 1955 the American economy had experienced a decade of relatively high-level prosperity since the end of the Second World War. Also, they felt that annual wage reopenings had produced substantial wage increases for workers, even during recessions.

Thus, employers wished to gain the benefits of long-term contracts with automatic wage adjustments. These contracts were seen by many workers as being more beneficial to their employers than themselves. Management had to make concession to gain the agreement of their workers. Often the annual improvement factor was greater than the expected rate of productivity advance and provided for higher wage increases than in the recent past. This was combined with a cost-of-living escalator.

Still it would have been a good deal for employers if prosperity and price stability had remained. They did not. The sharpest decline in business activity since the Second World War, until that time, had begun toward the end of 1957. Profit margins were under pressure and foreign competition was becoming stronger. At the same time the rate of inflation was substantially higher than management had anticipated, resulting in higher than expected cost-of-living allowances. Management's harder line in the late 1950s was in response to the new economic situation and the higher than expected costs of their labor agreements.

Increased cooperation was seen among employers in several major industries. The purpose of this cooperation was to limit the gains of unions rather than to eliminate unions altogether. There was more interfirm cooperation in the steel and auto industries. Mutual assistance pacts and strike insurance plans were developed in the airline, railroad and newspaper publishing industries. Under these plans, non-struck firms would provide financial assistance to those firms facing strikes in order to strengthen their will at the bargaining table.

Employers were interested in both slowing wage gains and increasing their control over the work process. Though most major strikes continued to be mainly over wage issues, conflicts over work rules, job assignments, automation and subcontracting dominated several major labor disputes in the airline, steel, railroad, glass and cement industries. Employers were trying to economize on labor costs and workers justifiably saw this as a threat to their job security.

Though rare, some major employers, such as the American Oil Company, Standard Oil of Indiana, United Aircraft Corporation (in 1960) and General Electric (GE) (1960) kept their plants operating during strikes. Not only did they emerge victorious from the strikes, but they also severely weakened their unions in the process.

CONCLUSION

At the close of the 1950s, unions were on the defensive. They were not fighting for their existence. Where they existed they were accepted by management. A stable framework for collective bargaining had evolved. They were struggling to maintain the gains they had achieved since the Second World War. These included improvements for workers in wages and fringe benefits and some say in personnel decisions and the organization of work. To a degree, they had infringed upon management prerogatives and management was trying to push them back. Yet, it was only to a degree for management still retained basic control over the operations of the firm.

To a large degree, the well-being of workers was tied to economic expansion. Though one goal of unions is to redistribute income from employers to employees, they seemed more successful at assuring that the workers received some of the benefits of economic growth. And in periods of economic expansion, employers were more willing to make concessions to their workers rather than suffer the cost of strikes. Economic prosperity lessened the severity of the conflict between labor and management. Though a basic power conflict remained, the stabilization of certain aspects of bargaining facilitated the production of goods and services, thereby facilitating economic growth. Furthermore, as workers' wages rose in step with the productive capacity of the economy, it helped to maintain an adequate demand for goods and services.

4. From Dollar Shortage to Dollar Glut

During the Second World War, policymakers in several countries developed alternative frameworks to govern monetary and financial relations between nations after the war. In 1944, representatives of 44 nations met at Bretton Woods, New Hampshire to create a new international monetary system. The Bretton Woods arrangements strongly reflected the preferences of the US government. This was not accidental. The United States was the dominant economic and military power at the time. The dollar was the key currency in the system; its value was tied to gold. All of the other currencies had fixed exchange rates relative to each other and relative to the dollar. But, it would be more than a decade before currencies would become fully convertible.

As with domestic economic policy, the expectation of a postwar depression colored the international economic policy discussion in the United States. There were several directions government policy could take. One was to push for a relatively closed economy whereby trade would occur only for those goods which could not be produced at home. Government macroeconomic policy and economic planning would serve to guarantee high employment levels and forestall economic downturns. This path was not chosen. Rather American policymakers pushed for a more open world where relatively free trade was to be the organizing principle. An export surplus would help to guarantee demand for American products, thus lessening the likelihood of a postwar depression in the United States.

Initially the export surplus was easy to attain. The European countries had to rebuild after the war and American firms were able to supply their needs. A dollar shortage emerged in Europe. Thus, in the late 1940s, American trade surpluses were financed by Marshall Plan aid. This aid was designed with several goals in mind, one of which was to reconstruct the European nations in accordance with American

83

designs and integrate them into a relatively open world economy dominated by the United States. When Marshall Plan aid ended, the export surpluses were funded by other government expenditures, including overseas military expenditures.

Though the United States ran balance of trade surpluses throughout much of the 1950s, the overall US balance of payments were generally in deficit. European governments initially supported such deficits since they enabled them to build up their dollar holdings. Eventually, toward the end of the 1950s, they began converting their excess dollars into gold, causing a run on US gold stocks. Europeans, rather than needing American goods, were now more successfully competing with American businesses on the world market. The US balance of trade temporarily turned negative in 1959 and the balance of payments deficit increased sharply toward the end of the 1950s. Strains were beginning to emerge in the international monetary system.

BRETTON WOODS

In July 1944, more than 700 delegates from 44 countries held three weeks of discussions in Bretton Woods, New Hampshire aimed at creating a blueprint for the postwar economic order. The war had not yet ended but the Allied nations were already planning for the future. The talks concerned relatively arcane international monetary arrangements. But behind the discussions was a prior question. Which country or groups of countries would dominate the postwar economic order? At the time of the conference, the United States was the strongest militarily and economically of the Allied countries. Its views would prevail and it would come to reap particular advantages from the postwar international monetary regime.

Prior to the conference, two major options had been advanced, one a British position developed by John Maynard Keynes and the second a US proposal presented by Harry Dexter White. Both argued for a relatively open international economy with trade flows being mainly determined by market forces. A supranational monetary institution would need to be created to guarantee conditions for relatively stable exchange rates across national currencies and determine the rules of international economic conduct. It would not unduly interfere with the traditional trading and financial activities of business people and bankers.

However, Keynes and White differed on the nature of the supra-national monetary institution and the rules of international economic conduct. Keynes wanted an international monetary regime that would enable Great Britain, as well as all other countries, to pursue full employment policies. He proposed an International Clearing Union, whose main function would be to provide credit to those nations running balance of payments deficits. These countries, and Great Britain was likely to be one of them, would feel little pressure to adjust their economic policies to eliminate the deficits.

Rather, the burden of adjustment would fall on countries, such as the United States, likely to run balance of payments surpluses. They would merely receive credits on the books of the International Clearing Union for their surpluses, not any goods or services. Countries running perpetual balance of payments surpluses would, in effect, be giving away a portion of their national production to countries running balance of payments deficits.

Thus, surplus countries would be induced to change their economic policies to reduce their balance of payments surpluses. More expansionary macroeconomic policies would likely be pursued, inasmuch as the demand for imports rises with economic growth. Rising imports would reduce the balance of payments surpluses. With countries running balance of payments surpluses being induced to expand economic activity and countries with balance of payments deficits feeling little pressure to shift their policy direction, a successfully functioning International Clearing Union would provide the basis for worldwide economic growth (Block, 1977, p. 48; Gardner, 1980, pp. 78–100).

Assuming the United States would be the dominant economy after the war and likely to run balance of payments surpluses, Keynes' plan implied that the United States would be forced to extend almost unlimited credit to the rest of the world and bear the brunt of the balance of payments adjustment. This was unacceptable to the US policymakers. In contrast to the Keynes plan, the White plan placed the burden of adjustment on countries with balance of payments deficits and provided for less liquidity to be made available to countries with temporary balance of payments difficulties.

White proposed the creation of an International Stabilization Fund. The members would contribute currencies and gold to the fund according to a system of quotas. Given that the fund would have substantially less at its disposal than would Keynes' International Clearing Union, the US contribution would be finite, not openended, and would be smaller than under Keynes' plan. Countries with temporary balance of payments deficits would be able to borrow needed currencies up to the amount of their quotas. The fund would have the right to strongly recommend changes in their domestic policies in order to correct the payments deficits.

Keynes and White negotiated to narrow the differences between their proposals. Out of their meetings came the Joint Statement of Experts, mainly based on the White plan. The Joint Statement, with minor changes, became the Articles of Agreement of the International Monetary Fund (IMF), approved by the participants of the Bretton Woods conference. The Articles of Agreement stated that the purpose of the IMF was to foster worldwide economic growth by facilitating the expansion of international trade, promoting exchange rate stability, eliminating foreign exchange restrictions, helping to establish a multilateral payments system, and providing assistance to member countries facing balance of payments disequilibria, particularly balance of payments deficits.

They laid the groundwork for the international monetary arrangements that would be in operation until August 15, 1971. The dollar, considered to be as "good as gold," was placed at the center of the international monetary system. The US government guaranteed to exchange any dollars held by foreign central banks for gold, at a price of $35 for one ounce of gold. This had been the price of gold since 1934. The dollar, being as "good as gold," provided a pillar of stability, at least for a while, for the international monetary system.

The value of all other currencies would be fixed relative to each other and relative to the dollar. With IMF approval, each member country would establish a par value, or exchange rate, for its currency. It would then be obligated to attempt to maintain that exchange rate (within a band of 1 percent on either side of parity) by appropriate intervention in the foreign exchange markets. Countries would intervene by buying or selling dollars against their own currencies. For example, assume Great Britain had been experiencing a balance of payments deficit. On the foreign exchange market, at the existing exchange rate, the supply of British pounds would exceed the demand for British pounds, causing downward pressure on the value of the pound. The British government would be expected to purchase the excess supply of pounds with dollars, it might have in reserve, thus maintaining the existing exchange rate. To change an exchange rate, a country would need to get IMF approval.

Such approval would only be granted if the country's balance of payments was in "fundamental disequilibrium." What a "fundamental disequilibrium" might be was not defined in the Articles of Agreement.

Thus, it was a system of relatively fixed exchange rates, with member countries being obliged to try, to the degree possible, to maintain their parities. But countries with large balance of payments deficits might run out of dollar holdings and not be able to support their currencies on the foreign exchange markets. They would then be able to turn to the IMF for assistance. The IMF would have at its disposal holdings of gold, dollars and other currencies subscribed by its members on the basis of their quotas. Based on its size in the world economy, each member country was assigned a quota payable partly in gold and partly in its own currency. The IMF would be able to lend to member countries in deficit, out of its holdings of gold and currencies. The maximum amount of a loan would be based on the size of the country's quota. Countries with chronic deficits would eventually lose the right to borrow from the IMF. At that point, the IMF would be able to intervene in the economic policies of the countries in question. IMF-set conditions would have to be satisfied prior to a country being able to again borrow funds from the IMF.

The total of the initial quotas subscribed by member countries was very small, equaling only $8.8 billion. This was about one-third of the amount of resources which Keynes wished to make available to countries with balance of payments deficits. The United States had the strongest economy at the time and was very influential in limiting the size of the initial quota. It wished to limit the extent to which American dollars, borrowed from the IMF, would support profligate behavior – the running of excessively large balance of payments deficits. Yet, American dollars would be needed for postwar reconstruction because war-torn countries would need to import substantial amounts of goods from the United States. The funds would be provided directly by the United States through the Marshall Plan. And with the Marshall Plan, the United States would have a major say in the rebuilding of postwar capitalism.

THE MARSHALL PLAN

Under the Marshall Plan, officially known as the European Recovery Program, the United States gave more than $13 billion between 1948 and 1952 to 16 Western European countries and West Germany. Over 90 percent of this aid was in the form of grants. At the same time, the IMF played a decreasing role in the world economy, with the IMF lending falling from $606 million in 1948, to $119.4 million in 1949, $52.8 million in 1950 and $28 million in 1951 (Wood, 1986, pp. 23, 29). The IMF complied with a US request that countries receiving Marshall Plan aid be declared ineligible for IMF loans, as long as that aid program existed (Eckes, 1975, p. 227). For the time being, the United States was pursuing its aims through bilateral aid rather than international organizations.

The Marshall Plan represented a resolution of an on-going debate over the nature of the postwar United States economy, the position of the United States in the world economy and the nature of that world economy. The debate was strongly influenced by a fear that the US economy would revert back to the depressed state present at the start of the war. While there was an awareness of the possibility of some pent-up demand forestalling the onset of the depression, it was feared that the pent-up demand would be satisfied relatively quickly. At that point, then, what new sources of demand for domestically produced goods and services would emerge?

Block (1977, 1980) distinguishes between two distinct policy positions in the debate, that of the national economic planners and that of the business community. The national economic planners had strong ties to the labor movement, particularly the new industrial unions of the CIO. The position of the national economic planners on the domestic economy was similar to that of the left coalition, discussed in Chapter 2.

Given that they pushed for government macroeconomic policy to guarantee full employment, they argued that the international economy should be organized along the lines of relatively closed, national economies. Most goods would be produced domestically, even if they could be purchased more cheaply from other countries. The benefits of full employment would justify import restrictions. Some products would not be able to be produced at home. For those items, bilateral trading arrangements between countries would be developed, with each nation being assured of a stable market for particular commodities. Most international capital flows would be eliminated. Any international investment that would occur would be done on the basis of international agreements. While the business community was divided on the question of international economic policy, they were very strongly opposed to the national economic planners. They did not support the political forces in the coalition with the national economic planners. Fully aware of the problem of inadequate demand for American-made products, they looked to foreign markets to guarantee economic prosperity, and their prosperity, after war.

Assistant Secretary of State Dean Acheson put it quite clearly when he testified before a special Congressional Committee on Postwar Economic Policy and Planning in November 1944. He stated:

> It seems quite clear that we are in for a very bad time, so far as the economic and social position of the country is concerned.... You don't have a problem with production. The United States has unlimited creative energy. The important thing is markets. We have got to see that what the country produces is used and is sold under financial arrangements which make its production possible.... You must look to foreign markets.... We could argue... that under a different system in this country you could use the entire production of the country in the United States... I take it the Soviet Union could use its entire production internally. If you wish to control the entire trade and income of the United States, which means the life of the people, you could probably fix it so that everything produced would be consumed here, but that would completely change our Constitution, our relations to property, human liberty, our very conceptions of law. (Quoted in Williams, 1962, pp. 235–236)

Thus, from Acheson's point of view the choice was between seeking out foreign markets or running the risk of an economic depression or experiencing significant social upheaval. Foreign markets were the more desirable outcome. Yet, foreign markets required foreign purchasing power and at the outset, at least, that would be lacking. He argued that private capital would not be able to provide the necessary credit to finance foreign purchasers. Thus, an alternative source of funds would be needed. That would eventually turn out to be the Marshall Plan.

The "export surplus" was at the heart of the business community's proposals for a prosperous US economy. To the extent that the value of goods and services exported from the United States exceeded the value of goods and services imported into the United States, that would complement the domestic demand for commodities produced in the United States. As such, it would serve to stimulate the economy and help to forestall another depression. Furthermore an export surplus would make an equivalent amount of federal governmental spending on goods and services unnecessary. This would lessen the need for a second New Deal and the policies of the national economic planners. The business community did not want the federal government to play as large a role in the domestic economy as it did during the Great Depression.

Given the desirablity of the export surplus, two questions needed to be answered. First, how should the international economy be organized to guarantee that foreign markets would be available for products made in the United States? Second, how would the export surplus be financed?

The answer to the first question was clear. Contrary to the national economic planners, the business community called for a world economy organized on an open, multilateral basis. Under such arrangements, the United States would not need to balance its accounts with each individual country as would be the case if the world economy was organized on a bilateral basis, as the national economic planners suggested. The United States would then be able to run export surpluses with many countries. Furthermore, an open world economy would provide maximum freedom for American firms wishing to pursue foreign investment opportunities.

The source of financing for the export surplus was less clear. With a US export surplus, countries would need a sum of dollars equivalent to the value of the surplus that they would not be able to obtain by selling goods and services to Americans. Initially it was thought that loans to war devastated nations would be sufficient. But loan financing raised the problem of repayment, not just of the principal of the loan but also the accrued interest. In the worst case scenario, new loans would need to be continually issued to pay off old loans, a never ending upward spiral of lending.

Eventually it was realized that "in fact, an outright gift, plainly labelled as such, may be the best solution in certain circumstances" (Eakins, 1969, p. 160). This was the position taken in a report written by Twentieth Century Fund's Committee on Foreign Economic Relations in 1947. On this committee sat leaders from the worlds of business, labor and academia. The Marshall Plan became the gift.

With the Marshall Plan, American policymakers wished to foster the growth of an open international economy under the leadership of the United States. They argued that two major tasks needed to be accomplished for this to be achieved. First, the rebuilding of European capitalist economies had to continue, but not along the lines of relatively closed national capitalisms based on state intervention and planning. Rather they believed that Europe should be organized along the lines of relatively open capitalist economies engaging in relatively unrestricted trade. According to Robert Hall of the British Treasury, "the Americans want an integrated Europe looking like the United States of America – 'God's own country.'" (Hogan, 1987, p. 427). Second, the influence of the Soviet Union needed to be contained.

European reconstruction required American aid to purchase food and materials on world markets. In 1946 and 1947, European exports to the United States covered no more than one-quarter of its imports from the United States. European countries were also running balance of trade deficits with the rest of the world. While some portion of these deficits were financed by loans from the United States, the gold and dollar reserves of Europe were being depleted. In 1946 and 1947 alone, the gold and dollar reserves fell by one-fourth (Solomon, 1982, p. 14). This situation could not continue. New sources of financing had to be found if European countries would be able to continue importing necessary goods and services.

Furthermore, while the United States was not being shut out of European markets, government policymakers feared that without American help, European nations would develop along the lines of relatively closed national capitalism. In 1947, American exports accounted for 27 percent of European imports, as compared to 10 percent in 1938 (Armstrong et al., 1984, p. 109). Still Secretary of State George Marshall worried in January 1948:

> There is no doubt that if the countries of Europe should be forced to meet their present problems without further assistance from this country the result could only be a radical increase in the restrictions and controls in force throughout the area affecting international trade and investment .... It is idle to think that a Europe left to its own efforts in these serious problems of recovery would remain open to American business in the same way that we have known it in the past. (Quoted in Wood, 1986, p. 39)

Given their shortage of dollars and gold, European countries placed restrictions on a wide variety of international economic transactions. Capital mobility was controlled so that money did not flow out of currencies perceived to be less stable and into currencies considered to be more stable, such as the dollar. There were import controls so that unacceptably large trade deficits did not arise and further deplete dollar and gold reserves. Much of the trade that did occur within Western Europe took place on the basis of country to country agreements designed to guarantee that exports would be paid for substantially by imports.

Some American policymakers feared that if the outflow of dollars and gold from Europe was to grow, European nations might consider implementing strict permanent controls on American exports and US investment in Europe. Not only did American policymakers see an open European economy as consistent with American economic interests, they also believed that such an arrangement was more conducive to European economic growth. While economic growth was a goal in its own right, it was also a means for mitigating conflicts between organized labor and organized business over the distribution of income. Such conflicts would be more severe in a stagnating or retrenching economy (Hogan, 1987, p. 428). And politicians of the Left were becoming more powerful. The politicians of the Right were often discredited because of right-wing collaboration with fascism. Left-wing politicians gained from the Left's participation in resistance movements during the war. The communists were the largest or second-largest parties in the parliaments of several European countries including France and Italy. According to American diplomat George Kennan, "economic maladjustment … makes European society vulnerable to exploitation by any and all totalitarian movements" (Kunze, 1997, p. 33). In other words, people who are suffering might vote for communists. The Marshall Plan was a form of containment of the Soviet Union.

On March 12, 1947, President Truman announced the Truman Doctrine, stressing the threat that totalitarian regimes posed to the security of European nations, declaring the Soviet Union to be the enemy and announcing the policy of containment. The Cold War had officially begun. The communists coming to power in Czechoslovakia in February 1948 increased the fear of the Soviet threat. At this time, the Marshall Plan was being debated in the US Congress. Conservatives argued against substantial funds for the Marshall Plan fearing that large-scale aid would bankrupt the US Treasury, create shortages, cause inflation and eventually lead to higher taxes or the imposition of economic controls (Hogan, 1998, p. 93). However, events in Czechoslovakia caused a scare in Washington DC and the Marshall Plan was approved with overwhelming support.

The Marshall Plan officially began on July 1, 1948. It was in operation for four years. In Europe, preliminary work for Marshall Plan aid had begun the year before. All European countries, including the Soviet Union, were invited to participate in the program. Though initially open to the possibility of joining, the Soviet Union eventually declined to participate and required all Eastern bloc countries to follow its lead. The Soviet Union did not wish to have its reconstruction plans dictated by the United States or the Western European countries. It did not want to be integrated into the capitalist trading sphere. Furthermore, it correctly feared that the issue of German reparations would be set aside. The question of the reparations was replaced by Marshall Plan aid to what would become West Germany.

It is likely that the United States knew from the very beginning that the Soviet Union would not accept Marshall Plan aid given the strings attached. In response, the Soviet Union set up Cominform, an organization designed to foster the development of the socialist countries. The Western bloc and the Eastern bloc were being solidified.

While the United States did not achieve all of its aims, the Marshall Plan did succeed on several levels. First, Marshall Plan aid fostered European economic recovery. The aid enabled European countries to maintain the flow of necessary imports, particularly imports priced in dollars. It also allowed European countries to maintain a high level of investment in new plant and equipment. Industrial productivity rose rapidly by 42 percent in the four years after 1947 (Armstrong et al., 1984, p. 126). Had this aid not been forthcoming, European countries would likely have had to take steps to reduce their trade deficits so as to limit the outflows of gold and dollar reserves. These might have included further controls on trade or restrictive macroeconomic policies designed to slow the economy to reduce the demand for imports. In the short term, neither of these policies would have been favorable for economic growth (Milward, 1984).

Second, the European economies did experience a great economic boom in the 1950s and 1960s. The US-led recovery policies attempted to put Europe on the path to more open, integrated economies. And the European Economic Community was eventually created in 1957. To the extent that the rapid economic growth of the 1950s and 1960s is related to the implementation of more open, integrated economic relations among European countries, then the Marshall Plan had a role to play in fueling European economic prosperity.

Third, while the United States wished to influence the long-term growth process in Western Europe, it also wanted to gain some short-term advantages for American businesses. There are many examples of specific benefits being carved out for American corporations under the rubric of the Marshall Plan. Agriculture was one privileged sector. Marshall Plan funds used for food imports had to be spent on American agricultural surplus items, even if cheaper commodities were available from other producers. In 1948, the Europeans requested wheat, but they were forced to accept one-fourth of their wheat shipment in the form of flour. The Europeans wished to build refineries so as to be able to import crude oil rather than the more expensive refined products. The United States approved relatively few expenditures for refineries. Thus, the Europeans had no choice but to purchase grossly overpriced oil from the US firms. And at least 50 percent of all goods purchased under the Marshall Plan had to be shipped in US boats, insured by American insurance companies, even if lower shipping costs could be found elsewhere (Kolko and Kolko, 1972, pp. 444–447; Milward, 1984, p. 121).

Fourth, the United States wanted to gain some long-term advantages for American businesses as well. The United States was interested in the raw materials available in the overseas colonies of European nations. Each aid treaty negotiated with a Marshall Plan recipient guaranteed potential American investors access "to the development of raw materials within participating countries on terms of treatment equivalent to those afforded to the nationals of the participating country concerned" (Wood, 1986, p. 42; Kolko and Kolko, 1972, p. 448).

The United States did not gain all of its aims under the Marshall Plan. When this program ended in 1952, the European economies were still not able to be fully integrated into the world economy. Restrictions remained on trade and capital flows. Currencies were not yet convertible. The European economies still needed more dollars than they were able to generate through exports and American private investment in Europe.

Nevertheless, the Marshall Plan helped to bring about Western European recovery and political stability. It helped to shift the European political climate in a pro-American direction and helped to create a status quo favorable to US interests, one which Charles Maier characterized as "consensual American hegemony" (Hogan, 1987, p. 444) since many Europeans welcomed American aid. And by creating orders for American goods it helped strengthen the United States economy.

After the Marshall Plan ended, US military aid for Europe took its place. In addition to recommending a substantial increase in military expenditures to fight the spread of communism and provide a floor under the US economy, National Security Council Document Sixty-Eight (NSC-68), written in 1950, argued that aid for European rearmament would increase the demand for goods and services in Europe and help to foster economic growth. Dollars for rearmament could be provided in various ways. First, they could be given directly to Western European governments. Second, large numbers of troops could remain stationed in Europe, who would spend dollars for local goods and services. Third, the United States could purchase weapons produced by one European country and provide them to another (Block, 1980, pp. 45–49). In each instance, additional dollars would flow into the coffers of the European governments. And the US Congress was much more likely to approve expenditures for rearmament to counter the threat of communism than additional funds for economic development.

THE BALANCE OF TRADE AND BALANCE OF PAYMENTS POSITION OF THE UNITED STATES

Marshall Plan aid and military expenditures supplemented European holdings of gold and dollars. They helped to allow the United States to run substantial export surpluses in the decade and a half after the Second World War.

With the ending of the Second World War, there was a strong foreign demand for US products. An export surplus in merchandise of $6.5 billion was achieved in 1946. This was equivalent to more than 3 percent of the Gross National Product (GNP). Foreign demand quickened in 1947 and by the middle of that year the export surplus was running at an annual rate of $20 billion. However, financing the export surplus became problematic with the slowing of US government aid to Europe and the drawing down of foreign country holdings of dollars and gold. The demand for exports sank rapidly in the second half of the year. Even so, in 1947, there was an overall merchandise export surplus of $10 billion, equivalent to more than 4 percent of the GNP (Block, 1977).

The slowdown in exports in the latter part of 1947 continued into 1948, setting part of the context for the Marshall Plan. It became apparent that further US aid would be necessary to maintain a large export surplus. While exports continued to exceed imports throughout the 1940s, the merchandise export surplus fell to $5.7 billion in 1948 and $5.3 billion in 1949. And the merchandise export surplus relative to the GNP declined accordingly to approximately 2 percent of GNP.

The latter half of the 1940s were a particularly distinctive period in postwar international trade relations. The United States dominated world markets in goods in a manner that it would not be able to replicate in the decades to follow. For example, the US share of major industrial countries' total manufacturing output was 62 percent in 1950. By 1960, it would shrink to 51 percent (Branson, 1980, p. 191). And while the United States would run merchandise export surpluses until 1971, they would rarely ever be as large as 1 percent of GNP (MacEwan, 1990, p. 88).

By 1950, after the immediate postwar reconstruction period had ended, a more long-term pattern in international trade began to emerge. In the 1950s, the United States ran growing surpluses on chemicals and capital goods while experiencing steadily shrinking surpluses on manufactured consumer goods, except automobiles. In fact, by 1959 the trade surplus on consumer items, except cars, had disappeared. (The balance of trade on cars was positive until 1968.) Imports of consumer goods were now exceeding exports. While trade in military goods was erratic, with a major expansion occurring during the Korean War, substantial surpluses were earned in this category throughout the 1950s (Branson, 1980).

The trade balance, though still positive, became a cause for concern by the end of the 1950s. It was not large enough to adequately offset large governmental military expenditures outside the United States, foreign aid and private investment abroad. And Europeans were becoming less interested in accumulating dollars just as the dollar outflow was increasing. The dollar shortage was turning into a dollar glut.

The merchandise trade surplus which averaged $3.1 billion between 1950 and 1957, dropped to $2.3 billion in 1958 and 1959. At the same time, net purchases of items by the United States armed forces stationed abroad from foreign suppliers rose steadily from $576 million in 1950 to $3 billion in 1958 and 1959. It is significant that this item continued to increase after the ceasefire in the Korean War. Government nonmilitary loans and grants continued to generate a deficit averaging $2.7 billion in the 1950s. More stable conditions abroad led to an increase in US private foreign investment. The flow of long-term private capital increased from a $900 million deficit in the early 1950s to $2.1 billion in 1958 and 1959 (Eckes, 1975, p. 243). The major growth area in the US direct investment was Europe. While Europe accounted for 15 percent of US direct investment in 1955, its share rose to 20 percent by 1960 (Branson, 1980, p. 243).

The overall US balance of payments deficit increased substantially toward the end of the 1950s. From 1950 to 1957, the balance of payments deficit, measured by the Gross Liquidity Balance, averaged $1.2 billion (Block, 1977, p. 160). However, at the time the US balance of payments was not characterized as being in deficit. Rather, the term that was used to describe this situation was "net transfers of gold and dollars to the rest of the world" (Solomon, 1982, p. 19). That, in fact, occurred and there was little questioning of it.

The rest of the world needed dollars to expand and regularize world trade. When a portion of these dollars was redeemed for gold, that tool was looked upon relatively favorably. The world gold supply was becoming less concentrated in the hands of the United States. In any event, the United States would always have adequate supplies of gold, or so it was thought. In 1953, for example, total dollar balances in the possession of foreign governments and international agencies amounted to only 57 percent of US gold reserves (Eckes, 1957, p. 249).

By the end of the decade, there was less need for dollars worldwide in the industrial countries. Europe had replenished its gold and dollar reserves and was better able to compete internationally. At the same time, however, the US balance of payments deficit was growing, increasing the outflow of dollars from the United States. From 1958 to 1960, the balance of payments deficit measured by the Gross Liquidity Balance averaged $3.6 billion, three times the annual deficit from 1950 to 1957 (Block, 1977, p. 160).

As the balance of payments deficits widened, the adequacy of US gold stocks came into question. By 1958, total dollar balances held by foreign governments and international agencies had risen to 86 percent of US gold reserves (Eckes, 1975, p. 249). And in that year, foreign governments, concluding that they had adequate dollar reserves and fearing that the dollar would eventually have to be devalued relative to gold, began converting dollars to gold in earnest. From 1958 to 1960, US gold holdings fell by $5 billion (Block, 1977, p. 157). By 1960, the amount of gold owned by the US Treasury, valued at the existing price of $35 per ounce, was less than the supply of dollars held abroad. The dollar was no longer, in effect, as good as gold.

CONCLUSION

The framers of the Bretton Woods agreements underestimated the time it would take to fully implement them. It was not until December 1958 that the Western European countries dismantled much of their exchange controls and made their currencies convertible in the foreign exchange market. Some restrictions still remained on international trade and some of these countries still retained some bilateral payment agreements. Three years later the major industrialized countries abandoned all restrictions on payments for current international transactions.

The United States had succeeded to a large degree in reestablishing liberal capitalism in Western Europe and placing international trade and payments on a multilateral basis. But at the same time as this was finally accomplished, one of the underpinnings of the international monetary arrangements – the fixed rate of exchange between the dollar and gold – was coming under stress. This pointed to a potentially fatal flaw in the Bretton Woods arrangements. There was a contradiction between the means for expanding international liquidity – the running of large balance of payments deficits by the United States – and the pledge by the United States to redeem all dollars held by foreigners for gold at a fixed price of $35 per ounce of gold.

The United States did run large balance of payments deficits and international liquidity did increase. Dollars provided approximately two-thirds of the world's growing monetary reserves. However, foreign governments began cashing in dollars for gold and the US gold stocks declined, undermining confidence in the ability of the United States to maintain the gold pledge. The risk of an international monetary crisis was now on the horizon.

If the United States was to decrease its balance of payments deficits, new means would have to be found for generating international liquidity to foster growing international trade. If the United States was to continue running large balance of payments deficits, the dollar would need to be devalued relative to gold or some steps would need to be taken to convince foreign governments to slow the rate at which they were redeeming dollars for gold.

However, the US balance of payments deficits reflected the global role of the United States. President Kennedy put it quite well when, shortly after taking office in 1961, he said:

> The surplus of our exports over imports, while substantial, have not been large enough to cover our expenditures for United States military establishments abroad, for capital invested abroad by private American businesses, and for government economic assistance and loan program. (Quoted in Eckes, 1975, p. 243)

The conflict between the global monetary arrangements created at Bretton Woods and the worldwide activities of the United States would take on importance in the 1960s.

PART III: STRAINS DEVELOPING WITHIN THE INSTITUTIONAL FRAMEWORK, 1960–71

5. From Guideposts to Controls: The Rise and Fall of Keynesian Demand Management Policy

During the 1960 presidential campaign, one of John F. Kennedy's favorite themes was the "need to get America moving again." But he did not believe that there were any major structural problems in the economy, nor did he feel that there were many major domestic problems which needed to be solved. However, this particular theme was not merely campaign rhetoric. It did capture some of the essence of the contemporary economic situation.

Economic growth slowed during the second half of the 1950s. By 1960, the economy appeared to be stagnating. There seemed to be a rising trend of unemployment. Though the rate of inflation was low, concern was raised over "creeping inflation." Balance of payments problems were becoming more apparent, and with them came a concern over the ability of the dollar to function as an international reverse currency.

Kennedy took office in 1961 and appointed economists to his administration who were steeped in Keynesian economics. With the proper use of fiscal and monetary policy, government policymakers argued that it was possible to "fine tune" the economy to achieve long-term economic growth with minimal unemployment and minimal inflation. This focus on economic growth and active Keynesian demand management policy differentiated them from the Eisenhower administration which emphasized passive Keynesianism in its attempt to minimize economic fluctuations, thereby stabilizing the business cycle.

The focus on economic growth mirrored that of the Truman administration but their active Keynesianism differentiated them from the passive Keynesianism of Truman. By the end of the decade, however, the optimistic viewpoint of the Kennedy economic policymakers would be demonstrated to be incorrect.

The longest cyclical upswing on record to that time, running for eight years, began in 1961. Keynesian expansionary macroeconomic policies, complemented by wage–price guideposts, were pushed by the Kennedy administration. In the first half of the 1960s, economic growth occurred with minimal inflation and labor strife. Unemployment fell, real wages grew, productivity increased and profits rose significantly.

Eventually, the situation changed dramatically. The growth in military spending due to the Vietnam War, during the Johnson administration, had an inflationary impact as taxes were not increased and other government expenditures decreased accordingly. In fact, with the War on Poverty and the Great Society, governmental social spending increased simultaneously with the military buildup. Strikes against the guideposts caused their elimination. Unemployment continued to fall, labor strife increased, the rate of growth of productivity slowed and profits were significantly squeezed.

The Nixon administration attempted to rebuild conditions for future profitability. Restrictive monetary and fiscal policies were utilized to fight inflation. Unemployment did increase, but inflation did not abate. The aggregative Keynesian macroeconomic policy tools were not suitable for fighting stagflation. The failure of this approach, together with serious balance of payments problems, business concerns with wage gains in the face of rising unemployment, and anticipated political problems during the presidential campaign of 1972 led to the New Economic Policy on August 15, 1971. Wages and prices were controlled and the dollar was no longer convertible for gold at a price of $35 per ounce of gold.

THE "NEW ECONOMICS"

Upon taking office in 1961, the Kennedy administration faced a troubling economic situation, both domestically and internationally. Domestically, the economy was in recession and many people were out of work. The unemployment rate was 8.1 percent in February 1961.

Though the rate of inflation was low, as prices had risen at an annual rate of 1.7 percent in 1960, the fear of "creeping inflation" was still present. Internationally, the United States had experienced growing balance of payments deficits toward the end of the 1950s. They did not appear to be the result of explicit US governmental policy, as earlier deficits were. Rather, they raised the specter of a weakening international competitive position.

The high rate of unemployment and the stagnating economy pointed to the need for expansionary macroeconomic policy to stimulate aggregate demand. With an increased demand for goods and services, production would be increased, more jobs would be created and unemployment would fall. From the standpoint of fiscal policy, a reduction in taxes or an increase in government expenditures or a combination of the two would be appropriate. If such a policy were pursued, however, the federal budget deficit would increase.

Macroeconomic policy is not undertaken in a political vacuum. And at the start of the Kennedy administration, there were several constraints, more of a political than economic nature, limiting the use of such a policy. First, economic orthodoxy in policymaking still pointed to the need for a balanced federal budget to maintain the price stability necessary for economic growth and a favorable balance of payments. And Kennedy, initially at least, accepted this orthodoxy partly due to his assessment of the political environment. He had been elected by just a very narrow margin over Richard Nixon and did not feel he had a mandate for a major change in economic policymaking. Furthermore, the US Congress was controlled by conservatives of both the Democratic and Republican parties.

Second, the business community did not support expansionary macroeconomic policy and Kennedy was quite eager to cooperate with them. For years, business leaders had argued that irresponsible union behavior was the major cause of inflation. And they feared that expansionary fiscal policy, by lowering the rate of unemployment, would increase the bargaining power of unions. A wage explosion would occur forcing prices to rise at a rapid rate. The increase in the rate of inflation would lead to a decline in international competitiveness. Sales abroad would diminish and there would be an increase in US imports.

Third, the fear of a decline in international competitiveness tied in with the fear of an overall growth in the balance of payments deficit. If it were true that American international competitiveness was deteriorating, that pointed to a worsening of the balance of payments deficit. And a growing US balance of payments deficit would cause international faith in the dollar to decline, possibly leading to a run on US gold stocks and an international financial crisis.

Thus, President Kennedy's first anti-recession program in early 1961 was firmly in line with orthodox economic ideas. He was committed, albeit with a lot of caveats, to fighting the recession within the confines of a balanced budget. To combat the recession, there was a speedup in government expenditures on goods and services and legislation was passed allowing states to temporarily extend unemployment benefits for an additional 13 weeks beyond the standard 26 weeks and provide aid to dependent children of the unemployed. The "counterrecession actions were not vastly different from those attempted in the two previous recoveries" (Lewis, 1962, p. 274) during the Eisenhower administration. The speedup in procurement to fight the recession was complemented by an increase in defense expenditures during the Berlin crisis of July 1961. Overall, government expenditures rose rapidly in 1961, primarily due to increased defense expenditures, and the economy showed signs of recovery.

However, by the Spring of 1962, the recovery from the 1960–61 recession was faltering. Fears were growing of a "Kennedy recession." A macroeconomic policy based on the economic orthodoxy of a balanced federal budget was shown to be a failure. On June 11, 1962, in a speech at Yale University, Kennedy debunked the economic mythology that had limited macroeconomic policy decisions:

> The myths persist that Federal deficits create inflation and budget surpluses prevent it.... Obviously deficits are sometimes dangerous – and so are surpluses. But honest assessment plainly required a more sophisticated view than the old and automatic cliché that deficits automatically bring inflation....
>
> .... What we need is not labels and clichés but more basic discussion of the sophisticated and technical questions involved in keeping a great economic machine going. (Quoted in Okun, 1970, p. 45)

A "new economics" was required.

The term "new economics" was coined by journalists. The economic concepts behind the "new economics" were not new; they had been known to economists for at least 20 years. What was new, however, was the incorporation of some of the lessons of Keynesian economics into macroeconomic policymaking. And it is important to stress that only some of the lessons of Keynesianism underlay Kennedy macroeconomic policy. It was a relatively conservative form of Keynesianism that was implemented.

The goal of macroeconomic policymaking was to change from smoothing the business cycle to fostering economic growth. In the language of the "new economics," the goal was to "close the gap" between the actual level of output and the economy's potential level of output. The potential level of output was that level of output able to be produced at "full employment." "Full employment" was defined, quite cautiously, as an unemployment rate of 4 percent. (This is similar to the Committee for Economic Development (CED) definition of high employment, as a 4 percent rate of unemployment, created in the mid-1940s.) This level of unemployment was initially considered to be an interim goal, achievable through the judicious use of fiscal policy. A lower rate of unemployment, requiring appropriate employment and training programs, was to be the ultimate goal. However, the 4 percent figure would eventually be, in effect, codified as "full employment" at least until the 1970s.

The potential level of output is an upward moving target. It will rise with labor force growth, investment in new plant and equipment, and technological change. Thus, even if the economy is growing there may still be a need for expansionary fiscal policy to stimulate aggregate demand to "close the gap" between the actual, though growing, level of GNP and potential GNP. Such fiscal policy may entail running a federal budget deficit during an economic expansion.

But the existing budget deficit (or surplus) is less important than what the deficit or surplus would be at "full employment," assuming the existing government expenditure programs and taking into account the higher tax revenues generated by the existing tax structure at the "full employment" level of income. Furthermore, the automatic increase in tax revenues will serve as a "fiscal drag" draining purchasing power out of the economy. This may cause the economic expansion to slow. To counter the "fiscal drag," "fiscal dividends" in the form of tax cuts or expenditure increases may need to be provided at appropriate times.

Evaluating the existing fiscal policy on the basis of the full (or high) employment budget was not a new idea. It had already been proposed by the CED in the 1940s. However, unlike the CED which argued for a fixed rule fiscal policy designed to yield a small budget surplus at high employment, the "new economists" did not specify that the full employment budget necessarily be in surplus. A full-employment budget deficit might be appropriate if, for example, monetary policy was too restrictive. Furthermore, while the CED wished to restrain the discretionary actions of fiscal policymakers, the "new economists" argued for a discretionary fiscal policy (Heller, 1967).

In theory, it is possible to "close the gap" with a fiscal policy emphasizing increased government expenditures on goods and services and transfer payments. In practice, however, the path of tax cuts was chosen. The Kennedy administration recognized that there were public needs not being met by the private sector. John Kenneth Galbraith, the Ambassador to India, had recently written of public squalor amidst private affluence in *The Affluent Society*. In addition, in 1962 in a memo to President Kennedy advancing the arguments for a tax cut, Walter Heller, the Chairman of the Council of Economic Advisers, wrote:

> ... our cities need renewal, our colleges and universities have no place for the flood of students about to inundate them, our mass transit system is in a sad state, our mental health facilities a disgrace, our parks and playgrounds inadequate, housing for many groups unsatisfactory. (Quoted in Rukstad, 1986, p. 217)

Even so, Heller called for tax cuts rather than large-scale government programs to attempt to remedy public needs. There was a stronger case politically for tax cuts rather than for expenditure increases. A growth of government expenditures would lead to charges of a "take-over" of the cities, the educational system and the housing market. Furthermore, tax-induced deficits would be more acceptable to the international financial community than expenditure-induced deficits. Thus, they would be less likely to cause a run on US gold stocks (Rukstad, 1986, p. 217).

The first tax cut was aimed at business and was designed to stimulate the rate of investment in new plant and equipment, thereby increasing the rate of growth of productivity and the rate of economic growth. Shortly after taking office, the Kennedy administration recommended an investment tax credit for investment in plant and equipment in excess of replacement investment. This was advanced at a time when the Kennedy administration was still concerned about balancing the budget. Thus, to regain some of the lost tax revenue, they proposed various tax reforms to close some "loopholes" benefiting business and wealthier members of society.

Conservatives did not object to the revenue losing part of the tax bill on the basis that the budget be balanced. However, the business community was successful in scuttling virtually all of the tax reform proposals designed to raise revenue and treat taxpayers evenhandedly. The bill which was passed – the Revenue Act of 1962 – essentially included just a 7 percent investment tax credit for any new investment in plant and equipment, not merely investment in excess of replacement investment. Earlier, by executive order, President Kennedy had liberalized depreciation allowances (Vogel, 1989; Stein, 1969).

In June 1962, after the passage of the Revenue Act of 1962, President Kennedy announced that he would propose additional tax legislation. At that time, there was fear of an imminent recession and tax cuts were being thought of as anti-recessionary measures. But by January 1963, when the administration's legislative proposals were unveiled, the threat of recession had passed and the economy was growing. The tax cuts aimed at both individuals and businesses were now designed to help the economy "close the gap" by eliminating "the unrealistically heavy drag of Federal income taxes on private purchasing power, initiative and incentive" (Vogel, 1989, p. 22). A budget deficit would intentionally be run even though the economy was not in recession. Tax reforms were also included to broaden the tax base and to make the tax system more equitable.

The Revenue Act of 1964, incorporating some of the components of the Kennedy program, was passed in February 1964 during the Johnson administration. (President Kennedy had been assassinated on November 22, 1963.) There were very few elements of tax reform; the business community had successfully lobbied against them. The new structure of tax rates was very similar to the proposals of the Kennedy administration. The new individual income tax rates ranged from 14 percent to 70 percent after 1964, down from 20 percent to 91 percent before the act. The maximum corporate income tax rate fell from 52 percent to 48 percent. A minimum standard deduction aided lower income people and removed 1.5 million individuals from the tax rolls.

It was the largest stimulative fiscal action taken by the federal government in relative peacetime, up to that point. Taxes were cut at a time when the federal budget was in deficit and federal expenditures were rising. Even so, the business community was essentially supportive of it. The dogma of the annual balanced federal budget was no longer subscribed to. Given the option of lowering their taxes or pushing for a balanced federal budget, the business community chose the former. However, conservative elements in the

US Congress were able to utilize the expected decline in tax revenues as a weapon to require that government expenditures be minimally cut. And their hope was that declining tax revenues would serve to limit government expenditures in the future.

The Revenue Act of 1964 represented the triumph of the "new economics." And perhaps it captures the essence of the "new economics" as well. That essence would be a very conservative form of Keynesianism, much modified from the American Keynesianism represented by the original version of the Murray–Wagner Full Employment Bill of 1945. This conservative form of Keynesianism emphasizes growth over redistribution, with the primary stimulus of fiscal policy being tax cuts. And to the extent that a redistribution of income occurred, it was toward the wealthy. The changes in federal revenue laws in 1962 and 1964 made the after tax distribution of income less equal (Hermansen, 1965; Pechman, 1965).

Yet, why was the route of increased government expenditure on goods and services not adequately provided by the private sector not taken? Was it a lack of political strength or a lack of political will? Heller argued that the Kennedy administration did not have the political power to push new spending programs through the US Congress. Furthermore, he believed that the way to higher domestic spending was through tax cuts. Cutting tax rates would lead to an economic expansion which would generate additional government revenues which could then be spent on new domestic social programs (Hargrove and Morley, 1984, pp. 200–201). However, Collins (1981, p. 184) believes that "to have battled for increased public investment rather than tax reduction would have required an ideological commitment to social welfare liberalism which was lacking in Kennedy and the New Frontier." Heller may have been correct that in this particular instance the Kennedy administration did not have the Congressional support for new spending programs. However, Collins' general argument captures the essence of Kennedy's conservative Keynesianism.

WAGE–PRICE GUIDEPOSTS

The Kennedy administration's expansionary macroeconomic policies were developed at a time when there was concern over "creeping inflation" and a growing balance of payments deficit. If inflation was to accelerate, it would limit the extent to which the government would be able to pursue its economic growth strategy and would weaken the international competitiveness of US firms, thereby serving to worsen the balance of payments situation. Thus, a policy was required to attempt to lessen the risk of inflation as the economy grew and unemployment declined.

The wage–price guideposts were that policy. They were designed to restrain wage and price increases in industries where unions had strong bargaining power and firms had strong market power. They did not have a legal status and, thus, were voluntary. But their aim was to set an overall framework for wage and price setting. They pointed to a government taking a more active role in wage and price setting than had normally been the case in peacetime.

The principle behind the guideposts was that if wages increased at the same rate as the long run economy-wide rate of growth of productivity, then unit labor costs would remain constant. If unit labor costs remained stable, then prices, on average, would remain stable as well. Initially, no specific figure was given for the recommended rate of wage increase, though a 3 percent increase was generally accepted as the standard. The guidepost for annual wage increases was eventually set at 3.2 percent in 1966. Assuming that wages are set on the basis of the guideposts, unit labor costs would rise in those industries with below average rates of growth of productivity and fall in those industries with above average rates of growth of productivity. Thus, prices would rise in the former set of industries while they would fall in the latter group. On average, then, prices would remain constant.

MACROECONOMIC POLICY AND THE BALANCE OF PAYMENTS

The discussion of the "new economics" ignored the role of monetary policy. While it was the case that the "new economists" emphasized fiscal policy rather than monetary policy, the balance of payments situation placed some restrictions on the use of expansionary monetary policy. The Federal Reserve allowed the money supply to expand to the degree necessary to accommodate the growing economy. However, it was concerned that short-term interest rates not decline to very low levels. As short-term interest rates fall, short-term capital has a tendency to leave the United States in search of higher returns elsewhere. To the extent that this occurs, the balance of payments deficit widens.

Thus, the Federal Reserve engaged in "Operation Twist" which was designed to increase short-term interest rates while keeping long-term interest rates low to stimulate private investment in the United States. In its open market operations, the Federal Reserve bought relatively more long-term bonds. As the demand for long-term bonds rises, bond prices increase and the effective interest rate declines. In addition, the US Treasury increased the share of new short-term securities in its regular offerings of new government securities. The increase in the supply of short-term securities caused their price to fall and the effective interest rate to rise.

THE ECONOMIC RECORD OF THE KENNEDY PROGRAM

In the first half of the 1960s, economic growth accelerated, unemployment fell and prices rose moderately. Real output grew by 22 percent from 1961 to 1965, or an annual rate of growth of better than 5 percent. The unemployment rate fell from 6.7 percent in 1961 to 4.5 percent in 1965. Even though the rate of unemployment was falling rapidly, the rate of inflation did not accelerate. Prices rose at an annual rate of 1.3 percent (*Economic Report of the President*, 1990, pp. 296, 338, 363).

The rise in labor productivity accelerated somewhat in the first half of the 1960s. Measured on the basis of cycle averages, the annual rate of productivity growth in nonfarm businesses was 2.82 percent from 1959 to 1966, in contrast to 2.07 percent from 1955 to 1959 (Naples, 1987, p. 159). Though the rate of productivity growth was rising, wages only increased at a relatively moderate rate. Total compensation per hour in the private economy rose at an annual rate of 3.6 percent from 1961 to 1965, a slower rate of increase than in the 1953–61 period when it grew at an annual rate of 4.2 percent. The annual rate of increase of prices was similar in the two periods as was the average annual rate of unemployment (Sheahan, 1967, p. 80). The rate of increase of compensation in the early 1960s was less than what might have been expected given the relationship between wages and unemployment that had existed in earlier postwar years.

The early 1960s were a profitable period for business. The net after tax rate of profit of nonfinancial corporations rose from approximately 6 percent in 1961 to approximately 10 percent in

1965 (Bowles *et al.*, 1990, p. 79). The rising rate of profit created and reflected a favorable business climate for investment in new plant and equipment. Real gross private domestic investment increased rapidly from $259 billion (1982 dollars) in 1961 to $367 billion (1982 dollars) in 1965. Real gross private fixed investment had hardly risen at all between the previous business cycle peaks of 1955 and 1959 (*Economic Report of the President*, 1990, p. 296).

The macroeconomic policies of the Kennedy administration worked as predicted. The tax cuts increased the after tax income of individuals. They responded by spending the additional income on consumer goods and services. The cut in corporate tax rates increased the after tax profits of business. The rise in after tax profits, the explicit investment incentives and the rise in sales induced business people to increase their rate of investment. The increase in demand for consumer and investment goods caused the economy to grow at a rapid rate.

The guideposts created an environment for wage restraint. They stiffened the backbone of employers by, in effect, setting a ceiling on the rate of increase of employee compensation. The major impact of the guideposts was felt by workers in some of the better organized manufacturing industries (Sheahan, 1967, p. 201). While organized labor was against the notion of maintaining the given distribution of income between wages and profits, as the guideposts were designed to do, unions did not, as of 1965, make any concerted efforts to bust the guideposts.

The guideposts also seem to have constrained, somewhat, the over-all rate of increase of prices. However, there was a sin of omission. Prices were not reduced in line with the guidepost criterion in firms and industries where productivity growth was particularly rapid.

There were no guideposts concerning the behavior of profits. It is likely that wages were restrained to a greater degree than prices because there was a dramatic increase in profits. Some of the growth of profits was due to the economic recovery. However, Sheahan (1967, p. 202) concludes that the rate of increase of profits was well beyond what would normally have been expected. Questions of the equity of the guideposts would soon be raised by the labor movement.

The apparent success of the "new economics" led to the belief that economists could "fine tune" the economy. With proper fiscal policy, the economy could be coaxed into that combination of rate of inflation and rate of unemployment that society deems optimal. The business cycle had been tamed. Recessions would be fewer and milder and the rate of economic growth would be higher than in the past (Heller, 1967, pp. 104–105). Less than a decade later, these beliefs would be shown to be wrong.

"GUNS AND BUTTER"

The period of strong economic growth amidst relative price stability came to an end in 1965. The economy continued to grow until the end of the decade. However, the rapid military buildup, due to the escalation of the Vietnam War, caused the rate of inflation to accelerate. The first American troops were sent to Vietnam in 1961. The US involvement in this country deepened in 1965. There was a sharp increase in military expenditures after mid-1965. Between the middle of 1965 and 1968, military spending increased by approximately $30 billion, or more than 60 percent (Gordon, 1974, p. 155).

How was the war to be financed? In previous wars, increases in taxes and cutbacks in nonmilitary governmental expenditures provided important sources of financing. But, it was not politically feasible to, initially, either cut nonmilitary governmental expenditures or raise taxes. The military buildup in Vietnam coincided with a "war" or more accurately a "skirmish" on the homefront – the War on Poverty. In May, 1964, at the University of Michigan, President Johnson stated that he would preside over the "Great Society" – great in the sense that it would eliminate poverty. His landslide victory in the presidential election of 1964 and the large Democratic majorities in the US Congress led to the passage of a wide variety of social legislation, including many poverty programs, the scope of which had not been seen since the New Deal of the 1930s. In January 1966, when it became apparent that there might be a potential conflict between funding the War on Poverty and the Vietnam War, President Johnson told the US Congress:

> I am unwilling to declare a moratorium on our progress toward the Great Society (in order to finance the war in Vietnam) .... Can we move ahead with the Great Society programs and at the same time meet our needs for defense. My confident answer is YES. (Quoted in Stevens, 1976, p. 53)

Thus, the claim was made that the economy through economic growth could produce both guns and butter.

In addition to ruling out cutting nonmilitary expenditures, at least for the time being, the government did not attempt to raise taxes. There were several reasons for this. First, the war was not a popular one. Second, President Johnson felt that if he had asked for a tax increase in early 1966, it would make it impossible to get the rest of the Great Society legislation passed. Third, the Johnson administration, partly by mistake and partly by design, underestimated the expected cost of the war. It was overconfident about a quick US victory and often claimed to see "the light at the end of the tunnel." It was interested in minimizing political opposition to the war and thus consciously minimized the expected cost of the war. By doing so, the administration made it appear that a tax increase was not necessary to fund the military buildup.

Given that taxes were not raised and nonmilitary expenditures were not reduced, the initial new military activities were financed by an increase in the federal budget deficit. This represented a growth in demand for goods and services. If the economy had substantial unused capacity and many unemployed people, the expansion of demand would have led to more jobs and more economic growth. But the increased deficit spending came at a time when the economy had little excess capacity and relatively low unemployment. By 1966, the unemployment rate had fallen to 3.8 percent and the rate of capacity utilization in manufacturing had risen to 91.1 percent, its highest level since the end of the Second World War (*Economic Report of the President*, 1990, pp. 330, 351). In such a situation, the federal government was competing with the private sector for the available output. The growth in spending exceeded the growth in output and the rate of inflation jumped to 2.9 percent in 1966 (*Economic Report of the President*, 1990, p. 363).

The rise in the rate of inflation and the unwillingness of the Johnson administration to push for legislation raising taxes or cutting expenditures led the Federal Reserve to implement a restrictive monetary policy. It represented the first time in the 1960s that the Federal Reserve tightened monetary policy to restrain aggregate demand. In December 1965, the Federal Reserve raised the discount rate – the interest rate it charges banks that borrow from it – from 4.0 percent to 4.5 percent. This was designed to make it more expensive for banks to borrow, and thus, provide an incentive to bankers to reduce their approval of new loans.

Early in 1966, through open market operations, the Federal Reserve began to slow the growth of the money supply. It did so by selling some of its holdings of US government bonds. By April 1966, the Federal Reserve Board concluded that further tightening of the money supply was required. In the second quarter of the year – April–June – the expansion of the money supply was brought to a halt. But, while the money supply was no longer growing, the demand for business loans was rapidly increasing. Interest rates rose dramatically.

Banks tried to find sources of funds for lending purposes. They increased their borrowing from the Federal Reserve. But even after doing so, there was a substantial demand for loans that banks were not able to satisfy. They then began selling their holdings of municipal bonds to come up with loanable funds. The price of municipal bonds declined and their effective yields rose. It became difficult to find buyers for newly issued municipal bonds. According to the Federal Reserve:

> At the depths of the gloom in the second half of August, conditions in the market for tax-exempt securities were on the verge of disorder and yields throughout short and long-term markets were at their highest levels in more than 40 years. (Quoted in Wolfson, 1986, p. 50)

In addition to the problems in the bond market, the housing market was in disarray. Mortgages were made more difficult to obtain and those that were provided were more costly for borrowers. Private housing starts fell more than 40 percent between February and October, 1966 (Gordon, 1974, p. 159).

There was talk of a financial panic. The "credit squeeze" was becoming a "credit crunch." The Federal Reserve was forced to loosen up on monetary policy. Through open market operations, the Federal Reserve bought US government bonds and the money supply was increased. Furthermore, banks were notified that if they stopped liquidating their holdings of municipal bonds and slowed their rate of expansion of business loans, the Federal Reserve would be more willing to approve their requests for loans to replenish their reserves. At around the same time, the federal government temporarily suspended the investment tax credit on machinery and equipment and the accelerated depreciation allowances on new buildings and reduced some nondefense spending. The actions of the Federal Reserve and the federal government, together with the slowing of the economy, restored calm in the financial markets. Interest rates began to decline. The first potential financial crisis of the postwar period was over.

In addition to triggering the "credit crunch" of 1966, the rise in the rate of inflation was one of the factors leading to the effective elimination of the wage–price guideposts. By 1966, the general attitude of unions toward the guideposts had turned strongly negative. While nominal wages had been rising in step with the guideposts, consumer prices were accelerating. Thus, real wages were not rising at the same rate as the rate of growth of productivity, as was one premise of the guideposts. However, corporate profits were growing at a very fast rate. And wages of nonunion workers were beginning to increase at a faster rate than those of unionized workers.

Prior to 1966, there had been no concerted effort on the part of the labor movement to bust the guideposts. In 1966, however, the legitimacy of the guideposts was on the bargaining table. The guideposts were defeated in a strike of airline machinists and ground service personnel against five of the national airlines. Though the airlines were heavily regulated by the federal government, their rates of profit were rising dramatically. Based on this strong economic position, the unions involved presented a set of wage demands which, though outside of the guideposts, could have been met without any increase in airline fares. A strike ensued and the government attempted to strengthen the hand of the airline negotiators. For example, the Civil Aeronautics Board allowed the struck airlines to lend airplanes to those still operating so that they could service some of their routes. Thus, the labor dispute was not just between airlines and their employees. It was now the workers versus the federal government and the employers.

It was a long strike. A settlement was finally achieved with an annual wage increase of approximately 5 percent, well above the 3.2 percent guidepost. The government tried to rationalize the settlement as being consistent with the guideposts, but the president of the International Association of Machinists knew better. He accurately claimed that the agreement "completely shatters" the guidepost notion (Sheahan, 1967, p. 60). The Johnson administration realized that its attempt to maintain the guideposts had prolonged the strike and concluded that new policies were required to restrain wages. While the guideposts were not officially jettisoned, they had, in effect, ceased to exist.

The restrictive monetary policy implemented in 1966 caused a slowdown in the economy in early 1967. However, by the middle of the year the economy began expanding again and the rate of inflation accelerated. Prices rose at an annual rate of 3.1 percent in 1967 (*Economic Report of the President*, 1990, p. 363). In 1968, the Johnson administration asked for a 10 percent temporary tax surcharge on personal and corporate income taxes to slow down the expansion and, hopefully, diminish the rate of inflation. The Revenue and Expenditure Control Act of 1968 was passed in June, with the temporary tax surcharge scheduled to expire on June 30, 1969.

But it was not merely a piece of tax legislation. It also required that the federal government cut $6 billion from nondefense expenditures. Cuts in social programs were demanded to appease conservatives for their support of the temporary tax increases.

The Tet offensive was launched by the Communists in South Vietnam in January 1968. Many cities, including Saigon, were attacked. It became very clear that the United States would not attain victory in a short period of time, if at all. The light at the end of the tunnel was flickering, if not going out. Lyndon Johnson chose not to run for reelection and Richard Nixon's victory in the presidential election returned the Republicans to power.

TOWARD THE NEW ECONOMIC POLICY

The temporary tax surcharge was too little, too late. The rate of inflation continued to accelerate, with prices rising at an annual rate of 4.2 percent in 1968 (*Economic Report of the President*, 1990, p. 363). And upon taking office in January 1969, the Nixon administration considered inflation to be the primary macroeconomic problem.

In addition to inflation, the Nixon administration was confronted with a "profit squeeze." The rate of profit had been falling since 1965. The net after-tax rate of profit of the nonfinancial corporate business sector rose steadily in the first half of the 1960s, peaking at approximately 10 percent in 1965. It steadily declined after that, falling to a level of approximately 7 percent in 1969 (Bowles *et al.*, 1990, p. 79).

The "profit squeeze" was the result of rising labor costs combined with a slowdown in productivity growth (Michl, 1988). The relative bargaining power of labor was strengthened in the second half of the 1960s by the low unemployment rates. Between 1966 and 1969, the unemployment rate remained below 4 percent, reaching a low of 3.5 percent in 1969 (*Economic Report of the President*, 1990, p. 363).

In such an environment workers were able to demand, and gain, large boosts in nominal wages. Employee compensation per person hour in the nonfarm business sector in 1969 was 30 percent higher than it had been in 1965. The rate of growth of productivity did not keep up with the rate of growth of compensation. Output per hour in the nonfarm business sector in 1969 was only approximately 8 percent higher than it had been in 1965. Thus, unit labor costs rose by approximately 20 percent between 1965 and 1969. This is in contrast to the first half of the decade when unit labor costs were essentially stable (*Economic Report of the President*, 1990, p. 346).

While prices were increasing, they were not rising in step with unit labor costs. One reason for this was that competition from imports limited the ability of domestic producers to raise prices. Thus, the rate of profit was falling.

The Nixon administration viewed the inflation as being caused by an excess demand for goods and services that had built up under the military and Great Society expenditures of the Johnson years. Their anti-inflation program emphasized cutting federal expenditures while terminating the investment tax credit and extending the temporary tax surcharge. The federal budget was no longer in deficit. In 1969, there was a $3.2 billion budget surplus (*Economic Report of the President*, 1990, p. 383).

Restrictive fiscal policy was complemented by tight monetary policy. The Federal Reserve described their program as a "very restrictive monetary policy" in order to "slow the expansion of aggregate money demands in the economy and to dissipate deeply rooted expectations of continued inflation" (Wolfson, 1986, p. 54). The discount rate was raised and open market sales of US government securities lowered the rate of growth of the money supply.

The restrictive monetary and fiscal policies led to a mild recession, as they were designed to do. The economy contracted in 1970 and the rate of unemployment rose from 3.5 percent in 1969 to 4.9 percent in 1970 (*Economic Report of the President*, 1990, p. 338). The recession and the associated increase in unemployment were designed to lower the rate of inflation and restore conditions for future profitability. With a higher rate of unemployment, workers would be less able to press their demands for higher wages, causing the rate of increase of wages to slow. Firms would feel less pressure to raise prices due to rising labor costs. And businesses would be less able to make price increases stick, given the decline in consumer demand

and increased product market competition. While the rate of profit might continue to decline during the recession, the decline in worker bargaining power due to increased unemployment would enhance the likelihood of improved profitability in the future.

However, this scenario did not play out as expected. While many lost their jobs, the rate of inflation did not slow. Prices rose at a 5.5 percent annual rate in 1969 and a 5.7 percent annual rate in 1970 (*Economic Report of the President*, 1990, p. 363). Workers did not behave as predicted. Even though unemployment was rising, workers successfully pushed for higher wages. In 1970, employee compensation per person hour in the nonfarm business sector rose by 7.1 percent (*Economic Report of the President*, 1990, p. 346). And the rate of increase of wages was fastest in the unionized sector of the labor force.

"Stagflation" characterized the economy. The standard policy tools did not seem to work. The business community was quite concerned by the apparent strength of the labor movement. They wanted the government to help them withstand the demands of their workers. The Nixon administration had officially ended the guideposts in 1969. In August 1970, the US Congress passed the Economic Stabilization Act of 1970. This legislation included the Democratic-inspired power to freeze wages, salaries, prices and rents. In signing this bill President Nixon said:

I have previously indicated that I did not intend to exercise such authority if it was given to me. (Quoted in Campagna, 1987, p. 358)

Within a year, he would exercise such authority. Wage and price setting would come under government control.

Not only was there a high rate of inflation occurring simultaneously with a high rate of unemployment, the balance of payments situation was rapidly deteriorating. The balance of payments had initially been a concern in the late 1950s. However, a growing balance of trade surplus in the early 1960s, temporarily at least, made the situation appear less problematic. But the annual balance of trade surpluses steadily declined in the second half of the 1960s. Prices in the United States were rising more rapidly than in other industrialized societies. US made goods were becoming less competitive with foreign goods, both at home and abroad. By 1971, the balance of trade had turned negative for the first time in the twentieth century.

The surplus in the balance of trade had been used to finance US activities abroad. Yet, at the same time as the surplus was shrinking,

US military expenditures abroad, especially in Asia, were rapidly growing. Balance of payments deficits were run throughout the 1960s. They grew toward the end of the decade. By 1971, there was a crisis of confidence in the dollar. Short-term capital fled from the United States. Foreign central banks were inundated with dollars as foreign holders of dollars converted their dollars into their home currency. For a long time, it had been clear that the US government did not have adequate gold stocks to redeem foreign holdings of dollars at the official rate of $35 per ounce of gold. But as long as foreign governments held the dollars, a crisis could be forestalled. And throughout the 1960s that is what occurred. But by 1971, confidence in the dollar had sunk.

On August 13, 1971, Great Britain asked to convert $3 billion of its dollar holdings into gold. Other countries were also contemplating doing the same. No country wished to be last in line because at that time there were $40 billion of foreign-held dollars and only about $12 billion in gold held by the United States (Campagna, 1987, p. 366). A run on US gold stocks had to be avoided.

THE NEW ECONOMIC POLICY

On August 15, 1971, President Nixon announced the New Economic Policy (NEP). It was designed to deal simultaneously with the problems of inflation, unemployment and the balance of payments. To the degree that the economic problems would be ameliorated prior to November 1972, the NEP had the additional goal of improving the prospect for President Nixon's reelection. The timing of the NEP was determined by the threat of a run on the "gold window." But the NEP went well beyond international matters.

The NEP involved direct government intervention into wage and price setting. Known as Phase I, wages, prices and rents were frozen for 90 days. While direct government intervention into economic decision-making goes against the grain of the free market ideology of the business community, business people largely supported the controls. From their perspective, there seemed to be no other way to handle, what they considered to be, excessive wage demands. Several days earlier, on August 9, the AFL–CIO Executive Council approved a resolution endorsing the principle of wage–price controls. But, they were critical of the wage–price freeze on the grounds that it was discriminatory against workers. Even so, organized labor would tacitly accept the program.

The labor leaders were correct in arguing that the freeze would be inequitable. With a wage–price freeze, all of the benefits of increased productivity would go toward increasing the rate of profit. However, it would only be a 90-day freeze. Phase I was designed to buy time for the Nixon administration as they developed the next stage of the NEP

In addition, the freeze was designed to break inflationary expectations and to deal with the potential inflationary consequences of the other elements of the NEP. The Nixon administration, concerned about the sluggish economy, proposed a set of tax reductions to stimulate the economy. The Revenue Act of 1971, passed in December by the US Congress, modified only slightly these proposals. The investment tax credit of 7 percent was reinstated. The excise tax on cars and trucks was repealed. Personal income taxes were slightly reduced. Tax breaks were provided to special subsidiaries of US firms set up to promote exports.

Internationally, the "gold window" was closed. The dollar was no longer convertible into gold at a price of $35 per ounce of gold. New international monetary arrangements would need to be created. The dollar would, in effect, need to be devalued.

But a dollar devaluation might be viewed in domestic politics as a "defeat". Thus, the Nixon administration went on the offensive. It imposed a temporary surcharge of 10 percent on dutiable imports. And it argued that any investment tax credit passed into law should not apply to imported machinery as long as the import surcharge was in effect. The administration demanded that countries with balance of payments surpluses revalue upward their currencies rather than having the United States devalue the dollar. Thus, the stage was set for international negotiations to begin over the new international monetary arrangements to replace the Bretton Woods Agreements.

CONCLUSION

A conservative form of Keynesianism dominated macroeconomic policymaking in the early 1960s. Government policymakers believed that if aggregative macroeconomic policy tools were suitably utilized the economy would be able to grow steadily with low rates of inflation and low rates of unemployment. However, by the early 1970s, this view was demonstrated to be overly optimistic. Monetary and fiscal policy alone were unable to deal with the simultaneous occurrence of high rates of inflation, high rates of unemployment and balance of payments deficits. Economic controls were imposed in 1971.

At the same time as the controls were announced, the "gold window" was closed. The Bretton Woods arrangements, based on the dollar being "as good as gold," were no longer appropriate for an evolving international economy no longer totally dominated by the United States. New international monetary arrangements would need to be created.

The accelerating inflation in the late 1960s reflected a growing imbalance between the claims being placed on the US economy and the economic resources it could deliver. Within the collective bargaining context, there were heightened tensions over the relative claims of employers and employees. In addition, increased demands were placed on the government by those benefiting minimally, if at all, from collective bargaining. The growing economic and social conflict was being played out against the backdrop of a relative decline in the international standing of the US economy.

The evolution of labor–management relations, governmental social initiatives and the international standing of the US economy in the 1960s and early 1970s are treated in the next three chapters.

6. Standoff at the Workplace

The "hard line" of management continued into the early 1960s. Contractually based work rules and noncontractual shop floor practices were in dispute. Employers wanted to increase the use of mechanization and introduce new automated technologies. Workers wished to protect their jobs and their power on the shop floor. Bargaining over compensation took place within the limits set by the guideposts. While the Kennedy administration wished to encourage the growth of collective bargaining, their guideposts set limits on the ability of unions to exercise their bargaining power, thereby reinforcing the hand of management.

Management's "hard line" melted as the economy strengthened and unemployment rapidly declined. Worker bargaining strength led to the effective elimination of the guideposts in 1966. And worker anger at pay levels and the degradation of working conditions resulted in an increase in the number of wildcat strikes, contract rejections and incumbent union leaders tossed out by the rank and file in the latter half of the 1960s.

By the early 1970s, two contradictory trends characterized labor management relations. On the surface, the labor movement appeared very strong. Employers unable to resist union demands for rapidly rising wages demanded the assistance of the government. Wages (and prices) were frozen by government edict on August 15, 1971. Yet, just below the surface another reality was emerging. A managerial resistance to new unionism, which first became apparent in the mid-1950s, continued to develop gradually in the 1960s. The perimeter of unionism was shrinking and the roots of a nonunion model were being laid.

124

MANAGEMENT'S "HARD LINE" AND LABOR'S RESPONSE

In the late 1950s and early 1960s, leaders of large mass production unions were in a somber mood. They had "become convinced the 'big corporations' have adopted a conscious ideology which, at the very least, looks to a drastic cutting down of union power and, at the most, offers a 'challenge to union existence'" (Barbash, 1961, p. 25). In retrospect, while employers made major efforts to cut down the power of unions, the continued existence of unions was never in doubt. Yet, that is in hindsight and may not have been apparent at the time.

The economy was stagnating. Pressured by increased domestic and international competition and dissatisfied with the level of profits, employers wished to raise labor productivity thereby lowering the costs of production and potentially increasing profits. Reforming rigid (from the employer perspective) work rules and accepted shop floor practices was one means of doing so. The introduction of new production technologies was another. Employer-induced changes in work rules and work practices may worsen working conditions for employees. These modifications, along with increased mechanization and automation, may lead to fewer workers being hired to produce the requisite output or may result in some members of the existing workforce being replaced by new hires with skills and capabilities more appropriate to the new technologies. Such were the fears of many unionized workers. At the same time that employers were pushing to raise productivity, many people were already out of work, further heightening worker concerns over job and income security.

The General Electric Company (GE) represented the epitome of a tough management line. Yet, in 1960 it was merely following an approach to collective bargaining that had been developed by the company over the past 15 years. It forced, or rather in the company's words "invested" in, a strike in 1960 (Brooks, 1971, p. 291). The company wished to dispose of excess inventory and increase its power inside the plants. The International Union of Electrical Workers (IUE) was in disarray. Some locals chose to strike while others wished to continue working. The company, communicating directly with its employees, reminded them that GE and its employees had worked together for many years before the 1930s without any unions. Furthermore GE kept its plants open for any employee who wished to work and guaranteed that he would receive all of the pay and benefit increases in the company's last offer prior to the strike. Many returned to work and the three-week strike was eventually settled on the terms of the company's last offer. GE clearly demonstrated the weakness of the IUE but did not choose to wring any further concessions from it. Pay was raised and a program was instituted which would provide severance pay to laid-off workers with three or more years of service. Even so, A.H. Raskin, the labor columnist for the *New York Times*, called this labor fiasco "the worst setback any union has received in a nationwide strike since World War II" (quoted in Kuhn, 1980, p. 237). The company, then, had a relatively free hand in introducing new productive machinery. And "the early 1960s saw the greatest burst of technological change in the industry in more than a generation" (Schatz, 1983, p. 238).

Other companies did not follow the "take it or leave it" strategy of GE. Yet, they too were interested in improving labor productivity and enhancing their control over the shop floor. And their attempt at doing so led to increased labor–management tensions. In 1963, Secretary of Labor Willard Wirtz observed:

Most of the recent controversies have involved basic issues of manpower utilization and job security. This has been true in the 1959 steel case, the 1961–62 airlines cases, the maritime cases, the longshore case, the New York newspaper case, and to a lesser degree, in most of the others. (Quoted in Barbash, 1970, p. 52)

Local issues became dominant in the worker's mind. The automobile industry provides a case in point. In 1961, the UAW and Ford and General Motors (GM) were able to reach an agreement at the national level providing for wage increases and improved supplemental unemployment benefits for autoworkers on layoff. Nevertheless, workers at the local level were not happy. Assembly-line workers were dissatisfied with production standards, relief time and working conditions. Strikes, unauthorized by the national union, broke out over plant level concerns. GM was presented with 19 000 local demands. Workers, having lost a large amount of shop floor control in recent years, wanted their working conditions protected through contract language. A similar pattern occurred in 1964 contract negotiations, though a week-long strike against GM took place over national issues such as wages and benefits. Following the settlement, a 31-day local issues strike by the rank and file occurred.

A particular concern was speedups. Also Ford was shut down for 20 days due to struggles over work rules (Livernash, 1967; Fairris, 1990, 1991; Lichtenstein, 1985). Disputes over local issues whereby local unions refused to accept the signing of company-wide agreements took place in other industries as well in the early 1960s.

While agreements varied across firms, disputes over the introduction of new technologies and changes in working conditions were generally settled with employers being allowed to make the desired changes subject to the normal grievance procedure. Unions were strong enough, however, to gain something in return. Workers often won improvements in severance pay or supplemental unemployment benefits, providing them with a greater degree of income security in the event of job loss. For example, in meatpacking, Armour agreed to provide members of the Meat Cutters and Packinghouse Workers unions with a 90-day notice of plant shutdown, with guaranteed earnings during this period and technological adjustment pay for those with five years of service who were subsequently laid off.

In other instances, employers agreed to protect the jobs of the existing workforce, reducing staffing levels merely by attrition, or to guarantee a minimum amount of paid annual hours of work. On the docks, containerization (the bulk loading of cargo in ready-packed trailer truck bodies or containers) threatened the jobs of longshore workers. Early in the decade, the International Longshoremen and Warehousemen's Union of the Pacific Coast and later in the decade the International Longshoremen's Association of the Atlantic and Gulf Coasts signed agreements accepting containerization in return for guarantees of annual earnings for many union members.

At times, unions tried to protect jobs by gaining a reduction in weekly hours of work without any cut in take-home pay or a reduction in annual hours of work through a lengthening of paid vacations. Reduced working hours were, it was argued, a way to guarantee the jobs of existing workers and perhaps open up positions for some of the unemployed. Reduced working hours were goals in and of themselves as well as tradeoffs gained from employers in response to shop floor changes. Perhaps the most innovative arrangement was negotiated by the United Steelworkers of America (USWA) in 1963. An agreement was reached with the steel companies providing for 13 weeks of paid vacation every five years to the senior half of each company's hourly workforce, in addition to the usual vacation during the other four years.

Though the early 1960s saw a continuation of the hard-line tactics of management begun in the late 1950s, there were relatively few strikes between 1960 and 1964. Work time lost due to strikes was at its lowest level in the postwar period (*Monthly Labor Review*, June 1965). Only approximately 8 percent of manufacturing workers in large-scale bargaining units whose contracts expired went on strike (Kaufman, 1978, p. 423). Workers, being on the defensive, were less likely to strike. And employers, more often than not, did not feel the need to force a strike. Furthermore, to the extent that they were adhered to, the guideposts of the Kennedy administration served to lessen the likelihood of strikes over questions of compensation.

THE LABOR POLICY OF THE KENNEDY ADMINISTRATION

The Kennedy administration sought to encourage the growth of collective bargaining. John F. Kennedy was elected with the strong support of the labor movement. The merger of the American Federation of Labor (AFL) and Congress of Industrial Organizations (CIO) in 1955 strengthened the labor movement's prowess in the political arena. The AFL–CIO's political arm, the Committee for Political Education, mobilized labor voters and led to the election of Kennedy and many liberal Democratic Congressmen and state legislators. In 1962, Kennedy issued an Executive Order 10988 providing for collective bargaining for federal employees. The order only covered federal workers. Nevertheless, it sent a message to state and local governments. They, too, should be willing to engage in collective bargaining with their employees.

The Kennedy administration also wished to foster collective bargaining in the private sector. Secretary of Labor Arthur Goldberg, a former lawyer for the USWA, set up the President's Advisory Committee on Labor–Management Policy, consisting of 19 representatives of labor, management, and the public, and the Secretaries of Labor and Commerce. Its goal was to create an environment for more cooperation between labor and management, thereby strengthening the industrial relations system. The fear was that bargaining relations were hardening, given the tough approach being taken by many employers in their dealings with unions (Stern, 1964; Ulman, 1963).

Kennedy appointees to the National Labor Relations Board (NLRB), such as Gerald Brown, supported encouraging collective bargaining. He saw the goal of the NLRB to be promoting a public policy which is "the encouragement of collective bargaining as the democratic method of solving labor problems" (quoted in Ulman, 1963, p. 250). Several decisions of the NLRB favored unionization and expanded the scope of collective bargaining. The NLRB placed some restrictions on employer "free speech" during union organizing drives. Previously, the NLRB tried to determine whether a particular employer statement or action was, on its face, coercive. Now, the NLRB was less concerned with whether a particular statement was intended to be a threat. Rather, the crucial issue was whether the employees would reasonably interpret it as a threat and thus be unwilling to vote for a union in a representation election. Employers who were actively persuading workers to vote nonunion were now more likely to be found in violation of the law (Grodin, 1964; Stern, 1964).

The NLRB broadened the range of issues subject to collective bargaining, thereby restricting the realm of "management rights." The landmark Borg–Warner US Supreme Court decision (NLRB v. Wooster Division of Borg–Warner, 1958) had been issued a few years earlier. In this case, the US Supreme Court distinguished between three types of subjects of bargaining – mandatory, permissible and illegal. Both labor and management are required to bargain over a mandatory subject until an impasse is reached. At that point, unions are legally allowed to strike. Permissible subjects can be raised during the course of bargaining. However, neither labor nor management can insist to the point of an impasse that the other party accept its proposal. Strikes over permissible subjects are illegal. Illegal subjects cannot be discussed during negotiations. While clear that there were three types of bargaining subjects, the US Supreme Court did not specify, very clearly, the components of each category. That would be left to the NLRB and future court decisions arising out of actions of the NLRB.

The Kennedy NLRB began to fill in the categories. Prior to the Kennedy administration, the NLRB had ruled that unless their actions were designed to destroy a union, employers were not required to bargain over such matters as the decision to subcontract, relocate operations or introduce new technologies. They were required, however, to bargain with their unions over the effects of their decisions. For example, if work was to be relocated, an employer would be forced to bargain over such questions as severance pay or worker transfer rights. The Kennedy NLRB reclassified a range of managerial decisions, previously thought to lie in the area of "management's rights," as mandatory subjects of bargaining. These included actions to terminate a department and subcontract its work, to consolidate operations through automation and to close one plant of a multiplant enterprise (St Antoine, 1981, p. 175).

In its Fibreboard decision (Fibreboard Paper Products Corporation v. NLRB, 1964), the US Supreme Court gave limited approval to this shift of direction by the NLRB. However, it made it very clear that there were limits, very strong limits, to the range of mandatory subjects of bargaining. Decisions fundamental to the "basic direction of a corporate enterprise" or requiring the "commitment of investment capital" shall not become mandatory subjects of bargaining (St Antoine, 1981, p. 175; Fairris, 1990, p. 30). While workers gained somewhat more input into corporate decision-making as a result of the rulings of the Kennedy NLRB, their input was circumscribed. Employers retained full control over decisions regarding the basic scope of the enterprise, notwithstanding the fact that workers were profoundly affected by such decisions.

While the Kennedy administration favored collective bargaining, it also sought to limit the ability of unions to exercise their bargaining power over matters of compensation. At a time when management was pursuing a hard line in bargaining, the Kennedy administration further strengthened the hand of management. It advanced a policy of voluntary guideposts, designed to slow down the rate of increase of wages, thereby slowing the rate of increase of prices.

Union leaders did not, in principle, have any objection to government intervention in wage bargaining, provided the intervention was equitable. In fact, Walter Reuther, in testifying for the AFL–CIO in congressional hearings on the *1964 Economic Report of the President* said:

> Although the guideposts for wage and price decisions first set forth by the Council of Economic Advisers in 1962 and reiterated in the Council's more recent reports may have contributed, as a result of misinterpretation, to a negative emphasis on wages as costs, there is actually no conflict between the guideposts and the kind of dynamic wage policy the AFL–CIO has been urging. (Quoted in Sheahan, 1967, p. 46)

Union leaders initially cooperated with the guideposts. There were relatively few strikes and strikes with general wage changes as a major issue hovered around 40 percent of total strikes between 1962 and 1965, well below their typical share (Wrenn, 1985, p. 99). However, while the guideposts, in theory, may have been consistent with the AFL–CIO approach to wage policy, in practice they did not work out to be "equitable." Unionized workers become dissatisfied with them. The guideposts were eventually broken.

LABOR DISSATISFACTION AND LABOR MILITANCY

The tough bargaining of management, reinforced by the guideposts, led to lower nominal wage increases than would otherwise have occurred. At the same time, price increases, though relatively moderate, were eating into real wage gains. And profits were rising at a very fast rate, so fast that even Gardner Ackley, the Chairman of the Council of Economic Advisers, was concerned whether this had negative implications for the long-term health of the economy. In 1966, he said:

> Now that profits after taxes are providing the highest sustained rate of return on owner's equity in our modern history, it is time to ask whether a further rise in the share of profits in the national income is in the interest either of the health of the nation's economy or in the interest of business itself. (Quoted in Brooks, 1971, p. 298)

From labor's perspective, the answer was clear. The guideposts must go. In 1966, a series of settlements outside of the range of the guideposts signaled their demise and ushered in a period of increased labor–management strife.

There was a sharp upsurge in the number of strikes. Between 1960 and 1964, there were an average of 3466 strikes per year. That figure rose to 4937 in the 1965–71 time period. And in 1970, there were 5716 strikes, more than in any other year in the postwar period, up to that time. In that year 66 000 000 workdays were lost due to strikes, a number exceeded only in 1946, the time of the Great Strike Wave, and 1959 (US Department of Labor, 1979, pp. 508–509). Approximately 17 percent of manufacturing workers in large-scale bargaining units whose contracts expired went on strike between 1965 and 1971 (Kaufman, 1978, p. 423).

It was not just that strikes at the end of a contract rose. There was also a sharp increase in strikes occurring while a contract was in force.

Intra-contractual strikes rose from roughly 1000 in 1960 to nearly 2000 in 1970. Some of these were legal, permitted under the terms of the agreement. But most were illegal, wildcat strikes. These intra-contractual work stoppages were indicators of worker dissatisfaction with the conditions of work.

Rank-and-file unhappiness was also manifested in an increase in contract rejections. The rate of rank-and-file refusal to ratify contracts rose from 8.7 percent of contracts negotiated in 1964 to 14.2 percent of contracts negotiated in 1967. That figure then began to decline to 11.2 percent in 1970 and 9.9 percent in 1971, when wage–price controls were in effect in the latter part of the year (Kochan, 1980, p. 46). Contract rejections were primarily due to worker displeasure over proposals regarding compensation (Simkin, 1970).

In addition to turning down contracts negotiated by their union leaders, workers also rejected their leaders. Between 1964 and 1969, union leaders were deposed in steel, electrical equipment and rubber. And major internal insurgencies occurred in many other unions including the miners, teamsters, postal workers and auto workers. At the local level, many local presidents were thrown out. For example, in the steel workers union, new local presidents were elected in 1100 of the union's 3800 locals in 1970 (Fairris, 1990).

The low unemployment rates during the latter half of the 1960s combined with the increased militancy of workers to strengthen the bargaining power of unionized workers. Unionized workers were angry. From 1964 to 1968, their earnings had been rising at a slower rate than those of nonunion workers, a reversal of the trend of the previous ten years. Given the decline in unemployment, nonunion employers paying market-based wages were forced to raise wages rapidly to retain their existing employees and hire additional workers. Unionized employers, paying wages above the market rate, were under somewhat less pressure to do so. Given the above-market compensation package, there would always be a queue, of varying length, of workers seeking to be hired. Furthermore, long-term contracts predominate in the unionized sector. Many were signed during the period of the guideposts and remained in effect after the guideposts ceased to exist. And while some contracts included a cost of living allowance, to partially protect workers from inflation, many did not. Overall, the degree of automatic adjustment of wages to price changes was inadequate to keep union wages rising at the same rate as nonunion wages (Mitchell, 1980).

Unionized workers were out to change this situation, and they did. Between 1968 and 1971, their earnings rose more rapidly than did the earnings of nonunion workers. Very large improvements in compensation appeared in collective bargaining contracts negotiated in 1969 and 1970. First year changes in wage rates in collective bargaining agreements covering 1000 workers or more negotiated in 1968–69 averaged 9.2 percent and in 1969–70 averaged 11.9 percent. And these figures do not include possible wage increases resulting from cost of living escalators.

While wages were rising throughout the unionized workforce, unionized workers in the construction sector were particularly successful at bettering their conditions. Their first year wage adjustments averaged 13.1 percent in 1968–69 and 17.6 percent in 1969–70 (Bosworth, 1972, p. 348). In 1969, in reaction to rapidly escalating construction worker wages, several major industrial companies formed the Construction Users' Anti-inflation Roundtable to lobby for policies in construction to benefit construction purchasers. (This group would eventually be merged into the Business Roundtable, an organization created in 1972 comprising chief executives of many of the largest corporations in the United States.) In 1970, industrial relations in construction were particularly tense. One-third of all contract negotiations resulted in strikes, more than 500 in all (Mills, 1972, p. 352).

Not only were wages rising rapidly, but the rate of growth of productivity was slowing. In fact, in 1969, output per person hour in the nonfarm business sector remained constant, while rising by a scant 0.9 percent in 1970 (*Economic Report of the President*, 1992, p. 349). Rising levels of militancy and shop floor confrontation played a significant role in the productivity slowdown in manufacturing (Flaherty, 1987) and in the nonfarm business sector as a whole (Weisskopf *et al.*, 1983; Bowles *et al.*, 1983). Unit labor costs rose as did prices. But profits were squeezed, as prices did not rise fast enough.

Labor's muscles were being flexed. Even GE was forced to capitulate. By the end of the decade, it was no longer able to pursue a "take it or leave it" bargaining strategy. The three unions which represented most of the workers at GE's plants – International Brotherhood of Electrical Workers (IBEW), International Union of Electrical Workers (IUE) and United Electrical Workers (UE) – coordinated their bargaining strategy in 1969. After some discussions with the union bargaining committees, the company announced its terms for a new labor contract. The unions rejected the company offer and a strike ensued in October 1969. The company argued that the union leaders were conducting "ideological warfare" (Kuhn, 1980, p. 246). And perhaps there was a grain of truth in that charge since the central issue of the dispute went far deeper than a mere wage increase. Rather the unions wished to show that the GE approach to industrial relations was no longer viable. Union leaders claimed that GE's demands were "union busting moves by the one major employer in the U.S. that persists in strike breaking as a matter of policy" (Kuhn, 1980, p. 246). They were particularly incensed by GE's apparent willingness to attempt to operate during the strike. Furthermore, the company's proposals for interfering with the right of workers to conduct a work stoppage after exhausting the grievance procedure and for eliminating the national contract, opening up the possibility for local agreements and increased inter-plant competition, were abhorrent. The strike lasted for 101 days. It was eventually settled after the unions and the company retreated from their initial positions. GE backed down from the two demands the unions found most offensive. Union leaders were pleased with the outcome, viewing it as the first fully negotiated contract with GE since 1946.

GE was just one manifestation of a labor movement with bargaining strength. The data on compensation changes in newly negotiated contracts clearly demonstrate that unions throughout the society were able to pressure their employers into hefty wage increases, increases that could not be fully passed along to the consumer. Organized labor was succeeding even as unemployment was rising. The Nixon administration was forced to intervene.

GOVERNMENT INTERVENTION

Wage settlements in construction evoked the most controversy. The Nixon administration was pressured by construction contractors and construction users to restore rationality (from their perspective) to the wage determination process in the industry. Business leaders argued that rapidly rising construction wages threatened to spill over into other sectors of the economy as workers in other industries tried to achieve similar gains. They feared a wage-push inflationary spiral emerging.

In March 1971, the Nixon administration established the Construction Industry Stabilization Committee, a tripartite body with labor, employer and public representatives on it. All newly negotiated collective bargaining agreements in construction would need to be approved by this body before becoming effective. It served to slow down somewhat the rate of growth of compensation. In the first six months of 1971, first year changes in wage rates in collective bargaining agreements covering 1000 workers or more averaged 13.4 percent, less than the 17.6 percent recorded in 1969–70 (Bosworth, 1972, p. 348).

But slowing the rate of growth of construction wages had no impact on wages outside of the construction sector. Negotiated wage increases were not abating. In fact, the settlement in the steel industry in early August 1971 included an estimated 16 percent hike in total compensation during the first year (Weber and Mitchell, 1978, p. 1). The business community was mounting pressure on the Nixon administration to do something to secure smaller wage and, thereby, price increases. Rising unemployment did not seem to be weakening worker bargaining power. Something further needed to be done. The wage–price freeze was announced on August 15, 1971.

A SLOW TRADE UNION DECLINE

In the early 1960s and the early 1970s, employers turned to the federal government for help in restraining wage growth. Union bargaining strength was too tough for them to handle alone. This obviously connoted a very strong labor movement, one able to achieve solid gains for workers. However, there were signs of storm clouds on the horizon for labor. The share of the workforce unionized fell during the 1960s, as it had since 1954. Union membership as a percentage of employees in nonagricultural establishments dropped from 31.4 percent in 1960 to 27.0 percent in 1970 (US Department of Labor, 1979, p. 507).

The relative decline in union membership was occurring just in the private sector. Public sector unions surged in the 1960s. During the mid-1960s through the early 1970s, union membership in the public sector more than quadrupled (Freeman, 1986, p. 44). The Kennedy administration had recognized federal worker unions. In step with federal policy, at the state and local level there were many legal changes favorable to public sector workers seeking unionization. And public sector employers did not fight unionization to the extent that private sector employers did.

Private sector employers, using legal and illegal tactics, often successfully opposed new organizing efforts. The legal tactics included delaying for as long as possible the holding of a representation election and, in the interim, doing all that was legally possible to sway workers to vote for the nonunion choice. Employer delaying strategies became more prevalent in the 1960s. There was a fall in the relative share of representation elections that were consent elections and an increase in the relative share of stipulated elections. Consent elections, whereby employers do not raise any objections concerning the holding of the election, generally occur within one month of the filing of an election petition. While they constituted 46 percent of all elections in 1962, they only were 26 percent of all elections in 1970.

On the other hand, stipulated elections, which require the NLRB to decide election related matters at the national level prior to the holding of an election, became more prevalent. The share of stipulated elections jumped from 27 percent in 1962 to 56 percent by 1970 (Prosten, 1979, p. 245). The length of time between the filing of an election petition and the holding of an election is much longer with a stipulated election than a consent election. And employers were the driving force behind the growth in stipulated elections. Employers were often trying to obtain a voting unit which they felt was more likely to vote against unionization, or were merely trying to delay.

Consent elections indicate employer acceptance of the legitimacy of unions, while stipulated elections point to employer resistance. Unions were more likely to win consent elections than stipulated elections. And workers were less likely to vote for a union the longer the delay in holding the election and the greater the extent of employer opposition to union representation of the workforce (Freeman and Medoff, 1984, pp. 234–235; Goldfield, 1987, pp. 204–205; Seeber and Cooke, 1983, p. 43).

Even where unions were chosen by workers, they had difficulty getting the employers to sign contracts. Thirty-five percent of the units that won in NLRB elections in 1970 were not under contract five years later (Prosten, 1979, p. 247). And the NLRB refused to have workers "made-whole" (or compensated) for an employer's refusal to bargain in good faith prior to the signing of the first contract. They ruled in this way in the Ex-Cell-O Corp. case, 1970, even though the employer's violation was "clear and fragrant."

In short, union avoiding employers could legally block the holding of an election for a long period of time. If, by chance, workers voted for union representation, they could legally forestall first contract negotiations for several years. Even though these legal avenues were open to employers, illegal strategies became increasingly more popular in the 1960s. Employers were willing to go to great lengths to avoid unionization. From 1960 to 1970, the number of cases brought to the NLRB alleging illegal firing for union activity rose from 6024 to 9290. Furthermore, there was a doubling in the number of workers – from 1885 to 3779 – deemed to have been fired illegally for union activities and ordered reinstated by the NLRB (Goldfield, 1986, p. 10).

At the same time as managerial opposition to union organizing efforts stiffened, unions devoted inadequate resources to organizing new members (Freeman, 1985). However, the drop in the success rate of unions in representation elections was due more to managerial action than union inaction. Overall, workers won by unions in organizing drives as a percentage of workers eligible to vote in representation elections fell from 59 percent in 1960 to 52 percent in 1970. And while unions organized 0.7 percent of the private wage and salary work force in new elections in 1960, that figure fell slightly to 0.6 percent in 1970 (Freeman, 1985, p. 46).

If faced with a representation election, most employers, of course, tried to prevail. But, for many the preferred course of action was to create conditions where there would be no representation election at all. And herein lies an additional factor behind the emergence of a growing nonunion sector in the 1960s. Within the United States, employer strategies included decentralizing production by building smaller factories for greater managerial control and locating them in weakly organized parts of the South or in semi-rural areas. When ready for operation, personnel managers would hire workforces without previous union experience.

Some of these new facilities were "runaway shops." A company would shut its unionized plants in the North. The entire operation would be shifted to nonunion facilities elsewhere. Runaway shops predominated in the more highly competitive industries such as clothing, shoes, toys and furniture.

Firms in the less competitive industries, interested in avoiding or shedding unionization, pursued a more sophisticated strategy. Their unionized operations would remain open though a process of disinvestment would often occur. A new duplicate production facility would be built elsewhere. This form of parallel production would work both to diminish the probability of unionization at the new facility as well as weaken the bargaining power of workers at the original plant. Workers at the new facility would be less likely to unionize to begin with. Workers at the old facility would be less able to strike or pursue other options to seek to have their demands met by their employer. If they were to do so, production might easily be redirected to the newer, equivalent facility (Bluestone and Harrison, 1982).

Within the United States, the relocation of economic activity began earlier. It first became apparent in the late 1940s. It grew more prevalent in the 1950s and 1960s. As a result, there was a significant age gap between union and nonunion manufacturing plants. The unionized facilities were much older with many of them being built before the mid-1950s (Klein and Wanger, 1985, p. 77; Kochan *et al.*, 1986).

One of the first industries to utilize parallel production was the electrical equipment industry. The strikes of 1946 convinced management that the large existing manufacturing facilities had become hotbeds of labor militancy. They were mainly located in the industrial belt of the Northeast and Midwest. Starting in the mid-1940s, "the corporations moved operations out of the older, large factories and into newer, smaller facilities in the border states; the South; the Pacific Coast; rural sections of New England, the Mid-Atlantic states, and the Midwest; Puerto Rico; and other countries" (Schatz, 1983, p. 233). GE went from a company which had all of its plants located in the Northeast in the 1920s to one which had 117 plants in 24 states in 1952 and 170 plants in 134 cities in 1961. And at that time there was a larger concentration of facilities in the South and West than before (Schatz, 1983, p. 235).

The geographic decentralization of operations also occurred in other industries. In meatpacking, firms closed many large urban-based operations in, for example, Chicago and built new smaller plants throughout the Midwest and Plains states. Between 1962 and 1971, 19 new rubber tire plants were built, mostly in relatively small towns in the South and West. There were no plant closings but it was very clear that Akron, Ohio's days as a center of tire production were numbered (Karper, 1987). In automobiles, GM followed what the UAW called its "southern strategy." Soon after the Second World War, GM began locating new plants in what were primarily "right-to-work" states (Bluestone and Harrison, 1982).

The decentralization of production did not guarantee that unions would be avoided. In fact, during the 1960s, the United Rubber Workers were able to organize the new plants quickly. However, it did make signing up new workers more difficult. This was quite apparent in the electrical equipment industry. Between 1958 and 1968, the three major unions – IBEW, IUE and UE – were able to organize only one out of every four new production workers in the industry. The primary reason was the difficulty the unions had in organizing new workers in the South (Kuhn, 1980, pp. 212–216).

Capital mobility did not stop at the borders of the United States. Companies based in the United States expanded in other parts of the world. The globalization of activities of manufacturing firms based in the United States accelerated during the mid-1960s (Barnet and Muller, 1974, p. 259). Often these new operations remained nonunion. Even if the workers were to unionize, it would be very difficult for workers in the United States to coordinate their actions with unionists elsewhere.

The shifting of operation (or differential expanding) into nonunion areas in the United States and abroad was one strategy of union avoidance. And if successful, employers had the opportunity of setting up low-standards shops, where wages would be low, fringe benefits nonexistent, working conditions poor and the threat of firing ever present. But, they need not follow such a policy.

Some large employers remained nonunion or diminished the extent of unionization by being a better-standards employer. By their actions, they tried to demonstrate to their employees that they had no need for a union. They would encourage two-way communication between workers and managers. Grievances would be attended to swiftly. Discipline and discharge would be handled according to carefully spelled out company policies. Layoffs and firings would be minimized. Compensation would, at least, be competitive in the local labor market, or at least be equivalent to that provided by any comparable unionized firm, if one existed, within the geographic area. DuPont followed such an approach. In 1946, 94 percent of DuPont's blue-collar workers were unionized. At that time, the company adopted a policy that all new plants would be nonunion. They became a better-standards employer and were quite successful in implementing their nonunion approach (Kochan et al., 1986).

It was not just in manufacturing where a managerial resistance to unionization appears to have evolved gradually in the 1960s. In construction, a sophisticated nonunion movement developed. The Associated Builders and Contractors, a trade association of nonunion commercial builders, was created. Focusing on labor relations, its

goal was to support nonunion contractors in resisting union organizing efforts or other types of union pressures (Mills, 1980). In addition,
one of the goals of the Construction Users' Anti-inflation Roundtable
was the enlargement of the nonunion sector in the construction
industry.

CONCLUSION

The second half of the 1960s and the beginning of the 1970s represented a time of strong bargaining strength for the labor movement.
Employers were unable to resist union demands for rapidly rising
nominal wages. Profits were squeezed as employers were unable to
gain improvements in labor productivity to slow the rise in unit labor
costs, nor fully pass on the increase in costs of production to consumers. Employers were forced to seek governmental assistance. And
the Nixon administration complied with the wishes of business by
freezing wages (and) prices on August 15, 1971.

Yet, while labor was doing well at the bargaining table, a managerial resistance to new unionism was gradually developing. The share
of the private sector workforce unionized was shrinking. While unions
in the most highly organized industries were still relatively protected
by their bargaining strength from the nonunion model, the roots of
the nonunion model were laid in the 1960s. They would take hold in
the 1970s and 1980s, during a more difficult economic environment,
catching American workers and their labor leaders by surprise.

7. The Persistence of Inequality and the Limits of Liberal Policy

Collective bargaining led to higher living standards for many union members, including black and white women and black men who were able to be employed in jobs organized by large industrial unions. But many other women and black men, benefiting little from the postwar economic prosperity, were left out. Many employers and unions persisted in racial and gender discrimination. Some employers, either on their own or in collusion with unions, only hired white men. Others, though willing to hire women and black men, often barred them from the more desirable positions. Even as late as 1960, some American Federation of Labor (AFL)–Congress of Industrial Organizations (CIO) affiliates were closed to blacks. Other affiliates restricted black workers to segregated locals.

During the 1960s, American society was forced to confront the issues of poverty and discrimination. Blacks deeply resented their second-class status. A major political mobilization emerged to guarantee the civil rights of the blacks. Women, too, pressed for an end to the discrimination they faced in the labor market.

The society responded, albeit haltingly. Racial and gender discriminations were outlawed by the Equal Pay Act and the Civil Rights Act but minimal resources were allocated for the enforcement of the new legislation. The anti-poverty policies of the War on Poverty emphasized changing the characteristics of the poor rather than restructuring the economy or significantly redistributing income. While transfer payments increased more than anticipated due to rising welfare caseloads in response to urban riots and a vocal welfare rights movement, a more liberal transfer payment policy was not a central element of the War on Poverty. Rather, anti-poverty policy assumed that with

141

better education and training the poor would be able to benefit from the opportunities provided by a growing economy. Economic growth rather than income redistribution lay at the heart of the government's anti-poverty strategy.

The 1960s were a period of strong economic growth and tight labor markets. Poverty did decline and women and black men did experience job and income gains. Yet, while some progress occurred much remained to be accomplished.

RACE, GENDER AND WORKPLACE DISCRIMINATION

Race and gender discrimination persisted in the workplace after the Second World War. Black workers, being among the last to enter the war-time industries, were among the first to be fired during the demobilization following the Second World War. In 1945 and 1946, the unemployment rate of nonwhites (hereafter referred to as blacks, since blacks constituted more than 90 percent of nonwhites) increased twice as fast as for whites. By 1947, the black unemployment rate was 5.4 percent in contrast to 3.3 percent for whites. At this time, the black unemployment rate was "only" 1.6 times the white one. The racial unemployment differential continued to rise. By the second half of the 1950s, blacks were more than twice as likely to be out of work as whites.

When they worked, blacks were concentrated in lower status, lower paying jobs. They were overrepresented among the working poor and had extremely low annual incomes. In 1960, one out of 12 male workers were black while one out of four men working in low-wage jobs were black. Black women comprised one out of eight working women, but one out of six women in low-wage jobs (Cummings, 1965, p. 830).

Their greater difficulty in finding work and their concentration in lower paying jobs translated into lower annual income for blacks than whites. From the end of the Second World War to 1960, black male median annual income typically fluctuated between 50 and 55 percent of white male median annual income. Black women also earned less than white women. But unlike in the case of men, there was a steady convergence in the annual incomes of black and white women. The ratio of black female to white female median annual income fluctuated around 50 percent in the late 1940s. It steadily rose in the 1950s and reached 70 percent by 1960 (Reich, 1981, p. 32).

The income convergence for women is significant in its own right. Yet, it is only part of the story of the labor market experiences of women. There was no convergence in the job prospects of men and women. There was a strong sexual division of labor in the postwar labor market.

Women were not able to retain the employment gains they had made during the war. While it is true that many quit their jobs after the war ended, they often left relatively low-paying industries such as food, apparel and textiles. Women who had moved into better paying jobs during the war wished to retain their positions. But, they were often unable to do so. From August 1945 to May 1946, women were laid off at a much higher rate than men in the heavy manufacturing industries such as iron and steel, petroleum, automobiles and machinery, to make room for returning veterans. They were just those industries where women had not been employed in significant numbers prior to the war (*Monthly Labor Review*, 1947; Kessler-Harris, 1982).

While some women left the labor force during the demobilization, many continued to be employed or seek employment. In fact, the labor force participation rate of women was 33.9 percent in 1950, higher than it had been in 1940 when 28.9 percent of women were in the labor force, though lower than it was at the end of the war (Blau, 1978, p. 36). Yet, while women were working after the war, they were working in different jobs than during the war. The sexual division of labor was reconstituted and women were back in "women's jobs." Many women found themselves performing clerical and office jobs. In 1950, 27.4 percent of women were clerical workers, well above the 21.5 percent of women workers doing such work in 1940 (Bancroft, 1958, p. 209). While women continued to enter the labor force in the 1950s and their labor force participation rate rose to 37.7 percent by 1960 (Blau, 1978, p. 36), the occupational segregation of women continued in force. A majority of women were employed in jobs stereotyped as female in 1960 (Kessler-Harris, 1982; Blau, 1978). With the growth in the number of clerical jobs, 30 percent of women were now holding such positions. In addition, a growing share of women were finding jobs in service work outside of the household.

Not only did women hold different jobs than men, they earned substantially less than their male counterparts. In 1960, the ratio of the median earnings of full-time, year-round women workers to those of full-time, year-round men workers was 64 percent for professional and technical workers; 58 percent for managers; 68 percent for clerical workers; 49 percent for sales workers; 60 percent for operatives; and 59 percent for service workers (US Bureau of the Census, 1983, p. 23). Even within the same broad occupational groups, men and women tended to be concentrated in different jobs or work in different industries.

The practices of employers and unions confirm what the data imply. Women and black men faced discrimination in the labor market. All unions were not racist. In fact some, for example the United Packinghouse Workers and the United Electrical Workers (UE), had strong commitments to racial equality (Rosen, 1968, p. 205). But many others, particularly the large industrial unions, accepted the racist status quo. This often entailed employer hiring practices restricting blacks to the lowest paying, least skilled jobs. Furthermore, existing discriminatory seniority and promotion arrangements served to limit the chances for black workers to move to higher paying, more highly skilled positions within the enterprise.

Worse still were the unions that segregated blacks into "auxiliary" locals or refused them membership altogether. Segregated locals were often accommodations to existing patterns and customs in the workplace or the local community. Blacks were refused entry into many craft unions in the building trades and on the railroads. For example, the requirement for membership in the Brotherhood of Locomotive Firemen and Enginemen were that an applicant be "white born, of good moral character, sober and industrious ...." (quoted in Hill, 1982, p. 18). Craft unions, through hiring halls and other referral systems, controlled access to employment and training opportunities. By refusing membership to blacks, they strongly limited black options in the construction trades.

The National Negro Labor Council was formed in 1951 to end the racist practices of employers and unions. Many of its actions were taken to increase black access to better jobs. A campaign was waged to force Sears Roebuck to hire blacks in clerical, sales and administrative positions. Ford Motor Company was pressured to employ more black office workers. Demands were made of the airlines for black pilots and flight attendants. Hotels in New York City were pressured into hiring black waiters and waitresses and upgrading black maintenance workers. A new General Electric (GE) plant was opened in Louisville and the company was convinced to hire black women as production workers. Other companies in Louisville, including Westinghouse, Reynolds and Ford, changed their hiring practices and utilized more black production workers. While some gains were made for black workers, the National Negro Labor Council ceased to exist in 1956. Given that some communists participated in the organization, the House Un-American Activities Committee hounded it out of existence (Foner, 1982, pp. 293–311).

It is apparent that blacks faced serious employment problems at the time of the merger of the AFL and the CIO. The actions of the AFL–CIO did little to quell the concerns of the blacks that they were being treated like second-class citizens by important segments of the labor movement. The AFL–CIO, at best, was able to get a token number of blacks admitted to formerly all white building trades locals. More often than not, "lily white" construction locals remained "lily white." In fact, blacks were not even allowed to do electrical work on the construction of the AFL–CIO headquarters in Washington DC. The jobs were reserved for members of the Washington DC local of the International Brotherhood of Electrical Workers (IBEW). All of the members of this IBEW local were white. In addition, in 1957, the AFL–CIO admitted two railroad unions, the Brotherhood of Locomotive, Firemen and Enginemen and the Brotherhood of Railroad Trainmen even though their constitutions refused the admission of blacks. And other affiliates continued to retain segregated locals for blacks.

Union controlled apprenticeship training programs remained the preserve of whites. A 1960 study by the National Association for the Advancement of Colored People (NAACP) found:

… Negroes make up only 1.69 percent of the total number of apprentices. The proportion of Negroes is actually less than 1 percent of the apprentice carpenters, electricians, machinists and plumbers. And the situation in the North is not very different from the South; it is nation-wide. (Quoted in Hill, 1982, p. 23)

The practices of employers and unions also restricted the job prospects of women. Where unions existed, it was often union–management collusion that reserved the better positions for men. But women also faced discrimination in areas where unions did not exist. Here, it was management, either acting alone or in deference to the wishes of male workers, which was responsible. The disproportionate layoffs of women in heavy industry at the end of the war was due to the use and abuse of seniority arrangements and job reclassifications.

Women, being among the last hired during the war, did expect to bear the brunt of the initial layoffs. Those with least seniority would be the first to go. And women accepted the fact that veterans who wished to come back to work in their previous jobs should receive seniority credit for the time spent in the military.

But there were many instances where women's job losses were due to the abuse of women's seniority rights. Separate seniority lists for men and women were not uncommon. Under such an arrangement, more senior women might be laid off before less senior men. Even when separate seniority list did not exist, men were granted "bumping" rights over women holding jobs classified as "male." And the sexual reclassification of jobs to "male" jobs was common in the postwar reconversion period (Milkman, 1980).

The nature of sex discrimination is illustrated by the following clause from a contract signed by a United Auto Workers (UAW) local with the Federal Mogul Corporation:

> There shall be separate and non-interchangeable seniority lists for men and women in accordance with their intra-plant seniority. Provided, however, that all female employees hired subsequent to July 1, 1942, shall be placed on a special seniority list and shall be considered as male replacements and as having been hired solely because of a shortage of male labor, and their tenure of employment shall be limited to the duration of the war, or as soon thereafter as they can be replaced by former male employees or other male applicants. In all cases of lay-offs due to the above reason, seniority provisions shall apply. (Quoted in Women's Work Project, n.d.)

In this instance, not only were women to be replaced by returning veterans previously employed by the firm but also by any male applicant. This contract may have been more blatantly discriminatory than most. But it reflected a "pattern that saw most unions unceremoniously discard their female members at war's end" (Kessler-Harris, 1982, p. 292).

It was not just in heavy industry that women faced discrimination. Many professional and managerial jobs were closed to them. In the late 1940s, medical schools still retained a quota of 5 percent on female admissions. Seventy percent of all hospitals did not accept women interns. Medical associations such as the New York Obstetrical Society did not accept women members. Very few women held high-level governmental positions. Business executives, when polled, expressed little confidence in the ability of women to perform well in managerial posts (Chafe, 1972, p. 185).

The prejudice against women was deep-rooted and continued into the 1950s. In manufacturing, women were still laid off when their jobs were reclassified as male jobs. There were agreements between union locals and managements forbidding the hiring or retaining of married women. Married women workers were viewed as a threat to the sanctity and stability of the family. Many shop stewards ignored inequities and failed to process grievances or support women in labor–management disputes (Women's Work Project, n.d.).

Jobs were sex-typed within the federal government. Supervisors were allowed to advertise for and hire only women for "women's" jobs and men for "men's jobs." In the private sector, job vacancies were also often sex-typed in newspaper want-ads.

Women were becoming impatient with their situation and wished to see an end to discrimination. Initially, the Kennedy administration argued that economic growth should be the primary vehicle for expanding opportunities for women (Kessler-Harris, 1982, p. 313). Yet, women would not wait for the economy to grow; neither would blacks.

ATTACKING PAY AND EMPLOYMENT DISCRIMINATION

Responding to pressure from women, the Kennedy administration outlawed discrimination in the federal civil service in 1962. Civil service hiring officers were now required to state their reasons when posting sex-specific requests for candidates to fill job vacancies. It became very clear, virtually overnight, that previous advertisements for women to fill certain jobs and for men to fill other jobs bore little relation to job content. Sex-specific vacancy notices fell to 1 percent of their previous level (Stevenson, 1975, p. 246).

But it was not merely within the federal civil service that women were facing restricted opportunities. Their options were limited in the private sector as well. Pay discrimination was outlawed in 1963 when the Kennedy administration pushed the Equal Pay Act through the US Congress. Employers were no longer legally able to pay differential wages to men and women doing equivalent jobs, unless these sex-based pay differentials were the result of a non-discriminatory seniority system or merit system. However, the legislation on equal pay was really quite limited. It addressed only one facet of women's unequal status in the labor market. It did not apply to, perhaps, the more basic problem women faced, that being the refusal of employers to hire or promote them. This would be taken up in the Civil Rights Act of 1964.

In his 1960 presidential campaign, Kennedy promised to push for major civil rights legislation designed to improve the lives of blacks. By the beginning of 1963, he had not yet done so. By this time, the civil rights movement was growing and becoming more militant. Furthermore, it was gaining acceptance among many whites living outside the South. The Kennedy administration was finally moved to act when 2500 blacks in Birmingham, Alabama rioted in the streets on May 11 protesting white racist violence and their lack of civil rights. Inspired by the example of Birmingham blacks, civil rights demonstrations began occurring in many southern and northern cities. Protestors demanded more jobs and better schools for blacks and an end to segregated accomodations. On June 19, 1963, Kennedy sent a civil rights bill to the US Congress incorporating many of the demands of the civil rights movement. On August 28, 1963, 250 000 people, blacks and whites, participated in the March on Washington demanding an end to racial discrimination. The Civil Rights Act of 1964 was passed by the US Congress and signed into law by President Johnson in July 1964 (Matusow, 1984).

This was a wide-ranging piece of legislation which, among other things, prohibited discrimination in public accommodations such as motels, restaurants and places of amusement and authorized the federal government to bring suits to desegregate public facilities and to provide aid to communities desegregating their schools. Title VII of the Civil Rights Acts outlawed discrimination on the basis of race, color, religion, sex or national origin in hiring, pay and promotion. The law applied to private employers, employment agencies and labor organizations. The Equal Employment Opportunity Commission (EEOC) was set up to enforce the law. Initially, it merely gathered information and tried to mediate disputes. In 1972, the law's coverage was extended to governments and educational institutions and the EEOC was given the right to bring federal court actions seeking remedies on behalf of those who had suffered discrimination.

The Civil Rights Act was complemented by two executive orders prohibiting discrimination by government contractors on the basis of

race, creed, color, sex or national origin. The Office of Federal
Contract Compliance (OFCC) was created in 1965 to enforce these
executive orders. It had the power to cancel, terminate, suspend or
delay a federal contract where the contractor was found to have discriminated. And as of 1972, it began requiring contractors who had
underutilized women or minority group members in comparison to
their proportions in the available labor force to develop an affirmative action program with goals and timetables for increasing the hiring of women and minorities. The contractor was required to make
a good faith effort to meet the goals set up but was prohibited from
setting rigid quotas (Eastwood, 1978, pp. 109–110; Levitan et al.,
1975, pp. 268–271).

ATTACKING POVERTY

Poverty existed in the 1940s and 1950s, and even before this time.
However, it was not viewed as a problem in the eyes of the public, nor
was it considered a problem to be solved by government policy. The
United States was considered to be an affluent society. Poverty was
"rediscovered" in the early 1960s and was placed at the center stage of
public policy discussions. *The Other America*, written by Michael
Harrington, appeared in 1962 and focused political attention on the
poor – the "other Americans" – and their condition. Harrington, a
democratic socialist, called for government action to solve the problem
of poverty. How many people were poor? Federal policymakers did not
know since at that time there was no official definition of poverty.

Even though there was no official measure of poverty in the early
1960s, it was apparent that poverty was widespread. In 1963, believing that the government had an important role to play in the amelioration of poverty, the Kennedy administration began developing a
policy agenda for the elimination of poverty. In part, this was
a response to the burgeoning civil rights movement. But the War on
Poverty was not primarily a response to the struggle for racial equality. Rather, it was the "invisible poverty" of whites in areas such as
Appalachia that provided the initial impetus for the War on Poverty.
While blacks were more likely than whites to be poor, they were only
a minority of the poor population (Davies, 1996).

With the death of President Kennedy, President Johnson made
fighting poverty a priority. The administration created a measure for

the "poverty line" designed to determine the number of people considered poor. However, while fighting poverty was to be a governmental priority, the official poverty measure was explicitly designed to minimize the number of people counted as poor. The government began with the US Department of Agriculture's "economy food plan" which was meant for emergency or temporary use when funds were low. It did not meet minimal nutritional standards over a long period of time. Based on a 1955 US Department of Agriculture study showing that families spent approximately one-third of their budget on food, the government set the poverty line at three times the cost of the "economy food plan," adjusted for differences in family size. The poor were those whose incomes fell below this line. However, the one-third estimate was probably outdated by this time. A more recent 1961 US Department of Agriculture study found that food expenditures were 24 percent of total expenditures. This implied a multiple of four (Ruggles, 1992). But a multiple of four would have led to more people being considered poor. This was unacceptable to the government.

Thus, the official poverty line was an arbitrary, low, absolute measure of poverty. Yet, is poverty a fixed condition or a condition of relative deprivation? If it is a condition of relative deprivation, then a relative measure of poverty, for example, a level of family income less than 1/2 of median family income adjusted for differences in family size, is required. A relative measure of poverty points to the need for income redistribution policies to make the income distribution more equal thereby reducing the extent of poverty. While income redistribution policies are not ruled out by an absolute standard of poverty, they are seen as less essential. With such a measure, economic growth by "raising all boats" is often given primary policy emphasis. The Johnson administration chose an absolute measure of poverty because "it meant that poverty did not necessarily require the rich to be cast down, only that the poor be raised up" (Matusow, 1984, p. 218).

Even with this official standard of poverty, in 1964, 36 055 000 or 19.0 percent of the population was officially considered to be poor. Approximately 69 percent of the poor were white. But blacks were concentrated among the poor. Forty percent of black families lived in poverty in contrast to 12 percent of white families (*Employment and Training Report of the President*, 1977, pp. 290–291).

In the State of the Union message on January 8, 1964, President Johnson said that it was time for the country to commit itself to an "unconditional war on poverty" (Chafe, 1986, p. 232). Within months, the Economic Opportunity Act (EOA), the centerpiece of the War on Poverty, was passed by the US Congress. The Office of Economic Opportunity (OEO) was established with a budget of $800 million.

The problem of poverty was viewed as one of inequality of opportunity, not inequality of result. This was made very clear in the preamble to the EOA where the country was committed to eliminating "the paradox of poverty in the midst of plenty ... by opening to everyone the opportunity to live in decency and dignity" (Chafe, 1986, p. 240). Thus, no attempt would be made to change, for example, the structure of the economy to try to lessen the number of low-paying jobs and increase the number of higher paying ones. In addition, explicit job creation programs were out of the question. The tax cuts, being implemented at approximately the same time, were to lead to economic growth and employment opportunities.

The poor must be willing and able to take advantage of the available, more than adequate opportunities. That they should be willing meant that handouts were not to be provided. It would have been possible to eliminate poverty (as officially defined) by giving the poor enough money so their income exceeded the poverty line. However, if that had been done, it was feared that the poor would have no incentive to try to improve themselves. Ruling out significant economic restructuring or substantially increased transfer payments left a policy whose major emphasis was on changing the characteristics of the poor. Job training and education, along with the enforcement of anti-discrimination legislation, would enable the poor to share in the benefits of economic growth.

The War on Poverty included programs administered by the OEO and programs run by other government agencies. It encompassed newly created initiatives aimed explicitly at the poor as well as the expansion of previously existing programs that were not, initially at least, necessarily focused on the poor. A wide variety of training programs, both institutional and on-the-job, were established or expanded to improve the job skills of the poor. The Job Corps sent high school dropouts to centers far away from their home for two years for job training and education in basic skills. The Neighborhood Youth Corps provided part-time employment in useful local projects during the school year and during the summer. Institutional training and education under the Manpower Development and Training Act began in 1962 and was initially aimed at those who lost their jobs due to technological change. By the mid-1960s, its focus was shifted to the

education and training of the poor. In 1968, a public–private part-
nership was created – Job Opportunities in the Private Sector –
under which firms provided jobs for the poor with the federal
government subsidizing the extra hiring and training costs.

Programs were developed and money was provided to improve the
education of children of the poor. For pre-schoolers, there was Head
Start. The children were provided food and academic activities
designed to improve their preparation for school. The Elementary
and Secondary Education Act of 1965 allocated money for compensatory education programs. Upward Bound was designed to find
underachieving high-school students, who might otherwise not have
been interested in furthering their education, and prepare them for a
college education. To further increase the likelihood of children from
low-income families attending college, the Higher Education Act of
1965 gave grants to colleges and universities for scholarships to full-
time students of "exceptional financial need."

To counter the diet deficiencies of poor schoolchildren, the school
lunch program was expanded and a school breakfast program was created under the Child Nutrition Act of 1966. To improve the health of
the poor and their job performance, Neighborhood Health Centers
and Medicaid were set up in 1966 to subsidize their medical expenses.

Overall, many new initiatives were created as part of the War on
Poverty. But, they were not adequately financed, leading to a sense
that the War on Poverty was not a war, but rather a mere "skirmish."
While the policy approach to poverty reduction emphasized education and training, the share of the federal budget devoted to education and training and other services designed to increase the earnings
capacity of the poor remained small. They accounted for 2.8 percent
of federal expenditures in 1971. That was up from their 0.6 percent
share of the budget in 1965 (Aaron, 1978, p. 12).

Transfers, both in kind and cash, to the poor were also growing
somewhat faster than overall federal expenditures. In-kind transfers
refer to expenditures to provide or subsidize the purchase of such
services as food, health care or housing. They rose from 0.3 percent
of the federal budget in 1965 to 2.3 percent of the federal budget in
1971. The share of the budget going to cash transfers for the poor
rose from 4.2 percent in 1965 to 5.7 percent in 1971. Overall, spending on the poor by the federal government accounted for 10.9 percent of all expenditures in 1971, in contrast to 5.2 percent in 1965
(Aaron, 1978, p. 12).

The funding goals of the new initiatives in the front-line of the War on Poverty were never reached. There were two reasons for this. First, many of the employment and training programs came to be viewed as ineffective in reducing poverty. Second, even though it was not the case, the poverty programs were seen as aiding blacks and not whites.

On the other hand, the funding levels of other programs, not directly related to the War on Poverty, but nevertheless of importance to the poor rose beyond expectations. This refers particularly to income transfers, especially Aid to Families with Dependent Children (AFDC). A welfare explosion was occurring.

RAPIDLY GROWING WELFARE ROLLS

In 1950, 635 000 families were receiving AFDC. By 1960, the number of families on the welfare rolls had risen to 745 000, a 17 percent increase. During the 1960s, welfare caseloads jumped 225 percent to more than 2 400 000 by the end of 1970 (Piven and Cloward, 1971, pp. 341, 351). And in the early 1970s, even more families came to receive welfare. By 1972, 3 000 000 families were AFDC recipients. The cost of welfare rose in step with the growth in the welfare rolls. Less than $1 billion was spent on AFDC in 1960 by the federal and state governments. That figure was $6 billion in 1972 (Katz, 1989, p. 106).

While there was some growth in caseloads in the early 1960s, more than 70 percent of the increase in the welfare rolls occurred in the four years after 1964. That coincided with the riots taking place in the black ghettoes of many of the major cities of the United States. Serious disorders occurred in Atlanta, Baltimore, Birmingham, Boston, Chicago, Cleveland, Detroit, Los Angeles, Miami, Milwaukee, Newark, New York, Oakland, Philadelphia, Phoenix, San Francisco, Tampa and Washington DC, among other cities. Blacks were expressing their anger and asserting their rights. Furthermore, a welfare rights movement was growing. The National Welfare Rights Organization and community action agencies, created under anti-poverty legislation, were asserting black rights to welfare and informing their clients of their eligibility for such assistance.

Many more poor families, of long-standing eligibility, were applying for welfare. And many more applications were being approved. The proportion of applicants being accepted rose from 55 percent in 1960 to 70 percent in 1968 (Piven and Cloward, 1971, p. 334) to

90 percent in 1971 (Katz, 1989, p. 106). Welfare administrators, responding to the troubles poor blacks were making, were more likely to approve their requests. Also, procedural safeguards were multiplying limiting the arbitrary denial of benefits.

Furthermore, changes in federal and state policy and several US Supreme Court decisions liberalized the eligibility requirements for welfare. In 1962, the US Congress passed legislation allowing, but not requiring, states to provide welfare to families with an unemployed father. Prior to that, only female-headed households were eligible for aid. In addition, some states loosened general eligibility standards.

Welfare rights advocates won three important US Supreme Court decisions which effectively extended benefits to hundreds of thousands of recipients. First, state laws requiring a minimum period of residence before being eligible for welfare were struck down (Shapiro v. Thompson, 1969). Second, the "man in the house" rule was declared illegal (King v. Smith, 1968). Prior to this decision, 19 states and Washington DC denied AFDC benefits to families where the mother had a sexual relationship with a man who was not the father of her children. The man had been viewed as a "substitute father," responsible for the financial support of the family. Third, welfare agencies were required to offer clients a hearing that met "minimal due process standards" before stopping benefits (Goldberg v. Kelly, 1970; Katz, 1989, p. 107; Piven and Cloward, 1971, pp. 306–312).

With the growth in the welfare rolls came a call for welfare reform. There were too many "welfare chiselers," "shiftless mothers," "deserting fathers" and illegitimate children. The welfare population was no longer the "deserving" white widows and their children as it had mainly been when the welfare program was begun in 1935. More and more recipients were black and an increasing proportion of cases involved families with divorced or unmarried women.

Thus, work incentives and work requirements were instituted as the welfare population changed from the "deserving" to the "undeserving" poor and the number of beneficiaries increased. Prior to 1967, welfare recipients would lose 1 dollar in benefits for every dollar that they earned and no allowances were made for work-related expenses. Thus, it was argued there was no incentive to find a job and attempt to earn enough to cease receiving AFDC. From 1967, states were required to exempt $30 per month and one-third of additional earnings and to allow itemized deductions for work-related expenses in determining AFDC allowances. This would serve as a financial inducement to find a job. Also, adult recipients unable or unwilling to find employment were required to participate in work and training programs. Refusal to do so would mean the loss of benefits.

Relatively few recipients enrolled in work and training programs. The turbulence in the ghettoes made enforcement very risky and difficult. Those that did enroll received training that did not seem to lead to steady work. The welfare rolls continued to rise.

ONE STEP FORWARD BUT A LONG WAY TO GO

As the economy grew, the proportion of the population with annual incomes below the poverty line diminished sharply. Nineteen percent of the population was officially living in poverty in 1964 when the War on Poverty was declared. That figure dropped to 11.9 percent by 1972. Blacks were still more likely to be poor than whites. In 1972, the poverty rate for blacks was 31.9 percent, substantially above the white rate of 9.0 percent (*Employment and Training Report of the President*, 1977, p. 291).

However, the growing economy itself had a minimal direct role to play in the lessening of poverty. Relatively few people were able to earn their way out of poverty (Aaron 1978; Schwarz, 1983). Rather the growing economy provided the resources enabling government transfer payments to grow. Those who were able to leave the ranks of the poor often did so as a result of government transfer payments unrelated to the War on Poverty. Social Security benefits, payable to those who retire after the age of 62 or who become disabled or who are dependents of deceased workers, were most effective in raising families out of poverty. Public assistance programs, such as welfare, were not particularly effective in doing so (Lynn, 1977). The benefit levels were too low. In 1972, AFDC and food stamps benefits for a family of four with no other income averaged 84 percent of the poverty line. This was higher than it had been in the 1960s but inadequate nonetheless (Cherry, 1989, p. 116).

The success of government transfer payments in reducing poverty contradicted one of the key premises of the War on Poverty. "Handouts," as transfer payments were often referred to, were not to be the main policy for poverty reduction. Rather education and training programs were to play that role. While some did benefit from these initiatives, the programs were not adequately funded and the initial premise of the War on Poverty was not particularly well thought out. Well-paying jobs demanding the services of those poor completing education and training programs did not automatically emerge. Instead, the unemployment rate began to rise after 1969 and many of the jobs that did exist did not pay enough to enable job holders to earn an annual income above the poverty level. Furthermore, the share of total income going to poorer members of society did not change. The poorest 20 percent of families in the United States received 5.2 percent of total income in 1964 and 5.4 percent in 1972. The government transfer payments merely counteracted the tendency toward increased inequality.

Though many of the poor were not able to earn their way out of poverty, the civil rights movement and the women's movement together with the strong demand for labor did open up some employment opportunities for women and black men. A small but growing proportion of black men came to hold the more desirable, higher paying professional, managerial and craft jobs. Even so, their representation in these occupations was still well below that of white men. Black men were 9.1 percent of employed men in 1962 and 9.6 percent of employed men in 1972. They accounted for 5.7 percent of all male professional workers in 1972, up from 3.6 percent in 1962. Black managers were 3.5 percent of all male managers in 1972, in contrast to 2.2 percent ten years earlier. The growth of black professionals and managers occurred primarily among the lowest paying jobs in these two broad occupational groupings (Reich, 1981, p. 30; Levitan et al., 1975, p. 162). Black men increased their share of male skilled craft positions from 4.7 percent in 1962 to 6.8 percent in 1972 (Garfinkle, 1975, p. 30). Overall, black male annual income rose relative to white male income. The black male to white male median income ratio increased from 49 percent in 1962 to 62 percent in 1972 (Reich, 1981, p. 32).

Black women also made strong job gains relative to white women. They were 12.6 percent of employed women in 1962 and 12.1 percent of employed women in 1972 (Garfinkle, 1975, p. 31). They moved out of domestic service and into clerical and professional occupations. While black women were still underrepresented in clerical work relative to white women, their share of female clerical jobs rose from 4.1 percent in 1962 to 8.2 percent in 1972. A similar though less dramatic trend occurred in professional work. Black women accounted for 9.4 percent of all female professional workers in 1972, up from 6.7 percent in 1962 (Garfinkle, 1975, p. 31).

Overall black female annual income rose sharply, relatively, to white female annual income. The black female to white female median income ratio increased from 67 percent in 1962 to 95 percent in 1972 (Reich, 1981, p. 32).

It was easier for black women to enter jobs, up to this time, reserved for white women than for women as a whole to enter jobs considered the preserve of white men. Women continued to enter the labor force with their participation rate rising to 43.9 percent in 1972. They were still concentrated in clerical and service jobs with 34.7 percent of women holding clerical positions and 17.5 percent of women doing nonhousehold service work. And they were still virtually excluded from skilled craft jobs with only 1.2 percent of women doing such work in 1972 (*Employment and Training Report of the President*, 1977, p. 162).

However, even though sex segregation continued to exist, women did increase their presence in a number of occupations where few had worked in the past. While women professional workers were still segregated into the predominantly female occupations of elementary and secondary school teaching, nursing, library and social work, they did make some gains in medicine increasing from 5.8 percent of all doctors in 1962 to 10.1 percent in 1972; in accounting from 18.7 percent to 21.7 percent; and in college and university teaching from 19.2 percent to 28.0 percent. Women moved into a variety of clerical jobs such as ticket and station agents, postal clerks, bill collectors and insurance adjusters in which their employment opportunities had been limited in the past. They also made substantial gains in such sales occupations as real estate agents (Garfinkle, 1975).

The enforcement of the legal prohibitions against discrimination was weak. The OFCC did not aggressively enforce regulations barring racial discrimination until after 1973 and did not even begin enforcing regulations against sex discrimination until 1974. The EEOC had minimal powers to attempt to uphold Title VII of the Civil Rights Act until 1972. Furthermore, it was very understaffed. Even so, the threat of OFCC sanctions or litigation under Title VII did seem to change employer and union practices and advance the employment of blacks and women. The employment share of blacks increased more in firms holding government contracts subject to affirmative action requirements than in firms without government contracts (Jaynes and Williams, 1989, pp. 316–317). Between 1967 and 1974, enforcement of Title VII narrowed the sex differential in earnings by 7 percentage points and sex differences in the probability of being employed in a male occupation by about 6 percentage points (Blau and Ferber, 1992, p. 225).

Legal changes began occurring in seniority rules, hiring and promotion practices and in the definition of discrimination. In the landmark US Supreme Court case Griggs v. Duke Power (1971), the justices ruled that those alleging discrimination need not prove that their employer intended to discriminate. Rather, all they had to show was that the actions of the company had an "adverse impact" on their employment opportunities. The company would then be obliged to prove that the particular practice in question was necessary for the safe and efficient operation of the business. Thus, it would become easier, at least for a while, to legally demonstrate the existence of discrimination. And employers would have to scrutinize more carefully their personnel policies. They would no longer be able to utilize employment exams, as screening devices, that did not have a direct bearing on job performance. These exams often had an adverse impact on blacks. They would now be more likely to be required to develop affirmative action programs to expand promotion possibilities for blacks (and by implication for women). The court also ruled that union contracts, though apparently neutral, "cannot be maintained if they operate to freeze the status quo of prior discriminatory employment practices" (quoted in Harris, 1982, p. 159). Thus, blacks can be promoted outside the existing seniority system.

This was not the first case questioning seniority arrangements, nor would it be the last. Many of the earliest cases filed under Title VII dealt with alleged discriminatory seniority systems. Unions tried to protect these arrangements, often siding with the employers against their own black union members. But the courts held that union negotiated seniority systems that were discriminatory must be changed in compliance with the requirements of Title VII.

For some blacks the issue was promotion, for others it was initial hiring. Segregated union locals were, by definition, deemed to be a violation of Title VII. Black workers in the International Longshoremen's Association, disturbed by segregated locals and racist job referral policies, successfully sued the union in federal court in the early 1970s. All-white construction craft unions were, of course, illegal. Many building trades locals were found to have engaged in widespread illegal discriminatory practices and the courts ordered sweeping relief to the black plaintiffs in the lawsuits (Hill, 1982, p. 45). Even so, many construction unions stonewalled the courts for as long as possible. Given that companies doing construction work for the government were forced to demonstrate that they had an integrated work force before bidding for contracts, firms began turning to black-controlled hiring halls. As a result, the share of jobs going to blacks in the construction trades increased.

It is undeniable that women and black men made slow but noticeable progress into traditional white male occupations, and black women moved into white female jobs such as clerical work. But this picture of progress must be tempered by the vast extent of racial and sexual inequality that still prevailed. The degree of sex segregation of work was mitigated only slightly (Blau and Hendricks, 1979). And the sex-based earnings differential did not narrow, but rather widened slightly. Except for professional and technical work, the ratio of the median earnings of full-time year-round women workers to those of full-time year-round men workers in similar broad occupational groupings was lower in 1970 than it had been in 1960 (US Bureau of the Census, 1983, p. 23). Women still experienced somewhat more unemployment than did men with the female unemployment rate equaling 6.6 percent in 1972, in contrast to the male rate of 4.9 percent.

Blacks were still much more likely than whites to be out of work. During the late 1960s, the unemployment rate fell below 4 percent, the "full employment" goal at the time, but many blacks failed to find work. In 1969, the overall unemployment rate was 3.5 percent while the rate for blacks was 6.4 percent. That level of unemployment surely did not represent a fully employed black community. Throughout the 1960s, black men were still more than twice as likely as white men to be unemployed. Yet, the problem of black male joblessness is not fully captured by the official measure of unemployment. Many out of work black men had ceased looking for work and thus were no longer counted among the unemployed. In 1960, approximately 83 percent of black and white men were in the labor force. By 1972, the black male labor force participation rate had fallen to 73.7 percent in contrast to the white male rate of 79.6 percent (*Employment and Training Report of the President*, 1977, pp. 143–144).

Black women also had more difficulty finding work than did white women. Many more white women entered the labor force in the 1960s. Their labor force participation rate rose from 36.5 percent in 1960 to 43.2 percent in 1972. The black woman participation rate remained virtually constant, being 48.2 percent in 1960 and 48.7 percent in 1972. At the same time as more white women were working, the racial unemployment differential remained wide. It hovered in the range of 1.8–2.0 in the 1960s (*Employment and Training Report of the President*, 1977, p. 166).

Overall, blacks were still concentrated among the working poor. Levitan, Johnston and Taggart create an employment and earnings inadequacy index which measures the number of workers who are unemployed, not looking for work because they feel they cannot find a job, involuntarily working part-time, and household heads earning too little to raise their families out of poverty. By this index, 25 percent of blacks and 10 percent of whites had inadequate employment and earnings in 1972 (Levitan *et al.*, 1975, p. 75).

In conclusion, the 1960s were a period of strong economic growth and tight labor markets. While a growing economy does not guarantee that poverty will diminish and tight labor markets do not guarantee that progress will be made against discrimination, they do provide an enabling atmosphere. Progress against poverty and discrimination seem less like a zero-sum game. The poor can be helped without taking from the wealthier. Opportunities for women and black men can be expanded without restricting, to a great degree, the options of white men.

But the 1960s left an ambiguous legacy. Some progress occurred but much remained to be accomplished. The rate of economic growth would slow in the 1970s. Cutbacks would occur in funding for transfer payments and other anti-poverty programs. Tensions would emerge over equal employment opportunity and affirmative action policies. The slowing in economic growth partly reflected the relative decline in the international standing of the US economy. As a basis for understanding the position of the US economy in the 1970s, the next chapter treats the evolving international economic position of the United States in the 1960s and early 1970s.

8. The Dollar: No Longer As Good As Gold

By 1960, the US balance of payments deficits were raising concerns regarding the stability of the international monetary system created at Bretton Woods. If large balance of payments deficits continued to be run and dollars continued to flow from the United States, would the dollar be able to continue serving as the international reserve currency with a value fixed relative to gold? Realizing that the balance of payments deficits reflected the global role of the United States, particularly its overseas military and foreign aid activities as well as the long-term foreign investment of American corporations, neither the Kennedy nor Johnson administrations were interested in developing balance of payments policies which might interfere with the worldwide aims of the nation. Rather a variety of *ad hoc* measures were taken to reduce dollar outflows, increase dollar inflows and induce foreign countries to continue holding dollars rather than redeeming them for gold. In addition, freer trade policies were advanced under the belief that liberalizing trade would serve to improve the US balance of trade since American goods and American know-how would capture many markets.

The *ad hoc* measures did buy some time. Furthermore, Western European countries with the exception of France were willing, at least for a time, to cooperate with the US attempts to maintain its hegemony. However, the balance of payments problems ultimately worsened. The economies of Western Europe and Japan had grown stronger relative to the United States. Products made in the United States became less competitive with foreign goods, both at home and abroad. Furthermore, the attempt to have both "guns and butter" during the Vietnam War and the inflation which ensued, further hurt American competitiveness. The balance of trade weakened, placing additional pressure on the balance of payments. The United States was finding it difficult to pay for its global military domination.

By the middle of 1971, it became apparent that the United States would record a balance of trade deficit for that year, the first one of the twentieth century. Large short-term capital outflows from the United States precipitated a balance of payments crisis in 1971. International faith in the dollar plummeted and countries were beginning to ask for gold in exchange for their dollar holdings at the still official price of $35 for one ounce of gold. However, the United States did not have adequate gold stocks. The situation was untenable.

Given the option of maintaining the existing international monetary regime or advancing the autonomy of the United States in domestic and international policy, the United States chose its autonomy. On August 15, 1971, the Nixon administration suspended the convertibility of the dollar into gold, thereby dismantling the international monetary system which had been created by the United States in the period of its maximum relative power. That such a step needed to be taken was an indication of the relative decline in the international standing of the US economy.

THE DOLLAR PROBLEM

By 1960, the United States was facing balance of payments deficits with potentially grave implications for the international monetary system. International faith in the dollar was weakening and American gold stocks were being drained. There was talk of the need to devalue the dollar. President Kennedy was seriously concerned about the balance of payments deficit. In fact, according to Arthur M. Schlesinger Jr:

> Kennedy ... used to tell his advisers that the two things which scared him were nuclear war and the payments deficit. Once he half-humorously derided the notion that nuclear weapons were essential to international prestige. "What really matters," he said, "is the strength of the currency." (Quoted in Wachtel, 1986, pp. 71–72)

President Kennedy was also aware that the balance of payments deficits reflected the global role of the United States.

Thus, any balance of payments policy would need to be consistent with maintaining the value of the dollar and facilitating the worldwide activities of the United States. Furthermore, it should not interfere with expansionary macroeconomic policy designed to pull the economy out of recession. However, the dilemma for the Kennedy administration was that the typical balance of payments policies of deflation, devaluation, or controls on trade and capital flows did interfere with the pursuit of these goals.

Restrictive fiscal and monetary policy, or deflation, may reduce dollar outflows and increase dollar inflows. With higher taxes or lower government spending, the economy will grow more slowly or even contract. As a result, personal income levels will grow more slowly or even decline, thereby reducing the demand for imports. With an economic slowdown, the rate of inflation may diminish or actual deflation occur, thereby increasing the demand for American exports. With restrictive monetary policy, interest rates may rise, thereby attracting foreign short-term capital to the United States. Less imports, more exports and more foreign short-term capital would improve the balance of payments. But the slowing of the economy would make it more difficult to "get America moving again."

Thus, deflation was not a particularly suitable option. Devaluation, as well, was also ruled out. If the dollar was to be devalued, the cost to Americans of imported goods would rise thereby decreasing the demand for imports. The cost to foreigners of American exports would drop, thereby increasing the demand for exports. However, the devaluation of the dollar would be at odds with the goal of maintaining a strong dollar. Furthermore, it would conflict with a central tenet of the Bretton Woods Agreements, that being the fixed rate of exchange between the dollar and gold and the fixed exchange rates between the dollar and other country currencies. Thus, rather than foster confidence in the international monetary system, in general, and the dollar, in particular, it might instead deal a blow to the Bretton Woods Agreements.

More direct intervention in international trade and capital flows had the potential to stem the dollar outflow. Import barriers could be raised and controls could be placed on the foreign investment activities of American individuals and corporations. But such a policy would be in conflict with free trade and free mobility of capital, central elements of the American vision of the world economy. Bringing home American troops based in other countries could complement these policies. But doing so would constrain American foreign policy.

The dilemma for the Kennedy administration was that the conventional, systematic policies for alleviating a balance of payments deficit were not available. But, ignoring the balance of payments problem did not appear to be feasible nor desirable. Rather the Kennedy administration and the Johnson administration thereafter continuously searched for *ad hoc* answers to what would eventually turn out to be a more systemic problem.

The Kennedy Administration initially argued that the best and most painless solution to the balance of payments problem would be to expand exports from the United States. Liberalizing world trade would be a means for doing so. Furthermore, moving toward a worldwide free market was consistent with a policy of renewing American world leadership and tightening the alliance between the United States and the Western European societies.

Several years before, on March 25, 1957, the Treaty of Rome was signed establishing the European Economic Community (EEC). The members of the EEC were Belgium, the Federal Republic of Germany, France, Italy, Luxembourg and the Netherlands. The goal of the EEC was to integrate the economies of the member countries by reducing internal barriers to trade and establishing a single EEC tariff against the commodities produced by the rest of the world. The first reductions in tariffs and import quotas among member countries occurred in 1959. Schedules were developed for successive tariff and quota reductions, with the end goal being their total elimination and the free movement of goods across country borders.

The United States supported the creation of the EEC, believing it would lead to stronger European economies. However, there was still a major concern. It was inevitable that the members of the EEC would trade more among themselves and less with the United States. However, would US-based producers experience great difficulty penetrating Western European markets? If this were to occur, would it encourage American firms to invest in Europe rather than export from the United States? Increased capital outflows and decreased exports would further worsen the balance of payments deficit.

Thus, the Kennedy Administration pushed for, and the US Congress approved, the Trade Expansion Act of 1962. This legislation had general clauses applying to trade between the United States and other countries and more specific clauses relevant for trade between the United States and the EEC. It provided the President with wide-ranging authority to negotiate reductions in tariffs. The President had the freedom to reduce existing tariffs by up to 50 percent in reciprocal negotiations with any country. The scope for tariff reductions with the EEC was even wider.

The government knew that all American workers and all businesses would not benefit from expanded world trade. Some workers would likely lose their jobs and some businesses would be forced to downsize or close entirely due to import competition. Thus, the Trade Expansion Act included trade adjustment assistance for workers and financial aid, technical assistance and tax concessions for businesses hurt by increased foreign competition. This provision was the price set by the AFL–CIO for its support of the trade expansion measure. The business community was split on the trade bill. The weak sectors of the US economy, such as textiles and other labor-intensive industries, opposed further trade liberalization. The stronger, more capital-intensive industries supported freer trade and were interested in expanding their markets, particularly in Europe. The financial sector strongly favored policies which expanded the freedom for global financial capital. The business opposition that did materialize was not strong enough to prevent the passage of the legislation.

By liberalizing trade, the Kennedy Administration hoped to improve the balance of payments. First, it was thought that reducing tariffs would increase the trade surplus by allowing exports to grow faster than imports since it was assumed that American firms would dominate most markets. Second, an improved trade environment would provide an inducement for US-based companies to export to foreign markets rather than locate production facilities abroad. Increased domestic investment would improve the competitiveness of the US economy and lead to an even more favorable trade balance in the future.

However, this was, at best, a long-term strategy for ameliorating the balance of payments. First, there was no guarantee that liberalizing trade would, in fact, improve the American trade surplus. Imports might increase more than exports. Second, any tariff reductions would need to be negotiated. This would not occur immediately, if it was to happen at all.

Thus, in the short run, more *ad hoc* measures were taken to attempt to quickly shrink the balance of payments deficits and improve international confidence in the dollar. Direct capital investment abroad by American corporations and short-term capital flows were two large negative items in the balance of payments. The United States took several unilateral steps to try to lessen the outflow of private capital.

Monetary policy was pursued by the Federal Reserve with an eye on the balance of payments. The Federal Reserve engaged in

"Operation Twist" (discussed in Chapter 5), designed to increase short-term interest rates while keeping long-term interest rates low. Operation Twist was complemented by a higher discount rate. On July 16, 1963, the Federal Reserve raised the discount rate from 3.0 to 3.5 percent in order "to minimize short-term capital outflows prompted by higher interest rates prevalent in other countries" (quoted in Solomon, 1982, p. 47). The Kennedy administration concurred with the Federal Reserve policy but believed it needed to be supported by additional measures.

On July 18, two days after the increase in the discount rate, the President proposed a temporary interest equalization tax on American purchases of foreign securities. The US capital market was by far the most well-developed in the world. Foreign governments, particularly those in Western Europe, and foreign corporations were searching for new capital and issuing securities in the United States. The Interest Equalization Tax, passed by the US Congress in August 1964, was designed to make foreign securities more expensive to US purchasers thereby serving to limit the outflow of capital from the United States.

Additional *ad hoc* measures were taken to stem the dollar outflow. The US Department of Defense was ordered to use domestic suppliers as long as their prices were no more than 50 percent greater than the cost of foreign suppliers. The duty-free allowance for returning American tourists was reduced. Tied assistance became more common, requiring that foreign aid dollars be spent on US-made items, even if the commodities could be purchased more cheaply elsewhere. In addition, President Kennedy reduced, though slightly, overseas military and civilian expenditures.

The preceding, mainly unilateral, policies were designed to diminish the US balance of payments deficit, thereby strengthening international confidence in the dollar. These more unilateral approaches were supplemented by more multilateral policies aimed at directly maintaining the price of gold at $35 an ounce. The United States had the responsibility of selling gold on the London gold market if the price of gold exceeded $35. However, if steadily rising demand for gold caused a sharp increase in the price, the declining gold stocks of the United States might come under extreme pressure.

The London Gold Pool was created to increase the potential supply of gold, thereby lessening the risk of a sharp drop in US gold stocks. The six members of the EEC, along with Great Britain and

Switzerland, agreed to work with the United States in stabilizing the price of gold. If the price of gold were to rise above the official price, these countries would provide half of the gold needed to push the price down to $35. They also agreed to purchase half of the gold necessary if the price of gold were to fall below $35. The Gold Pool began operating in November 1961.

Overall, these various *ad hoc* policies bought the US time. The balance of payments deficits stabilized during the Kennedy years. And time was all that American policymakers believed was required to improve the US balance of payments position. With time, increased investment, rising productivity and continuing cost and price stability would improve the international competitiveness of the American economy. However, this forecast would prove to be overly optimistic.

Not only were the various *ad hoc* measures unable to turn around the balance of payments situation, some of them were not even consistent with the government's often stated goal of creating an integrated world economy based on free trade and the free mobility of capital. While explicit capital controls were not implemented, they would come later, the Interest Equalization Tax did try to indirectly restrict capital flows from the United States. And the manipulation of short and long-term interest rates represented an attempt to somewhat insulate the US capital market from international conditions.

In 1964, the merchandise trade balance improved by $1.6 billion to $6.8 billion, the largest it had been since 1947 (*Economic Report of the President*, 1995, p. 394). Nevertheless, the government faced a balance of payments issue. Outflows of long and short-term capital were rising, two-thirds of which were going to Europe. The government decided to supplement the Interest Equalization Tax by voluntarily limiting capital outflows. In February 1965, the Johnson Administration introduced the Voluntary Foreign Credit Restraint Program requesting corporations and banks not to increase their export of funds by more than 5 percent above the levels outstanding as of December 31, 1964. Capital outflows did decline in 1965. However, the merchandise balance of trade surplus declined by $2 billion, placing continued pressure on the overall balance of payments.

Throughout the second half of the 1960s, the merchandise balance of trade surplus steadily diminished. The declining merchandise trade balance, along with the increased overseas military costs related to the Vietnam War, meant the balance of payments continued to be a concern to American policymakers. They continued to try to buy time since they believed the problems were temporary and would cease with the end of the war.

The United States tried to induce other countries not to turn in their dollars for gold since it had become clear that American gold stocks were far short of what would be required if countries simultaneously demanded gold for their dollars. Western Europe (primarily West Germany), with the exception of France, and Japan were willing to underwrite an incontrovertible dollar. According to Benjamin Cohen:

> America's allies acquiesced in a hegemonic system that accorded the United States special privileges to act abroad unilaterally to promote U.S. interests. The United States, in turn, condoned its allies' use of the system to promote their own economic prosperity, even if this happened to come largely at the expense of the United States. (Quoted in Gilpin, 1987, p. 136)

The United States tolerated discrimination against its exports by the European Economic Community and the Japanese as well as aggressive export expansion strategies. In return, the United States was able to pursue its domestic and worldwide political objectives.

Over time, this situation would prove to be less satisfying to American allies. They would come to view sympathetically the French criticism of US behavior. Unlike West Germany and other advanced industrialized societies, France was not interested in collaborating with the United States to maintain the existing international monetary system. Rather the French felt that the Bretton Woods arrangements provided the United States with privileges which were not available to other nations. In February 1965, Charles DeGaulle argued that as long as countries were expected to hold American dollars rather than exchange them for gold, they were unwilling creditors of the United States. And by doing so, they were participants, however unwilling, in a process leading to the selling off of their businesses to American investors for nothing in return. The dollar outflows coincided with substantial American direct investment in European firms. Furthermore, the United States was more able to pursue its foreign policy objectives than were other countries. Foreign policy goals often entail expenditures in other lands. Countries, other than the United States, facing balance of payments deficits resulting from their foreign activities might be forced to cut back on these ventures in order to maintain the exchange rates of their currencies. On the other hand, to the extent that other countries held dollars rather than turn them in for gold, the United States was free to pursue its international objectives. And, at the time, France was quite critical of American foreign policy. Overall, the French point of view implied that "America's monetary hegemony reflected a political relationship between Europe and America that was growing increasingly inappropriate" (Calleo, 1982, p. 47).

Given the French approach, it was not surprising that the French would opt out of the Gold Pool in June 1967. Later in 1967, speculators anticipating a devaluation of the British pound sold large amounts of pounds on the international currency market. In November 1967, the pound was devalued by 14.3 percent. Speculators then attacked the dollar. To moderate the speculative attack on the dollar, on January 1, 1968, President Johnson announced a new program of mandatory capital controls. No new capital could leave the United States to be invested in continental Europe. Thus, to save Bretton Woods, the United States was breaking more and more of its rules. Bretton Woods was designed to promote the free flow of capital. The United States, in order to save Bretton Woods, was now restricting private capital exports (Borden, 1989, p. 84).

But the speculation against the dollar continued. The latest balance of payments figures, announced in February 1968, showed a larger than expected deficit in 1967 and one which was growing rapidly in the last quarter of the year. By March, there was a massive rush to sell dollars for gold on the London gold market. The London gold market was closed on March 15. The Gold Pool was then disbanded and the United States announced it would no longer support the price of gold in the market. Rather a two-tier system would be set up. Official transactions between central banks would still take place on the basis of the official price of gold. However, the free market price of gold would be allowed to reach its own level based on the demand and supply of gold. The London gold market was reopened on April 1. The two-tier arrangement was a step on the road to the total elimination of the official dollar price of gold. The United States unilaterally repudiated its responsibility under the Bretton Woods Agreements to maintain the market price of gold at the official level. While there was still an official price of gold, it was unclear whether it would truly be operational.

Shortly thereafter, the pressure on the dollar subsided. The US balance of payments began to improve as short-term capital began flowing to the United States. There were several reasons for the return of short-term capital to the United States. First, the Federal Reserve instituted a tight monetary policy as an anti-inflationary tool. Interest rates began to rise, thereby attracting short-term capital from other countries. Second, Europe was experiencing serious political upheavals. In May 1968, a student revolt and, then, a general strike of workers occurred in France, nearly toppling the DeGaulle government. Furthermore, in August the Soviet Union invaded Czechoslovakia in order to oust the Dubcek government and replace it with one more to its liking. The United States appeared to be a more favorable place for portfolio investment and foreigners sharply increased their net purchase of stock in American corporations. Thus, even though there was a sharp decline in the US trade surplus in 1968, the overall balance of payments position did not present a problem. The same held for 1969.

However, by 1970, economic conditions had changed. During the recession of 1970, interest rates fell as the Federal Reserve turned to easy monetary policy to help to stimulate the economy. While interest rates were falling in the United States, they were rising in Europe. Dollars flowed from the United States in response to higher interest rates elsewhere. And foreigners were less interested in placing their funds on the New York Stock Exchange since stock prices were declining. Overall, short-term US capital flows shifted dramatically from a positive (inflow) $5.8 billion average for 1968–69 to a negative (outflow) $6.5 billion in 1970 (Guttmann, 1994, p. 142). The overall balance of payments deficit rose to an unprecedented $9.8 billion.

The flight from the dollar continued in the first half of 1971. The balance of payments deficit increased from $5.4 billion in the first quarter of 1971 to $6.5 billion in the second quarter. Close to 40 percent of the deficit in the second quarter was accounted for by "errors and omissions," unrecorded and quite likely speculative outflows of dollars (Rukstad, 1992, p. 505). Further complicating the situation were data being released on the balance of trade. It was becoming apparent that the US trade balance was about to record a deficit, the first one since 1893.

The data provide a backdrop for the May 28 speech of Treasury Secretary Connally to the International Banking Conference of the American Bankers Association in Munich. In discussing the US balance of payments deficit, he emphasized that American inflation, though a factor, was not the only factor. Rather he focused on the failure of Europe and Japan to share defense burdens adequately and to ease their import restrictions. He stated:

> Specifically, we today spend nearly 9 percent of our gross national product on defense – nearly 5 billion dollars of that overseas, much of it in Western Europe and Japan. Financing a military shield is part of the burden of leadership; the responsibility cannot and should not be cast off … [But] the nations of Western Europe and Japan are again strong and vigorous, and their capacities to contribute have vastly increased.
>
> I find it an impressive fact, and a depressing fact, that the persistent underlying balance of payments deficit which causes such concern is more than covered, year in and year out, by our net military expenditures abroad, over and above amounts received from foreign military purchases in the United States.
>
> A second area where action is plainly overdue lies in trading arrangements. The comfortable assumption that the United States should – in the broader political interests of the free world – be willing to bear disproportionate economic costs does not fit the facts today … .
>
> The question is only – but the "only" is important – whether these nations, (Common Market, Japan, Canada) now more than amply supplied with reserves as well as with productive power should not now be called upon for fresh initiatives in opening their markets to the products of others. (Quoted in Sweezy and Magdoff, 1971, p. 12)

In essence, the Treasury Secretary was calling for a new political–economic policy, one designed to force the countries of Western Europe, Japan and Canada to revalue their currencies upward, share the burden of policing the world and change their trade policies in a way that would favor the United States. What that policy would be remained to be seen.

THE MERCHANDISE BALANCE OF TRADE

Treasury Secretary Connolly pointed out what had already become known. The economies of Western Europe and Japan had grown stronger relative to the United States. The process had begun in the 1950s, after the immediate postwar reconstruction period, and continued apace in the 1960s. By 1971, the earlier optimism among policymakers regarding the international position of the US economy had given way to serious concern. Several months after Connolly's speech, President Nixon would announce a new economic strategy, having as one of its goals the reversal of the relative decline of the American economy.

The United States emerged from the Second World War with its industrial base intact. In the early postwar period, its relative economic strength was overwhelming. In 1950, the United States accounted for 62 percent of the manufacturing output of the ten largest industrialized countries. But this was a transitory situation. The economies of Western Europe and Japan were rebuilt and their manufacturing capacity grew. As would be anticipated, the US share of manufacturing output declined during the 1950s. But the American share continued to slide during the 1960s. By 1970, it had shrunk to 44 percent from 51 percent in 1960. West Germany and Japan experienced rapid growth in manufacturing with a concomitant increase in their relative shares of manufacturing output. West Germany's share rose from 10.1 percent in 1950 to 17.2 percent in 1960 and then remained constant in the 1960s. The Japanese share rose from 2.1 percent in 1950 to 6.3 percent in 1960. During the 1960s, Japanese industrial growth was far more rapid than in the other advanced industrialized societies. By 1970, Japan accounted for 13.1 percent of the manufacturing output of the ten major industrialized countries (Branson, 1980, p. 191).

Not only did the US share of world manufacturing production decline, but the American share of the world market for manufactured goods shrunk as well. The United States had pushed for freer trade but other countries seemed to gain more as trade barriers were partially dismantled and a boom in world trade emerged. In 1953, 29.4 percent of total world exports of manufactured products were from the United States. By 1971, that figure had fallen to 13 percent. At the same time, West Germany and Japan became more formidable competitors on the world market. Their shares of manufactured exports rose rapidly. West Germany's share of manufactured exports climbed from 9.7 percent in 1953 to 15.6 percent in 1959 and stayed around that level throughout the 1960s. Japan was a minor participant in world trade in the early 1950s. In 1953, it accounted for only 2.8 percent of world manufactured exports. By 1959, its share had risen to 4.9 percent. Continued steady growth in manufactured exports resulted in a doubling of the Japanese share by 1971, reaching a level of 10.0 percent (Branson, 1980, p. 196).

Along with the decline in the presence of US-made manufactured goods on world markets came an increase in the penetration of the American market by foreign made products. During the 1960s, Americans began purchasing growing amounts of imported manufactured goods. Import penetration of manufactured goods, defined as imports as a percentage of domestic production of manufactures plus imports, equaled 2 percent for the United States in 1950. This figure rose to 3 percent in 1963. But by 1971, it had reached 8 percent (Armstrong *et al.*, 1984, p. 215).

In 1960, when Americans went to buy a car 95 times out of 100 they returned with one built by General Motors (GM), Ford, Chrysler or American Motors within the borders of the United States. Americans shopping for clothes, footwear or consumer electronics, such as radios and televisions, also virtually always returned home with an American-made product. The same held for American firms in the market for items such as steel, electrical components, industrial chemicals and machine tools.

But, during the 1960s, American consumers and American firms changed their buying habits. They began looking more favorably on imported products. American producers, while still the major players in these product areas, were no longer as dominant in the domestic market. The American producers' US market shares, defined as domestic producers' percentage of total sales, fell in automobiles from 95.5 percent in 1960 to 82.6 percent in 1970, in apparel from 98.2 percent to 94.8 percent, in footwear from 97.7 percent to 85.4 percent, in consumer electronics from 94.4 percent to 68.4 percent, in steel from 95.8 percent to 85.7 percent, in electrical components from 99.5 percent to 94.4 percent, in industrial chemicals from 98.0 percent to 91.5 percent, and in machine tools from more than 96 percent to approximately 91 percent (Guttmann, 1994, p. 463).

A growing openness to imports together with increased competition on world markets points to the likelihood of a diminishing balance of trade surplus or perhaps, even, an eventual balance of trade deficit. In fact, this is just what occurred. The merchandise balance of trade went into deficit in 1971 for the first time in the twentieth century. This trade deficit was an important symbol of change in the international status of the US economy. The United States, no longer, totally dominated the international economy.

Several factors were responsible for the worsening merchandise balance of trade. The timing of the deterioration in the balance of trade was directly connected to the Vietnam War-related inflation. From 1960 to 1964, a period of very low inflation in most advanced industrial nations, prices of American exports rose at approximately the same rate as prices of exports from other industrialized societies. And during this period, the surplus in the US balance of trade rose by about $2 billion, from $4.9 billion to $6.8 billion (*Economic Report of the President*, 1995, p. 394). The US trade surplus dropped by about $6 billion from 1964 to 1968. And during these years, the US export prices rose by about 10 percent, well above the 3 percent increase in export prices for other industrialized societies. Thus, US-made products became less competitive with foreign goods, both at home and abroad. Between 1968 and 1971, the prices of American exports rose at the same rate as the prices of exports from other industrialized nations. Thus, the United States was unable to regain any lost ground before 1968 (Ackerman and MacEwan, 1972, pp. 16–17).

While the timing of the decline in the merchandise balance of trade was related to the more rapidly rising prices in the United States than in its trading partners, more long-term factors were also at work. There was the improving international competitiveness of Western European countries and Japan. Firms in these nations were investing in new plant and equipment at a faster rate than were companies located in the United States. Between 1955 and 1970, the capital stock in US manufacturing grew by 57 percent; in the major European countries (e.g. Great Britain, France, West Germany and Italy) the rise was 116 percent and in Japan it was 500 percent. The growth in the capital stock outpaced the increase in employment. Each manufacturing employee was thereby working with more capital. However, the capital stock per worker grew more rapidly in Europe and Japan.

Not surprisingly, productivity in manufacturing rose faster in Europe and Japan than in the United States. Nevertheless, even in 1970, American manufacturing workers were still producing more per hour than their European and Japanese counterparts. However, the productivity differences were narrowing and labor costs in Europe and Japan were still far below those in the United States. Overall, European and Japanese plants were more likely to utilize the most modern of technology than were manufacturing facilities located in the United States (Armstrong *et al.*, 1984).

But the international competitiveness of a nation is not equivalent to the international competitiveness of firms owned by citizens of a nation. At the same time as signs were pointing to a decline in the international standing of the US economy, American multinational corporations were widening their presence throughout the world. US direct foreign investment grew from $11.8 billion in 1950 to $31.9 billion in 1960 to $78.2 billion in 1970 (Branson, 1980, p. 237).

The pace of American foreign investment was more rapid than domestic investment. Between 1950 and 1972, direct private investment assets abroad doubled from 5 percent to roughly 10 percent of total corporate investment assets (at home and abroad). And the foreign operations were profitable, earning average rates of profit exceeding those earned on domestic operations. The share of foreign profits in total after-tax corporate profits rose from roughly 7 percent in 1950 to about 25 percent in 1972. It was the largest American corporations that were most heavily involved in foreign economic activity (Edwards *et al.*, 1978, pp. 476–477).

As the globalization of American corporations progressed, they began to serve world markets more from their foreign operations and less from their plants in the United States. While the share of world exports of manufactured products produced in the United States peaked in 1953, falling steadily thereafter, the share of world exports of manufactured goods from foreign located affiliates of US multinational corporations was steadily rising from 5.8 percent in 1957 to approximately 9 percent in the early 1970s (Duboff, 1989, p. 155).

Furthermore, manufacturing was the most rapidly growing sector of the US foreign investment. The value of foreign investment in manufacturing was 34.0 percent of the total US foreign investment in 1955. By 1970, it had reached 41.3 percent. American firms were seeking out cheaper labor abroad and were attempting to gain a foothold in foreign markets. They were particularly increasing their presence in Western Europe. With the creation of the Common Market in 1957 and the convertibility of European currencies shortly thereafter, American firms rushed to Western Europe, setting up branches to gain access to what was to be a large tariff-free market. American investment in manufacturing in Europe rose from 25.7 percent of total American direct investment in foreign manufacturing operations in 1955 to 42.4 percent in 1970 (Branson, 1980).

The US overseas investment was facilitated by the role played by the dollar in the international monetary system. The dollar was the international reserve currency and its value was fixed relative to the other currencies. As would become apparent by the end of the 1960s, the dollar was overvalued. While the overvalued dollar made it more expensive for foreigners to purchase goods made in the United States, it led to lower costs for American companies buying or building facilities in other lands.

The consequences for the US economy of direct foreign investment by American multinationals became hotly debated as the balance of trade surplus declined. Trade union leaders were disturbed by the export of unionized jobs overseas. They could point to many examples of production transfers throwing people out of work.

Westinghouse closed its Edison, New Jersey TV plant and moved production to Canada and Japan. Emerson Radio closed down its Jersey City plant and transferred production to Admiral's operation in Taiwan. General Instrument transferred its TV-tuner production from New England plants to Portuguese and Taiwanese factories .... (Barnet and Muller, 1974, p. 305)

The list could go on and on. The AFL–CIO argued that multinationals negatively affected the balance of trade. They exported American technology through branch planting and licensing agreements making it easier for foreign firms to compete with American-made products. Furthermore, they imported substantial amounts of products into the United States from their plants overseas.

The multinationals, themselves, and their supporters countered by arguing that the globalization of American corporations created substantial numbers of jobs in the United States and improved the balance of trade. Without the direct foreign investment, American corporations would have lost markets to foreign competitors. And American firms operating abroad purchased capital goods produced in the United States and helped to promote the sale abroad of US-made products (Block, 1977; Barnett and Muller, 1974).

Ultimately, it is extremely difficult to determine the impact of American multinationals on the US balance of trade. The conclusions reached are directly related to the assumptions made. For example, if American multinationals did not operate overseas would the markets be lost or would the markets be served from plants located in the United States? Nevertheless, it does seem plausible that the activities of American global corporations negatively affected the merchandise balance of trade. Had more attention been devoted to facilities located in the United States, there would have been more investment in new plant and equipment, further modernizing American factories. And more technologically advanced plants in the United States would likely have been able to successfully sell to many overseas markets, particularly since multilateral negotiations completed in 1967 – the Kennedy Round – resulted in tariff reductions on the order of 36–39 percent, mainly on manufactured goods, by all major industrial countries.

But the tariff reductions came too late to slow the flow of direct foreign investment from the United States. And the US trade surplus did not improve. Foreign firms seemed more able to take advantage of trade liberalization than the US-based businesses. In the United States, a backlash emerged against trade liberalization and government policy was developed to attempt to reverse the decline in the international trade position of the United States.

THE NEW ECONOMIC POLICY

During June and July 1971, the Nixon Administration was quite concerned about the stagflation afflicting the economy. The recovery from the recession was slow, unemployment remained high and inflation was persistent. Though still more than a year away, President Nixon understood that without an improving economy his chances for reelection in November 1972 were slim.

The President would have preferred not to be bothered about the balance of payments and he did not want domestic economic policy, nor foreign policy for that matter, to be constrained by balance of payments considerations. However, throughout June and July, there was substantial selling of the dollar on international financial markets. Almost daily, news stories reported purchases of dollars by foreign central banks in order to "support the dollar." Speculators running the gamut from individuals to treasurers of large multinational corporations were anticipating that the dollar would be devalued and did not want to be caught with excess dollars.

The run on the dollar continued into August. Throughout the year, foreign central banks had been accumulating dollars but generally not redeeming them for gold. No one country wanted to be the one to potentially undermine the international monetary system by demanding gold. However, demands for gold were building from some small countries. Furthermore, France made it known that it intended to convert some of its dollars to gold so as to repay a loan from the IMF. And on August 13, Great Britain requested the United States to guarantee the value of its dollar holdings of about $3 billion. The disturbed state of the financial markets and the requests for gold and guarantees set the stage for the final abandonment of gold convertibility.

On August 15, 1971, President Nixon announced an economic strategy designed to increase his chances for reelection and help to guarantee that economic and foreign policy would not be held hostage to balance of payments considerations. It was called the New Economic Policy (NEP) and was aimed at both the domestic and international economy. Domestically, the goal was to increase employment and decrease inflation. (The domestic aspects were discussed in Chapter 5.) Internationally, the NEP had several aspects.

First, the role of gold was to be reduced in the international monetary system. The President stated that he was suspending "temporarily the convertibility of the dollar into gold or other reserve assets except in amounts and conditions determined to be in the interests of monetary stability and in the best interests of the United States" (Rukstad, 1992, p. 499). For all practical purposes, the gold window was now closed and the United States would no longer have to worry about potential runs on American gold stocks.

Second, the international competitiveness of American manufacturing needed to be restored. A temporary additional tax of 10 percent was placed on goods imported into the United States. This 10 percent surcharge on dutiable imports was not the only protectionist measure in the NEP. The 10 percent Job Development Credit, a tax credit for investment in new equipment, would only apply to capital goods manufactured in the United States. The import surcharge, in particular, was to be a bargaining chip in negotiations to come with Europe and Japan over trade concessions and exchange rate revaluation.

Third, and somewhat related to the previous policy, the dollar would need to be devalued. Though President Nixon did not call for a devalued dollar in his speech, he did state that the import surcharge was "an action to make certain that American products would not be at a disadvantage because of unfair exchange rates. When the unfair treatment is ended, the import tax will end as well" (quoted in Rukstad, 1992, pp. 499–500). The term "unfair exchange rates" was a euphemism for an overvalued dollar.

The international aspects of the NEP represented a strong assertion of US nationalism. The United States had unilaterally repudiated the international monetary arrangements it had earlier created in the period of its maximum relative power. American policymakers had concluded that the Bretton Woods Agreements were no longer supporting the interests of the United States. They were aware that the Bretton Woods system had provided more flexibility to the United States than to other countries. In a 1969 report to President Nixon written by a group of policymakers headed by Paul Volcker, then Undersecretary for Monetary Affairs in the Treasury Department, they noted:

> The present system has permitted financing some 70 percent of our cumulative balance of payments deficits (on the liquidity basis) of $24 billion over the past decade with increased foreign official and private liquid dollar holdings .... The available financing for our deficits has permitted the United States to carry out heavy overseas military expenditures and to undertake other foreign commitments, and to retain substantial flexibility in domestic economic policy. (Quoted in Gowa, 1983, p. 63)

However, by August 1971, the Nixon Administration had concluded that the Bretton Woods system had outlived its usefulness for the United States. The United States did not have the option of altering the exchange rate of the dollar as did other countries regarding their currencies. The United States also needed to be concerned by the gold convertibility requirement while other countries did not. An unnamed State Department official in describing President Nixon and others involved in the creation of the NEP stated:

> They thought they were freeing America from the bondage of the dollar commitment to uphold the Bretton Woods system – a feeling that they needed more room in domestic policy to deal with recession, to deal with trade problems, military costs, a whole variety of things. (Quoted in Gowa, 1983, pp. 158–159)

President Nixon presented the closing of the gold window as a bold new initiative, a victory for the United States. But it remained to be seen whether it was truly a victory or rather, in some ways, a defeat.

PART IV: THE UNMAKING OF AN INSTITUTIONAL FRAMEWORK AND THE RECREATION OF ANOTHER, 1971–2000

9.   Stagflation, 1971–80

During the 1970s, the US economy suffered from stagflation. The simultaneous occurrence of high rates of inflation and high rates of unemployment were the outward manifestation of a more fundamental problem, the decline of the US dominance in the world economy. At the same time as the rate of economic growth was slowing, foreigners were, in effect, increasing their claims on the real output produced in the United States. Western European and Japanese firms were becoming more formidable competitors on the world scene. Oil producing countries were demanding a larger share of world output. If the increased claims of foreigners were to be satisfied, in the context of a slowly growing economy, a noninflationary situation required the claims of those living in the United States to be scaled back (Rosenberg and Weisskopf, 1981).

But business was attempting to rebuild profits after the profit squeeze of the late 1960s. And workers were not willing to voluntarily accept a decline in the rate of improvement of their real income, let alone an actual decline in their standard of living. Furthermore, beneficiaries of government programs wished to see the real value of their benefits grow as well. A political–economic stalemate emerged as each group had the necessary economic or political power to press their claims in terms of higher prices, higher negotiated wages and higher benefits. But given that the level of real output was inadequate to satisfy the claims, and monetary growth validated the claims, inflation was the result.

Income policies, both voluntary and involuntary, and more conventional monetary and fiscal policies were tried to ameliorate stagflation but to no avail. Even a strong dose of monetarism toward the end of the 1970s was not up to the task. The rate of inflation remained high throughout the decade and restrictive macroeconomic policies served to stifle economic growth.

Furthermore, the rapidly changing international economic environment worked against the government's anti-inflation efforts.

The demise of the Bretton Woods monetary agreements led to the creation of a new international monetary system minimizing the role of gold and maintaining flexible exchange rates. "What had been a gold and dollar standard evolved into a pure dollar standard" (Kunz, 1997, p. 222). With the ending of the Bretton Woods monetary system, the dollar was no longer the explicit international reserve currency. Nevertheless, the dollar continued to be, de facto, the international reserve currency. The United States was able to retain its financial hegemony. Even though countries such as Japan and West Germany were gaining in relative economic strength, the United States was still the strongest industrial and financial power in the world. In addition, the United States was the strongest military power in the alliance against the Soviet Union.

While the United States retained its financial leadership, its relative decline in international economic dominance necessitated policies to deal with the balance of trade and balance of payments deficits. These policies had inflationary implications. First, the dollar was devalued against other currencies, particularly the West German mark and the Japanese yen. The drop in the value of the dollar relative to other foreign currencies was designed to increase US exports by lowering their prices and decrease imports into the United States by raising their prices. Second, complimenting the devaluation of the dollar were explicit efforts to expand agricultural exports, an area in which the US producers were particularly strong. Poor worldwide harvests together with the explicit agricultural export policy resulted in a substantial increase in food exports. As food exports rose, so did the domestic price of food. Rapidly rising food prices were one of the important elements in the inflation of the 1970s.

Domestic oil prices rose as well. The strengthening of the bargaining power of the Oil Producing Exporting Countries (OPEC), due to the decline in US hegemony and an increased ability to manipulate competitive relations among advanced industrialized societies, led to substantially higher oil prices. The oil price increase was equivalent to placing a large tax on oil consumption and transferring large sums of purchasing power to oil producing nations. Less real resources were then available for domestic use in the United States.

By the end of the decade, economic conditions deteriorated. The rate of inflation peaked at 13.5 percent in 1980, the highest annual rate of increase in the postwar period. And in the same year, the rate of unemployment was 7.1 percent, higher than in any postwar year prior to 1975.

Which groups in society would bear the burden for the decline in the relative strength of the United States in the world economy? It was not clear. Ultimately for there to be a way out of stagflation, the economy would need to grow more rapidly and the claims being placed on economic output would need to be brought more in line with the available goods and services. This chapter focuses on the US government policymakers' attempts to "grow the economy" in a time of stagflation and changing international realities. The next chapter looks at attempts of workers (organized and unorganized), civil rights organizations and the state to cope with the potential deleterious consequences of stagflation on the living standards of Americans.

WAGE–PRICE CONTROLS

As part of the Nixon administration's New Economic Policy (NEP), all wages and prices (except those of raw agricultural products) were frozen for 90 days beginning August 15, 1971. This was Phase I in the struggle against inflation. It was designed to stop prices from rising and help break the psychology of inflation. There was a high degree of compliance with the freeze and the rate of inflation slowed significantly. A secondary goal of Phase I was to buy time for what was to follow. When the freeze was announced, government policymakers did not have a well thought out anti-inflation strategy.

Phase II began on November 15, 1971. Wages and prices were no longer frozen. However, changes in wages and prices would be regulated by the government. A Pay Board, composed of 15 members with equal representation of labor, business and the public, was created to oversee wage determination. All three parties on the board agreed that overall wage increases should be based on the economy-wide trend rate of growth in productivity and an expected increase in the cost of living. Except for the allowance for expected inflation, the logic of this wage standard was the same as the basic concepts underlying the voluntary guidelines of the early 1960s. At that time, however, the goal was price stability and there was no allowance for anticipated inflation. By 1971, government policymakers had concluded that price stability was unattainable. Now the goal was merely slowing the rate of inflation.

The standards set by the Pay Board limited annual wage increases in new contracts to 5.5 percent. This assumed an annual rate of increase in productivity of approximately 3 percent and a target rate of inflation of 2.5 percent. The logic of the Pay Board's standard pointed to unit labor costs rising by about 2.5 percent. Under regulations promulgated by the Price Commission, the annual rate of inflation was expected to approximate 2.5 percent. Firms would be permitted to pass on cost increases in their prices. However, limits would be placed on their profit margins.

There was substantial compliance with the wage and price controls. By suppressing the rate of inflation, the controls created an environment conducive for expansionary fiscal and monetary policy. Concerned that dissatisfaction over the performance of the economy would lead to Richard Nixon's defeat in the 1972 Presidential election, the administration urged heads of federal departments to increase and speed up their spending. Additional transfer payments, such as Social Security benefits and veteran's benefits, and increased grants-in-aid to states and localities were provided right before the election. The Nixon administration had been pressuring the Federal Reserve to loosen up the money supply and the Federal Reserve eventually responded. Expansionary monetary policy complemented the expansionary fiscal policy. The strategy worked. Real Gross National Product (GNP) was increasing, unemployment was declining, prices were rising quite slowly, real wages were growing as were corporate profits. President Nixon was reelected.

Phase II was still in effect as Richard Nixon prepared for his second term in office. Wage and price increases seemed to have moderated during Phase II. Even so, on January 11, 1973, Phase II was ended. The Nixon administration had a distaste for controls and feared that resource allocation decisions would be adversely affected by continuing them. Phase III, a gradual decontrol of the economy, was begun. While controls remained on food, health care and construction, outside of these three sectors, business and labor were expected to voluntarily comply with general wage and price standards. Phase III was a total failure. Rather than being the first step on the path toward a totally decontrolled economy, it was the first step on the road back toward a controlled economy. Prices began to rise rapidly. Between January and May, the Consumer Price Index (CPI) rose by 3 percent (over 7 percent at an annual rate), as food prices alone jumped by 8.7 percent (or over 22 percent on an annual basis) (Campagna, 1987, p. 375). Fuel prices were also rising rapidly. The Nixon administration was under pressure to do something about the rapidly deteriorating inflationary situation.

A price-freeze was reinstalled in June 1973. But wages were not frozen again, since the government saw wage settlements moderating. The price-freeze was a disaster. Prices of raw farm products, left uncontrolled, continued to rise but food processors and distributors were not able to pass along their increased costs in higher prices. Processors cut back on production and shortages of foodstuffs emerged. The freeze was lifted in August 1973 when it was replaced by Phase IV. New controls were placed on all sectors of the economy, strictly regulating price setting and profit margins. Once that was done a process of selective decontrol was begun on a sector by sector basis, in the hope of preventing a rapid bulge in prices. Phase IV ended on April 30, 1974 when Congressional authorization for controls expired. Prices continued to increase rapidly during Phase IV, with the CPI rising at a 12.2 percent annual rate. The rate of inflation in wholesale prices was even higher, an annual rate of 21.9 percent. The prices of oil and crude materials were rising rapidly (Campagna, 1987, p. 378). Wholesale price inflation pointed to rapid price increases at the retail level, once controls were removed.

AUSTERITY

Given the failure of wage and price controls, albeit ones implemented by policymakers who did not believe in the desirability or efficacy of controls, the Nixon administration believed only one policy option remained – austerity. Austerity causes financial and emotional pain. The administration was aware of that, but so be it. Herbert Stein, the Chairman of the Council of Economic Advisers, succinctly put it:

> Demand would have to be restrained by fiscal and monetary policy and the resulting unemployment and other pain would have to be accepted until the inflation was substantially eliminated. (Stein, 1984, p. 184)

And many would lose their jobs; the unemployment rate would eventually rise to a level not experienced (up to that time) since the Great Depression.

Reversing themselves completely from the spending policies prior to the election, the Nixon administration began utilizing restrictive macroeconomic policies in the early months of 1973. Bills passed by

Congress were vetoed by the administration on the grounds that they were too costly. Funds allocated by Congress for approved projects were impounded by President Nixon and not spent. While expenditures were being cut, taxes were going up both by action and inaction. Social Security taxes were increased. Federal income taxes were effectively raised due to inflation. The federal personal income tax structure was progressive and not indexed for inflation. Those with rising nominal incomes, though not necessarily rising real incomes, were pushed into higher tax brackets.

Restrictive monetary policies complemented restrictive fiscal policies. The rate of growth of the money supply slowed and interest rates went higher. Given that prices continued to rise, monetary policy was tightened further precipitating a credit crunch in 1974, which included the failure of Franklin National Bank. At that time it was the 20th largest bank in the United States.

Richard Nixon did not remain in office to see the full impact of his policies. Under the threat of impeachment due to the Watergate affair, he resigned on August 9, 1974. Gerald Ford became President on that same day. Fighting inflation would be his number one economic priority. Though the economy was contracting, his anti-inflation program emphasized restrictive macroeconomic policies. On October 9, 1974, President Ford asked the US Congress to place a tight limit on spending and pass a temporary 5 percent tax surcharge on upper-income families and corporations. Buttons were also part of the program. He concluded his presentation to Congress by asking the country to "whip inflation now" (WIN) and saying:

> I say to you with all sincerity, that our inflation, our public enemy number one, will, unless whipped, destroy our country, our homes, our liberties, our property, and finally our national pride, as surely as any well-armed wartime enemy. (Quoted in Campagna, 1987, p. 400)

Shortly thereafter, WIN buttons were passed out to all Americans interested in enlisting in the anti-inflation army.

But, it would take more than buttons to whip inflation. Even the sharpest recession up to that time, since the postwar demobilization, would not accomplish it. The contractionary macroeconomic policy combined with the sharp OPEC oil price increases to withdraw a substantial amount of purchasing power from the economy.

Real GNP declined in 1974 and 1975. The rate of unemployment rose from 4.9 percent in 1973 to 8.5 percent in 1975. Yet, the rate of inflation accelerated. In 1973, consumer prices rose by 6.2 percent. Double-digit inflation emerged in 1974 when the rate of inflation jumped to 11.0 percent. The following year prices were still rising rapidly at an annual rate of 9.1 percent (*Economic Report of the President*, 1990, p. 363). Now high rates of inflation were coexisting with high rates of unemployment. To use the rhetoric of President Ford, stagflation should have been considered public enemy number one.

However, it was not. The problem of unemployment was deemed to be less serious than inflation. According to Alan Greenspan, the Chairman of the Council of Economic Advisers, as long as "the response to these higher levels of unemployment was remarkably mild" (quoted in Hargrove and Morley, 1984, p. 445), the Ford administration was able to pursue restrictive macroeconomic policy. And at the same time as unemployment was rising, the administration was redefining the notion of full employment. The full employment level of unemployment was no longer 4 percent, the interim goal of the Kennedy administration. Now the full employment level of unemployment was an unemployment rate of 4.9 percent (or even 5.5 percent) (Brown, 1983, p. 180). By calling for a higher full-employment unemployment rate, the administration was, in effect, attempting to minimize the unemployment problem.

Furthermore, it tried to shift the blame for the rising unemployment away from their macroeconomic policies and toward the unemployment insurance system. The administration argued that the high rate of unemployment was partly due to the extension of unemployment insurance. Rather than enabling people to search for appropriate jobs, in their view unemployment insurance unnecessarily lengthened the duration of a spell of unemployment thus increasing the overall level of unemployment. It was the case that the maximum duration of unemployment benefits was temporarily extended to 65 weeks from the standard 26 weeks, or 39 weeks if one was receiving extended benefits. But this did not have a major impact on the extent of joblessness. The unemployment that existed was a direct result of the austerity program pursued by the government.

Though the Ford administration tried to define away the problem of stagflation, the public knew better. Gerald Ford was defeated by Jimmy Carter in the 1976 presidential election. The Democrats returned to power.

A RESPITE FROM AUSTERITY BUT ONLY TEMPORARILY

The Carter administration took office in January 1977. At that time, the rate of unemployment was 7.4 percent, a level of joblessness which it considered to be unacceptably high. Lowering unemployment became a central goal of macroeconomic policy. Inflation was less of a concern. The administration believed that as long as so many were out of work inflation would not revive.

Taxes were cut and government expenditures increased. The Tax Reduction and Simplification Act of 1977 was passed in May increasing the personal standard deduction and providing additional funds to states and localities. Later, higher spending on public works was approved. Furthermore, in contrast to the Ford administration which would have partially phased out public service employment had it been returned to office, the Carter administration made it a central component of its program to encourage economic expansion. These positions, in state and local governments and in nonprofit organizations, were funded under the Comprehensive Employment and Training Act of 1973. Funds were provided for more than doubling the number of posts to 725 000 by March 1978.

The economy grew and the number of jobless declined. Real GNP expanded at a rate of 5.5 percent in 1977 and 4.8 percent in 1978. Though still quite high, the unemployment rate fell from 7.7 percent in 1976 to 6.1 percent in 1978. But the focus on economic growth through expanding the demand for goods and services was relatively short-lived. The rate of inflation began to accelerate, rising from 5.8 percent in 1976 to 7.7 percent by 1978 (*Economic Report of the President*, 1982, pp. 235, 269 and 295). It was soon to reach double-digit levels once again. Of secondary importance was a shift in the perspective of policymakers. Economic problems came increasingly to be seen as rooted in the supply side of the economy. The assumption was that policies must be developed improving the business climate, since private enterprise was the primary engine for economic prosperity.

The 1978 Revenue Act represented a turning point in tax politics and marked the policy debut of what would come to be known, during the 1980s, as supply-side economics. In 1978, though prices were rising relatively rapidly, there still was political pressure to stimulate the economy. The tax structure was changed to foster "capital formation," a phrase which according to Charls Walker, the head of the

American Council for Capital Formation, quickly "entered the lexicon of 'good words'" (quoted in Vogel, 1989, p. 175). Personal and business taxes were reduced with a disproportionate share of the benefits aimed at the very wealthy and the corporations. Corporate income tax rates were cut. The 10 percent investment tax credit, slated to fall to 7 percent by 1981, was expanded and made permanent. The effective tax rate on capital gains was reduced by about one-third (*Economic Report of the President*, 1979, p. 130). Proponents argued that the changes in tax policy by lowering the cost of capital and raising the expected after-tax rate of return would have a positive impact on investment in new plant and equipment, or, to put it another way, on "capital formation." At this time, this was speculation, mere rationalization for a shift in the tax burden away from the wealthy.

This tax program was implemented at a time when business investment in plant and equipment was stagnating and there was a sharp slowdown in the rate of growth of productivity. Since 1973, productivity growth in the private nonfarm sector had averaged less than 1 percent per year, well below the 2.6 percent rate of growth per year between 1948 and 1965, and the 2.0 percent rate of growth between 1965 and 1973 (*Economic Report of the President*, 1979, p. 67). An increase in the rate of investment would make an important contribution to productivity growth.

By the end of 1978, reducing inflation became the top economic priority. The rapid inflation was partially the result of a sharp rise in food prices and a fall in the value of the dollar on world currency markets. A weaker dollar leads to higher import prices and higher import prices allow more rapid price increases for goods produced in the United States which compete with imports. But according to the Carter administration the inflation more fundamentally reflected a sharp rise in employee compensation at a time of stagnant productivity growth. Compensation per hour went up from a 7.6 percent annual rate of increase in 1977 to a 9.8 percent rate during 1978. As a result, the rate of increase of unit labor costs rose from 6.3 percent in 1977 to 8.9 percent in 1978 (*Economic Report of the President*, 1979, pp. 56–57).

A three-part anti-inflation program was put forward in October 1978 designed to lower the rate of increase in unit labor costs. The first component was restrictive fiscal and monetary policy. Growth in federal spending was curtailed. At the same time, the Federal Reserve was restraining the growth of the money supply and interest rates were rising. Higher interest rates were both a part of an anti-inflation strategy and a part of a policy to support the value of the dollar on overseas currency markets. However, the rate of increase of prices and wages appeared to be relatively impervious to declining demand for goods and services. Thus, unless the Carter administration was willing to create the conditions for a deep, long recession, which it was not, restrictive macroeconomic policy needed to be complemented by some additional anti-inflation measures.

The second component of the anti-inflation strategy was voluntary wage–price guidelines. The compensation standard was set at 7 percent. To induce workers to respect the pay standard, the Carter administration proposed that the US Congress pass a program of real wage insurance. Those workers who complied with the pay standard would receive a tax credit if the rate of inflation exceeded 7 percent. (Real wage insurance was never passed by the US Congress.) Firms were asked to meet either a price or a profit margin standard. The rate of price increase should not be more than 0.5 percent below a firm's average annual rate of price increase during 1976–77. Firms unable to meet this standard, due to, for example, uncontrollable increases in the cost of inputs, were asked to limit their profit margins so that their profit margin did not exceed the profit margins for two of the last three years prior to October 1978 (*Economic Report of the President*, 1979, pp. 80–84).

The third prong of the anti-inflation program was regulatory reform. It, like the 1978 Revenue Act, foreshadowed the "supply-side" economics of the 1980s. In recent years, a wide variety of laws had been passed and agencies created to regulate the activities of business, especially where businesses did not take account of the social costs of their profit-making activities. The new agencies created included the Environmental Protection Agency designed to lessen environmental pollution and the Occupational Safety and Health Administration having the goal of protecting workers' health and safety at the workplace. The business community was united in opposing the wide variety of social regulation. The Carter administration accepted their claims that these regulations were responsible for the productivity slowdown, created unnecessary paperwork, stifled innovation, delayed plant construction and expansion, and raised the cost of production of consumer goods and services, and pointed to the connection, in its view, between social regulation and inflation. By decreasing productivity, social regulations increased unit labor costs and by increasing the cost of production they led to higher prices. When the increase in the cost of living became incorporated into higher wages, costs of production were further pushed up with prices rising once again. Thus, as part of the fight against inflation, the Carter administration wished to minimize the costs of regulatory actions. Regulatory agencies were required to periodically review existing regulations to see which could be eliminated or simplified, thus reducing the costs of regulation to business.

The three-pronged anti-inflation program was a failure. The rate of inflation accelerated in 1979 and 1980. Nevertheless, this program was significant in two respects. First, it represented the last time that the federal government would attempt to utilize an incomes policy, albeit a weak, voluntary one to slow the rate of increase of prices. Rather an all-out resort to austerity would follow, inflicting much pain on many members of society. Second, the regulatory "reform" of the Carter administration laid the basis for a major assault on social regulations during the 1980s. Regulatory "reform" would be replaced by regulatory "relief."

Double-digit inflation emerged in 1979. Prices rose at an annual rate of 11.3 percent. Energy prices jumped by more than 25 percent, housing costs by 15 percent and food prices by more than 10 percent. These price increases were being incorporated into higher labor compensation while the productivity of labor fell slightly. Overall unit labor costs rose by more than 10 percent.

At the same time as prices were rising rapidly, there was turmoil in the international financial markets. The value of the dollar had been dropping sharply since the summer and fall of 1977. By the summer of 1979, dollar holders were panicking, fearing a free-fall in the value of the dollar. While the fall in the value of the dollar partially reflected conscious policy of the Carter administration to attempt to halt the decline in the international competitive position of the United States, the results were unexpected. World financial markets were in turmoil. In August 1979, Paul Volcker, a man well-known to other central bankers, was appointed chairman of the Federal Reserve. President Carter hoped that Volcker would be able to find a solution to the problem of stagflation, and restore the world's confidence in the dollar and stability in the international money markets.

Volcker's policy was advanced as monetarism, said to represent a change in the operating procedure of the Federal Reserve. But, in reality it was austerity, a program quite familiar to the Federal Reserve. The Federal Reserve would no longer attempt to target interest rates by manipulating the discount rate or engaging in open market operations. Rather, now it would set targets for the growth of the money supply and allow interest rates to be determined in the financial markets. If there were to be rapid fluctuations in interest rates, this would merely reflect the workings of the free market, a negative side-effect of monetarism, perhaps. But there would be little that could be done about it, or so it was claimed.

The proclamation of monetarism was the political cover for a program of rapidly rising interest rates. Interest rates skyrocketed, reflecting the tight monetary targets that were set. Interest rates on short-term US Treasury bills rose from 9.67 percent in the third quarter of 1979 to 14.39 percent by the fourth quarter of 1980, and on long-term US government bonds from 9.03 percent to 12.74 percent. Mortgage interest rates averaged 11.13 percent in the third quarter of 1979. By the fourth quarter of 1980, they had risen to 15.1 percent (Campagna, 1987, p. 443).

The high interest rates helped to push the economy into recession in 1980. Interest-rate dependent sectors were particularly hard hit. Real fixed investment in plant and equipment declined by 7 percent. Real inventory investment fell by close to 8 percent as businesses relying on bank credit for day-to-day financing of inventories faced burdensome credit costs. Real expenditures on new housing construction fell by 20 percent as developers faced extreme difficulty in borrowing money for new projects (Campagna, 1987, p. 444). This policy had its strongest impact in the second quarter of 1980 when the level of economic output declined by 9.9 percent. Overall, real GNP fell by 0.2 percent for the year and the rate of unemployment rose from 5.8 percent in 1979 to 7.1 percent in 1980.

The high interest rate policy did stop the fall in the value of the dollar. With interest rates higher in the United States than in the rest of the industrialized world, short-term foreign capital flowed into the United States. This increased flow of foreign capital represented an increase in the demand for dollars. The value of the dollar rose accordingly. For example, the dollar rose from a low of 177 yen and 1.7 German marks in January 1980 to over 210 yen and 2 marks by January 20, 1981, the day of Ronald Reagan's Presidential inauguration (Kuttner, 1991, p. 78).

While the policy of monetarism succeeded in restoring international confidence in the value of the dollar, it did not initially, at least, succeed in eliminating stagflation. Many lost their jobs, a predictable side-effect of a tight monetary policy, but the rate of inflation did not abate. Double-digit inflation continued with prices rising at a 13.5 percent rate in 1980. The Volcker strategy assumed that by generating unemployment the power of labor would be eroded, the rate of increase of wages would slow, the rate of growth of productivity would rise and the rise in unit labor costs would slow. However, at least in 1980, that did not occur. Output per hour continued to decline while compensation per hour rose by approximately 10 percent. Unit labor costs rose by somewhat more than 10 percent. And the prices of food and energy continued moving upward.

THE UNITED STATES AND INTERNATIONAL ECONOMIC RELATIONS

The stagflation was the outward manifestation of unresolved conflicts within the United States and throughout the world. The domestic economy, in particular, and the world economy, in general, were not growing fast enough to satisfy the claims being placed on them. The production and distribution of real income within the United States, to be discussed in the following chapter, and the share of world real income controlled by the United States, to be discussed below, were at issue.

The devaluation of the dollar

In announcing the NEP, the Nixon administration made it clear that the United States wanted to reform the international monetary system and revamp trade relations between the United States and Europe and Japan. Exchange rates would need to be realigned, particularly the dollar relative to other currencies and trade barriers reduced. Furthermore, defense burdens would need to be shared more equitably. President Nixon believed that "as we move into the post-Vietnam world military confrontation will be replaced by economic competition and we had to assure the competitive position of the United States" (quoted in Kunz, 1997, p. 218).

While the United States had these three aims, it quickly became apparent that the realignment of exchange rates would take center stage. Which countries should bear the burden of the realignment? Negotiations among the G-10 countries – the United States, Canada,

Japan and the major European economies – began in September 1971. The US opening position was that it needed a $13 billion improvement in the current account of the balance of payments. If this was to occur, the growing export of capital by American multinationals would be able to continue. It would then be financed mainly from a current account surplus rather than entail an endless piling up of dollars in foreign central banks abroad.

Such a turnaround in the current account required a sharp drop in the value of the dollar relative to foreign currencies, so as to expand US exports by lowering their prices and diminish American imports by raising their prices. The US trading partners were disturbed by the Nixon administration's import surcharge and aghast at the implications of a large decline in the value of the dollar for their own balance of trade. Furthermore, they believed the United States should also contribute to remedying the situation. They demanded that the United States be willing to devalue the dollar in terms of gold by raising the official dollar price of gold.

The ongoing negotiations were the first ever conducted to adjust exchange rates on a multilateral basis. The Smithsonian Agreement was finally reached on December 18, 1971. The exchange rates of the currencies of the G-10 countries were raised relative to the dollar though by an amount less than what the United States desired. The extent of upward revaluation varied by country ranging from 7.5 percent for the Italian lire, 13.6 percent for the German mark and 16.9 percent for the Japanese yen from the rates which prevailed on May 1, 1971. The system of fixed exchange rates was made somewhat more flexible than under the Bretton Woods Agreements. Now, the "band" for permissible currency price fluctuations was widened to plus or minus 2.25 percent from the set level. Originally, it had been plus or minus 1 percent. The dollar price of gold was increased from $35 to $38 per ounce. But the dollar was still not officially convertible to gold.

With the signing of the Smithsonian Agreement, the United States ended the 10 percent import surcharge and the requirement that the Job Development Credit only apply to domestically produced capital equipment. The United States now had minimal negotiating leverage to convince Europe and Japan to change their trading practices and bear more of the defense burden. Little was accomplished on these fronts.

The exchange rates set up by the Smithsonian Agreement did not last long. By March 1973, the major economic powers gave up trying to maintain the existing arrangements. The Paris Agreement of March 1973 established a system of floating exchange rates for the leading currencies of the world. The value of the dollar would now be set in the international financial markets. The Bretton Woods era of fixed exchange rates was over.

Dollar depreciation and macroeconomic stimulation: an unusual policy mix

With the demise of the Bretton Woods Agreements, the explicit role of the dollar as the international reserve currency ended. However, the United States was still the strongest industrial and financial power in the world and the dollar continued to be, de facto, the international reserve currency. This was apparent as the Nixon administration pursued a policy of dollar depreciation and macroeconomic stimulation. Normally, countries experiencing large balance of payments deficits are expected to combine currency devaluation with restrictive macroeconomic policy so as to diminish balance of payments deficits. A fall in the value of the currency, for example, would be anticipated to improve the trade balance. Restrictive macroeconomic policy, by slowing the growth of national income, would decrease the demand for all goods and services, including imports, thereby further helping the balance of trade and, as a result, the balance of payments.

Yet, during the period from August 15, 1971 to early 1973, the Nixon administration combined a strategy of dollar depreciation with expansionary macroeconomic policy. The trade and current account deficits grew and dollars continued to leave the United States. Foreign central banks were willing to add to their dollar holdings even though the United States was no longer even pretending that foreign holdings of dollars would eventually be convertible into gold. First, they earned interest on their dollar balances in New York banks. Second, the dollar continued to be the favored currency for international transactions. Third, had they sold substantial amounts of dollars and bought their own currencies, the value of their currencies would rise even more, thereby likely further improving the international competitiveness of the US economy. And the Japanese and Germans, in particular, preferred instead to continue reaping the benefits of large export surpluses.

At this point there were no individual currencies available to challenge the dollar as the principal reserve currency. While the Japanese and German economies were strong and growing stronger, the legacy of the Second World War was still powerful enough to negate the possibility of the yen or the mark replacing the dollar even if the Japanese or the Germans wished this to occur. In fact, they did not fearing that if their currencies began playing more central roles in international commerce the demand for their currencies would rise, and thereby their values with possible negative repercussions on their export industries. Thus, even though there was a shift to floating exchange rates, the US dollar remained the dominant currency in the world. Also, the floating of major currencies removed the original basis for attempting to restrict capital outflow from the United States. Capital controls were lifted in early 1974.

Food

Devaluing the dollar while maintaining its reserve currency status was part of the government's strategy to strengthen the US international economic standing. But the devaluation, while significant, was likely not large enough, in and of itself, to generate the $13 billion turnaround in the current account of the balance of payments pushed for by Treasury Secretary Connolly. Strengthening the trade balance in specific sectors would be needed. Agriculture was one area in which the US producers were particularly strong. The Nixon administration pursued an agricultural export policy. It was integrally related to the wage and price controls of the NEP. Agricultural output needed to expand faster than domestic consumption of agricultural goods, thus freeing up goods for export. Prices of unprocessed agricultural commodities were not regulated, while prices were controlled on inputs in the production of farm products. As a result, there was a high likelihood that profit margins would rise on raw agricultural goods, thereby serving as an incentive to increase output. At the same time, domestic food processors and retailers were not allowed to fully pass along all price increases on agricultural products used in food production to the final American consumer. However, price controls did not apply to imports or exports. Thus, domestic food processors would be strongly inclined to sell in foreign markets, given the higher profit margins able to be obtained in the uncontrolled export sector.

Furthermore, the wages of American workers were being controlled. Thus, if prices of raw agricultural products were to rise, as they did quite substantially, American workers would not be able to afford their historical share of domestic agricultural production. By December 1973, retail prices for meat, poultry and fish were 26.4 percent higher than a year earlier, cereals and bakery products were up 28.2 percent, dairy products 22.5 percent, and all food at retail 20.1 percent. (Hathaway, 1974, p. 69). Agricultural exports rose strongly partly, though not entirely, due to large wheat sales to the Soviet Union. Overall, the trade surplus on agricultural goods improved from $1.56 billion in 1972 to $10.53 billion in 1974 (Branson, 1980, p. 209). Such a dramatic improvement, while heavily dependent upon a series of crop failures around the world and rapidly rising food prices, was facilitated by the government's export promotion policy (Crotty and Rapping, 1975; Boddy and Crotty, 1975).

Oil

The agricultural export policy was necessitated by a decline in US international economic dominance. The oil price explosion was facilitated by a decline in US hegemony. During the 1950s and 1960s, the US-based oil companies were able to negotiate highly profitable arrangements with conservative Middle Eastern governments. The oil business was dominated by seven major oil companies, five of whom were American, one was British and one was Anglo-Dutch. Oil producing countries were dependent on these companies for access to technology, refining facilities and markets. Further working in the companies' favor was the fact that these governments were dependent on the United States and European political and military power for protection against external and internal threats.

By the end of the 1960s, this situation began to change. First, the dominance of the oil market by the seven major companies began to erode. Producing countries set up their own companies. Several American independent companies began playing larger roles in the world market. They were joined by European companies, some state-owned, based in countries other than Great Britain and the Netherlands. These firms were willing to cut deals providing the producing countries with a larger share of the oil profits. And European governments and Japan were interested in negotiating special arrangements with oil producing nations guaranteeing oil supplies for their domestic markets.

At the same time as there was increasing competition among buyers of oil, there was growing coordination among the producing countries. A watershed event was the Libyan coup of 1969 when Colonel Muammar Qaddafi overthrew King Idris. The new Libyan government wanted larger oil revenues from the companies working the Libyan oil fields and a more anti-Western stance taken by Arab governments. Able to play one company off against another, it succeeded in 1970 in pushing up the price of a barrel of oil. Seeing the Libyan example, the members of OPEC then demanded new price negotiations with the major oil companies. OPEC was successful and the price of oil rose in 1971.

Thus began a process which would lead to higher oil prices, a growing share of ownership of the oil companies by the host governments and a strong ability of producing countries to link the sale of oil to political demands. In October 1973, war broke out between Israel and several Arab nations. To reduce support for Israel OPEC, some but not all of whose members were Arab countries, announced a 10 percent across-the-board reduction in oil exports (later increased to 25 percent) and an oil embargo against the United States and the Netherlands, two strong supporters of Israel. The supply of oil on world markets diminished. Over a span of two months, OPEC was able to raise the price of a barrel of oil from $3.01 to $11.65. In March 1974, the embargo on the United States was lifted, though OPEC oil production was still just 85 percent of September 1973 levels. The oil price hikes and the use of oil as a political weapon represented a challenge by oil producing nations to the US dominance.

The oil price increase was equivalent to placing a large tax on oil consumption and transferring large sums of real purchasing power to oil producing nations. The quadrupling of oil prices raised oil producers' annual revenues by $64 billion, enough to buy $1\frac{1}{2}$ percent of world output (Armstrong et al., 1984, p. 310). Their revenues grew so rapidly that OPEC nations were not able to immediately spend the majority of their additional income. Instead, the current account surplus of the OPEC nations grew from $9 billion in 1973 to $62 billion in 1974 (Solomon, 1982, p. 317). This represented a decline in world demand for goods and services. Moreover, many oil importing countries pursued restrictive macroeconomic policies to combat accelerating inflation and deteriorating trade balances resulting from OPEC's price hikes. In 1974–75, the world experienced the deepest recession since the Second World War.

For each oil consuming nation, including the United States, the jump in oil prices represented a decline in terms of trade. Ultimately, this would mean that more goods would need to be exported to acquire a given quantity of imports. Less real resources would then be available for domestic use.

The consolidation of the dollar standard

Even though the United States experienced a larger trade deficit in fuels and lubricants due to the more expensive oil, the overall current account balance improved in the period 1973–75. The surplus in the current account was particularly large in 1975. While this turn-around in the current account would prove to be temporary, that was not apparent at the time. This improvement in the balance of payments together with the expectation that Europe and Japan would face enormous economic difficulties due to their dependence on imported oil set a context in which the United States wielded considerable power in international monetary deliberations.

At an International Monetary Fund (IMF) conference in Jamaica in January 1976, the existing arrangements concerning gold and exchange rates were institutionalized by amending the original IMF articles. The changes to the IMF articles strongly reflected the viewpoint of the United States. The United States wanted to eliminate any rivals to the dollar and to maintain the existing system of floating exchange rates. The dollar was strengthened as the dominant reserve currency while the role of gold was diminished. By this time the official price of gold was far below the free market price of gold. Thus, the official price of gold was abolished and gold was demonetized. All references to gold were eliminated from the IMF Charter.

The fixed, though adjustable, exchange rate mechanism of the original IMF Articles was superseded by the existing floating exchange rate system. Any return to the original arrangements would require an 85 percent vote in the IMF, effectively giving the United States veto power. The IMF would have the right to try to guarantee the orderly evolution of exchange rates by consulting with the relevant countries.

The upshot was that there was now institutionalized a de facto dollar standard and floating exchange rates. As a result, the US government would be more able to bring about the adjustments in international exchange rates it desired. Whether these adjustments would be to the disadvantage of the United States' major competitors in the international market remained to be seen.

"Benign neglect" or "malign neglect?"

From late 1973 until the spring of 1977, the United States followed a policy of "benign neglect" toward the exchange rate of the dollar. The United States did not try to influence the exchange rate set in the international currency markets. During this period, the value of the dollar rose slightly relative to the German mark and the Japanese yen and even more relative to other currencies.

But the policy approach changed by the summer of 1977. The Carter administration had concluded that the dollar was overvalued. As evidence, they could point to the US merchandise balance of trade which had weakened considerably since late 1975. In the fourth quarter of 1975, there was a balance of trade surplus of $8.9 billion. One year later, it had become a deficit of $14.4 billion. And imports continued to grow faster than the value of exports in 1977. During the fourth quarter of 1977, there was a trade deficit of $35.5 billion (Lawrence, 1978, p. 159).

The "benign neglect" approach was replaced by an "open mouth" policy. In June 1977, the US Treasury Secretary W. Michael Blumenthal stated that the dollar was overvalued, hoping to "talk down" its value so as to improve the international competitive position of the United States. The dollar began dropping sharply on the international monetary market. From summer 1977 through October 1978, the value of the dollar relative to the trade weighted average of the currencies of the 15 major US trade partners fell by more than 10 percent. The devaluation relative to the mark and yen was about 20 percent (Parboni, 1981, p. 127). The Europeans viewed this with alarm and argued that a policy of "malign neglect" had supplanted the policy of "benign neglect." Furthermore, foreign central banks felt compelled to purchase substantial amounts of dollars to keep the exchange rate of the dollar from declining even further. The Carter administration finally abandoned its policy of "talking down" the dollar on November 1, 1978 but the dollar continued to decline in value.

The weakness of the dollar annoyed oil producers since they were being paid in dollars for their oil. Furthermore, there was a strong demand for oil. At the same time, the supply of oil declined due to the Iranian cutbacks as a result of the Iranian Revolution. In 1979, OPEC raised the price of oil from $13 per barrel at the end of 1978 to $22 by October 1979.

By the end of 1979, it had become clear that the world's confidence in the dollar was shaken, thereby threatening its status as the international reserve currency. People were turning to gold as the most attractive store of value. The price of gold more than doubled from $200 per ounce at the end of 1978 to $450 per ounce in October 1979. OPEC announced that it wished to be paid with a combination of currencies rather than dollars. The movement away from the dollar represented a negative statement toward further dollar depreciation. This was the context surrounding Volcker's strategy of monetarism, having as one of its goals restoring the world's confidence in the dollar.

The merchandise balance of trade and US international competitiveness

In 1971, the United States recorded its first merchandise trade deficit, albeit small, in the twentieth century. One of the goals of the NEP was to improve the competitiveness of the US-based producers thereby returning to running surpluses on the balance of trade. However, notwithstanding conscious policies to devalue the dollar and promote exports, imports exceeded exports in all but two years – 1973 and 1975 – during the 1970s. And toward the later part of the 1970s, the size of the trade deficits grew substantially. In 1977, 1978 and 1979, trade deficits averaged approximately $30 billion annually. In magnitude this was approximately 1.3 percent of GNP. This is in contrast to the $2.2 billion trade deficit which had raised such concerns in 1971 (*Economic Report of the President*, 1990, p. 410). Central to the rising trade deficit was oil. While oil imports had exceeded exports since 1958, the deficit widened dramatically after 1973.

At the same time as the trade deficit was growing, the terms of trade were shifting against the United States. The dollar price of imports rose more rapidly than the dollar price of exports. Export prices were 151 percent higher in 1979 than in 1969, while import prices rose by 230 percent (Clarke, 1980, p. 33). The rise in import prices was directly due to the devaluation of the dollar and higher oil prices. The shift in the terms of trade implied that in price terms the US-made products had become more competitive both at home and abroad. Nevertheless, consumers and firms in the United States did not see it this way. An import revolution was in progress. Imports, though relatively more expensive, were rapidly penetrating many key markets. A few examples will suffice. The US producers' domestic market shares, defined as domestic producers percentage of total sales fell in automobiles from 82.8 percent in 1970 to 72.9 percent in 1980, in footwear from 85.4 percent to 66.6 percent, in consumer electronics from 68.4 percent to 53.1 percent, in electrical components from 94.4 percent to 78.9 percent, in industrial chemicals from 91.5 percent to 76.2 percent, and in machine tools from approximately 91 percent to approximately 77 percent (Guttmann, 1994, p. 463).

Not only did domestic producers face stiffer competition from foreign producers for the American market, they were also finding it impossible to maintain their relative standing in international markets. Their world market shares, defined as the US exports as a percentage of world exports, were dropping in many sectors. And this was occurring at the same time as the dollar was depreciating in value relative to the currencies of the major competitors of the United States. The world market shares of American producers fell in motor vehicles from 17.5 percent in 1970 to 11.4 percent in 1980, in aircraft from 66.5 percent to 52.2 percent, in organic chemicals from 25.7 percent to 15.3 percent, in nonelectrical machinery and appliances from 24.1 percent to 16.6 percent, and in agricultural machinery from 29.6 percent to 24.9 percent (Guttmann, 1994, p. 463).

It is apparent that competitiveness depends on factors other than just the exchange rate. During the 1970s, European and Japanese firms continued to strengthen relative to US-based businesses. Capital stock per worker in manufacturing continued to grow more rapidly in Europe and Japan. Capital stock per worker rose at an annual rate of approximately 6 percent for Japan, 5 percent for Europe and 4 percent for the United States (Armstrong *et al.*, 1984, p. 367). And output per person hour in manufacturing increased at a more rapid rate in Europe and Japan than in the United States.

At the same time as firms located in the United States faced growing competition from foreign companies, competition among the world's largest multinational corporations became more intense. The world economy was growing more slowly, as was world trade. Excess capacity was mounting. According to West German Chancellor Helmut Schmidt, there was an "intense struggle for the world product" (The *Business Week* Team, 1980, p. 144). As a result, American multinational corporations were just able to maintain their share of world exports of manufactured goods. This was unlike during the 1950s and 1960s when the share of world exports of manufactured goods from foreign located affiliates of US multinational corporations steadily rose (Duboff, 1989, p. 155).

Though the world economic environment was more difficult, the globalization of American economic activity continued in the 1970s, albeit at a slower real rate than during the 1960s. The US direct foreign investment increased from $78.2 billion in 1970 to $192.6 billion in 1979 (Branson, 1980, p. 237; MacEwan, 1981, p. 120). As in earlier decades, foreign investment grew more rapidly than domestic investment and profits from abroad continued to rise as a share of total after-tax corporate profits. The very largest US corporations earned a disproportionately large share of the foreign profits. Overall, the income from foreign investment as a percentage of after-tax corporate profits averaged 21.0 percent in the 1970s, as compared to 13.4 percent in the 1960s (MacEwan, 1981, p. 121).

American multinationals expanded their presence in Europe. Europe's share of direct foreign investment went from 31 percent of the total in 1970 to 42 percent of the total in 1979 (Branson, 1980, p. 243; MacEwan, 1981, p. 119). And the US corporations continued locating their foreign manufacturing plants in Europe. In 1977, 47.9 percent of total American direct investment in foreign manufacturing operations was located in Europe in contrast to 42.4 percent in 1970 (Branson, 1980, p. 240). The relocation of the US multinational activities to Europe occurred in the face of a sharp decline in the dollar relative to the major European currencies. The falling dollar pushed up the cost to the US firms of investing in Europe. Nevertheless, Europe offered political stability and the expectation of growing markets.

Corporations from countries other than the United States also participated in the globalization of economic activity. In fact, multinational corporations based in Europe and Japan had higher growth rates of foreign direct investment than did American multinational corporations. As a result, the US corporations' share of total direct foreign investment flows of the 13 countries in the Organization for Economic Cooperation and Development (OECD) which kept such records fell from an average of 61 percent during 1961–67 to 30 percent during 1974–78 (Bluestone and Harrison, 1982, p. 142).

The growth of global competition came amidst serious economic problems for the United States and many advanced industrialized societies. From some of the leading US firms came cries of "unfair competition." The domestic steel industry was a case in point.

Led by US Steel, it argued that foreign – mainly Japanese – steel companies were "dumping" excess steel output on the US market, at prices below the cost of production. The Carter administration in 1977 introduced a minimum floor price for steel. Furthermore, the US Congress did not feel that the general anti-dumping legislation that had been on the books since 1921 was being adequately enforced. The 1979 Trade Agreements Act was designed to toughen US unfair trade enforcement.

Pressure for protectionism emerged outside the United States as well. Voluntary export restraints became more common, particularly concerning trade between the EEC and Japan, though the United States also engaged in such policies. It was estimated that the proportion of manufactured trade covered by some form of control rose from about 13 percent in 1974 to approximately 30 percent in 1982 (Armstrong *et al.*, 1984, p. 374).

These more defensive strategies were complemented by more offensive strategies to gain trade advantages. They included indirect subsidies to exporters, investment incentives, government funded consortiums to develop leading industries in emerging growth industries and trading off political support, arms aid or other government help in exchange for favorable deals for national companies. Many American multinational executives believed that the US government needed to create strong, offensive policies to match those government policies supporting their competitors. And *Business Week* predicted that during the 1980s "world markets will be marked by increasingly naked use of power by national governments to secure advantages for their respective national companies" (The *Business Week* Team, 1980, p. 160).

CONCLUSION

During the 1970s, the US economy suffered from stagflation. The stagflation was the outward manifestation of unresolved conflicts over the production and distribution of goods and services within the United States and throughout the world. Economic output, both worldwide and domestically was not growing fast enough to satisfy the demands, made with political power or economic power, being placed upon it. Inflation was the result.

Internationally, the US economic dominance was being challenged. Western European and Japanese firms were becoming more formidable competitors on the world scene. Oil producing countries were demanding a larger share of world output. While the United States was losing some of its economic predominance, it still was powerful enough to retain financial hegemony. Under the new international monetary arrangements replacing the Bretton Woods Agreements, the dollar continued to serve de facto as the international reserve currency and the new monetary arrangements were quite to the liking of the United States.

The more difficult international economic environment was the backdrop for business–labor relations. A stalemate emerged between employers and workers over who would bear the brunt of the relative decline of the United State in the world economy. Furthermore, the federal government became an increasingly significant arena for conflict over the distribution of income. The income distribution became more explicitly politicized and as the negative effects of stagflation were felt throughout the society, government policies to improve equity and equality came to be seen more as zero-sum. A political and economic stalemate emerged.

10. The Economic and Political Stalemate, 1971–80

Given the decline of US dominance in the world economy, the American economy was not growing fast enough to satisfy the claims being paced on it by those living in the country. Labor and management were struggling over the production and distribution of income. American workers wanted higher living standards. Though many were jobless in the 1970s, organized labor still maintained enough bargaining power to push up nominal wages and widen the pay gap between union and nonunion workers. Nevertheless, while nominal wages rose, real wages did not. Employers were trying to improve their real return from profits. Conflicts between labor and management emerged over the work process and the rate of production. Employers were able to maintain profit rates but were not able to raise them to levels existing before the "profit squeeze" of the late 1960s.

Relations between organized labor and the business community became increasingly tense. Employers stepped up their resistance to unionization. The percentage of the labor force in unions continued to fall and with it came a decline in the political power of labor. The labor movement tried to gain an improved economic and legal environment for union organizing and collective bargaining. An unprecedentedly broad coalition of business groups came together to defeat labor's efforts.

The federal government became an increasingly significant arena for conflict over the distribution of income. The income distribution became more explicitly politicized as federal governmental transfer payments rose relative to the national income and governmental anti-discrimination efforts opened up opportunities for minorities and women. However, as the negative effects of stagflation were felt throughout the society, governmental policies to improve equity and equality came to be seen more and more as effectively zero-sum. Demands of the poor, particularly welfare recipients, were viewed as having less legitimacy and cries of "reverse discrimination" by aggrieved white men were beginning to be listened to more sympathetically.

ECONOMIC AND POLITICAL STALEMATE BETWEEN BUSINESS AND LABOR

The economic stalemate

An economic stalemate emerged between the labor movement and the business community. It was manifested by a price–wage spiral. Initially, it seemed that labor had the upper hand in the bargaining relationship. But, that situation would only last for a short period of time. Rather by the end of the decade, "concession bargaining" would begin.

During the period of controls, the price–wage spiral was muted. Nominal wage growth slowed appreciably. First year wage rate adjustments in major collective bargaining agreements averaged 7.3 percent in 1972, down from more than 11 percent in 1970 and 1971. Wage growth slowed further in 1973 when first year wage rate adjustments in major collective bargaining agreements averaged 5.8 percent (US Department of Labor, 1983, p. 305).

Overall strike activity also declined. There was an annual average of 5167 strikes in the period 1971–73, down from 5716 strikes in 1970 (US Department of Labor, 1979, p. 509). Given that improvements in wages and salaries and fringe benefits were regulated by the government, nonwage issues such as job security, work rules, work scheduling and work hours increased in importance as causes for labor disputes.

While strikes at the end of a contract diminished in number, intra-contractual strikes did not. From 1971 to 1973, they averaged nearly 2000 annually, similar to what had occurred at the end of the 1960s. Worker dissatisfaction over the conditions of work were at the heart of these disputes. Two of the most celebrated wildcats took place at General Motors (GM) factories in Lordstown, Ohio and Norwood, Ohio. The strikes were provoked by the company's attempts to spur labor productivity by increasing the speed of the assembly line. The Lordstown plant had typically produced 60 cars per hour. With the 1972 model changeover in the summer and fall of 1971, the company was now demanding that 100 cars be produced per hour.

To achieve that goal, the company tried to eliminate the shop floor agreements between line foremen and workers, providing workers with some flexibility in how work was to be performed. Rather, GM was demanding a strict interpretation of the contract clause giving it the right to direct production.

During the fall, the workers conducted an in-plant strategy against the speedup. Gary Bryner, the president of the Lordstown union local, explained the union's response to the management initiatives:

> In November and December people refused to do extra work. The more the company pressured them, the less work they turned out. Cars went down the line without repairs. The repair lot began to fill up. Soon the company began to retaliate by sending us home early. (Quoted in Aronowitz, 1973, p. 42)

The in-plant strategy did not slow the assembly line. Eventually, in March 1972, the workers went on strike for three weeks to protest the heightened intensity of work and the layoff of 350 workers. The issues were similar at Norwood. Here workers struck for 174 days to protest speedups and the layoff of approximately 400 workers. The strikes were, at best, standoffs for the union locals involved.

While relatively little public attention was given to the wildcats of the late 1960s, the labor strife at the Lordstown and Norwood plants received much play in the media. The young, white autoworkers were angry (as were their black counterparts). Their attitudes reflected the outlooks of many young workers in the society. Survey results showed that workers under age 30 were the most dissatisfied workers in the society (US Department of Health, Education and Welfare, 1973). They wanted interesting and meaningful work, jobs on which they could control the style and pace of work. However, the strikes at Lordstown and Norwood did not presage a coming revolt of young workers against all dehumanizing work. The labor revolts burned out during the recession of 1974–75.

With the ending of wage–price controls on April 30, 1974, and a rapidly rising rate of inflation, unions sought to gain major improvements in compensation. Strike activity sharply increased. In 1974, there were 6074 strikes, more than would occur in any year to follow. Wages rose rapidly, particularly in contracts negotiated after April 30. Overall, first year wage rate adjustments in major collective bargaining agreements averaged 9.8 percent. Nominal wages continued to rise rapidly in 1975, with wage gains averaging 10.2 percent in the first contract year (US Department of Labor, Bureau of Labor Statistics, 1983, p. 332). Furthermore, workers wished to improve their protection from inflation. COLA (cost-of-living allowance) coverage in labor contracts expanded with 51.5 percent of unionized workers covered by COLAs in 1975, up from 25.9 percent in 1970 (Flanagan, 1984, p. 198).

Wages were increasing rapidly in the face of growing unemployment. This was consistent with the pattern first seen prior to the imposition of wage–price controls in 1971. And it was contrary to the situation during the 1950s and 1960s, when rising unemployment seemed to dampen wage growth (Tsuru, 1991; Buchele and Christiansen, 1993). A fundamental shift in bargaining power in favor of labor seemed to be occurring.

In the second half of the decade, nominal wages continued to rise, though at a slower rate. Between 1976 and 1979, first year wage increases in major collective bargaining agreements averaged 7.8 percent. Federal governmental pressure supported employer attempts to limit wage hikes. However, COLA coverage steadily widened. By 1979, 58.9 percent of unionized workers benefited from COLAs. With the high rates of inflation, they saw their nominal wages grow more rapidly than the specified negotiated wage adjustments. But explicit COLAs are rare in nonunion compensation packages and nonunion workers did not receive as large wage boosts as did unionists. The union/nonunion wage differential grew from 19 percent in the 1965–75 time period to 30 percent during 1976–80, its highest level in the post Second World War period (Freeman and Medoff, 1984, p. 53).

There were fewer strikes. After reaching a peak of 6074 in 1974, the number of work stoppages averaged 5048 between 1975 and 1979, with strike activity declining toward the end of the decade. In addition, strikes during the term of an agreement diminished sharply. There were nearly 2000 of them in 1976. They would drop in number to approximately 800 by 1979 (Wrenn, 1985). Thus, unlike during the late 1960s when rising levels of organized militancy and shop floor confrontations, as evidenced by wildcat strikes, played a significant role in the productivity slowdown, this was not the case for the post-1973 period. While the rate of growth of productivity declined appreciably, so did intra-contractural strikes.

Nevertheless, while measures of organized resistance to conditions of work diminished, worker job satisfaction did not improve. Rather

212   AMERICAN ECONOMIC DEVELOPMENT

worker dissatisfaction increased appreciably. A large-scale study funded by the US Department of Labor revealed that between 1973 and 1977 there was a pervasive decline in job satisfaction. According to Graham Staines, a principal author of the study:

> The sky has finally fallen. Workers in virtually all occupational and demographic categories evidenced appreciable declines in job satisfaction along with other, quite unmistakable manifestations of rising discontent. (Staines, 1979, p. 39)

A portion of the decline in productivity growth was likely due to increased worker dissatisfaction. Bowles *et al.* (1983) found that declining work intensity explained approximately 20 percent of the productivity slowdown from 1973 to 1979, a not inconsequential amount.

The productivity slowdown worsened the distributional conflict between workers and owners. Nominal wages rose rapidly as did prices. However, real average hourly wages in private nonagricultural industries declined by 9 percent from 1973 to 1980, from $8.55 to $7.78 (1982 dollars). But employer contributions for social security, health and disability, pension and other fringe benefits rose much faster than the rate of inflation. Thus, there was a real increase in total hourly compensation of 1.4 percent from 1973 to 1980 (*Economic Report of the President*, 1994, pp. 320, 322). Firms could not reduce real hourly wages fast enough to compensate for the growth in their real cost of benefits. At the same time, the increased employer cost for fringe benefits did not translate dollar for dollar into an improved benefits package for workers.

Furthermore, energy costs were escalating as were the costs of all products utilizing petroleum, international competition was becoming more severe and imports were sharply rising. With the slack in the economy, firms were unable to fully pass along the increased costs of production into higher prices for goods and services. Profit rates were under pressure. While the Carter administration did provide tax breaks to businesses and did try to restrain wage growth, the economy-wide after-tax rate of profit remained relatively low. The average net after-tax rate of profit during the business cycle from 1974 to 1979 was 5.7 percent. By contrast, the average net after-tax rate of profit in the 1959–66 cycle was 8.2 percent (Bowles *et al.*, 1986, p. 155).

In the decade to follow, both government policy and corporate strategy would be aimed at raising the average rate of profit.

In retrospect, the concessions made by the United Auto Workers (UAW) to Chrysler Corporation in November 1979, January 1980 and January 1981 foreshadowed the "concession bargaining" of the 1980s. Chrysler was on the verge of bankruptcy and the federal government was providing loan guarantees to save the company. The union agreed to reopen the contract in November 1979. Wages were frozen with the parties deciding to defer payment of the annual improvement factor and the scheduled COLA. Further pressure from the federal government led the union to agree in January 1980 to extend the deferrals through 1980 and to reduce the number of paid personal holidays. The company's financial difficulties continued and in January 1981 the UAW agreed to cancel the remaining annual improvement factor and cost-of-living increases. As a result, the hourly pay of Chrysler workers was $2.50 below the pay received by workers at Ford and GM (Katz, 1987). In return for these concessions, UAW President Douglas Fraser was given a seat on Chrysler's Board of Directors.

The UAW initially said that the concessions at Chrysler were unique, required by the weak financial condition of the company. But automobile industry executives were less certain. A Ford spokesman said:

You can bet we're watching Chrysler's efforts with a good deal of interest. We haven't done it [asked for concessions] yet, but we'll see what happens on this go-round with Chrysler. (Quoted in Slaughter, 1983, p. 11)

The continuing trade union decline

As in the 1960s and early 1970s, during the stagflation period of the 1970s there was evidence of a strong labor movement. The union–nonunion wage differential was rising and the Carter administration felt compelled to take steps, albeit "voluntary" ones, to restrain wage growth. The concessions granted to Chrysler by the UAW appeared, at the time at least, to be an isolated incident determined more by the economic problems of a particular company rather than a harbinger of the "concession bargaining" of the 1980s.

However, just as in the previous decade, while there was an outward semblance of a strong labor movement, the overall economic and political power of labor was slowly being undermined. The share of the workforce unionized continued to fall during the 1970s, just as it had since 1954. Union membership as a percentage of employees in nonagricultural establishments dropped from 27.0 percent in 1970 to 23.2 percent in 1980

Employers continued by legal and illegal means to counter union organizing drives. Legally, to a greater degree than during the 1960s, employers delayed the holding of representation elections. The relative share of representation elections that were consent elections continued declining while the relative share of stipulated elections continued growing. While consent elections constituted 15.9 percent of all elections in 1972, they were only 4.5 percent of all elections in 1980. The share of stipulated elections jumped from 63.4 percent in 1972 to 76.6 percent in 1980. While unions were likely to win somewhat more than 60 percent of all consent elections, they were victorious in somewhat less than 50 percent of all stipulated elections (Goldfield, 1987, pp. 203–204).

Even though employers had legal means for avoiding unions, many turned to potentially illegal strategies. From 1970 to 1980, the number of cases brought to the National Labor Relations Board (NLRB) alleging illegal discharges for union activity doubled from 9290 in 1970 to 18 317 in 1980. Furthermore, there was a more than doubling in the number of workers – from 3779 to 10 003 – deemed to have been fired illegally for union activities and ordered reinstated by the NLRB. And backpay awards rose even more sharply during the 1970s, indicating that employers were keeping illegally fired union supporters off the job for longer periods of time (Goldfield, 1986, p. 10).

While management was devoting increasing resources to stifling union organizing, the American Federation of Labor (AFL)–Congress of the Industrial Organizations (CIO) was not responding accordingly. Rather the labor leadership was fairly complacent in the face of this management strategy. In general, unions continued to devote inadequate resources to gaining new members. Real expenditures on organizing per nonunion employee, a measure of organizing effort, steadily declined from the 1950s through the 1970s (Freeman, 1985).

Unions continued to fare poorly at winning new members. Workers won by unions in organizing drives as a percentage of workers eligible to vote in representation elections fell from 52 percent in 1970 to 37 percent in 1980. This, combined with the fact that the number of representation elections did not keep pace with the growing work force and the average number of workers eligible per representation election steadily declined, had grave implications for unions. New workers won to unionism as a result of NLRB elections as a share of the private wage and salary work force fell from 0.6 percent in 1970 to 0.2 percent in 1980. The rate of decline quickened in the 1970s relative to the slow decline experienced during the 1960s (Freeman, 1985, p. 46).

The increased employer opposition to unionism, as manifested in managerial behavior around representation elections, was a major factor behind the diminished success of unions in organizing drives in the 1970s (Goldfield, 1987; Freeman and Medoff, 1984; Freeman, 1985). The relative failure of labor in representation elections was an important factor in the shrinking realm of unionization during the 1970s. In addition, employment was growing more slowly in union than in nonunion plants. Management was increasingly disinvesting from unionized factories in Northern urban areas and relocating operations to the South or rural areas in the hope of avoiding unions and lowering labor costs. According to Kochan *et al.* (1986, p. 71), companies such as General Mills, Pepsi-Cola, Mead Paper, International Paper, Weyerhauser, Mobil Oil, Goodyear, Firestone, General Tire, Uniroyal, Corning Glass, Cummins Engine, Pratt and Whitney and Piper Aircraft opened nonunion facilities rather than expand their existing union facilities during the 1970s.

The relocation of economic activity did not guarantee that workers would remain unorganized. GM is a case in point. In the mid-1970s, it opened several nonunion plants in the South. The UAW was not able to organize most of the plants. As a result of union pressure, in 1976 GM agreed to remain neutral in organizing campaigns occurring in the new southern plants. However, the union still lost many of the representation elections and was convinced that GM had, in fact, not acted in a neutral manner. In 1979, the company agreed that the UAW would automatically be recognized as the bargaining agent in any of the new facilities whose output was similar to that in existing unionized plants. Finally, in 1982, GM agreed to automatically recognize the UAW where it could show that a majority of the workers favored unionization. A representation election would not be required to be held. By the end of the year, all of GM's nonunion facilities were organized (Katz, 1987, pp. 21–22).

But the GM case was more the exception than the rule. It was more common that the nonunion plants remained nonunion. The rubber industry is a particularly stark example. The UAW was able to organize all of the 21 new plants opened during the 1960s. But of the 19 plants constructed between 1970 and 1985, only one operated as a union plant. At the same time all of the 22 plants shut down during the 1970s were organized. Furthermore, the more obsolete bias ply tire production was concentrated in the older, unionized plants while the new radial tire production took place in the new, nonunion southern plants (Jeszeck, 1986).

The political stalemate

Neither the labor movement nor the business community had the political power to initiate major changes in the country's labor laws or overall approach to employment policy. Thus, a political stalemate emerged. But, it was less a stalemate between two equally powerful forces, likely to remain in balance in the near term. Rather, it was a reflection of a more cohesive business community with growing political clout and a weakening labor movement with less influence within the Democratic Party, its traditional political ally. The labor movement pushed on two fronts: labor law reform and job creation. It was completely defeated on labor law reform. While legislation purporting to address the question of full employment was signed into law by President Carter, it was quite different from the proposals initially advanced by the labor movement and its allies.

Labor law reform was viewed as crucial by organized labor. Legislation was needed to counter employer strategies, both legal and illegal, which were subverting the underlying premise of the National Labor Relations Act, that being workers have the right to organize unions of their own choosing and to engage in an ongoing collective bargaining relationship with their employers. The Labor Law Reform Bill of 1978 was designed to rectify the situation. The procedures of the NLRB would be streamlined, thereby shortening the time delay in holding a representation election or in adjudicating an unfair labor practice complaint relating to dismissal for union organizing activities. The compensation to be paid to illegally fired workers would be increased. Furthermore, those employers found to have refused to bargain in good faith for an initial contract would face increased penalties. Their workers would be "made-whole" (or compensated) by receiving an amount based on the average wage settlements negotiated by workers at similar plants where collective bargaining had proceeded lawfully. This would reverse the Ex-Cell-O decision (Gould, 1986, pp. 122–131).

From labor's perspective, the labor law reform was a modest proposal aimed at allowing the NLRB to administer labor law more properly and stifling the activities of those companies which flagrantly violated labor law. Thus, they were shocked by the extent of the business opposition to this legislation. Not surprisingly, the owners of small nonunion businesses mobilized in opposition. They were joined, however, by the Business Roundtable, many of whose members were large corporations with longstanding relations with unionized workforces. The legislation was defeated by this unprecedentedly broad coalition of business groups.

While reforming the rules explicitly regulating labor–management relations was one political priority of labor's, job creation was another. The Equal Opportunity and Full Employment Act was introduced into the US Congress in 1974 and 1975 during the height of the recession. It was to amend the Whittington–Taft Employment Act of 1946 by putting some "teeth" into it. It called for the guarantee of useful paid employment at fair rates of pay to everyone able and willing to work. Those not able to find private sector employment would be guaranteed public sector jobs. This was to be achieved by governmental planning of production and investment to meet social needs and guarantee employment. Wages in these public sector jobs would be equal to prevailing regional pay levels for similar work, the minimum wage or existing collective bargaining agreements, whichever was highest. Those unable to find work would have the right to sue the government in federal court for a job. Goals other than full employment, such as price stability, were of distinctly secondary importance. Rather than the traditional obligatory words of support for private enterprise, this bill accepted the notion that the private sector did not meet social needs nor provide adequate employment opportunities (Currie, 1977).

This piece of legislation was not enacted into law. The negative reaction to it was quite strong. The objections were numerous but they could be boiled down to one essential notion. It was not the role of the federal government to guarantee full employment at fair wages. The bill began to be watered down to increase its probability of passage. The process by which the proposed piece of legislation guaranteeing employment was transformed into a law guaranteeing some level of unemployment was eerily similar to what occurred 30 years before when the Murray–Wagner Full Employment bill eventually became the Whittington–Taft Employment Act of 1946.

In 1978, the Full Employment and Balanced Growth Act, more commonly known as the Humphrey–Hawkins Act, was passed by the US Congress and signed into law by President Carter. It bore little resemblance to the Equal Opportunity and Full Employment Act. Its name was changed as was its contents. The goal of full employment, of everyone wanting a job being able to find one, was dropped. The new goal was an overall rate of unemployment of 4 percent by 1983. Gone as well from the legislation was any notion of government planning to meet social needs and guarantee employment, nor any governmental requirement to create public service jobs. The President would be able to modify the timetable for reaching an unemployment rate of 4 percent if the President believed it impossible to achieve without jeopardizing reasonable price stability. Reasonable price stability was defined as a rate of inflation of 3 percent, also to be achieved by 1983. And this timetable as well could be modified with proper justification. Thus, the goal of a low rate of inflation could infringe upon the goal of job creation (Campagna, 1987, pp. 434–435).

In short, however, the Full Employment and Balanced Growth Act provided little solace for those out of work or soon to be unemployed. No new jobs need be created. And it provided little hope for those employed in low-wage positions. Public sector jobs at fair rates of pay were not part of this legislation. That the Humphrey–Hawkins Act was passed at all might be viewed as a victory for organized labor, since the labor movement had devoted much energy into the struggle for an increased government commitment to job creation. But the content of the law was quite in line with a corporate vision of the economy, a vision which did little more than admit that unemployment would continue to be a problem for many years to come.

THE GOVERNMENT, INCOME CLAIMS AND THE LABOR MARKET

The growing politicization of the income distribution

During the 1960s, various groups increasingly turned to, or strongly pressured, the federal government to intervene in the economy on their behalf. The political upheavals of the 1960s led to a whole host of federal anti-poverty strategies. Demands for political and economic equality led to Civil Rights legislation and anti-discrimination programs. Struggles over the quality of life both inside and outside the workplace led to the creation of the Environmental Protection Agency and the Occupational Safety and Health Administration in the early 1970s.

The push for social, economic and political equality continued into the 1970s. Increasing claims on economic resources were being placed through the government. The federal government became more heavily involved in determining the ultimate distribution of income. Therefore, the income distribution became more explicitly politicized. Transfer payments are, perhaps, the clearest indicator of this process. Comparing federal transfer payments to national income provides a measure of the extent to which income generated through the market process is reallocated by the transfer payment policies of the federal government. During the 1960s, federal transfer payments averaged 5.7 percent of the national income. This is in contrast to 9.8 percent of the national income in the 1970s. During the first half of the 1960s, transfer payments grew at approximately the same rate as the national income. Beginning in 1966, transfer payments outpaced national income, peaking in 1975 at 11.8 percent of national income. In the second half of the decade, the rate of growth of transfer payments was less than that of national income. At the end of the decade, federal spending on transfer payments equalled 10.4 percent of national income (*Economic Report of the President*, 1985, pp. 255, 322).

Transfer payments are visible and often controversial, particularly those provided to the poor. However, the federal government directly affects the income distribution in another manner, less well understood, less visible and thereby less controversial, though by no means less important. This is through the use of "tax expenditures", also known as tax incentives, tax subsidies or, somewhat pejoratively, tax loopholes. Tax expenditures refer to losses in tax revenues due to special or selective tax relief for individuals or businesses. They are similar to transfer payments in that they increase the after-tax incomes of recipients. Officially defined in the 1974 Congressional Budget Act, by 1978 they were an amount equal to 7.2 percent of national income (Peterson, 1982, p. 147). In 1978, federal expenditures on transfer payments combined with federal tax expenditures were a sum equal to 17.5 percent of national income. In effect, the federal government was explicitly reallocating $0.17 out of every $1.00 generated by the economy.

The data on transfer payments clearly demonstrate a growing federal presence in the income distribution process. During the first half of the 1970s, there were several policy changes which improved federal assistance for the poor and nonpoor. In 1971, food stamp benefits were increased and indexed for food price inflation. From 1971 to 1976, monthly food stamp benefits increased by 54 percent due to the rapid rise in food prices (Browning, 1986, p. 147). In 1973, the federal government required all areas of the country to participate in the food stamp program. Prior to that time, counties were able to distribute food rather than food stamps.

On January 1, 1974, the Supplemental Security Income (SSI) program was created. It federalized three federal-state grant-in-aid programs for the blind, the aged, and the disabled. Previously, each state had its own program and there were widely differing benefit levels across states. With the federalization of the program, benefit levels were improved. This represented the first federal cash income floor for a broad group of adults, dependent only upon need. The Earned Income Tax Credit (EITC) was created in 1975. It was designed to encourage poor people with children to seek employment. Those without earnings would not benefit from the EITC. But parents with low earnings would be eligible for a tax credit. The tax credit would be gradually phased out as earnings grew.

Food stamps, SSI and the EITC are means-tested programs. Improvements also occurred in programs which were not income-conditioned but rather social insurance transfers. Social Security benefits were increased by 15 percent in 1969, 10 percent in 1971, and 20 percent in 1972. In 1972, legislation was passed linking Social Security benefits to the Consumer Price Index (CPI).

In addition, transfer payments were expanded for those who lost their jobs during the 1973–75 recession. The maximum duration of unemployment benefits was temporarily lengthened. Furthermore, in 1974, the US Congress, overriding objections from the Ford administration, included provisions in the Trade Act of 1974 making it easier for workers who lost their jobs due to imports to qualify for Trade Adjustment Assistance.

The growth in federal transfer payments in the first half of the 1970s was partly due to explicit policy changes creating new programs and improving benefits provided under existing programs. They also were an automatic response to the serious recession of 1973–75. During recessions overall expenditures on income conditioned transfer payments rise as more people, given the economic difficulties they face, become eligible. Also social insurance expenditures related to job loss rise as more people become unemployed.

But the second half of the decade represented a change in policy. While the benefits received by the elderly did not decline in real terms, the benefits received by the poor did. The political power of the poor diminished. There were cutbacks in selected means-tested programs, particularly Aid to Families with Dependent Children (AFDC). Real wages were stagnating and families were sending more workers into the labor market. Many Americans came to believe that AFDC recipients were choosing not to work. That was particularly galling to them as many were having difficulty making ends meet while working. There was strong support for reducing government outlays on AFDC. Many states tightened up eligibility standards and caseloads did not grow. Nominal benefits did not keep pace with inflation. Therefore, the real value of assistance declined sharply. In 1976, a "typical" single-parent family of four with no income could get the equivalent of approximately $8800 (in 1984 dollars) in combined annual AFDC and food stamp benefits. This was slightly less than the real value of benefits in 1972. By 1980, a single-parent family of four with no income could get the equivalent of approximately $7300 (in 1984 dollars) in combined annual AFDC and food stamp benefits, a decrease of 17 percent, adjusting for inflation (Ellwood, 1988, p. 58).

The 1960s were a period of steadily declining poverty rates. But the stagflation of the 1970s, along with the cutbacks in means-tested benefits for the poor, stopped the progress against poverty in its tracks. The official poverty rate was 13.0 percent in 1980, above the 12.6 percent level of 1970 (*Economic Report of the President*, 1993, p. 380).

The welfare reform stalemate

The urban unrest and the growing numbers receiving AFDC convinced President Nixon that welfare reform was necessary. Not wishing to repudiate the government's role in the amelioration of poverty, he proposed a guaranteed minimum income for all families with dependent children. This represented the first attempt to significantly change the social welfare system, initially developed during the Great Depression. On August 8, 1969, President Nixon introduced the Family Assistance Plan (FAP). All low-income families with dependent children would be eligible for cash payments from the federal government. The amount of the payment would depend on family size. The first two family members would receive $500 per person per year and each family member thereafter would receive $300 per year.

The basic family benefit for a family of four, with no earnings, would be $1600.

Individuals would be encouraged to find work. All families would be allowed to earn $720 annually and still receive full benefits. The effective tax rate on any additional earnings would be 50 percent. For every dollar earned, the family would lose 50 cents in benefits. With high enough earnings, the benefit would fall to zero. The FAP was structured so as to guarantee that any family with an employed member would be economically better off than one just receiving the basic federal benefit.

However, these monetary incentives might not be strong enough to induce low-income individuals to seek and find work. Thus, they were supplemented by a work requirement. All employable benefit recipients would be required to register with the Employment Service and accept training or employment or lose their portion of the family benefit. Exempt from this work registration requirement would be any woman who had a pre-school child, any woman who had an unemployed husband since the husband would be expected to satisfy the work requirement, or any woman who was over the age of 65. As part of the FAP, additional funds were to be allocated to increase training opportunities and child care services for benefit recipients.

Under the existing AFDC system, welfare payments varied widely by state. The FAP would place a floor under welfare benefits throughout the country. It would effectively replace the AFDC system in states where benefit levels were below those to be provided under the FAP. These 16–18 states were mainly located in the South. Where the FAP benefits were below the existing AFDC benefits, the states would be required to supplement the FAP benefit so that no one would receive less under FAP than they were currently receiving under AFDC.

The FAP was passed by the US House of Representatives but was was defeated in the US Senate. There was opposition from both liberal and conservative legislators. Liberals, supported by the National Welfare Rights Organization and welfare mothers, argued that the work incentive was too punitive and the benefit levels too low. Conservatives felt that the work requirements were too weak. Opposition from Southern Senators was particularly intense. They feared what the FAP would do to the Southern way of life in general and the Southern labor market in particular.

Wages in the South were below those in the rest of the country. Wages in the urban South were kept low by the large numbers of people leaving the farms and seeking work in the cities. The FAP was expected to expand welfare rolls substantially, particularly in the South. And Southerners would receive higher benefits under the FAP than they were getting from AFDC. Given the weak work requirements and the large number of people exempted from them, many Southerners, it was claimed, would prefer to remain in rural areas and live off the FAP benefit rather than seek work in the cities. The labor supply to urban areas would diminish thereby driving up wages particularly in low-wage jobs (Quadagno, 1994, p. 130). Lester Maddox, the Governor of Georgia, put it quite succinctly:

> You're not going to be able to find anyone willing to work as maids or janitors or housekeepers if this bill goes through. That I promise you. (Quoted in Moynihan, 1973, pp. 378–379)

While the business community was divided on the FAP, the strong opposition provided by the US Chamber of Commerce complemented that of the Southern Senators. The US Chamber of Commerce was critical of the notion of a guaranteed income provided by the government, the lack of strong work requirements and the likely growth of the welfare rolls.

The FAP unambiguously represented an improvement in public assistance for the poor. But whether it would lead to better job prospects for the poor remained an open question. If the Southern conservatives were correct, then the FAP would indirectly cause wages to rise in the low-wage sector of the labor market. If they were wrong and the work requirements were to prove effective, then the supply of labor would increase to low-wage jobs, thereby serving to hold down wages. Overall, however, by emphasizing work requirements and lacking a jobs component, the Nixon administration made it easy to construe the problems of poverty in terms of deficient individual characteristics of the poor and not as a consequence of inadequate job opportunities for the poor.

The work issue was crucial in the welfare reform proposals of the Carter administration. Unlike the FAP, the Program for Better Jobs and Income (PBJI), proposed in 1977, did contain a jobs component. Like the FAP, the PBJI would have entailed broadening access to welfare benefits and spending more on the poor. However, the PBJI met the same fate as the FAP. It did not gain Congressional approval.

The PBJI would have replaced AFDC with a system of nationally uniform cash payments to low-income people including the working poor. The size of the basic benefit was dependent on family size and employability. In order to maintain incentives to work, those considered "unemployable" – the aged, disabled or single parents with children under six years of age – were to receive substantially larger basic grants than those considered "employable" – all families with children with two able-bodied adults and single-parent families with no children under six years of age. The income grants for the "unemployables" were substantially larger, in real terms, than the benefits proposed under the FAP. For example, a family of four headed by an "unemployable" would receive a benefit of $4200 per year. The equivalent family headed by an "employable" would only receive an annual benefit of $2300.

Earnings of the "employables" below a base level would not be taxed and above that would be taxed at 50 percent. For those expected to work, job search assistance would be provided to help in finding an unsubsidized private or public sector job. Those unable to find such positions would be given federally subsidized training or a public service job paying slightly above the minimum wage. Financial incentives were to be provided to people to find unsubsidized jobs in the private or public sectors.

The Carter administration insisted that the PBJI emphasized work and incentives to work. However, recipients were not to be forced to work and the government had a responsibility to guarantee that jobs would be available for welfare recipients expected to work. It represented the last major federal attempt to expand welfare. After failing to have the PBJI passed into law, the Carter administration continued to propose, albeit unsuccessfully, limited welfare reform. Perhaps, most importantly, toward the end of its term in office, the Carter administration began calling for cuts in AFDC outlays. This about face foreshadowed the approach to be taken by the Reagan administration in the 1980s.

Equal employment opportunity and affirmative action:
seeming more like a zero sum game

Racial tensions were one element behind the strong push to limit eligibility for and reduce the real value of AFDC payments. Disproportionately African–American and single mothers, AFDC recipients were viewed by many as undeserving of society's largesse. Racial tensions also colored conflicts over equal employment opportunity and affirmative action policies. But the situation was even more complex. Questions of gender discrimination were also at issue. Both white women and members of minority groups would challenge employment discrimination and press the government (and employers and unions) to take action.

From 1972 to 1975, the federal government pressured many major corporations to face up to their past and present discriminatory personnel policies and take steps to rectify the situation. American Telephone and Telegraph (AT&T) was one of them. At the time, it was the largest private employer in the United States. Though the biggest, its employees did not consider AT&T to be the best employer. In fact, many of them sought the aid of the Equal Employment Opportunity Commission (EEOC) in their struggle against institutionalized discrimination at the company. At one point, 7 percent of the cases at the EEOC came from complaints brought by AT&T employees. Rather than settle them on a case by case basis, the EEOC decided to confront the company directly. Facing the threat of legal action, in 1973 AT&T signed a consent decree with the federal government. It agreed to provide $38 million in backpay and wage adjustments to several groups of female employees and to implement a broad affirmative action plan.

Though the lawsuit filed by the EEOC was on behalf of women workers, the affirmative action plan concerned the transfer and promotion rights of all employees. The goal was to improve the representation of women, members of racial minority groups and even white men in jobs where these groups had been underrepresented. More men were to become telephone operators and clerical workers. More women were to be seen working on telephone poles and repairing telephones. And managerial ranks were to become more open to women. The consent decree represented an attack on racial and gender stereotyping throughout the company.

AT&T was the first major corporation to sign a wide-ranging consent decree with the EEOC. It would not be the last. After successfully suing Bethlehem Steel and United States Steel individually, the federal government gained a consent decree from the entire steel industry in 1974. Successful suits against several trucking companies led to a consent decree with 250 trucking companies in 1974. Consent decrees were also reached with large companies such as Uniroyal, Bank of America, United Airlines, El Paso Natural Gas and Pacific Gas and Electric. These highly publicized actions sent a message to the entire business community. Voluntarily deal with race and gender discrimination or else face the risk of major litigation and costly back pay settlements.

Many consent decrees were entered into at the same time as the economy went into recession. As unemployment rose and remained high, many white men became particularly angered by what they perceived to be "reverse discrimination." For them, racial and gender progress had become a zero sum game. The recession made more apparent the potential contradiction between affirmative action policies and long-standing personnel practices involving seniority. Where there was a collective bargaining agreement, worker seniority, be it plant-wide, departmental or occupational, often was a major criterion in determining eligibility for upgrading, promotion and transfer, and the likelihood of layoff. Yet, the consent decrees called for changes in company personnel policies. At times this required the overriding of existing seniority arrangements to remedy the underrepresentation of women and racial minorities throughout the company or within the more desirable occupations. If there was a clash between affirmative action policies and existing seniority practices, which should prevail?

For the union movement, the answer was clear. It should be seniority unless through voluntary collective bargaining management and labor agree otherwise. Seniority arrangements are not inherently discriminatory. Rather, they limit the possibility of management using favoritism in work allocation and layoffs.

Employers also benefited from seniority arrangements. A seniority system generally results in smoother labor relations, as the rules and regulations are clearly stipulated in the contract. Seniority leads to less worker turnover and lower hiring and training costs. Employers tried to defend existing seniority procedures when brought before the EEOC or faced with legal action.

However, the EEOC was generally more critical of existing seniority provisions. The conflict between seniority and affirmative action often ended up in the courts. The legal system vacillated on this question, in some cases giving primacy to seniority considerations and in other cases favoring affirmative action. The earliest court rulings in the late 1960s and early 1970s repeatedly found a variety of discriminatory seniority systems codified in union contracts and demanded they be changed. Often these cases dealt with questions of job assignment and job promotion with African–Americans being trapped in the least desirable, lowest paying positions.

Attacks on seniority systems increased during the recession of 1973–75. With employment being reduced, layoffs under the last-hired first-fired principle, a principle common to virtually all seniority systems, resulted in the loss of newly won jobs by minorities and women. Assuming there was past racial or gender discrimination in hiring, laying off on the basis of least seniority was perpetuating the effects of such discrimination.

The Jersey Central Power and Light Company needed to reduce its employment levels by 10 percent. An earlier consent decree with the EEOC required the company to hire more women and minorities. Furthermore, it stipulated that in the event of a layoff, the newly hired women and minorities should not bear a disproportionate share of the job loss. But this aspect of the consent decree violated the union seniority system. In 1975, a federal court of appeals found in favor of the seniority system even though it may operate to the disadvantage of women and minority groups as a result of past employment practices.

Subsequent court decisions affirmed and extended this view. In 1977, the US Supreme Court found that TIME–DC, a large trucking firm, had discriminated against minority drivers by assigning them to lower paying, short-distance city jobs instead of higher paying, long-haul routes. Furthermore, there were separate seniority lines for the two types of work. Thus, any employee, quite likely a minority, who shifted from the short-haul to the long-haul jobs would lose any accumulated seniority with the firm. Nevertheless, the US Supreme Court ruled that "an otherwise neutral legitimate seniority system does not become unlawful simply because it may perpetuate" discrimination that occurred prior to the 1964 Civil Rights Act (*Wall Street Journal*, June 1, 1977).

However, explicit discrimination occurring after the 1964 Civil Rights Act went into effect was handled somewhat differently. The seniority system could be overridden for any individuals who could prove they were not hired due to discrimination. In 1976, in Franks v. Bowman, the US Supreme Court ruled that any African–Americans who could demonstrate they were denied jobs on the basis of race must be awarded retroactive seniority once they are able to be hired. Thus, assuming such an individual is hired, any white who was hired after the African–American's initial job application but before the African–American was given a job, would now have less seniority and job protection than previously.

This decision raised the specter of "reverse discrimination" in some quarters. Some white men felt they were being forced to give up rights in favor of minorities or women when they themselves did not actively discriminate against minorities or women nor benefit from any discrimination which may have occurred. They would go to court to protect their rights. Brian Weber, a white male, worked at the Gramercy, Louisiana plant of the Kaiser Aluminum Company. In the early 1970s, the company faced numerous Title VII suits alleging discrimination against African–Americans. In response, in 1974 Kaiser and the United Steelworkers of America, through voluntary collective bargaining, created a craft training program for plants throughout the country. It was designed to increase the representation of minorities in better paying craft positions. Half of the slots would be reserved for minorities. Trainees would be chosen based on their relative seniority within their racial group. Brian Weber had relatively little seniority for a white worker but more seniority than several African–Americans chosen for the program. He was not allowed to enter the program. He sued both the company and the union alleging "reverse discrimination" against all white workers. Even though Kaiser Aluminum had never admitted to practicing discrimination in the past, the US Supreme Court held in 1979 that employers and unions were free to take race-conscious steps to remedy "manifest racial imbalance." And by implication, the seniority system can be overridden in such instances.

Thus, at the end of the decade, there was still controversy over the proper relationship between seniority systems and affirmative action. However, the potential conflicts between affirmative action and collective bargaining should not be overemphasized, particularly when thinking about racial and gender discrimination in the society as a whole. Relatively few workers were covered by collective bargaining agreements. And the underrepresentation of women and minorities was often the greatest in upper level professional and managerial positions. Employers, for the most part, select workers for those jobs. Nevertheless, the conflict between seniority and affirmative action was important because it signified the fraying of relations between organized labor and the civil rights movement. Though they were allies on a wide variety of economic issues and worked together for the passage of the Civil Rights Act, they often ended up on different sides of the seniority dispute. The Weber case was significant since in this instance the labor movement took an unequivocal position against Weber's opposition to affirmative action. Rather, it supported the use of voluntary collective bargaining to remedy racial injustice. But this case was more the exception than the rule.

For some white men the push for equality had gone too far. If the economy did not improve in the 1980s, many predicted that there would be a rash of "reverse discrimination" lawsuits filed by aggrieved white males. But minorities and women still had a long way to go to reach equality with white men.

Race, gender and the labor market

The federal government more effectively enforced affirmative action after 1973. Still, the likelihood of a firm being reviewed by a government compliance officer was low. And if judged in violation of the law, the penalties imposed were often minimal. Nevertheless, between 1974 and 1980 the employment of women and African–American men increased faster in firms which were federal contractors than in those without federal contracts (Leonard, 1984).

In addition to improving access to jobs, affirmative action is designed to open up promotion possibilities for minorities and women. Affirmative action was more effective in facilitating occupational upgrading for African–Americans than for white women. Leonard (1990) finds that between 1974 and 1980 African–American males' share of employment increased faster in federal contractor than in non-contractor firms in every broad occupational group except laborers, a very low-paying position, and white-collar trainees. Affirmative action also contributed to the movement of African–American women up the occupational ladder. They increased their employment share faster in contractor enterprises than in noncontractor firms in all occupations except technical, craft and white-collar trainee. For white women the story was different. For the most part, their occupational upgrading was not directly related to affirmative action (Leonard, 1989).

Technically, it was only federal contractors who were required to develop affirmative action plans. However, Title VII of the Civil Rights Act and the activities of the EEOC apply to virtually all companies, except for the very smallest. Title VII and the EEOC had an independent effect, above and beyond that of affirmative action, in improving the job prospects of women and minorities. By the late 1970s, most large corporations had formal equal employment opportunity programs and had changed their personnel policies in order to attempt to diversify their work forces. As long as these programs were not complete shams, they likely opened up some opportunities for women and minorities.

While the equal employment opportunity and affirmative action policies of the federal government did benefit some African–Americans and white women during the 1970s, the overall impact was limited. Large wage and employment disparities between women and minorities and white men still remained.

In general, in the 1970s, black men made some job gains relative to white men, thus continuing the trend seen in the 1960s. However, African–American men progressed up the occupational scale at a slower rate than during the 1960s. While they increased their relative presence in the more desirable, higher paying professional, managerial and craft jobs, they were still underrepresented in these occupations as compared with white men. African–American men were 8.6 percent of employed men in 1972 and 8.4 percent in 1980. They accounted for 4.4 percent of all male professional and technical workers in 1980, up from 4.0 percent in 1972. (Due to changes in the Census Bureau's occupational classification scheme, the data for the period 1972–80 are not strictly comparable to data presented for earlier time periods.) African–American male managers were 3.2 percent of all male managers in 1980, in contrast to 2.6 percent eight years earlier. However, as during the 1960s, the growth of black male professionals and managers occurred primarily among the lowest paying jobs in these two broad occupational groupings. African–American men increased their share of male craft positions from 6.2 percent in 1972 to 7.0 percent in 1980 (Westcott, 1982, p. 32). Unlike during the 1960s, however, black male annual income did not rise relative to white male annual income. In 1972, the black male to white male median income ratio was 62 percent. In 1980, it was 63 percent (Reich, 1988, p. 148).

While there was a reduction in the level of racial segregation among male workers, the greater decline in racial segregation occurred among women workers (King, 1992). African–American women continued moving into traditionally white female occupational categories. They were 11.0 percent of employed women in 1972 and 10.6 percent of employed women in 1980. While African–American women were still underrepresented in clerical work relative to white women, their share of female clerical jobs rose from 7.2 percent in 1972 to 8.9 percent in 1980. Relative to white women, African–American women increased their presence in professional jobs. In 1972, African–American women held 8.0 percent of professional jobs held by women. Though still underrepresented in this occupation, the African–American female share of this occupation rose to 8.8 percent in 1980. As with African–American men, the growth in professional occupations among African–American women proceeded at a slower pace than in the 1960s. However, in contrast to African–American men, African–American women increased their presence significantly throughout most of the professional job categories. African–American women also made limited gains in managerial positions. At the other end of the occupational spectrum, they moved out of low-paid private household work at a faster rate than white women. However, they were still disproportionately concentrated in this sector. African–American women were 31.9 percent of female private household workers in 1980, down from 39.8 percent in 1972 (Westcott, 1982, p. 32). Overall, African–American female annual income did not rise relative to white female annual income. In 1972, the black to white female median income ratio was 95 percent. In 1980, it was 96 percent (Reich, 1988, p. 148).

As during the 1960s, African–American women had more success in being hired into positions, up to this time, reserved mainly for white women than did women, as a whole, in finding work in occupations considered the preserve of white men. Women entered the labor force in droves. Their labor force participation rate rose from 43.9 percent in 1972 to 51.5 percent in 1980 (US Department of Labor, 1983, p. 17). In 1980, women were still concentrated in clerical and service jobs with 35.1 percent of women holding clerical positions and 17.0 percent of women doing nonhousehold service work. And craft jobs remained a male bastion, with only 1.8 percent of women doing such work (US Department of Labor, 1983, p. 46). These figures had hardly changed since 1972.

While jobs were strongly gender segregated, women did make some inroads into male occupations during the 1970s. Overall, gender segregation within occupations decreased more rapidly during the 1970s than during the 1960s (King, 1992). The decline in occupational segregation occurred mainly in traditionally male professional and managerial positions. While women were still segregated into the predominantly female occupations of elementary and secondary school teaching, nursing, library and social work, they did make some gains in lawyers rising from 5 percent of all lawyers in 1970 to 14 percent in 1980; in operations and systems researchers and analysts from 11 to 28 percent; in pharmacists from 12 to 24 percent; and in veterinarians from 5 to 13 percent (Blau and Ferber, 1987, p. 40). And their presence continued to grow in accounting, college and university teaching and medicine. Many more women were holding managerial positions in public administration, public relations, financial services and retail trade. The more educated women were the major beneficiaries of the decline in gender segregation in professional and managerial occupations. However, women did not make much progress in integrating the traditionally male-dominated blue-collar occupations (Blau and Ferber, 1987; Gatlin, 1987).

While progress was made, considerable sexual and racial inequality remained. There was still a vast amount of sex segregation. More than 60 percent of women (or men) would have had to change jobs in 1981 for the occupational distribution of men and women to be the same (Blau and Ferber, 1987, p. 41). The sex-based earnings differential did not narrow. Within broad occupational groupings other than crafts and services (excluding private household services), the ratio of the median earnings of full-time year-round women workers to those of full-time year-round men workers was the same or lower in 1980 than it had been in 1970 (US Bureau of the Census, 1983, p. 23). In addition, women were still more likely to be jobless than men. In 1980, the unemployment rate of women was 7.4 percent while for men it was 6.9 percent.

Black men were still twice as likely to be out of work as white men. Furthermore, their labor force participation rate declined more than that of white men during the 1970s. The labor force participation rate of African–American men was 71.5 percent in 1980, in contrast to 78.2 percent for white men (*Employment and Training Report*, 1981, pp. 157, 190). Thus, despite anti-discrimination efforts, African–American men were much less likely to hold jobs than their white counterparts.

Finding work was also more difficult for African–American women than white women. During the 1970s, white women entered the labor force at a faster rate than did African–American women. Their labor force participation rate jumped from 43.2 percent in 1972 to 51.2 percent in 1980 while that of African–American women rose to 53.6 percent in 1980 from 48.8 percent in 1972. At the same time as more white women were finding work, the racial unemployment differential remained high. African–American women were slightly less than twice as likely to be unemployed as their white counterparts (*Employment and Training Report of the President*, 1981, pp. 157, 190).

Overall, African–Americans continued to be concentrated among the working poor. Classifying low earnings as an annual earnings level below the poverty level for a family of four, African–Americans were much more likely to have low earnings than whites. Looking at those individuals with year-round full-time attachment to the labor force, 25.1 percent of African–American men in contrast to 12.2 percent of white men, and 37.1 percent of African–American women as compared to 28.0 percent of white women had low annual earnings (US Bureau of the Census, Current Population Reports, series P60-178, 1992, p. 23).

CONCLUSION

During the 1970s, stagflation characterized the US economy. A political and economic stalemate occurred between business and labor. Nominal earnings rose but real earnings did not. Many found their living standards stagnating. Profit rates were maintained but they still remained below the levels of the first half of the 1960s. Labor tried to make gains through the political process but the business community was able to rally political support in opposition to labor. The Labor Law Reform Bill of 1978 was defeated and the Humphrey–Hawkins Full Employment legislation was significantly watered down prior to passage.

There was a growing politicization of the income distribution. Transfer payments took up an increasing share of the federal budget. Federal governmental expenditures on programs not exclusively for the poor rose rapidly, particularly transfer payments for the elderly. Spending on the poor was reduced. Women and minorities continued their push for equality. While they did make some employment gains, partly resulting from equal employment opportunity and affirmative action, discrimination still existed. Given the stagflation, government anti-discrimination and anti-poverty initiatives took on the appearance, and for some the reality, of a zero-sum game. Racial tensions escalated and a backlash began to take shape.

Ultimately, for there to be a way out of stagflation the economy would need to grow more rapidly and the claims being placed on economic output would need to be brought more in line with the available goods and services. Yet, what should be the economic growth strategy and whose claims should bear the brunt of the adjustment?

11. Restructuring the Economy: The Market-Based Conservative Strategy, 1981–92

Seeking to reverse the economic decline of the 1970s, raise the average rate of profit and improve the overall productive efficiency of the economy, the Reagan administration, having a conservative Republican bent, pursued a policy agenda designed to restructure the economy by freeing up market forces. Ideologically, the federal government was attacked as the most important cause of the economic problems facing the United States, both domestically and internationally. Programmatically, this attack on the state, on the one hand, translated into reducing tax and regulatory burdens faced by businesses along with taxes on the wealthy. On the other hand, it also led to a weakening of the minimal social protection policies benefiting workers in general and the poor in particular. Two thrusts of state labor market policies were apparent. The first was to increase competition in the labor market at a given level of unemployment, by reducing the social wage and lowering the effective minimum wage. The second was to reduce union power through higher aggregate levels of unemployment, increased labor market competition and the reinterpretation of existing industrial relations legislation in a pro-business manner.

Internationally, the Reagan administration wished to restore American political and economic supremacy. Militarily, the administration wanted to carry a "big stick." Economically, it hoped to strengthen and stabilize the value of the dollar on world currency markets, thereby reinforcing the ability of the dollar to remain the principal currency for international and financial transactions. However, the "high flying" dollar would be one of the factors making it more difficult for the US-based firms to compete in world markets.

The market-based conservative strategy was closely aligned with an ongoing corporate restructuring. Facing growing domestic and international competition, US-based corporations were trying to become more low-cost producers. Federal governmental policy weakening the bargaining power of organized and unorganized workers alike was just what many employers desired. Wishing to dominate labor, many employers became more adversarial in their relations with their workers. More often than not employers gained wage and work rule concessions from their employees. The share of employees who were unionized steadily declined and aggressive anti-union management behavior was an important factor in the shrinking perimeter of unionism.

The market-based conservative strategy for restructuring the economy reached its limits during the Reagan years. The Bush administration acted as a caretaker for the Reagan Revolution, albeit while being forced to deal with some of its excesses. Its results were decidedly mixed.

After the recession of 1981–82, the economy did expand, unemployment did decline, the rate of inflation was reduced, and firms became more profitable. The dollar did retain its role as the primary currency for international transactions. However, the conservative economic agenda did not lead to a more well-functioning economy. The rate of economic growth did not accelerate and an investment boom did not materialize.

What "supply-side" economics did lead to was growing economic inequality and growing economic deprivation. The number of people in poverty increased. The average economic status of blacks relative to whites deteriorated. However, countering the trend toward increased inequality was the narrowing of the pay gap between men and women. Overall, the rich were getting richer and the poor were becoming even more destitute. For many in the middle, the 1980s was a lost decade, lost in terms of improvement in their living standards.

SUPPLY-SIDE ECONOMICS AND MONETARISM

Upon taking office in 1981, the Reagan administration faced a troubling economic situation both domestically and internationally. Domestically, the economy had been in recession in 1980 and many people were out of work. Though there was large-scale unemployment, prices were rising rapidly. As a result of the monetary policies of the Federal Reserve, interest rates were at an unprecedented height. Internationally, US-based corporations were finding it more difficult to maintain their standing in world markets. The United States had become increasingly dependent on imports of petroleum and other vital raw materials and natural resource producing countries had become more assertive in controlling and pricing their raw materials. The Soviet Union remained a formidable military presence, able to challenge American influence throughout the world.

On February 18, the President announced a new economic policy designed to reduce the rate of inflation and lay the foundation for future economic growth. It was called *America's New Beginning: A Program for Economic Recovery*. And it argued that this "new beginning" represented a break with the past, the now discredited policies of Keynesianism. The key elements of the program included cutting the rate of growth of federal spending, reducing personal and business tax rates, providing relief from burdensome government regulations and, in cooperation with the Federal Reserve, developing a monetary policy that would restore a stable currency and healthy financial markets.

Though serious inflation and widespread unemployment were occurring simultaneously, priority was placed on slowing the rise in prices. The Reagan administration turned to the Federal Reserve for leadership in the fight against inflation. A restrictive monetary policy, together with falling world prices for food and energy, resulted in the rate of inflation dropping from 13.5 percent in 1980 to 3.2 percent in 1983.

But American workers paid dearly for this. The unemployment rate reached heights not experienced since the Great Depression of the 1930s. The 1981–82 recession was deeper than any downturn since the 1930s, with the real Gross National Product (GNP) falling by 2.2 percent in 1982 and the unemployment rate rising to 9.7 percent. Although unemployment rose throughout the economy, it was centered in mining, construction and manufacturing, those areas where unions have traditionally been the strongest. For example, within manufacturing, by December 1982 the unemployment rate had reached 23.2 percent in the motor vehicle industry and 29.2 percent in the primary metals industry (*Economic Report of the President*, 1983, p. 46).

The joblessness and the lost output which resulted from the anti-inflationary monetary policy was, in the administration's view, a mere short-term cost to pay for the long-run benefit of lower inflation. With high and varying rates of inflation, economic uncertainty increases and more and more resources are devoted to speculative activities designed to "beat inflation," rather than to long-term investments in new plant and equipment. A lower rate of investment leads to a lower rate of future economic growth and reduces future living standards. Thus, a low and stable rate of inflation is necessary, though not sufficient, for an expanding economy.

In addition, government policy needed to be redefined if long-term economic growth was to be attained. "The most important cause of our economic problems has been the government itself." (*America's New Beginning*, 1981, p. 4). The burdensome, intrusive role of the government must be reduced thereby freeing the creativity and ambition of the American people. It was a call for a more laissez-faire approach to government macroeconomic and microeconomic policy, thereby reversing, to a degree, the policies of previous administrations. This approach was philosophically opposed to the Keynesian ideas which had influenced macroeconomic policy making in the 1960s, and to a much lesser degree in the 1970s. According to the Keynesian perspective, the government can play a positive role in the economy. And the primary way for the government to affect the level of economic output is by influencing the demand for goods and services. With a higher level of demand, the additional supply would be forthcoming. The Reagan administration countered by emphasizing the negative role of the government. And it argued that changing the incentives to produce goods and services was the most effective way for growing the economy. If the additional supply was created, the necessary demand would be forthcoming.

Across-the-board cuts in personal income tax rates were at the heart of the Reagan approach to the "supply-side" of the economy. Lower tax rates would provide people with strong incentives to work, save and invest more thereby increasing the supply of goods and services. As personal income tax rates decline, the after-tax hourly wage rises, for any given pre-tax hourly wage. Thus, people would wish to work longer hours or accept more demanding jobs. Similarly, cutting personal tax rates raises after-tax interest income thereby inducing people to save more of their money rather than spend it for current consumption. And lower tax rates increase people's willingness to place money in risky, though potentially rewarding investment ventures. Furthermore, with greater savings the supply of funds available to be loaned out by banks grows, thereby reducing the interest rates charged to borrowers. Lower interest rates further increase the willingness of entrepreneurs and corporate managers to borrow for investment in new plant and equipment.

Yet, there was no guarantee that this rather indirect approach to increasing investment would be adequate. Thus, individual tax cuts were to be complemented by business tax cuts and by regulatory relief. At least for a time, direct incentives for investment, through tax credits and accelerated depreciation, would be provided to businesses which invest in new plant and equipment. Regarding government regulations, the administration argued, as did the Carter administration previously, that these regulations imposed excessive burdens on business. The result was a slowing of the rate of economic growth and an increase in the rate of inflation. Regulatory relief would reduce the cost of compliance thereby lowering the costs of goods and services and freeing up resources which could be used more productively by American businesses, for example in research and development. Furthermore, rationalizing the regulatory process would lower the administrative outlays of governmental regulatory agencies. The resultant savings would be passed on to individuals and businesses in the form of lower taxes.

It was not merely expenditures on regulatory programs which the Reagan administration argued should be reduced. They also called for slowing the rate of growth of government spending in general. Philosophically, they argued that most individuals know best what they want and how to attain it. Therefore, individual decisionmaking, coordinated via free markets, will "generally result in the most appropriate distribution of our economic resources" (*Economic Report of the President*, 1982, p. 78). With this perspective in mind, the administration concluded that the size and scope of the federal government had grown too large. Furthermore, it believed that resources left in the private sector can more effectively generate growth and productive employment than resources moved to the public sector. And they asserted that "uncontrolled growth of government spending has been a primary cause of the sustained high rate of inflation experienced by the American economy" (*America's New Beginning*, 1981, p. 10). Without a credible program to slow the growth of the government, people will continue to expect persistent, and possibly higher, rates of inflation.

Between 1965 and 1981, the federal budget grew from 18 percent of GNP to 23 percent, doubling in real terms from $330 to $660 billion (in 1981 dollars). At the same time, there was a shift in budgetary priorities. Spending on defense oriented activities – including national defense, international affairs and veteran's benefits and services – fell from 50 percent to 29 percent of the budget. Social welfare expenditures, broadly defined, took up a growing share of the budget, doubling from 25 to 50 percent. Within this category, health expenditures – largely Medicare and Medicaid – grew most rapidly, consuming 10 percent of the budget in 1981, in contrast to 1.4 percent in 1965. They were followed by outlays on education, training, employment and social service programs which grew from 1.9 percent to nearly 5 percent of the budget. Programs that provide cash transfers or access to goods and services such as Social Security, Unemployment Insurance (UI) and Aid to Families with Dependent Children (AFDC) increased from 22 to 35 percent of the budget (Danziger and Haveman, 1981, p. 6).

Thus, the Reagan administration wanted to slow the growth of government spending while, at the same time, shifting spending priorities. Viewing the federal budget as a '"coast to coast soupline' that dispenses remedial aid with almost reckless abandon" (Stockman, 1981, p. 18), the administration cut back social programs thereby freeing up funds for strengthening national defense. Along with the election of President Reagan came the most politically conservative US Congress in a generation. The US Congress accepted most of the recommendations of the Reagan administration. The Omnibus Budget Reconciliation Act was passed in June 1981 and the Economic Recovery Tax Act (ERTA) was approved in August 1981. Overall, the US Congress approved almost 80 percent of the cuts in 1982 nondefense outlays requested by the administration. At the same time, additional funds were provided for defense.

After the passage of the budget legislation, attention then turned to taxes. ERTA was the centerpiece of the supply-side economics program of the Reagan administration. Strongly influenced by ideas pushed by representatives of major business organizations, ERTA included substantial tax breaks for individuals and businesses. Individual income tax rates were reduced 23 percent, 5 percent as of October 1, 1981 and 10 percent as of July 1, 1982 and again as of July 1, 1983. The top marginal tax rate was quickly dropped from 70 percent to 50 percent as of January 1, 1982, as was the maximum capital gains tax rate from 28 percent to 20 percent. Beginning in 1985, the personal income tax structure would be indexed for inflation. People would move into higher tax brackets only if their taxable incomes rose faster than prices, not just because inflation led to higher dollar values for the same real incomes. Wealth taxes were also cut with estate and gift tax rates reduced (Campagna, 1987, p. 496).

ERTA also made major changes in the taxation of business income, all designed to increase the rate of return from investment in plant and equipment, thereby spurring new investment spending. The most important change was the more generous treatment of depreciation – the writing off of the cost of new plant and equipment against income. The act shortened the period over which assets could be fully depreciated. A second change was to increase the investment tax credit for some types of equipment (*Economic Report of the President*, 1982, pp. 122–127).

The 1981 tax cuts were unprecedented in magnitude though, at least in regard to cutting business taxes, they were a continuation of a trend begun during the Carter administration. They were advanced by a President who, during the campaign for the Presidency and upon taking office, continually argued that reducing federal budget deficits and eventually balancing the federal budget were of utmost importance. Yet, how would it be possible to simultaneously cut tax rates, build up national defense and balance the federal budget? It soon became clear that it would not be possible to cut taxes, increase defense spending and balance the budget at the same time. It is even questionable whether many in the administration believed this was possible. It is more likely that the cut in tax rates were part of a long-term plan to reduce nondefense governmental expenditures, particularly social expenditures, and reshape the role of the federal government in American society. David Stockman, the director of the Office of Management and Budget, admitted the tax cuts were designed to deprive the government of revenue thereby requiring cutbacks in the scope of governmental activities. He wrote "The Reagan Revolution, as I defined it, required a frontal assault on the American welfare state. That was the only way to pay for the massive Kemp–Roth tax cut" (Stockman, 1986, p. 8).

Shortly after the 1981 tax cuts went into effect, it became very clear that something was awry. The economy continued to perform miserably, largely as a result of the tight monetary policies of the Federal Reserve. The federal budget deficit, rather than beginning to decline, was projected to grow rapidly. While taxes were somewhat raised in 1982 and 1983, the federal budget deficits continued to grow. The federal budget deficit was $72.7 billion in fiscal year 1980 (October 1979–September 1980), the last full fiscal year of the Carter administration. This amounted to 2.7 percent of GNP. From fiscal year 1982 through fiscal year 1986, the federal budget deficits averaged 5.3 percent of GNP, reaching a level of $238 billion in 1986 (*Economic Report of the President*, 1993, p. 435). This was the first time in the post Second World War period that the federal budget deficit was of a magnitude greater than 5 percent of GNP.

Even though the Reagan administration claimed to support a balanced federal budget and the federal budget deficits were large, it was still against lowering the budget deficits by further increasing tax revenues. Rather large federal budget deficits continued to be the administration's major weapon in its attempt to reduce nondefense government spending. In the debate surrounding the Tax Reform Act of 1986, the administration argued that any changes in the tax code should be expected to leave total tax revenue unchanged. The Tax Reform Act of 1986 was projected to be revenue neutral. While it reduced the tax bill of individuals, it raised the tax bill of corporations. Individual income tax rates were lowered. Prior to the legislation, there were 14 tax brackets, with tax rates ranging from 11 percent to 50 percent. Under this bill, there would be only four tax brackets, with the marginal tax rate rising from 15 percent to 28 percent to 33 percent, but then falling back to 28 percent for the highest income taxpayers. The very poorest of taxpayers also gained substantially lower tax rates. By raising the income level below which no taxes are paid, approximately 6 000 000 low-wage workers were removed from the income tax rolls.

While taxes paid by individuals fell, corporate taxes rose. As with individual tax rates, corporate tax rates declined and the number of tax brackets diminished. The top corporate tax rate was now 34 percent, below the former top rate of 46 percent. There would now be only three corporate tax brackets rather than the previous five. In order to finance the lower rates for corporations and individuals, several corporate tax breaks were repealed. The investment tax credit was eliminated. Depreciation allowances were made less generous for equipment and much less generous for real estate. A large number of tax shelters for particular industries were abolished or reduced. And a minimum tax of 20 percent of taxable income was imposed designed to remedy the fact that many corporations had been paying minimal taxes or even avoiding taxes altogether.

Conservative legislators supported this bill because it was consistent with a conservative administration's approach to "supply-side" economics. Personal marginal tax rates and corporate income tax rates were lowered. Eliminating the investment tax credit and making less generous depreciation allowances creates a "more level playing field." And on a more "level playing field," investment decisions will be based more on economic rationality and less on inappropriate incentives created by misguided government policy. It appealed to liberal legislators since it abolished some tax loopholes for the wealthy and lowered the taxes of low-wage workers. The business community was divided. Firms in capital-intensive industries, such as manufacturing, mining and construction, lobbied against the revoking of the investment tax credit and the changes in the tax code regarding accelerated depreciation. However, trade associations representing apparel manufacturers, electronics firms, supermarkets, wholesalers, retailers and trucking companies favored the legislation. Companies in these industries had effective tax rates which exceeded the average for all businesses and they did not benefit very much from the accelerated depreciation provisions of the ERTA. Their main interest was in lowering overall corporate income tax rates. Thus, the Tax Reform Act of 1986 was able to be passed by the US Congress and signed into law.

Government efforts to improve corporate profitability extended beyond tax code changes. They also included reducing the federal regulation of business. On January 22, 1981, the day after his inauguration, President Reagan announced the creation of a Task Force on Regulatory Relief whose goal would be to review existing regulations to see which needed to be revised or eliminated. Of particular importance were those regulations deemed to be "particularly burdensome to the national economy or to key industrial sectors" (*America's New Beginning*, 1981, p. 19). Furthermore, it would review all major regulatory proposals by regulatory agencies.

A month later the President issued an Executive Order requiring all regulatory agencies to utilize cost–benefit analysis before developing any new rules. If the potential benefits to society of the new regulatory objectives exceed the potential costs, then the most cost effective method of reaching any given regulatory objective should be chosen. Furthermore, existing regulations were to be reviewed in light of the potential costs and benefits to society. While in principle the utilization of cost–benefit analysis need not lead to deregulation, in practice it often did.

The administration quickly made other changes in regulatory policies. The President froze many of the "midnight" regulations announced during the last days of the Carter administration and requested that no new regulations be issued for the next 60 days. In addition, appointees to head the regulatory agencies shared this deregulatory philosophy. Anne Gorusch, the head of the Environmental Protection Agency, while a member of the Colorado state legislature, had opposed many of the environmental regulations imposed on states by the federal government. Thorne Auchter, previously a manager of a family construction firm that had faced difficulties from the Occupational Safety and Health Administration, was chosen to head this agency. The size and budgets of the regulatory agencies were cut, reversing a trend which had begun during the Nixon administration.

THE LABOR AND SOCIAL POLICY AGENDA

Two of the explicit goals of supply-side macroeconomic policy were raising the average rate of growth of productivity and the average rate of profit. Though never stated explicitly, these were also two of the central aims of the labor and social policy agenda of the Reagan administration. They were to be achieved by weakening the bargaining power of both organized and unorganized workers. Here, too, a deregulatory politics was followed, one designed to expose workers more fully to the competitive forces of the labor market. In some respects, the actions taken were merely an extension of those of the Carter administration. However, on balance, a more conservative trend in social policy took hold (Rosenberg, 1983, 1988, 1989, 1994).

The push for labor market efficiency via deregulation represented a decline in labor standards. The effective minimum wage declined. Unemployment insurance, trade adjustment assistance and AFDC were reduced. Public service employment programs were ended. The government policies aimed at introducing a more competitive mode of regulation of the labor market served to weaken unions. Government industrial relations policies, setting a union busting tone, did the same. These policy changes took place in a period of high unemployment and large-scale joblessness weakens the bargaining power of employed workers.

Declining real minimum wage

The growth in the number of unemployed constitutes, in and of itself, an increase in competition in the labor market. A decline in the real value of the federal minimum wage has the same effect on low-wage workers. The floor of the wage structure falls and their wages become more determined by market forces than by government legislation The Reagan administration would have preferred to eliminate the federal minimum wage entirely. However, this was not politically feasible and was, thus, never attempted. Rather, throughout the eight years that Ronald Reagan was in office the minimum wage remained at $3.35 per hour, the value set in 1981. This represented the longest elapsed time without a minimum wage increase since the passage of the Fair Labor Standards Act of 1938, enacting the federal minimum wage for the country as a whole. At the same time prices were rising, causing the real value of the minimum wage to fall. For example, the nominal value of the federal minimum wage was $2.90 per hour in 1979. This is equivalent to $4.86 in 1989 dollars. In 1989, however, the minimum wage was only $3.35 per hour (Mishel and Frankel, 1991, p. 116). Furthermore, the minimum wage fell relative to the average wage. After hovering around 50 percent of average hourly earnings in private nonagricultural industries during the 1950s and 1960s, the minimum averaged 45 percent in the 1970s. By 1985, it had declined to about 39 percent of average wages (Smith and Vavrichek, 1987).

Unemployment insurance cutbacks

At the same time as the number of unemployed was rising, the federal government was cutting back on UI. Given the example set by the federal government, many states also did the same. UI provides a cushion for workers as they search for work. That cushion was totally withdrawn for some and partially withdrawn for others.

The weakening of the unemployment compensation system began during the Carter administration. The program enabling unemployment benefits to be paid for up to 65 weeks was allowed to expire in January 1978. In addition, the tax-exempt status of UI was ended. Legislation was passed to tax the unemployment benefits of individuals who receive a combination of income and unemployment benefits exceeding a base amount. The Reagan adminstration continued with this policy thrust. As did the Ford administration, it claimed that overly generous UI lengthened the duration of a spell of unemployment. Wishing to force workers to lower their job expectations and accept whatever work was available, the administration, with the approval of the US Congress, increased the income taxes on unemployment compensation and made "extended benefits" (EB) more difficult to attain. By 1986, all recipients of UI regardless of their income were taxed on their benefits. By redefining the conditions under which EB were to be paid, fewer workers were able to qualify for the program. To the extent that workers reacted as the administration wished, the effective supply of labor for low-wage jobs would increase, serving to keep wages down.

Subject to minimal federal standards, states set qualifying requirements for UI, benefit levels and benefit duration. Changes at the state level also made it more difficult to qualify for standard UI. Many states increased the number of weeks worked and the amount of earnings required to collect benefits or changed formulas to yield lower benefits. Most states implemented policies generally denying benefits altogether to those who quit their jobs voluntarily (Baldwin and McHugh, 1992).

The upshot was that the share of the unemployed collecting UI declined during the 1980s. In 1975, when the unemployment rate was 8.5 percent, 76 percent of the unemployed received UI. During 1982, with a higher unemployment rate than in 1975, only 45 percent received compensation (Levitan *et al.*, 1986, p. 165). Later, in 1987 and 1988, approximately 32 percent of the unemployed received a benefit, compared to 40–45 percent of the jobless during similar periods in the 1960s and 1970s (Baldwin and McHugh, 1992).

Trade Adjustment Assistance (TAA) cutbacks

While the UI system was partially eroded, TAA was sharply cutback. TAA was received by workers whose unemployment was deemed to be in part due to imports. The payments were for more per week and for longer periods than people received for UI. In addition, training opportunities, and relocation and job search allowances were also granted. Most of the TAA payments went to unionized industrial workers, mainly steel, automobile, and clothing and textile workers, in the mid-Atlantic and North Central regions. During the Carter years, many workers were certified to receive TAA.

In 1981, the Reagan administration developed, and the US Congress passed, legislation increasing the difficulty of qualifying for TAA, limiting the size of the benefit and shortening its duration. Similar to its position on UI, the government argued that TAA enabled workers to avoid adjusting to industrial decline brought on by international competition. The changes made effectively gutted the program. Even though the 1980s was a decade of very high trade deficits, virtually no worker received TAA. From 1976 to 1980, there was an annual average of 199 000 workers receiving TAA. This is in contrast to 1986–90 when 37 000 workers received TAA annually (Friedman, 1991).

Elimination of public service employment

Not only were alternative sources of income to private sector wages scaled down, but alternative sources of jobs outside of the private sector were eliminated. Public service employment programs (PSE), funded by the federal government, providing for positions in state and local governments and in nonprofit making organizations were ended. The positions had been funded under the Comprehensive Employment and Training Act of 1973.

The basic reasoning behind PSE is that it could quickly increase the employment of selected workers. The Carter administration made PSE a central component of its employment strategy. When Ronald Reagan entered office in 1981, 309 000 PSE positions existed, approximately 85 percent of which were held by people officially considered to be living at or below the poverty line. None remained by the end of the year as the funding was eliminated. The workers who had been holding these positions were thrust back into the labor market, thereby providing low-wage employers with an increased supply of labor. At the time when it ended PSE, officials in the administration were making the case that an expanding private economy was a necessary – and in most cases sufficient – condition for reducing long-term unemployment (Moran, 1982, p. 402).

"Welfare reform"

While voluntary PSE programs were ended, mandatory public employment programs for welfare recipients were developed. Mandatory "workfare" complemented welfare changes that limited the number of people eligible for assistance and the amounts they received. During the Carter administration, AFDC benefits did not keep pace with inflation. Furthermore, there had been no growth in welfare caseloads since the early 1970s (Ellwood, 1988, p. 59). The Reagan administration further cut the welfare program. In 1981, the means test for eligibility for welfare was tightened. In addition, qualifying families had limitations placed on the amount of work related expenses they were able to deduct in determining their net income and, thus, their AFDC needs.

Up to 500 000 AFDC families may have lost eligibility as a result of the policy changes (Pierson, 1994, p. 118). The cutbacks in the welfare program were occurring at a time when the number of people in poverty was growing. According to official measures of poverty, 15.2 percent of the population was poor in 1983, the highest level it had been since 1965 (*Economic Report of the President*, 1986, p. 286). As a result of the changes regarding the welfare program, the real value of AFDC and food stamps was lower in 1990 compared to 1980 and these benefits were phased out more quickly at low levels of earnings (Mishel and Frankel, 1991, p. 191). The net effect of the AFDC policy changes was to shorten the amount of time both working and nonworking people received welfare. Thus, the welfare reforms likely helped to increase the supply of labor to low wage jobs. However, women who had their AFDC benefits reduced or eliminated were economically worse off though their monthly earnings may have increased (*Focus*, 1985).

The Reagan administration continually proposed legislation requiring states to develop mandatory "workfare" programs, imposing work requirements for AFDC recipients. States already had the option of doing so, and many, though not all, did implement "workfare" of one form or another. Rather than provide welfare recipients with an incentive to work, the Reagan administration argued they should be forced to work. It took eight years but in October 1988 the administration was finally successful in having the US Congress pass legislation forcing all states to develop "workfare" programs by 1990.

Weakening and busting unions

The large number of unemployed and the cutbacks in the minimum wage and the social wage hurt unions. Government policy, setting a union busting tone, did the same. In its first year in office, the Reagan administration fired the 11 000 striking air traffic controllers and had the Professional Air Traffic Controllers Organization decertified. The administration was able to do this because federal government employees are legally forbidden to strike. This action sent a clear message to employers; they should feel free to bash unions.

Furthermore, the Reagan administration's appointments to the National Labor Relations Board (NLRB) were designed to create a majority who would roll back many of the gains made by the labor movement. Donald Dotson, named chairman of the NLRB from 1983 to 1987, had a very low opinion of the virtues of collective bargaining. He had said that "collective bargaining frequently means ... the destruction of the marketplace" and that "the price we have paid is the loss of entire industries and the crippling of others" (AFL–CIO Committee on the Evolution of Work, 1985, p. 11). According to William Gould, appointed by President Clinton to head the NLRB, the NLRB in the early years of the Reagan administration "was relentless in reversing precedent more than any board even under Eisenhower, Nixon or Ford" (Tasini, 1988). By June 1984, it was estimated that the NLRB had recast nearly 40 percent of the decisions made since the mid-1970s that conservatives had found objectionable (*Business Week*, 1984, p. 122).

The anti-union perspective of the NLRB made it more difficult for union-organizing drives to succeed and for unions to achieve their goals at the bargaining table. As a result of NLRB rulings, employers became more able to use misleading information to try to influence the outcome of a representation election (Midland National Life Insurance Co. case, 1982). Employers were more able to engage in unfair labor practices designed to stop a union victory in a representation election without suffering negative consequences (Gourmet Foods, Inc. case, 1984). The National Labor Relations Act (NLRA) protection provided to individual employees during organizing drives, as well as generally, was eroded even further. Workers who protest extreme unfair labor practices and were fired lost their right to reinstatement if they engaged in "excessive" behavior. This held even if they could demonstrate that they had been provoked by their employer into engaging in nonflagrant misconduct (Clear Pine Moldings case, 1984).

These decisions, taken together, made it much easier for an employer to defeat an organizing drive and terminate employees active in the organizing effort. Workers could be misled during the campaign. Organizers could be let go and if they responded in an "excessive" fashion they would lose their rights to reinstatement. And unfair labor practices resulting in less than a majority vote for a union would not lead to a union being certified as the duly chosen bargaining agent of the workers. An existing organizing drive would fail and there would be little chance of success in the future.

The NLRB decisions also made it more difficult for unions to gain their demands at the bargaining table. Employers were now more able to move union jobs to nonunion locations. Previously, the NLRB had found that as long as a collective bargaining agreement was in effect, an employer was prohibited from moving work to a nonunion facility. A company would now be able to move work during the life of a contract unless there was a clause in the contract explicitly prohibiting such action. All the company needed to do, if the move was designed to lower labor costs, was to bargain over the decision and its effects (Milwaukee Springs case, 1984). Yet, there was no requirement that an agreement be reached or that the work remain at the unionized plant. And if the movement of work hinged on factors other than cutting labor costs, there would be no requirement to bargain at all (Otis Elevator case, 1984).

The NLRB rulings also make it more difficult for a union to succeed with a strike. Most labor contracts include a general no-strike clause during the life of the pact. Previously, the NLRB had ruled that sympathy strikes were not covered by the no-strike clause. Thus, workers had the right not to cross another union's picket line. Now workers agreeing to a general no-strike clause would not have the right to honor another union's picket line (Indianapolis Power and Light case, 1985).

Furthermore, unions could no longer fine workers who resign their union membership during a strike and return to work in violation of union rules. In upholding an earlier NLRB decision, the US Supreme Court determined that any union rules limiting the freedom of workers to resign during or just prior to a strike may be illegal (Pattern Makers' League of North America case, 1985) (*Business Week*, 1984; Taub and Needleman, 1984; Craver, 1993).

THE "HIGH-FLYING" DOLLAR AND ITS DESCENT

Not only did the Reagan labor and social policy agenda attack the bargaining power of workers, the strong dollar policy did the same.

The "high-flying" dollar was one of the factors lying behind the declining international competitiveness of the US-based firms.

Since fiscal policy was expansionary, monetary policy was relied on to slow the economy in 1981–82 and reduce the rate of inflation at that time, as well as to keep inflation rates low thereafter. The growth rate of the money supply was sharply reduced. Interest rates in the United States remained high. The interest rate differential between the United States and other advanced industrialized societies widened attracting substantial amounts of foreign funds to the United States. Given the increased demand for dollars, the value of the dollar rose by 32 percent on international currency markets from 1980 to 1982 (*Economic Report of the President*, 1986, p. 373).

As a result of the decline in the rate of inflation, the Federal Reserve abandoned its tight monetary policy and experiment with monetarism in July 1982. Rather now their focus was the fragility of the banking and financial system and the overall health of the economy. The strains in the banking system were highlighted by the collapse of the Penn Square National Bank of Oklahoma City on July 5, 1982. It was a rather obscure financial institution which had originated billions of dollars of oil loans. Given the depressed state of the oil industry, these loans turned out to be worthless. Many large and well-known banks were involved with Penn Square. What would be the ripple effect of the Penn Square bankruptcy? Which bank would be the next to collapse?

US banks did not just face the risks of their domestic borrowers defaulting on their loans. American banks had lent huge sums of money to Third World nations. Some of these countries were finding it difficult to repay their loans, particularly since the banks were no longer lending additional funds so easily. For example, in June 1982, the Mexican government faced the prospect of being unable to arrange financing for a large volume of bank loans coming due during the summer.

The message was clear. Without an economic recovery, the banking system would be in serious jeopardy. Monetary policy was eased. Expansionary fiscal and monetary policy provided the impetus for the economic recovery which began in 1983. More and more US Treasury bonds were issued to raise money to fund the growing federal budget deficits. Given the increased supply of bonds, interest rates remained high to induce individuals and institutions to purchase them. The differential between interest rates in the

United States and interest rates in other advanced industrialized societies widened even further, at least until June 1984.

The relatively higher interest rates continued serving as a magnet attracting funds from other countries. Yet, higher interest returns were not the only reason for placing capital, both short-term and long-term, in the United States. The US economy recovered earlier than did the economies of other advanced industrialized societies. And the pro-business Reagan administration, together with the ongoing weakening of the labor movement, was viewed quite favorably by those interested in pursuing direct foreign investment in the United States. Thus, there was a strong demand for dollars further pushing up the international exchange rate of the dollar. By 1985, the value of the dollar was 56 percent above its level in 1980 (*Economic Report of the President*, 1986, p. 373).

But economic fundamentals were not the only factors behind the dollar's ascent. The interest rate differential peaked in June 1984, and then began to move in the opposite direction. But the dollar continued to appreciate. Now the dollar was being carried along by simple speculation in the currency market. The momentum was upward, speculators were purchasing dollars and jumping on for the ride.

Until 1985, the Reagan administration took a laissez-faire approach to the international currency markets. From their point of view, the rising dollar reflected approval of their sound economic policies. In addition, a strong dollar helped in the fight against inflation. With imports becoming substantially cheaper, domestic producers in trade-dependent sectors were forced to cut costs, improve product quality and restrain their urge to raise prices. Furthermore, given the inadequate amount of domestic savings, the United States needed to sell increasing amounts of government bonds to foreigners to fund the federal budget deficit. A strong dollar made foreigners more willing to purchase US government bonds. They had little fear that the dollar would depreciate, thereby reducing their overall returns.

But by 1985, the negative aspects of the laissez-faire approach to the skyrocketing dollar became more apparent. First, the "speculative bubble" might burst. Speculators might conclude simultaneously that the dollar was overvalued. And to avoid being caught holding depreciating dollars, they might all try to sell dollars at the same time. The end result would be a free fall in the exchange rate of the dollar. Should this occur, foreigners would be less willing to place their funds in the United States. Interest rates in the United States would spike up rather quickly.

That the "speculative bubble" might burst was not a completely far-fetched possibility. By February 1985, the dollar's ascent had ended. Speculators were now focusing on the implications for the value of the dollar of the rapidly growing US balance of trade deficit. And herein lay the second negative effect of the overvalued dollar. That US-based producers were having difficulty competing in world markets had become quite apparent in the 1970s. The overvalued dollar further hastened the decline in international competitiveness by making exports more expensive and cheapening imports. There was a rapid growth of imports and a much slower growth of exports. The merchandise trade deficit steadily increased from $28 billion in 1981 to $122 billion in 1985 (*Economic Report of the President*, 1988, p. 364). Trade-dependent sectors were depressed. Pressure was growing for a depreciation of the dollar from business leaders in manufacturing and agriculture and from the labor movement. Some were calling for import restrictions as well.

Third, it was not just the balance of trade which was running large deficits. The balance on the current account was sharply in the red as well. In 1981, the first year of the Reagan administration, the current account showed a $7 billion surplus. By 1985, that surplus had turned into a $116 billion deficit. A deficit on the current account of such magnitude was previously unimaginable. And in 1985, it was reported that the United States had become so dependent on foreign capital to finance its trade and budget deficits that it was now a debtor nation. The value of foreign owned assets in the United States exceeded the value of US-owned assets abroad. This was the first time the United States had found itself in this situation since the First World War.

The rising budget and trade deficits and the fear that the "speculative bubble" might burst forced the Reagan administration to change its attitude toward the dollar. No longer was a laissez-faire policy appropriate. Rather, a coordinated effort with the leading economic powers was required to bring down the dollar and guide overall exchange rates. On September 22, 1985, finance ministers and central bank governors of West Germany, Japan, France, Great Britain and the United States met at the Plaza Hotel in New York. In the Plaza Accord they agreed to try to bring down the value of the dollar. The dollar had already fallen by 13 percent from its peak in February. And after the Plaza Accord, the dollar continued its gradual depreciation. By January 1986, the dollar was on average 25 percent below its peak levels a year before. Along with the decline in the dollar was the hope that the trade deficit would also be reduced gradually by boosting exports and cutting imports.

During 1986, the dollar continued to decline. After 18 months of constant depreciation, the value of the dollar was 40 percent below its peak. There seemed to be no end in sight to the dollar's slide. The US trade deficit was growing even larger. And foreigners were cutting back on their purchases of dollar-denominated assets fearing future losses if the dollar continued to lose value.

This set the stage for the Louvre Agreement reached in February 1987 among the Group of Seven. Included were the five countries involved in the Plaza Accord, joined by Italy and Canada. They had decided that the dollar had declined enough and they committed themselves to stabilizing exchanging rates at the existing level. This represented a rejection of the floating exchange rate system, which had characterized international monetary relations since the demise of Bretton Woods.

They also agreed to cooperate more closely in their macroeconomic policies. Fiscal and monetary policies would be designed with an eye on reducing trade imbalances, particularly among the United States, Japan and Germany. The United States was able to convince Japan and Germany, two countries with very large trade surpluses, to stimulate their economies. As they reached higher rates of growth, they would be more likely to boost imports, perhaps even imports from the United States. The United States, for its part, agreed to lower the federal budget deficit, thereby reducing the overall demand for goods and services, including imports. If this policy coordination worked as predicted, the trade deficit of the United States would shrink, as would the trade surpluses of Japan and Germany. There would then be less pressure on the dollar.

The Louvre Accord marked a sharp move away from the unilateral policies and free-floating exchange rates espoused by the Reagan administration. And while the US unilateralism did not restore global economic order, more closer cooperation among the leading industrial nations would turn out to be easier to espouse than to implement. By the fall of 1987, the US trade deficit had not improved. The US policymakers, led by Treasury Secretary James Baker, were certain that the other G-7 countries were not doing enough to expand their economies. And these countries, for their part, were not convinced that the United States was serious about shrinking the federal budget deficit. Tensions arose in September when interest rates increased slightly in Japan and West Germany, contrary to what would be expected to occur with expansionary monetary policy. The US Federal Reserve then moved quickly to raise interest rates, as well, in order to protect the value of the dollar.

On October 15, the US Department of Commerce reported an unexpectedly large trade deficit for the month of August. During the weekend of October 17–18, Treasury Secretary Baker threatened Germany with renewed dollar depreciation unless Germany eased its credit policy. It appeared as if the Louvre Accord was unraveling, pointing to increased tensions between the governments of the major advanced industrialized societies over matters of interest rates and currency policy. The following day, October 19, the stock market crashed in the United States with the Dow Jones Industrial Average, an index of the stock prices of 30 of the leading US corporations, losing more than 22 percent of its value. Would this be a repeat of 1929? It would not but that was not known at the time.

NOT A GREAT DEPRESSION, BUT STAGNATION AND RECESSION

Owners of corporate stock saw $500 billion worth of asset value wiped out by the stock market crash. A high level of anxiety pervaded Wall Street. To rebuild confidence in the financial system, Alan Greenspan, the head of the Federal Reserve, announced the Federal Reserve's willingness to meet all liquidity needs. Through open market operations, the Federal Reserve quickly increased the money supply. And the Federal Reserve informed banks that it expected them to continue to provide credit to firms in the financial sector facing hard times due to the crash.

The economy did not go into a slump. Rather the rate of economic growth was higher in 1988 than in 1987, and the unemployment rate continued to decline as it had since 1983. By 1988, the unemployment rate was 5.5 percent, considered quite low by conventional wisdom. It was an export-led growth. The sharply devalued dollar resulted in the US merchandise trade deficit narrowing for the first time in eight years – to about $127 billion from a record $160 billion in 1987 (*Economic Report of the President*, 1994, p. 386).

The growing economy and the declining joblessness helped George Bush be elected President in November 1988. He ran for office as the guardian of the Reagan Revolution, albeit while promising to deal with some of its excesses. He wanted to make the United States a "kinder, gentler" society. However, he proposed few new initiatives of note. Perhaps most memorable was his pledge to the Republican national convention: "Read my lips, no new taxes."

While vowing to hold the line on taxes, he pledged to close the federal budget deficit by implementing a "flexible freeze", whereby total government spending would rise no more than the rate of inflation. Economic growth would generate additional tax revenues. With spending being limited, eventually the federal budget would be in balance. However, his pledge on taxes would return to haunt him and the economy would not grow rapidly enough to balance the budget.

In fact, during the Bush Presidency the economy remained in a period of protracted economic stagnation. Monetary policy contributed to the flat economy. By March 1988, the Federal Reserve determined that the economy had successfully survived the stock market crash. In their eyes, the problem was now the risk of inflation. Tight monetary policy was introduced to accomplish a "soft landing" – moderate growth with low inflation. Interest rates rose and the rate of economic growth slowed from 3.9 percent in 1988 to 2.5 percent in 1989. By the middle of 1990, the economy would go into recession.

The weakening economy negated Bush's strategy for balancing the budget. The federal budget deficit did not decline. Rather it widened from $169.3 billion in fiscal year 1987 to $206.1 billion in fiscal year 1989. By fiscal year 1990, the federal budget deficit would reach $277.0 billion, a sum equal to 5.1 percent of GNP (*Economic Report of the President*, 1991, p. 375). The federal budget deficit was now virtually as large relative to the GNP as it had been from fiscal year 1982 through fiscal year 1986. Thus, while balancing the budget was an often stated goal of the Reagan and Bush administrations, no apparent progress had been made toward reaching this goal.

In addition to a stagnating economy, the high cost of the savings and loan bailout was another factor behind the growing federal budget deficit during the early years of the Bush administration. Historically, banks known as savings and loans (S&Ls) provided the bulk of mortgage financing for home ownership. The mortgages were long term, often 15–30 years in length. With the rise in interest rates in the late 1970s and early 1980s, S&Ls found themselves in a difficult situation. They needed to pay high interest rates to attract deposits. And while they were able to issue new mortgages at even higher interest rates than they were paying to attract funds, their existing mortgage portfolios contained older mortgages with interest rates below the current cost of funds. Furthermore, the sharp recession of 1981–82 caused many people to default on their mortgages. The upshot was that many S&Ls were experiencing large losses and a growing number were insolvent. The number of insolvent S&Ls rose from 43 in 1980 to 415 in 1982 (Wolfson, 1994, p. 132). The Federal Savings and Loan Insurance Corporation (FSLIC), the government agency insuring deposits at S&Ls, saw its revenues decline rapidly as it closed and paid off depositors, or subsidized the merging of insolvent S&Ls.

After 1982, the federal government realized that the FSLIC, itself, would become insolvent if it continued closing or subsidizing the merging of every insolvent S&L. Thus, the number of operating though insolvent S&Ls rose to 705 by 1985 (Wolfson, 1994, p. 132). And the federal government deregulated S&Ls allowing them to place their funds in riskier ventures than home mortgages in the hope their returns would grow, enabling them to escape insolvency. Instead, as S&Ls diversified their loan portfolios, they ended up with a credit quality problem as the number of bad loans escalated.

This approach would only further increase the cost of the eventual S&L bailout. The FSLIC became insolvent in 1986. By 1989, the situation could no longer be ignored. On August 9, 1989, the S&L bailout bill – Financial Institutions Reform, Recovery and Enforcement Act – was passed by the US Congress. Fifty billion dollars were initially authorized for the task of closing bankrupt S&Ls and paying off their depositors. This amount was not enough and more money was eventually needed. The federal budget deficits continued to grow.

The federal budget deficit took center stage in the debate over economy policy and tested President Bush's resolve on his "no new taxes" pledge. He was forced to renege. On October 28, 1990, the 1990 Budget Agreement was passed by the US Congress. Characterized as the biggest deficit reduction package in history, it included spending cuts and tax increases, including a rise in personal income tax rates. This was particularly damaging to President Bush, given his earlier pledge on taxes.

Coming as they did when the economy was entering into recession, the tax increases and spending cuts contributed to the depth and length of the recession. The real Gross Domestic Product (GDP) declined by 0.7 percent in 1991. The federal budget deficit did not shrink. Rather, reflecting the continuing costs of the S&L bailout and the recession, the federal budget deficit was $321.7 billion in fiscal year 1991 and in fiscal year 1992 it was 340.5 billion. Over these two years, the federal budget deficits averaged 5.7 percent of the GDP, well above the levels of the Reagan years (*Economic Report of the President*, 1994, p. 359). (The government was now using the GDP to measure economic output instead of the GNP.)

The economic contraction ended by the latter part of 1992. Superficially, at least, the recession did not appear dramatically different from the average recession of the post Second World War period. And in contrast to the most recent recessions of 1981–82 and 1974–75, it appeared, on the surface at least, to be milder. The production of goods and services declined at a more rapid rate in the 1981–82 and 1974–75 recessions. And the rates of unemployment in 1991 and 1992 – 6.7 percent and 7.4 percent, respectively – were well below the average unemployment rates in the two earlier recessions.

But these facts notwithstanding, there was a distinct malaise characterizing the society. Allan Greenspan, not known to be a doomsayer, said in Congressional testimony in March 1992:

> There is a deep-seated concern out there which I must say to you I haven't seen in my lifetime. People can get past short-term hardships but if they think that they are not short-term but something fundamental to their future, then a deep-seated concern arises.

Combine a protracted recession and no signs of an improving economy with the legacy of the 1980s, as we will see, a decade of growing inequality and, at best, stagnating living standards for many, and it becomes easy to comprehend the malaise afflicting the US society.

UNPRECEDENTED BALANCE OF TRADE AND BALANCE OF PAYMENTS DEFICITS

Contributing to the concern of many workers were the trade problems facing many US corporations. Whole sectors of American industry seemed unable to match up to the foreign competition. Factories were closing, workers were being laid off. The United States appeared to be an economy in decline.

The US balance of trade first went into deficit in the 1970s. But what was, in retrospect, a trickle of red ink turned into a flow of red ink in the 1980s. The merchandise trade deficit steadily increased from $28 billion in 1981 to $160 billion in 1987, a magnitude equalling approximately 3.4 percent of GDP. This is in contrast to the late 1970s when the trade deficit averaged 1.3 percent of GNP. While the trade deficit did improve after 1987, it was still $96 billion in 1992, approximately 1.5 percent of GDP (*Economic Report of the President*, 1998, pp. 280, 398).

The persistent balance of trade deficits pointed to an ongoing relative decline in the international competitiveness of the US-based firms or US-based operations of American multinational corporations. This was occurring even though the US employers succeeded in lowering labor costs. During the 1980s, real hourly compensation of manufacturing workers dropped in the United States while rising in other advanced industrialized societies. While labor productivity, or output per person hour, in manufacturing increased more rapidly in Japan and such European countries as Germany, France, Italy and the United Kingdom than in the United States, overall unit labor costs still fell in the United States relative to those in other societies (Blecker, 1996; Buchele and Christiansen, 1999). Nevertheless, large balance of trade deficits remained.

Japan and many Western European countries were improving their utilization of capital and labor more rapidly than was occurring in the United States (Spero and Hart, 1997; Buchele and Christiansen, 1999). However, measures of productivity represent only one facet of business performance. They do not tell the entire story of international competitiveness. A 1989 study of the US industrial strength argued:

> In such areas as product quality, service to customers and speed of product development, American companies are no longer perceived as world leaders, even by American consumers. There is also evidence that technological innovations are being incorporated into practice more quickly abroad, and the pace of invention and discovery in the United States may be slowing. (Dertouzos *et al.*, 1989, p. 26)

Among the advanced industrial countries, the United States ran the largest trade deficits and had the most serious trade conflicts with Japan. The bilateral trade deficit with Japan equaled $10.5 billion in 1980. By 1987, it had risen to $56.9 billion. It then diminished slightly to $50.5 billion in 1992. The trade deficit with Japan did not seem particularly related to exchange rate fluctuations. Underlying the strong Japanese trade performance was a rapid rate of growth of investment in manufacturing and a well-functioning strategic industrial policy. During the 1980s, the manufacturing capital stock increased by more than 6 percent annually in Japan while in the United States it only grew by slightly more than 2 percent annually (Armstrong et al., 1991, p. 238). In addition, active Japanese government industrial policy promoted the development of strategic economic sectors. First, it was basic industry such as steel and then it was consumer durable industries such as automobiles. Once the Japanese became internationally competitive in these areas they then turned to high technology sectors such as capital goods, electronics products and computers. These long-term development policies bore fruit in the 1980s, a time when the Japanese share of world manufacturing exports rose from 11.1 percent in 1980 to 12.5 percent in 1988 while the US share of world manufacturing exports fell from 13.1 percent to 11.3 percent (Armstrong et al., 1991, p. 296). Complementing Japanese export prowess was a domestic market relatively closed to imports, particularly manufactured goods. It would be the goal of the US policymakers to open up the Japanese market to products made in the United States.

In addition to Japan, a group of newly industrializing countries in East Asia, including Taiwan, China, South Korea, Singapore and Hong Kong, ran large trade surpluses with the United States during the 1980s and early 1990s. In the newly industrializing countries, living standards were far below those in the United States. By importing relatively advanced technology, often from Japan, these countries were able to combine low wages and high productivity in modern industries and gain significant advantages in unit labor costs. Initially, they attained a large and growing world market share at the expense of the advanced industrialized societies, including the United States, in labor intensive products such as textiles, footwear and leather goods. Eventually, they were able to break into more technology intensive sectors such as electronics and computers. Overall, South Korea, Hong Kong, Taiwan and Singapore increased their share of world exports of manufactured goods from 5.4 percent in 1980 to 9.7 percent in 1988 (Armstrong et al., 1991, p. 296). They sold large amounts of consumer goods to the United States and Western Europe with whom they ran large trade surpluses while buying capital goods from Japan with whom they ran large trade deficits.

The trade situation led to calls for protectionism which the Reagan administration, initially, often opposed. Nevertheless, in 1981, in response to proposed legislation to limit Japanese imports the Reagan administration negotiated a voluntary restraint agreement with Japan restricting the number of Japanese cars imported annually into the United States to 1.8 million. In 1982, an agreement was reached with the European Community limiting steel exports to the United States. Two years later, voluntary export restraints were negotiated with additional steel exporting countries. Trade in textiles was regulated by the Third Multifiber Arrangement during Reagan's first term. In 1984, it was estimated that about one-third of American manufactured goods were covered by voluntary quotas and other restrictions (Kunz, 1997, p. 311).

These trade arrangements aside the US trade deficit continued to grow. As a result, between 1984 and 1988, the United States shifted more toward a policy of "fair trade" rather than "free trade." On September 23, 1985 President Reagan, in restating the US commitment to free trade said, "if trade is not fair for all, then trade is 'free' in name only" (*Economic Report of the President*, 1986, p. 105). In 1988, after three years of work, the US Congress passed the Omnibus Trade and Competitiveness Act (OTCA). Aimed mainly at Japan, although not in name, it required the US trade representative to identify countries discriminating against the US producers of goods and services, specify the nature of the discrimination and begin negotiations to seek removal of these practices. If these discussions failed, the President had the right, but not the obligation, to impose trade sanctions which would limit access to the US market. In addition, trade relief would be made available to industries hurt by foreign competition, provided these industries were willing to take steps to improve their international competitiveness. Retraining money would also be provided for workers displaced by imports. Given the increased presence of foreign multinationals in the United States, the President was given the authority to block foreign acquisitions of US firms that threatened national security. Lobbyists for foreign countries spent more than $100 million in trying to defeat the bill. Many countries criticized the legislation as protectionist and objected to the United States being able to unilaterally determine what was fair in trade matters. Yet, what was considered to be protectionist by the US trading partners was considered the beginning of a policy of "fair trade" by US policymakers (Kaplan, 1996).

Not surprisingly, Japan was one of the first countries named an "unfair trader" under OTCA. In May 1989, Carla Hills, the US Trade Representative, threatened to impose duties of 100 percent on some Japanese goods in retaliation for Japan's unwillingness to open its telecommunications market. An agreement was eventually reached and, on April 27, 1990, Japan was taken off the list of countries subject to economic reprisals as a result of "unfair" trade practices.

There would continue to be strong resentment in the United States against Japanese trade practices. However, calls for protectionism were necessarily tempered by the fact that the Japanese were buying significant amounts of US government bonds funding the large federal budget deficits and Japanese corporations were investing heavily in the United States. If the Japanese ceased their purchases of government bonds and were not replaced by other bond buyers, or sold their bonds en masse, interest rates would sharply rise, thereby slowing the US economy. In addition, state and local officials wishing to attract Japanese firms to their locality would often think twice before bashing Japan.

Foreign direct investment in the United States by Japanese as well as Western European business was a relatively new phenomenon. Prior to the 1980s, there was little activity of this sort. In 1980, the United States had about $83 billion in foreign direct investment. By 1992, this had grown to $420 billion. In 1970, the stock of direct foreign investment in the United States was only about 20 percent of the US direct investment abroad. By 1992, this figure was about 86 percent. And in the late 1980s, the flow of direct foreign investment into the United States exceeded the outflow for the first time in US history (Spero and Hart, 1997, p. 107). European and Japanese corporations had become more internationally competitive and were seeking to locate in the United States to make further inroads into the huge US market. Furthermore, producing in the United States guaranteed access to the American market in the event of more stringent protectionist policy.

"CONCESSION BARGAINING"

By the end of the 1970s, employers had become more confrontational in collective bargaining. The increased competition, both foreign and domestic, felt more strongly during the serious recession of the early 1980s, together with the rising union–nonunion wage premium provided the economic incentives for employers to demand concessions from their workers. The macroeconomic, industrial relations, employment and social policies of the government served to weaken union and nonunion workers alike. A labor movement on the defensive together with the general excess supply of labor increased the opportunities for employers to gain their demands. In an era of increasing competition and pressure on profits, employers wished to lower wage and benefit costs, change work rules and gain flexibility in scheduling daily and weekly working hours. In addition, they also wanted workers to bear more of the burden of economic uncertainty.

A central feature of collective bargaining prior to the 1980s had been the Annual Improvement Factor and Cost of Living Adjustment (COLA) clauses, initially negotiated between General Motors (GM) and the United Auto Workers (UAW) in 1948. During the 1980s, however, both of these clauses diminished in importance as wage increases slowed, patterns were eroded and agreements became more company and plant specific. In essence, companies were questioning previous understandings made with their unionized workforces.

The Chrysler settlement of 1979 set the stage for the concession bargaining of the 1980s. While it was not unknown, it had been highly unlikely for unionized workers to accept labor contracts freezing or cutting wages. But during the first half of the 1980s, unprecedented numbers of union members received modest wage increases or experienced no increases or even wage reductions. Between one-third and one-half of the workers covered by major collective bargaining agreements experienced a wage cut or wage freeze (Mitchell, 1985, p. 577).

Initially in 1981–82, the wage and benefit concession began in a narrow range of companies facing severe economic difficulties. These companies were located in such industries as metals, motor vehicles, machinery, meatpacking, airlines, printing and publishing, health care, lumber, ordnance and retail food stores. But by 1984–85, the situation had changed. Concessions were now being granted in virtually every industry with a unionized labor force. Even profitable firms were getting on the bandwagon and pressing their workers for givebacks (Winter, 1984; Mitchell, 1985; Moody, 1988).

Not only were wage settlements low, previous wage bargaining patterns were eroded. Unions wanted to take wages out of competition by pursuing pattern bargaining. However, in the first half of the 1980s, many employers sought to break out of existing patterns so that wage settlements were more firm-specific. This would enable them to take advantage of any specific wage concessions they might be able to negotiate. Patterns eroded in such industries as tires, trucking, meatpacking, airlines and autos, among others. Multiemployer bargaining ended in some industries, for example in steel. And in other instances, for example, trucking, some companies withdrew from multi-firm agreements (Capelli, 1990; Katz, 1993; Slaughter, 1983).

As part of the trend toward more company-specific agreements, COLA clauses were eliminated from many contracts. In 1977, 61.2 percent of the workers under major contract agreements had COLA clauses in their contracts, whereas by 1987 only 40.4 percent had them (Borum et al., 1988). This percentage would continue falling reaching a level of approximately 20 percent in 1992 (Sleemi and Brown, 1993).

In addition to seeking to change compensation levels and compensation practices, many employers aggressively sought work rule changes. Their concern with work rule concessions was unprecedented in the post-Great Depression period. Management was looking for increased flexibility so as to lower costs of production. This took the form of attempting to gain "broader job classifications, more managerial discretion in the allocation of overtime, more liberal subcontracting rights, and restrictions on voluntary transfers or other movements across jobs" (Kochan et al., 1986, p. 118). While it is very difficult to generalize as to the extent to which work rules have in fact changed, according to 1983 Conference Board survey data, 63 percent of the surveyed firms said they had received work rule concessions in recent bargaining (Kochan et al., 1986, p. 118).

While bargaining over wages and working conditions can lead to a lower cost structure, company working time policy can have the same effect. Many employers responded to the more difficult economic environment by lengthening weekly or annual working time without necessarily increasing pay accordingly, pushing for more flexibility in scheduling work and replacing full-time, full-year, long-term workers by part-time, part-year, contingent workers.

In the 1960s and 1970s, there were many instances of unions successfully negotiating for working time reductions, without any loss in pay on a weekly or annual basis. But during the severe recession of the early 1980s and in the years that followed, many of the unions which had earlier emphasized the shortening of working time as a means of job creation granted concessions in the area of paid time off.

Ironically, unions justified the lessening of paid time off by arguing that it would preserve jobs by lowering production costs. In 1982, the UAW agreed to give up paid personal holidays for workers in the auto industry. These holidays were the equivalent of approximately two weeks of paid time off annually. In 1983, in negotiations with major steel producers, the United Steel Workers of America (USWA) was forced to give up the extended vacation plan, vacation bonuses and one paid holiday. Paid holidays and paid vacation time were also reduced in the rubber industry, agricultural implements industry and retail food stores. In 1982, the Teamsters union agreed to change the national trucking agreement so that drivers were paid for time spent actually driving rather than for a specified number of hours per trip. Similar changes occurred in airlines. Airline pilots provided airlines with a variety of working time concessions increasing the proportion of flight time to paid hours (Rosenberg, 1991).

In addition to the length of working time, the daily and weekly scheduling of working time was also in dispute. For management the issue was scheduling flexibility. For workers, the result was at times a decline in overtime pay and/or the elimination of premium pay for Saturday and Sunday work, and more inconvenient work schedules. This occurred in such industries as tire, aluminum, retail food stores, steel, trucking and textiles (Rosenberg, 1991, 1993).

Not only did employers push for longer and more flexible hours from their full-time workers, they also tried to create a "just-in-time" cheaper workforce. Some unionized full-time, long-term workers found themselves being replaced by nonunion, contingent employees having only a short-term relationship with the firm. A Bureau of National Affairs survey of more than 400 firms reported a marked increase in the period 1980 to 1985 in the number of enterprises making use of agency temporaries, short-term hires, on-call workers, administrative/business support contracts and production subcontracting (Abraham, 1990, p. 92). US Bureau of Labor Statistics survey data on contracting out behavior of manufacturing firms showed that between 1979 and 1986 firms reported an increasing propensity to contract out at least some janitorial work, machine maintenance work, engineering and drafting work, accounting services work and computer service work (Abraham and Taylor, 1996).

Throughout the economy the issue was temporary work. Temporary jobs were growing more rapidly than overall employment. Employment in the temporary help supply industry grew from

0.5 percent of total employment in 1982 to 1.0 percent of total employment in 1992. And these figures do not include temporary workers hired directly by the company they work for (Rosenberg and Lapidus, 1999). Employment growth in the temporary help supply industry was directly related to the decreasing ability of unions to block the increasing usage of temporary workers (Golden and Appelbaum, 1992).

Even as the economy strengthened in the second half of the 1980s, with the unemployment rate falling from 9.6 percent in 1983 to 5.3 percent in 1989, the labor movement remained on the defensive. Work rules continued to be the major battleground in US labor disputes. Harley Shaiken, then a labor specialist at the University of California, San Diego, in commenting on the labor disputes occurring in 1986 argued "every major strike or labor dispute today has work rules at its core" (Kotlowitz, 1986, p. 1). The work rules concessions that were granted at the plant and local levels further undermined pattern bargaining and the trade union principle of common work standards for workers performing similar tasks. In fact, employers increasingly used the threat and actuality of plant closings to have plants compete with each other to see which ones would offer the best deals on work rules to the company. GM was a leader in the use of this strategy. By 1987, 12 of GM's 22 assembly plants had "competitive" agreements, in most cases because the local union agreed to reopen local contracts before the September 1987 expiration of the national agreement with the UAW (Moody, 1988, p. 184).

Normally, during a time of economic growth and declining unemployment, unions would be expected to be able to negotiate substantial improvements in pay. Yet, that did not occur. While the extent of wage cuts and wage freezes did decline in the second half of the 1980s (Mitchell, 1994) between 1983 and 1989, annual wage changes in major collective bargaining agreements only ranged between 2.3 and 4.0 percent (Mitchell, 1994; Sleemi and Brown, 1993; Vroman and Abowd, 1988). Furthermore, wages rose more slowly in union bargaining situations than elsewhere in the private sector. Thus, the union–nonunion pay differential narrowed in the 1980s (Vroman and Abowd, 1988).

Unlike during the 1970s, high levels of unemployment seemed to dampen compensation growth (Tsuru, 1991; Buchele and Christiansen, 1993). However, declining rates of unemployment did not lead to much improved wage settlements. The employer offensive of the 1980s, which produced unprecedented wage and work rule concessions, pointed to a fundamental shift occurring in the system of industrial relations. The bargaining power of labor was significantly weakened and the norms governing labor–management relations in the post Second World War era were undergoing fundamental changes.

A RAPID TRADE UNION DECLINE

The spread of concession bargaining from companies in financial distress to highly profitable enterprises was facilitated by a deterioration in the bargaining strength of organized labor. One manifestation of a weaker labor movement was that labor was much less able to use the strike to further its goals. There was a sharp decline in the number of major strikes – those involving 1000 or more workers – in the 1980s. (During the Reagan administration, the federal government ceased collecting data on total strikes.) In 1980, there were 187 major work stoppages. Since 1947, there was only one year, 1963, when there had been fewer major work stoppages. By 1990, however, the number of major work stoppages had fallen even further to 44 (US Department of Labor, Bureau of Labor Statistics, 1983, p. 379; Jacobs (ed.), 1997, p. 287).

Furthermore, many employers heeded the message sent by President Reagan in the air traffic controllers dispute. They, too, permanently replaced their striking employees. They included Phelps Dodge, Greyhound, Continental Airlines, the International Paper Company, Boise-Cascade, and the Tribune Company, owner of the Chicago Tribune. Many other employers, including the Pittston Coal Company, threatened to replace workers on strike but ended up dismissing the replacements upon settling the strike. While there are no annual data on striker replacement, a US General Accounting Office study found a growing willingness of employers to hire permanent replacements for striking workers (Kilborn, 1991). The shift in employer strategy had a chilling effect on workers' willingness to strike.

Declining union density was a further sign of the weakening bargaining power of organized labor. A fall in union density may not be synonymous with a decline in the ability of unions to achieve their goals. For example, during the late 1960s, the share of private sector workers in unions was falling while unions were quite successful at the bargaining table. However, this was not the case in the 1980s. In 1980, 23.2 percent of the work force was unionized. By 1989, that figure had dropped to just 16 percent, and in the private sector only 12 percent of the work force was organized. Union coverage continued to shrink in traditional union strongholds such as manufacturing, mining, construction and transportation (Freeman, 1988). The 1980s represented a period of the deunionization of the American labor force.

Aggressive anti-union management behavior lies behind the shrinking perimeter of unionism. As evidence of the growing opposition of employers to unions, a Conference Board Survey found that 45 percent of firms in their Personnel Practices Forum gave "operating union free" as a labor policy goal in 1983 compared to 31 percent in 1977 (Freeman, 1988, p. 79). Employers continued their tactics of delaying for as long as possible the holding of a representation election, while trying to convince workers to vote against union representation. The share of representation elections which were consent elections continued to steadily decrease so that by 1991 they represented only 1.0 percent of representation elections. This is in contrast to 1962, as was shown earlier, when they constituted 46 percent of all elections. Stipulated elections increased to more than 80 percent of all elections during the 1980s, while in 1962 they accounted for just one-fourth of all elections. The union victory rate steadily declined the longer the delay in holding a representation election (Friedman and Prosten, 1993).

While employers had ample opportunity to resist unionization in legal ways, for some this was not enough. Their chosen strategies included activities determined to be illegal. In the mid-1950s, the NLRB annually directed the reinstatement of roughly 1000 workers illegally fired for supporting a union. By the mid-1980s, approximately 10 000 workers were being reinstated annually by the NLRB, due to being fired illegally. This result is even more noteworthy since there were many fewer representation elections in the 1980s than in the 1950s and even fewer people who had supported unions in representation campaigns. By the late 1980s, unlawful employee terminations occurred in one of every three representation elections (Craver, 1993, p. 49). Of further significance was the fact that the reinstatements during the 1980s were being ordered by an NLRB appointed by President Reagan, notorious for its overall anti-union perspective.

Unions fared poorly in representation elections in the 1980s, so poorly that very few workers were organized via this process. Fewer workers participated in such elections. The percentage of private nonagricultural workers covered by such elections dropped from

0.5 percent in 1980 to less than 0.3 percent in 1989. And new workers won to unions via representation elections dropped from an already low 0.2 percent in 1980 to around 0.1 percent in the years following in the 1980s (Edwards, 1993, pp. 87–88). During the 1980s, unions won fewer than one new member for every thousand workers employed in the private sector.

THE BLOW TO EQUAL EMPLOYMENT OPPORTUNITY AND AFFIRMATIVE ACTION

In its macroeconomic, industrial relations, employment and social policies, the Reagan administration pushed for a return to the "free market." In such a "free market," there is no room for equal employment opportunity and affirmative action policies. And, in any event, they believed that racial and gender discrimination was no longer prevalent.

The administration attempted to eviscerate the EEOC and to eliminate governmental enforcement of affirmative action. The EEOC had been underfunded in the past and was facing a backlog of cases. Nevertheless, the administration sharply cut its budget, forcing a reduction in staff at the agency. While the administration tried to seriously weaken the EEOC, it wished to eliminate affirmative action altogether. However, it was not successful. Not surprisingly, adjusting for inflation, expenditures declined for the OFCCP. In August 1985, the administration called for revoking the use of goals and timetables and any other rules that "discriminate against or grant any preferences to any individual or group" in recruitment, hiring, promotion, transfers and pay (quoted in Power, 1989, p. 201).

However, these proposals did not become official policy. Civil rights groups made their opposition known. But these groups, alone, would not have been politically powerful enough to block the proposals. Somewhat unexpectedly, medium- and large-scale companies opposed ending federally established goals and timetables. Both the National Association of Manufacturers and the Business Roundtable wanted them to remain. On the other hand, small businesses represented by the US Chamber of Commerce and the Associated General Contractors of America backed the administration's efforts to end affirmative action. The larger firms had adapted their personnel policies to the affirmative action mandates. Had they supported the administration, they would have faced strong resentment from their female and nonwhite male employees.

While the administration never officially changed the affirmative action guidelines, the legal system turned out to be its primary venue for attacking affirmative action. The US Department of Justice's Civil Rights Division files suits for the federal government in discrimination cases. William Bradford Reynolds, the head of the Civil Rights Division, was strongly opposed to affirmative action, characterizing it as a "racial spoils system" that violated basic American concepts of fair play (quoted in Schiller, 1995, p. 284). Under Reynolds, the federal government often entered court cases on the side of white males charging reverse discrimination. The government filed a brief in Williams v. City of New Orleans, a private suit against the New Orleans police department, arguing that racial goals and quotas were illegal. They followed this brief with one in Firefighters Local No. 1784 v. Stotts (1984), a case involving a court order requiring the Memphis city government to lay off more senior whites while retaining African Americans with less seniority. The federal government urged the court to override the earlier decision, thereby allowing the local government to abide by the existing last-in-first-out provision of the collective bargaining agreement.

The US Supreme Court supported the federal government's position. After this case was adjudicated, the US Department of Justice then announced that race-conscious affirmative action policies were dead. It began a process to reverse existing consent decrees with many public employers in order to eliminate their goals and timetables. And the government continued arguing against race-conscious relief in Title VII cases and voluntary affirmative action plans with racial or gender goals.

With the Reagan administration's judicial appointments came a series of US Supreme Court decisions in 1989 which changed the rules, at least temporarily, regarding affirmative action. White male employees alleging reverse discrimination could force a reopening of court-approved consent decrees favoring African–Americans in promotion (Martin v. Wilks, 1989). Women and minorities would find it more difficult to win discrimination cases. Previously, they could rely on statistics demonstrating disparities in the number and nature of jobs held by white men and those held by women and minorities. Now, such data would not be sufficient. They would need to prove that companies have consciously chosen to discriminate. And they would need to demonstrate that the employer has no business reason for utilizing the particular personnel practices in dispute (Wards Cove v. Atonio, 1989). It would now be easier for companies to show that their refusal to promote a woman or an African–American was based on a legitimate business reason (Price Waterhouse v. Hopkins, 1989). And there would now be fewer laws which could be used to support a charge of racial discrimination. Minorities would no longer be able to use an 1866 civil rights law to seek damages for racial harassment or other discrimination by an employer after a person is hired. Now plaintiffs would only be able to use Title VII of the Civil Rights Act of 1964. They would not be able to collect monetary damages under Title VII (Patterson v. McLean Credit Union, 1989).

These US Supreme Court rulings all came within a span of six weeks. They signified that women and minorities alleging discrimination would now have a tougher time in court. Those dissatisfied with these decisions would now pressure the US Congress to pass a law to effectively overturn them.

COUNTERING US SUPREME COURT DECISIONS ON CIVIL RIGHTS

In his 1990 State of the Union address, President Bush issued a call to "condemn racism, anti-semitism, bigotry and hate." Civil rights groups along with Democrats and liberal and moderate Republicans in the US Congress challenged President Bush to back up his words with deeds. Shortly after his address, the legislators introduced a bill aimed at overturning the effects of the US Supreme Court decisions which made job bias more difficult to prove and limited the remedies available to those experiencing discrimination.

A lengthy debate ensued. In October, President Bush vetoed a civil rights bill on the grounds that it would force employers to utilize quotas in hiring and promotion. Eleanor Holmes Norton, who headed the EEOC under President Carter, argued that the Bush administration "raised and shamelessly exploited the racially polarizing issue of quotas .... The quota issue poisons the racial atmosphere already polluted by the mutual suspicion that is the legacy of the 1980s" (Norton, 1991, p. A17). The US Senate failed by one vote to override the President's veto.

Even though the bill was vetoed, there was still strong pressure for new civil rights legislation. Eventually, the Bush administration changed their position and in late 1991 the Civil Rights Act of 1991 became law. The bill restored rights that were available to victims of racial discrimination as recently as 1989. Employers would now have to prove there was a business necessity for the personnel practices in question, thus negating the decision in the Wards Cove case. The law made it more difficult for employers to demonstrate there was a legitimate motive for discriminating, thus raising the Price Waterhouse-required burden of proof. Court approved consent decrees could no longer be reopened by white men alleging reverse discrimination, thereby negating the ruling in the Martin case. An 1866 civil rights law was deemed applicable to cases alleging racial and other forms of discrimination by an employer after a person is hired, thus overturning the ruling in the Patterson case.

Furthermore, women gained a new right. They would now be able to sue for punitive damages, in addition to compensatory damages, where they could prove intentional sex-based employment discrimination. Previously, punitive damages were only potentially available for those alleging intentional racial discrimination.

The Civil Rights Act of 1991 would not end the societal debate on equal employment opportunity and affirmative action. Rather, the law would now need to be interpreted by the legal system.

A NARROWING BUT STILL PERSISTENT GENDER GAP, A WIDENING RACIAL GAP

The weakened federal commitment to enforcing equal employment opportunity certainly hurt women. Nevertheless, women continued to make gains in the labor market. The growing political power of the women's movement influenced employers to act in a less discriminatory fashion. And by the 1980s, the movement of women into professional and managerial positions may have taken on a momentum of its own.

Women continued to enter the labor market. Their labor force participation rate rose from 51.5 percent in 1980 to 57.8 percent in 1992 (*Economic Report of the President*, 1997, p. 343). But they were still concentrated in administrative support, including clerical, and service jobs. In 1992, 27.5 percent of women workers were holding administrative support positions and 16.3 percent were doing non-household service work. It was still rare to find women in the skilled trades – precision production, craft and repair jobs. Only 2.1 percent of women were doing this work (*Employment and Earnings*, January 1993, p. 194).

Nevertheless, women continued making inroads into male occupations. But the rate of decline in gender-based occupational segregation slowed during the 1980s (Spain and Bianchi, 1996; King, 1992). As in the previous decade, the decrease in occupational segregation occurred mainly in professional and managerial positions. Still, women were quite likely to be managing other women. Women managers were found in fields with proportionately large numbers of women employed below the managerial level. Health care and education are two cases in point. In 1992, women held 65.8 percent of all managerial positions in health care and they accounted for over half of all managers in the education field (US Bureau of the Census, *Statistical Abstract of the United States*, 1993, p. 405).

Not only did women make some further, though limited, progress in entering male dominated occupations during the 1980s, the gender-based earnings differential narrowed as well. Unlike in previous decades, the ratio of the median weekly earnings of full-time women workers to those of full-time men workers was higher in 1992 than in 1983 within many broad occupational groupings. In 1992, the weekly earnings of women who were professional workers were about 76 percent of those of men. Women managers earned 66 percent as much as male managers. For those in craft positions, the ratio was 67 percent. In occupations traditionally dominated by women, such as administrative support jobs, they made about 80 percent of the earnings of men (US Department of Labor, Report 872, 1994). Overall, among full-time, year-round workers, the median annual income of women was 71 percent that of men in 1992, up from 60 percent in 1980. This is particularly noteworthy since the ratio of women's to men's earnings among full-time, year-round workers had hovered around 60 percent throughout the 1960s and 1970s (Spain and Bianchi, 1996, p. 111).

Women also made relative gains on the jobless front. Until the early 1980s, women were more likely to be unemployed than men. But during the 1980s, that situation reversed itself. In 1992, the unemployment rate of women was 7.0 percent while for men it was 7.9 percent. There was substantial job growth in industries more likely to employ women while industries that tended to hire men experienced declines in employment.

Undoubtedly, there was progress. However, considerable gender inequality remained. Gender segregation among occupations was by no means a thing of the past. Between 55 and 60 percent of women (or men) would have had to change jobs in 1990 for the occupational distribution of men and women to be the same (King, 1992, p. 33; Spain and Bianchi, 1996, p. 94). That it is taken as a sign of progress when full-time, year-round working women earn 71 percent as much as their male counterparts is a stark indication of how much further women needed to go to reach equality with men.

The Reagan and Bush administrations created an overall political and economic climate that was not favorable to African–Americans. Federal governmental enforcement of affirmative action virtually ceased. The social spending cuts during the Reagan era were popular because they appeared to be (and were) hurting minorities more than whites. Being more likely to hold low-wage jobs, the falling real value of the minimum wage hurt African–Americans more than whites. The anti-union message of the federal government and the accompanying deunionization made it more difficult to retain the gains made by African–Americans who were able to get higher paying union jobs in the 1960s and 1970s. The economic situation of blacks relative to whites deteriorated. The policies of the federal government, while not the only causal factors, certainly contributed to the more difficult economic environment faced by African–Americans.

Between 1983 and 1992, African–American men increased their share of the employed male labor force. They were 9.2 percent of employed men in 1992, in contrast to 8.4 percent in 1983. Nevertheless, they made minimal job gains relative to white men during the 1980s. The extent of occupational differentiation by race among men decreased at a much slower rate than during the 1970s (King, 1992). As in the previous decade, African–Americans increased their relative presence in professional and managerial positions. However, they were still substantially underrepresented in these occupations. African–American men were 5.3 percent of all male professional workers in 1992, in contrast to 4.5 percent in 1983. They were 4.8 percent of all male executives in 1992, as compared with 3.8 percent in 1983. And their share of male craft positions rose from 6.8 percent in 1983 to 7.2 percent in 1992 (US Department of Labor, 1988, pp. 665, 666; *Employment and Earnings*, 1993, p. 194).

Black male unemployment rates increased relative to white males throughout much of the 1980s. From 1984 to 1989, African–American men were 2.5 times more likely to experience unemployment than white men. By 1992, however, the black–white unemployment rate gap returned to its more typical relationship. In that year, African–American men were somewhat more than twice as likely to be out of work than white men. Their labor force participation rates remained low. The labor force participation rate of African–American men was 70.7 percent in 1992, in contrast to 76.5 percent for white men (*Economic Report of the President*, 1997, pp. 344–345).

Continuing the trend seen in the 1970s, the black male annual income did not rise relative to the white male annual income. In 1980, the black male to white male median income ratio was 60 percent. In 1992, it was 61 percent (US Bureau of the Census, Census Population Reports, Series P60-206, 1999, p. B-12). Thus, African–American men entered the 1980s at a disadvantage relative to white men. And the lack of progress for many during the 1980s made the situation seem ever more permanent.

What about African–American women? They increased their share of the employed female labor force. In 1992, African–American women were 11.3 percent of employed women, as compared to 10.5 percent in 1983. However, in striking contrast to the 1960s and 1970s, there was minimal further reduction in the overall level of racial segregation among women workers (King, 1992). African–American women were still underrepresented in professional and managerial jobs. They were 8.7 percent of women professional workers in 1992, slightly more than their 8.4 percent share in 1983. They increased their relative presence among women executives from 6.5 percent in 1983 to 7.1 percent in 1992. They continued moving into clerical jobs. They were 10.6 percent of women holding administrative support positions, up from 9.0 percent in 1983. And although still disproportionately concentrated in low-paid private household work, they moved out of these positions at a fast rate. African–American women were 18.4 percent of female private household workers in 1992 (US Department of Labor, Bureau of Labor Statistics, 1988, Bulletin 2307, pp. 665–666; *Employment and Earnings*, January 1993, p. 194).

Both African–American women and white women increased their presence in the labor force. The labor force participation rate of white women rose from 51.2 percent in 1980 to 57.7 percent in 1992 and for African–American women from 53.1 percent to 58.5 percent. Though equally likely to be in the labor force, African–American women were more likely to be jobless. Furthermore, as with men, the racial unemployment differential widened during the 1980s. From 1983–90, the female racial unemployment differential fluctuated between 2.3 and 2.5, meaning that African–American women were much more than twice as likely to be out of work than white women. By 1992, the female racial unemployment differential fell. At that time, African–American women were somewhat more than twice as likely to be unemployed as white women (*Economic Report of the President*, 1997, pp. 344–345).

While the racial unemployment gap widened among women, that was only one sign of the more difficult conditions facing many African–American women. More striking was the sharp, unprecedented, decline in the average annual income of African–American women relative to white women. In 1980, the black to white female median annual income ratio was 93 percent. By 1992, it had fallen to 81 percent (US Bureau of the Census, Current Population Reports, Series P60-206, 1999, p. B-13).

The widening racial income gap was not due mainly to changing labor market conditions. The racial unemployment gap did not widen sufficiently to cause such a sharp relative fall in annual income. And of those who worked year-round full-time in 1992, African–American women earned 91 percent as much as their white counterparts, just slightly below the 93 percent figure of 1980 (US Bureau of the Census, *Statistical Abstract of the United States*, 1996, p. 469).

Rather it was the result of cutbacks in government transfer payment programs such as AFDC. African–American women were more likely to be single mothers living in poverty. Thus, they were more likely to be receiving AFDC and more vulnerable to reductions in benefits. In 1992, 54.5 percent of African–American families with children under the age of 18 were headed by a single mother in contrast to 16.5 percent of white families. In addition, in 1992, 57.4 percent of African–American single mothers were living in poverty as compared with 39.6 percent of white single mothers (Dalaker, 1999, pp. B-12, 14, 15). The decline in the median annual income of African–American women relative to white women began in the first half of the 1980s, the same time as the first round of retrenchment in government transfer payment programs, such as AFDC, providing income to the poor.

At the close of the decade of the 1980s just as at the beginning of the decade, African–Americans were concentrated among the working poor. Looking as those individuals with year-round, full-time attachment to the labor force, 27.7 percent of African–American men in contrast to 17.3 percent of white men and 34.8 percent of African–American women as compared to 29.9 percent of white women had low earnings. The racial differentials did narrow during the 1980s. However, this represented a spurious form of relative progress for African–Americans. Overall, 31.0 percent of African–Americans were earning low wages, slightly higher than in 1979. Reflecting the overall decline in real wages in the 1980s, the share of whites earning low wages jumped sharply. The overall percentage of whites with low earnings was 22.1 percent in 1989, in contrast to 17.8 percent in 1979 (US Bureau of the Census, Current Population Reports, Series P60-178, 1992, pp. 22–23).

CONCLUSION

Stagflation was the legacy of the 1970s. The Reagan administration blamed the country's economic problems on misguided federal governmental policy. Nothing short of a total reorientation of government policy was called for. The government would no longer have the main responsibility for maintaining employment and economic security. Rather, government policy should be designed to free up market forces, to provide a stable environment in which private individuals can confidently plan and make appropriate decisions. And the assumption was that a deregulatory approach to domestic government policy would improve the overall productive efficiency of the economy.

In revamping government policy, the Reagan administration was interested in fostering ongoing changes occurring within the private sector. The aim of corporate restructuring was to raise the average rate of profit throughout the economy. And the restructuring was to take place on terns set, to a large degree, by employers. Government macroeconomic, employment and social policy was designed to "knock the props" out from under workers, serving to weaken the bargaining power of union and nonunion workers alike. The real value of the minimum wage declined. There were cutbacks in UI, TAA and AFDC. Federal industrial relations policy took on a more pro-employer bent. And, as part of the fight against inflation, unemployment rates rose to their highest levels in the post Second World War period. Real hourly wages fell for the bottom 60 percent of employees over the 1979–89 time period (Mishel et al., 1997, p. 143).

Supply-side economics, together with the employer offensive, did not seem to lead to a more well-functioning, efficient economy. The rate of economic growth did not accelerate in the 1980s. Comparing business cycle peaks shows that from 1979 to 1989, the US economy grew at an annual rate of approximately 2.5 percent, the same as from 1973 to 1979. While the after-tax corporate profit rate did rise, an investment boom did not materialize. The rate of capital accumulation was slower in the 1980s than in the period after 1973. However, labor productivity did increase slightly faster in the period 1979–89 than from 1973–79, though at a much slower rate than in earlier years in the post Second World War period.

What the conservative economic agenda did lead to was growing income inequality, reversing the trend toward less income inequality over the postwar period into the 1970s. The rich became richer, the poor became poorer and many in the middle were forced to work longer and harder, just to pay their bills and maintain their standard of living. Between 1979 and 1989, the top 20 percent of families with the highest incomes saw their income share rise from 41.7 percent to 44.6 percent of total income generated in the economy. The 20 percent of families with the lowest income saw their income share fall from 5.2 percent in 1979 to 4.6 percent in 1989. The share of income gained by families in the middle 60 percent of the income distribution dropped as well (Mishel et al., 1997, p. 53).

Not only did the distribution of income become more unequal, the 20 percent of families with the lowest incomes actually lost ground in the 1980s. Real family income of those in the lowest fifth of the income distribution fell by 0.4 percent annually. Families in the middle of the income distribution experienced very modest gains in real income. Only the wealthy saw significant improvements in their living standards. The wealthiest 5 percent of families saw their real incomes rise by 2.3 percent annually, a more rapid rate of improvement than the 1.7 percent annual real income growth experienced by families in the top fifth of the income distribution.

Federal governmental tax and transfer payment policies exacerbated the trend toward growing inequality. Between 1980 and 1990, the share of federal governmental transfer payments received by those with low incomes declined while the share received by those with high incomes rose. Federal taxes also became less progressive over the decade. About 40 percent of the increase in inequality can be attributed to changes in federal governmental tax and transfer payment programs with the rest being the result of increasing inequality of market income (Gramlich *et al.*, 1993).

The 1980s was a decade of growing inequality and, at best, stagnating living standards for many. This legacy, along with the recession which followed under the Bush administration, made many Americans angry. They would want a relief from the Republican-led, business-dominated restructuring of the economy.

12. Toward the Twenty-first Century: A Reinvigorated Economy, 1993–2000

In his 1992 run for the Presidency, William Clinton stated that the critical issue of his campaign was the economy. Rather than leading to strong economic growth benefiting the entire population, the policies of the Reagan and Bush administrations contributed to rising inequality amidst economic stagnation. What was needed was a new economic program, one which "put people first," one which "put America back to work" (Clinton, 1992). He emphasized economic growth, a quite conventional goal, to occur by fostering free enterprise and free trade, quite conventional means to achieving growth. Nevertheless, in contrast to the Republican push for a more laissez-faire economy, the Clinton program allowed for a more activist government that would spur the economy. Furthermore, if elected, Clinton would force the wealthy to pay their fair share of taxes, thereby reversing some of the excesses of the Reagan years. The middle class would receive tax breaks, and tax credits would provide the poor with stronger incentives to work.

While claiming, if elected, there would be a break with the past, soon after taking office it quickly became apparent that the Reagan–Bush legacy would strongly influence the policy debate, the Clinton policy program and the nature of the economic recovery. The Clinton administration did initially emphasize investment – investment in people, investment in public infrastructure and investment in technology. The assumption was that additional expenditures in these areas would improve the overall productive efficiency of the US economy, thereby raising living standards. However, federal budget deficit reduction

279

quickly became the primary focus of the Clinton administration's overall economic strategy, and public investment was "crowded off" the policy agenda.

Not only was the macroeconomic policy strongly influenced by the results of Reaganomics, social policy and labor policy, as well were linked to Reaganism. The Reagan attack on Aid to Families with Dependent Children (AFDC) was carried to its conclusion. Vowing to end "welfare as we know it," the Clinton administration did not undertake a "war on poverty" but rather a "war on welfare." The right to AFDC would no longer be guaranteed. The Clinton administration was more favorably disposed to the labor movement. However, Clinton was the least pro-union Democratic President in the post Second World War period, perhaps reflecting the decline in the economic and political strength of labor, a legacy of the Reagan–Bush era.

Believing that the US market was more open than those of other countries, the Clinton administration pushed free trade, a policy anathema to the labor movement. If trade liberalization were to occur and exports were to rise, the living standards of American families would improve.

Having emerged from recession in 1991, the economy continued to expand. By 1999, the rate of unemployment had fallen to its lowest level in 30 years and inflation was negligible. Real wages were on the rise and labor productivity was improving. The federal budget was generating a surplus. Consumer and business confidence was up. The US economy appeared strong in the face of world financial tremors, a crisis hurting some of the other advanced industrial economies. The US worldwide political economic dominance was continuing to strengthen.

These developments notwithstanding, the economic expansion of the 1990s was marked by increased economic inequality and high poverty rates, continuing the pattern of the 1980s. Corporate profits surged while real wages grew more slowly. Job security declined despite improvements in the unemployment rate. The forces set in motion in the 1980s which weakened the bargaining power of union and nonunion workers alike continued to be felt by many workers in the 1990s.

For some, the 1990s represented the beginning of a "New Economic Paradigm," able to propel the economy on a path of long-term prosperity well beyond the millennium. And some Americans did experience sharp gains in income and living standards. But for many other working and nonworking Americans alike, the 1990s were, for the most part, merely an extension of the 1980s, a time of stagnant living standards and economic stress. The "New Economy" was something they only heard about on the news.

THE POLITICS OF FEDERAL ECONOMIC AND SOCIAL POLICY IN THE 1990s

The Clinton administration, at least early on, wished to shift the overall direction of government economic policy and correct the economic failures of 12 years of Republican rule. The administration argued that the misguided government policies of the Reagan–Bush years contributed to the following: (1) an exceptionally slow economic recovery from the 1990 recession; (2) the continuing slow productivity growth; (3) stagnation in average incomes and the greatest increase in inequality since, at least, before the Second World War; (4) large federal budget deficits and mounting national debt; and (5) the failure to use borrowed funds productively, reflected in an unwillingness to spend on infrastructure and education.

On February 17, 1993, President Clinton presented his economic plan to Congress. Labeled *A Vision of Change for America*, it was designed to undo 12 years of largely laissez-faire policy. It contained two parts. The first was a $30 billion short-term stimulus package consisting of $16 billion of spending increases and a temporary investment tax credit to boost the economy. The additional spending would be primarily on infrastructure such as highways, bridges and high technology projects. Money not devoted to infrastructure would go to unemployment insurance, worker retraining and summer jobs for youth.

The second part represented the more long-term goals of the Clinton administration. In his campaign for the Presidency, Clinton downplayed budget cutting and reducing the federal budget deficit. Nevertheless, desiring to "impress the financial markets," deficit reduction was at the center of the overall Clinton economic plan. Arguing that large and growing federal budget deficits were keeping interest rates high, thereby reducing (or "crowding out") investment in new plant and equipment, shrinking the federal budget deficit was crucial for lowering long-term interest rates thereby leading to increased investment in the future. Expenditures would be cut including for defense and a variety of entitlement programs. The federal workforce would be reduced. Taxes would be raised particularly for the wealthy, those who benefited most from the tax cuts of the early 1980s. Clinton proposed raising the top marginal income tax rate from 31 percent to 36 percent for households with taxable incomes of $140 000 or more. There would be a 10 percent surtax on top for households with taxable incomes of $250 000 or more. Thus, the effective top marginal income tax rate would be 39.6 percent.

Corporate taxes would also be raised. The president's economic plan called for the top corporate tax rate to rise from 34 to 36 percent. A temporary investment tax credit for increased equipment purchases and a permanent research and development tax credit would somewhat offset higher corporate tax rates and foster new investment and technological and product advances leading to improvements in productivity.

Higher income taxes for the wealthy would also be a step toward reducing income inequality. Increasing the Earned Income Tax Credit (EITC) for low-income workers with at least one dependent child would be another. The credit offsets income taxes that eligible workers would otherwise have to pay. And if a family's tax liability was less than its credit, it would receive a refund. Thus, the credit would increase the after-tax income from working.

On the face of it, there would seem to be a contradiction between deficit reduction and economic stimulus. Economic stimulus incorporates tax cuts and spending increases thereby increasing the demand for goods and services while budget deficit reduction, by raising taxes and cutting government spending, reduces the demand for goods and services. The Clinton administration was aware of this potential contradiction. It admitted that the economic stimulus program might temporarily increase the budget deficit. Thereafter, the deficit reduction program would take over. Furthermore, the administration anticipated that a deficit reduction policy, credible in the financial markets, would lead to a substantial lowering of long-term interest rates thereby having an expansionary effect on the economy.

Whether the programs would have been contradictory would never be known. Even though there was a Democratic majority in Congress, it soon became clear there was only tepid support for economic stimulus. There were charges that much of the projected spending would be wasteful. And, anyway, the economic stimulus package would interfere with deficit reduction, a goal of higher priority. Adding to the lack of interest in economic stimulus was the business community's opposition to the investment tax credit, which they deemed to be too small to do them much good.

The economic stimulus program was a central element in the Clinton administration's plans to increase public and private investment. Its failure clearly demonstrated that the investment agenda would be distinctly secondary to deficit reduction. Introduced into Congress as the Omnibus Budget Reconciliation Act (OBRA) of 1993, the deficit reduction program was passed in August 1993, albeit by a very narrow margin. Particularly controversial were the tax increases for the very wealthy. The supply-side economics rhetoric of Reaganomics had so influenced the policy debate that an income tax increase narrowly focused on the top 1.2 percent of taxpayers had great difficulty being passed by a Democratic majority in Congress.

By the 1998 fiscal year, OBRA was projected to reduce the federal budget deficit by $146 billion, approximately evenly divided between spending cuts and tax increases. There were cutbacks in defense spending and in the Medicare programs, and the number of federal government employees was reduced. Overall, nominal levels of discretionary spending were frozen for five years, thereby implying real declines in spending in the event of inflation.

While the rich would see their tax rates increase, those earning wages at the bottom of the pay structure would benefit from improvements in the EITC. More families became eligible for the EITC and the payments to recipients increased. By effectively increasing the after-tax hourly wage of low-paid workers, the expansion of the EITC provided positive work incentives to many of the lowest paid workers or those whose only option was low-paid work. As such, it represented a first step toward welfare reform.

With the Clinton administration's credible focus on deficit reduction, long-term interest rates began to decline. They fell sharply from January to October, before rising toward the end of 1993. With the stress on deficit reduction, the financial markets believed that macroeconomic policy would not be overly expansionary, thereby minimizing the risks of inflation. The economy would not grow too rapidly, and the rate of unemployment would remain high as would excess capacity. While interest rates fell, the economy remained sluggish. Real Gross Domestic Product (GDP) grew by only 2.3 percent in 1993. Unemployment remained high with the unemployment rate falling to 6.9 percent in 1993 from 7.5 percent in 1992.

Nevertheless, on February 4, 1994, the Federal Reserve began raising short-term interest rates in a preemptive move against inflation. While unemployment was high and there was substantial excess capacity, the economy had grown rapidly, by 5.3 percent in the last quarter of 1993. The Federal Reserve believed that a continuation of such a rapid rate of growth would be inflationary. Monetary policy was tightened further in five subsequent Federal Reserve actions over the course of the year, with short-term rates rising steadily.

Even though interest rates were increasing in 1994, the economic recovery continued. Real GDP grew by 3.5 percent, faster than in the preceding year. As the economy expanded, more people found work and the unemployment rate fell to 6.1 percent. Inflation was steady as prices rose at an annual rate of 2.7 percent, the same as in 1993.

Nevertheless, many people were dissatisfied; they felt left out of the economic recovery. While profits were up, paychecks were not. Adjusted for inflation, average weekly earnings were $256.73 (in 1982 dollars) in 1994, well below their level of $264.22 (in 1982 dollars) in 1989, at the end of the previous economic expansion. Job insecurity was reaching beyond younger, less educated, blue-collar workers who constituted a large share of the workers laid off in the 1980s. Now, as corporations slashed costs, layoffs extended to older, more educated, better paid, white-collar workers, people who had believed that job loss would not be a concern of theirs. Not only was job insecurity more widespread, the average duration of unemployment was lengthening and the share of unemployed workers reporting permanent job loss was rising. And even though the economy was into its third year of expansion, the poverty rate in 1994 – 14.5 percent – was still 1.7 percentage points higher than it had been in 1989 (*Economic Report of the President*, 1999, pp. 366, 382).

Real median family income was stagnating and, in fact, was still below its 1989 level. The real median family income of $42 000 (in 1997 dollars) in 1994 was approximately $2300 below the real median family income of $44 284 (in 1997 dollars) in 1989. Only a few were reaping the benefits of economic growth. The rising tide was not lifting all boats. In fact, more than a few boats remained under water. Between 1989 and 1994, the share of total family income declined for the bottom 80 percent of the income distribution. And virtually all of the gain in the share of income going to the top 20 percent of the income distribution was accounted for by the income gains of the top 5 percent, those families earning $127 090 or more in 1994. In that year, they had 20.1 percent of all income, well above the 17.9 percent earned by the top 5 percent in 1989 (US Bureau of the Census, *Statistical Abstract of the United States*, 1998, p. 473).

Economically-strapped Americans were less willing to pay for social programs for the poor, a group becoming more and more stigmatized as "other" – another race, immigrants, or those who behaved differently. They were open to calls for cutting taxes, cutting government expenditures and eliminating government waste. In the 1994 elections, conservative Republicans running on a platform entitled a "Contract with America" regained control of the US Senate and House of Representatives. Large numbers of non-college educated white men and women whose living standards had declined over the past 15 years deserted the Democratic Party (Teixeira and Rogers, 1995).

Many of the Republicans were newly elected legislators, deeply disappointed by what they believed to be the limited results of the Reagan Revolution. They wished to return economic policy to the stated goals of Reaganomics. The Contract with America included provisions for tax cuts and spending reductions, a moratorium on new government regulations and a constitutional amendment to balance the federal budget. While its sponsors denounced the welfare state, the Contract with America explicitly called for reductions in spending in only two areas: AFDC and social spending initiatives included in the 1994 anti-crime bill. Not surprisingly, the cuts in benefits would apply to the stigmatized poor.

While attacking the welfare state and spending for the poor, the Republicans were promising a wide variety of new social benefits for the more well-off members of society. These benefits would take the form of tax credits and tax incentives. There would be tax credits for families with children, tax incentives for child adoptions, an elderly dependent care tax credit, and a cut in taxes on Social Security payments for wealthier seniors. Higher income individuals in higher tax brackets benefit disproportionately from any general social policy emphasizing tax incentives and tax credits. In addition to these tax credits, the Contract with America proposed an old Republican staple – capital gains tax cuts. Such a policy would benefit the very wealthy who reap the bulk of the capital gains in the economy.

The extensive proposed tax breaks combined with the call for a balanced federal budget pointed to significant unspecified future spending cuts. The logic was clear. Tax cuts would be used to reduce tax revenue and create budgetary pressures which, in turn, would lessen resistance to significant reductions in government expenditures on a wide variety of social programs. The Reagan administration had pursued this strategy, though not particularly successfully in the eyes of the newly elected, ideologically conservative Republicans.

The first-term Republican legislators came to Washington DC in January 1995 committed to rolling back the New Deal and the War on Poverty. They called for the elimination of federal entitlements to public assistance, Medicaid and food stamps, programs benefiting the poor. They also proposed the partial privatization of Social Security and Medicare.

They would not achieve all of their goals, but they would shift the Congressional debate sharply to the right. The struggle over the federal budget initially took place around the Balanced Budget Amendment to the Constitution which required a balanced budget by 2002. Passed by the US House of Representatives, it failed in the US Senate by one vote.

The Republicans then attempted to have their spending reductions and tax cuts incorporated in the fiscal year 1996 budget bills. Here, too, they called for a balanced budget by 2002. The Republican-sponsored Fiscal Year 1996 Reconciliation Bill cut spending by approximately $900 billion and taxes by $245 billion over seven years. No longer would federal social program expenditures necessarily increase in step with inflation and the number of program beneficiaries. Nearly half of the savings would come from entitlement programs benefiting the poor, even though these programs represented only 25 percent of total entitlement spending. They also proposed to sharply cut back the EITC. They projected Medicare cuts totaling $270 billion over seven years. Legal immigrants were also singled out. They would no longer be able to receive food stamps, Medicaid and other assistance. Overall states would have more responsibility for funding and running programs serving the poor such as Medicaid, food stamps and AFDC. On the other hand, much of the benefits of tax reduction would go to business and the wealthy in the form of reductions in the capital gains and estate taxes.

The Clinton administration fought the Republican proposals. The disagreement between the White House and the US Congress over the budget proposal resulted in two partial federal government shutdowns in late 1995 and early 1996. Public opinion blamed the extremism of the Republicans for interfering with the functioning of the federal government. The negative public opinion forced the

Republicans to back off from their original proposals. However, the final spending bills were not passed until April 1996, more than six months after the start of the fiscal year.

President Clinton won the budget battle not by criticizing the political philosophy of the Contract with America but rather by pointing out the pain the Republican proposals would cause to the affected groups. Ultimately, the battle over the budget was fought on the Republican terms and President Clinton would accept the notion that the federal budget should be balanced in seven years.

The extent to which the Republicans had shifted the terms of the social policy discussion became quite apparent later in 1996 in the deliberations over welfare reform. While President Clinton wished to "end welfare as we know it," he would end it with a bill incorporating many of the conservative Republicans' ideas about the poor and public policy. Both social conservatives and fiscal conservatives shaped the Republican approach to welfare reform. For social conservatives, the poor, themselves, were the issue; they would need to change their lifestyles. Furthermore, federal welfare policy, which supported the improper behavior of the poor, would need to be substantially reformed. Any government aid provided to poor families with dependent children should come with strings attached, strict rules regarding the behavior of recipients in such areas as work, school attendance and out-of-wedlock births. Welfare payments should not be generous, and recipients should be forced to work or train for a job to remain eligible for government assistance.

While well-conceived, well-developed government training and work programs cost money, the fiscal conservatives would be primarily concerned with budget cutting. They were not particularly interested in welfare policy but rather in reducing expenditures on social programs as much as was politically feasible.

The Republican state governors also weighed in on welfare reform. They were tired of responding to directives from Washington DC. Rather they wished the federal government to just provide the financial resources and allow the states to determine the substance of welfare policy.

After vetoing an earlier version of the bill, President Clinton signed the Personal Responsibility and Work Opportunity Reconciliation Act (PRWA) on August 22, 1996, in the midst of the 1996 Presidential campaign. The act repealed AFDC and replaced it with Temporary Assistance for Needy Families (TANF). TANF ended the entitlement status of AFDC. Under AFDC, the term "entitle-ment" had meant two things. First, all single-parent families with chil-dren and all two-parent families with children where the second parent was unemployed were guaranteed assistance by the federal government if their incomes were below State-set limits. Second, the federal government guaranteed to match dollar for dollar state fund-ing on welfare. Under TANF, states now decide which categories of needy families to assist and they are no longer obligated to provide help to all eligible families. Furthermore, the federal government no longer provides matching funds to the states. Rather, federal matching funds are now replaced by a block grant. Initially, the states received a larger sum of money under the block grants than they would have received in matching funds. However, the amount of funding in the federal block grant is to stay effectively fixed for six years.

Not only was the "entitlement" to welfare ended, a strong work requirement was imposed. States were required to have 25 percent of all beneficiary families participating in "work activities" by 1997 and 50 percent by 2000. Welfare recipients who failed to engage in "work activities" within two years were to be denied TANF benefits. In most instances, people would not be able to receive welfare benefits for more than five years over their lifetime.

In addition to work requirement for welfare recipients, TANF included specific requirements for unwed mothers under the age of 18. In order to receive TANF benefits, they had to live with an adult and those who were high school dropouts had to attend school. Further-more, the states were given the right to deny benefits to women who had additional children while on welfare.

The PRWA was touted as a piece of welfare reform legislation. But it did more than merely replace AFDC. Included within it were benefit cuts and work requirements quite unrelated to welfare reform. Two groups – legal immigrants and food stamp recipients – were sin-gled out for special attention. Riding the wave of anti-immigrant sen-timent, the PRWA sharply limited the access of legal immigrants to federal assistance. New legal immigrants would not be eligible for most federal means-tested benefits for five years. Most legal immigrants liv-ing in the United States as of August 22, 1996, who had not yet become citizens, would lose their eligibility for Supplemental Security Income (SSI) and food stamps. States would also be able to deny them Medicaid and welfare. Thus, certain individuals lawfully living in the United States and paying taxes would not be able to access social benefits, when needed, merely because they had not yet become citizens. (Opposition to this facet of the legislation was particularly fierce and a year later legal immigrants residing in the United States as of August 22, 1996, once again became eligible to receive SSI.)

In addition to noncitizen legal immigrants, citizens of the United States also bore the brunt of cutbacks in food stamps. Many working families saw their food stamp benefits reduced as a result of legislated changes in the way benefits were calculated. Furthermore, particularly stringent was a new work requirement for adults under the age of 50 who were not raising children. They would only be able to receive food stamps for three months out of every 36 months while unemployed or not working at least 20 hours a week or not participating in a work training program. According to the Center on Budget and Policy Priorities, a Washington DC think tank, this is "probably the single harshest provision written into a major safety net program in at least 30 years" (Edelman, 1997, p. 48).

Clinton's capitulation to Congressional conservatives on welfare reform and budgetary principles represented major defeats for liberal Democrats and their supporters, including the labor movement. It marked the continuation of the Democratic party's shift to the right begun two decades earlier in the second half of the Carter administration.

Yet, these were not the only defeats suffered by the labor movement during Clinton's first term in office. The American Federation of Labor (AFL)–Congress of Industrial Organizations (CIO) had been thrilled with the election of Bill Clinton in 1992 and was optimistic for the prospects for its legislative agenda. At the 1993 AFL–CIO convention, President Clinton stated:

> I became president because I wanted a new partnership for the labor movement of America. We are replacing a government that for years worked labor over with a government that works with labor. (Quoted in Galenson, 1996, p. 74)

Soon after taking office, President Clinton signed the Family and Medical Leave Act, which had been supported by the AFL–CIO and vetoed by President Bush. This law applied to public employees and those working for firms with 50 or more employees. It provided for unpaid but protected leave for the birth or adoption of a child or serious illness of a child, spouse, parent or the employee concerned.

However, as time went on the labor movement experienced one setback after another. Important parts of its legislative agenda went down to defeat. Blocking the approval of the North American Free Trade Agreement (NAFTA) was of particular importance to the labor movement. Through the phased elimination of tariffs and non-tariff barriers, NAFTA was designed to increase the flows of goods and services between Mexico, the United States and Canada. The flow of capital between the three countries was to be facilitated by removing all barriers to investment facing investors in the three countries. Given the low labor costs and high unemployment in Mexico, the AFL–CIO vehemently opposed NAFTA, fearing that it would lead to the export of unionized jobs to Mexico and serve to place downward pressure on wages throughout the United States.

The AFL–CIO underestimated the support of the Clinton administration for freer trade. The NAFTA was signed on December 17, 1992 by George Bush and the leaders of Mexico and Canada. Legislation needed to be passed to implement NAFTA. The labor movement organized marches and rallies across the country opposing such legislation. The business community were strong supporters of NAFTA, seeing many investment opportunities in Mexico. First, large US-based multinational corporations hoped passage of NAFTA would further enable them to buy Mexican state-owned enterprises such as airlines and telephone companies at reasonable prices. Mexico had already begun the process of selling off state-owned companies to private investors. Second, corporate executives anticipated cutting labor costs by shifting some jobs from the United States to Mexico.

In November 1993, the battle over NAFTA took center stage in the US Congress. Clinton blamed the labor unions for pressuring Congress into defeating NAFTA. The president asked the business community to strongly lobby for passage of the legislation. Many business executives and factory workers, given time off from their jobs, came to Washington DC to lobby Congress. Laurence Bossidy, the chairman of Allied Signal, Inc. and head of USA–NAFTA, a coalition of thousands of companies and trade associations favoring NAFTA, said: "I think we have done more on NAFTA than on any legislative issue in history" (Kaplan, 1996, p. 151).

President Clinton complemented the efforts of the business community. Many wavering Congressmen were called to the White House and promised *quid pro quos* if they supported NAFTA.

Republicans voting in favor of NAFTA were promised his support in the next election if they were challenged on their NAFTA vote. These efforts paid off and the NAFTA legislation was passed. Given that many Democrats voted against NAFTA, it was the Republicans who gave Clinton his margin of victory. The labor movement was stunned.

In addition to freer trade, the labor movement was concerned about the use of strikebreakers. Employers were more prone to hire permanent replacement workers during strikes in the 1980s than they had been at any prior time in the post Second World War period. Along with the defeat of NAFTA, the passage of the Workplace Fairness Act was at the top of labor's legislative agenda. This piece of legislation prohibited the hiring of permanent replacement workers during a strike. Companies still would have the right to utilize temporary replacements. However, at the end of a strike, the strikers would have the right to return as long as they accepted the employer's terms and conditions of employment. The employer would retain the right to determine that post-strike business conditions did not require the rehiring of all of the strikers.

Even though this legislation did not guarantee the jobs of all of the strikers, the AFL–CIO was firmly behind it. The bill was passed by the US House of Representatives but, in the face of strong lobbying by employers, it ran into difficulty in the US Senate. While President Clinton claimed to support the bill, he did not utilize the same political arm twisting as had been done to generate support for NAFTA. In July 1994, opponents of the bill in the US Senate were able to filibuster it to death.

On March 8, 1995, less than a year after the failure to pass the Workplace Fairness Act, President Clinton issued Executive Order 12954 barring government contractors from utilizing permanent replacements for strikers. This Executive Order applied to all federal contracts of $100 000 or more. Companies holding such contracts retaining permanent replacement workers rather than rehiring strikers would lose such contracts and would not be able to receive future contracts. Employers challenged the legality of the Executive Order and the Court of Appeals in the District of Columbia overturned it. The end result was that the labor movement was back to where it started. Employers could continue hiring permanent replacement workers during strikes without facing any governmental penalties.

THE LABOR MOVEMENT AT A CROSSROAD

Thus, three years into President Clinton's first term, the labor movement found its legislative agenda stymied. The failure of labor's political program led to a leadership battle within the AFL–CIO. John J. Sweeney, the head of the Service Employees Union (SEIU), challenged Thomas R. Donahue, who had taken over as president of the AFL–CIO on August 1, 1995. The SEIU was known for its organizing prowess. During Sweeney's 15-year tenure as the head of the SEIU, it had grown from 625 000 members to 1.1 million members. And this was at a time when many unions were shrinking in size and the share of the overall workforce unionized was declining. Important in the growth of the SEIU were successful campaigns to organize public employees, health care workers and janitors working in large cities. Sweeney ran on the New Voice Platform whose main slogan was "America Needs a Raise." A revitalized labor movement, relevant to the mass of American workers, was of crucial importance if American workers were to get a significant raise. Sweeney called for sharply increasing the attention and resources devoted to organizing, particularly of low-paid workers, constructing a vibrant labor movement that can change workers' lives, creating a strong, progressive voice that can help redefine America's perception of the labor movement and developing a democratic movement that speaks for all workers, not merely those in unions. For the first time since its inception, a contested election was held at the October 1995 convention of the leadership of the AFL–CIO. The Sweeney slate was elected by a 56 to 44 percent margin over one led by Donahue.

Organizing was uppermost on Sweeney's agenda. By 1995, union members had fallen to 14.9 percent of wage and salary workers and only 10.3 percent of private wage and salary workers. The steady decline in the unionized share of the work force would need to be addressed. Yet, even where unions won representation elections, they still faced great difficulty coming to agreement with management over a first contract. Between 1993 and 1996, approximately one in four first contract negotiations did not produce an agreement. Many of these negotiations were highly adversarial. Management was much more likely to threaten and utilize replacement workers in first contract negotiations than in contract renewal negotiations. Similarly, the threat to close a plant was much more likely to be made in a first contract negotiation than a contract renewal situation (Cutcher-Gershenfeld et al., 1998).

Even in long-standing collective bargaining relationships, workers were often on the defensive. Many unionized workers were quite reluctant to strike to achieve their goals. In 1995, the number of major work stoppages fell to 31 (*Statistical Abstract of the United States*, 1998, p. 443).

Labor certainly did not lose every major strike. The length of the work week, work scheduling and job security continued to be strongly bargained over. Paid overtime hours increased sharply in the 1990s. In 1994, production workers in manufacturing were averaging 4.7 hours of paid overtime per week. At GM's Buick City plant in Flint, Michigan some workers had been working six days a week and up to 12 hours per day. One Flint worker said, "I like working at GM, but I don't want to live there" (Moody and Sagovac, 1995, p. 7). The company had not hired any long-term hourly workers since 1986. On September 27, 1994, 11 500 workers walked off their jobs. They wanted forced overtime reduced and permanent hires. The four-day work stoppage ended with the company agreeing to hire more than 500 new long-term employees and to stop using nonunion temporary workers.

Saving full-time jobs was at issue in the 24-day Teamsters strike in 1994, the longest national trucking strike in the union's history. On April 6, 70 000 Teamsters struck the three major national trucking companies. Employers wanted to replace many full-time workers on the loading dock with part-timers earning about half the union rate. The companies eventually backed down, to a large degree, on the part-time question.

These victories notwithstanding, unions suffered some major setbacks in some highly publicized, lengthy labor disputes. Three of these defeats occurred in Decatur, Illinois, a small industrial city of 84 000 located in central Illinois. To many workers this town became known as "The War Zone." The managements of A.E. Staley, a corn miller owned by the British conglomerate Tate & Lyle, the Japanese-owned Bridgestone/Firestone tire company, and Caterpillar, a US-based multinational producer of earth moving, farm and construction equipment, unleashed an entire anti-union arsenal to achieve their goals. At the height of the labor disputes, approximately one-third of Decatur's manufacturing work force was either locked out or on strike.

Though their demands varied, in general the three companies wanted to institute 12-hour shifts that require workers to rotate between working days and nights. These longer shifts would likely be accompanied by mandatory overtime. Management also wanted to reduce pay and time off and cut health benefits. Also on the list of demands was more freedom to subcontract work, often to lower wage, nonunion firms. Union members believed these companies collaborated in their attacks on their workers.

The labor contract at A.E. Staley expired in 1992. Fearing that they would be replaced if they struck, workers began to "work to rule" and instituted a corporate campaign against the company. Production dropped and in June 1993 the company locked out the workers. The lockout went on for more than two years. Eventually, the workers were forced to acquiesce.

The United Rubber Workers (URW) and Bridgestone/Firestone began contract negotiations in March 1994. No agreement was reached and on July 12, the URW struck company tire plants in Decatur and elsewhere. On August 18, the company began using replacement workers at three struck facilities including Decatur. The workers struck for ten months and then agreed to return to work under the terms of the company's last offer. However, the company announced that it intended to retain the replacement workers. The company eventually began rehiring the strikers but often into lower level jobs than they had prior to the strike. The URW, severely weakened by its disputes with Bridgestone/Firestone and other tire companies, was forced to merge with the United Steelworkers of America (USWA). Eventually, on November 7, 1996, the USWA and the company reached an agreement which provided for the return of all of the strikers to their original jobs. Workers gained improved pensions and wages and the restoration of holidays. The firm won the right to operate its factories around the clock with rotating shifts.

On November 4, 1991, workers went on strike at two Caterpillar plants in Illinois. The UAW wanted the company to sign a contract patterned on one negotiated with Deere & Co., the other major agricultural implement producer. The company refused and the strike spread. However, on April 14, 1992, the strike ended in the face of a company threat to hire permanent replacement workers. The workers returned to work under terms imposed by the company.

Two years passed without a contract agreement. Workers utilized an in-plant campaign designed to force the company back to the bargaining table. The UAW and Caterpillar brought a rash of unfair labor practice complaints to the National Labor Relations Board (NLRB). An agreement was not reached; a second strike began on June 20, 1994. Now the company did bring in replacement workers, from as far away as Mississippi to work in plants in Illinois and

Pennsylvania. They complemented management and office employees assigned to production duties, new permanent hires and union members who crossed picket lines. Production levels were maintained and high profits were earned. In early December, 1995, after striking for 17 months, the union rank-and-file rejected Caterpillar's contract proposal to end the strike. It was very similar to one presented by the company prior to the start of the strike. It included the replacement of the guaranteed annual wage increase, a contract provision of crucial importance for the UAW, by two lump-sum payments over six years plus cost-of-living payments. It also contained a two-tiered wage scale which lowered the pay for newly hired workers, restrictions on union activities and increased flexibility for management to introduce alternative work schedules including 12-hour shifts without overtime. Nevertheless, the UAW called off the strike and the workers returned to work. The UAW's retreat constituted a major defeat both for itself and the American labor movement.

Reversing labor's decline in the collective bargaining arena would be a long-term project with no guarantee of success. A stronger presence for the labor movement in the political process would be easier to attain. Labor's new leaders began speaking out about living standards and income security. Raising the minimum wage was one of labor's central goals. For more than five years, the minimum wage had remained at $4.25 per hour, and its purchasing power had fallen to a 40-year low. There was strong public support for raising the minimum wage. While many Americans were critical of the welfare system and looked down upon long-term welfare recipients, they sympathized with low-wage workers trying to support a family on a minimum wage job. The Clinton administration and the Congressional Democratic leadership supported labor's push for a higher minimum wage. After stalling for a while, the Republicans eventually went along, not willing to go against public opinion in an election year. In the summer of 1996, legislation was passed raising the minimum wage to $4.75 an hour on October 1, 1996 and to $5.15 an hour on September 1, 1997.

The labor movement also tried to mobilize voters to reelect Bill Clinton in November 1996 and restore the Democratic majority in Congress. The AFL–CIO spent $35 million on legislation and political activity in 1996, raising the ire of the business community. There were calls for restricting the ability of the labor movement to utilize funds for political campaigns. Yet, corporations still outspent labor by a ratio of 11 to 1 (Rosenthal, 1998, pp. 100–101). Clinton was reelected and while the labor movement did not succeed in returning the Democratic Party to control of the US House of Representatives, many anti-union members of the US House of Representatives were defeated. The Republican Party had come close to losing control of the US House of Representatives. The Contract with America was taken off the legislative table.

A LONG, STRONG ECONOMIC EXPANSION

The economic expansion continued in the second half of the 1990s, with the rate of economic growth accelerating as the decade came to a close. Real GDP rose by 3.7 percent in 1996, 4.5 percent in 1997, 4.3 percent in 1998 and 4.1 percent in 1999. The economy grew particularly rapidly in the last two quarters of 1999, with real GDP rising by 5.7 percent in the third quarter and 8.3 percent in the fourth quarter (*Economic Report of the President*, 2001, p. 279).

As the economy expanded, more people were hired and the unemployment rate fell to levels not seen since the late 1960s. The unemployment rate steadily declined from 5.4 percent in 1996 to 4.2 percent in 1999. The labor force participation rate in 1999 was 67.1 percent, the same as in 1997 and 1998. This represented the highest rate of labor force participation in the post Second World War period (*Economic Report of the President*, 2000, pp. 352, 354).

Even though the economy was growing and unemployment was dropping, inflation remained subdued. The rate of inflation fell from 3.0 percent in 1996 to 2.2 percent in 1999 (*Economic Report of the President*, 2000, p. 377). Falling import prices, a still weak labor movement and rising productivity growth helped keep inflation low in a low unemployment environment.

With the rise in the value of the dollar, import prices fell. Reversing its decline in the first half of the 1990s, the value of the dollar in 1999 was 16 percent above its 1995 level (*Economic Report of the President*, 2000, p. 430). Falling import prices serve to lower the rate of inflation in two ways. First, domestic producers of goods competing with imports are discouraged from raising prices. Second, since the price of some imported goods are included in the Consumer Price Index (CPI), falling import prices lead to a slowdown in the rate of inflation as measured by the CPI.

Even though the rate of unemployment was steadily falling which typically implies stronger worker bargaining power, most workers, union and nonunion alike, were accepting modest wage increases. Unions remained weak as the share of the work force unionized continued to decline. By 1999, only 13.9 percent of wage and salary workers were unionized. In the private sector, this figure stood at 9.4 percent. Major work stoppages were rare, there being only 17 in 1999 (*Statistical Abstract of the United States*, 2000, pp. 444–445).

With rare exception, nonunion workers were also reluctant to push for higher wages. Federal Reserve Board Chairman Greenspan attributed this to workers' anxieties over potential job loss even at a time of falling unemployment. A survey of 444 large companies carried out by International Survey Research showed that in 1986 only 20 percent of the respondents feared being laid off. This number rose to 46 percent in 1996 (Bluestone and Rose, 1998). Yet, the unemployment rate in 1996 was 5.4 percent, below the 7.0 percent of 1986. Corporate downsizing in the face of a strong economy and strong profitability certainly fostered job insecurity. The increasing prevalence of contingent employment relationships did the same (Rosenberg and Lapidus, 1999). The share of the work force employed in the temporary help industry rose from 1.3 percent in 1992 to 2.2 percent in 1997. Similarly, workers with contract agencies were also growing in importance. In 1992, employment in the personnel services industry accounted for 1.5 percent of total employment. By 1997, this number had risen to 2.4 percent (Mishel *et al.*, 1999, p. 249).

At a time when family life was under increased stress as two earners were increasingly required to support an adequate lifestyle, job stability was declining and job insecurity was rising. Thus, low unemployment notwithstanding, it is not surprising that workers were settling for modest wage increases. While real earnings began rising reversing the trend of the earlier years of the expansion, their slow rate of growth meant that it was not until 1998 that the average real weekly earnings of $268.32 (in 1982 dollars) exceeded their level of $264.22 (in 1982 dollars) in 1989, at the end of the previous economic expansion. And in 1999, the rate of growth of real weekly earnings slowed to 1.1 percent (*Economic Report of the President*, 2000, p. 360).

Since real wages were stagnating, family members had to work longer hours to maintain their desired living standards. A rising sense of job insecurity leads workers to work as long as possible when jobs are available in anticipation of the time when they would be unemployed. As a result, since 1982 there has been a rise in annual hours of work reversing the trend of declining work hours between 1967 and 1982. Thus, even though the unemployment rate fell to low levels in the second half of the 1990s, widespread bottlenecks did not arise and there was enough additional labor supplied by existing workers to meet the needs of most employers (Bluestone and Rose, 1998). Rapid increases in wages did not emerge.

Productivity gains also served to dampen inflationary pressures. Labor productivity grew more rapidly in the second half of the 1990s than it had in the two preceding decades. Between 1973 and 1995, labor productivity growth in the nonfarm business sector averaged 1.4 percent annually. In contrast, between 1996 and 1999, the annual average rate of labor productivity growth was 2.7 percent (*Economic Report of the President*, 2000, p. 59; *Economic Report of the President*, 2001, p. 333). The more rapid improvements in productivity combined with slowly growing compensation served to moderate labor cost growth. From 1996 to 1999, unit labor cost growth averaged less than 1.5 percent annually. In fact, in the last two quarters of 1999 unit labor costs actually declined as productivity gains outpaced improvements in compensation.

Slowly rising unit labor costs at a time of improving labor productivity point to the fact that the typical worker was not sharing fully in the benefits from improved productivity. Since 1982, productivity grew faster than wages or total compensation. This divergence in the rate of growth of wages and total compensation and the rate of growth of productivity widened in the 1990s. Continuing a trend begun in the 1980s, there was a redistribution of income from wages to capital income (Mishel *et al.*, 1999, p. 69). One of the key characteristics of the expansion of the 1990s has been a sharp increase in corporate profitability.

Overall, corporate earnings more than doubled from 1989 to 1999. A measure of corporate profitability is the ratio of after-tax profits to stockholder equity. From 1994 to 1999, this measure for manufacturing corporations reached levels rarely seen in the previous 50 years. During this time, this measure of manufacturing profitability averaged 16.3 percent annually. Prior to 1994, there were only three years in the post Second World War period where the ratio of after tax profits to stockholder equity even reached 16 percent for manufacturing companies (*Economic Report of the President*, 2000, p. 413). Historically unprecedented high profit rates were also earned in the corporate sector outside of manufacturing (Mishel *et al.*, 1999, p. 69).

Strong corporate profitability helped to drive the lengthy economic expansion. Rapidly rising business investment in computer equipment and software, together with strong household consumption expenditures, offset the drag on growth caused by slowing federal government spending and the rising trade deficit. New information technologies were developed in the 1980s and early 1990s. And there was ongoing technological innovation throughout the 1990s. Corporate leaders did not wish to be left out of this technological revolution. Firms flush with cash and wanting to implement the latest technologies to increase productivity and raise profitability sharply increased their investment spending on software and information processing equipment. Further stimulating spending was the sharp fall in the prices of computers and semiconductors, adjusted for quality improvements. Real spending on information processing equipment and software grew at a rate of 19 percent per year from 1993 to 1999. Overall, the share of real investment in real GDP rose dramatically as did the share of high technology investment in total investment (*Economic Report of the President*, 2000, p. 29).

Investment spending contributed more to the long expansion of the 1990s than it did to the lengthy expansions from 1982 to 1990 and 1961 to 1969. Consumption spending also played an important role. For seven years, beginning in 1993, households steadily increased their rate of consumption out of their disposable income. The personal savings rate, correspondingly, fell from 8.7 percent in 1993 to 2.4 percent in 1999 (*Economic Report of the President*, 2000, p. 243). The decline in the savings rate was due to several factors. First, families were attempting to maintain their customary standard of living in the face of declining real family income. While the economy pulled out of a recession and began growing in 1992, it was not until 1998 that real median family income exceeded its level of 1989, the end of the previous expansion.

Yet, the savings rate continued falling after 1997, pointing to additional factors responsible for its decline. Beginning in 1995, household wealth grew faster than personal income. By 1999, household net worth was nearly six times annual personal income, up from approximately 4.75 times annual personal income in 1989 (*Economic Report of the President*, 2000, p. 55). Thus, people were willing to spend a larger proportion of their personal income since they felt wealthier and were wealthier, at least on paper. For most people their home is their most valuable asset. And the housing market was strong for most of the second half of the 1990s. Yet, for the very wealthy the stock market represents an important source of their wealth. And from 1995 to 1999, stock market performance was quite exceptional. It provided a total return of nearly 200 percent, or 24 percent per year on average (*Economic Report of the President*, 2000, p. 67). The strong profit performance of American corporations provided an underpinning for stock prices. Yet, stock prices rose more rapidly than did profits. Strong current profitability likely led to expectations of even stronger future profitability, thus furthering the desire to own corporate stock. Nevertheless, it did seem as if part of the run up in stock prices, particularly among high technology companies, represented a "speculative bubble" not likely to last.

Be that as it may, rising stock prices provided a boost to the assets of the very wealthy. Even though more and more Americans were caught up in the "bull market" frenzy of the 1990s, most of them owned small amounts of corporate stock. The top 1 percent of wealth holders in the United States owned 47 percent of total net financial assets in 1995; the top 10 percent of wealth holders owned 83 percent (Bluestone and Harrison, 2000, p. 117). Thus, rising stock prices enabled the very wealthy to consume a larger proportion of their real disposable income. And if the very wealthy felt confident enough to buy a new luxury car or take an additional vacation at a luxury resort some of that added spending would trickle down to the workers who made the tires and glass for the car, assuming the car was made in the United States, or the clerks and chambermaids in the resort hotel assuming the vacation was taken in the United States. The economy would continue to grow, generating further increases in income and consumption expenditures.

Much of the additional consumption and investment spending was spent on goods and services produced in the United States. Nevertheless, throughout the economic expansion there was strong import growth, counterbalanced though not fully for a time by increasing exports. From 1992 to 1997, the trade deficit constituted a small drag on economic growth. Yet, with the financial tremors shaking the world economy beginning in Asia in July 1997, and then spreading to Russia, Brazil and several other Latin American countries in 1998 and early 1999 and coming dangerously close to a financial catastrophe in the United States in autumn 1998, this situation dramatically changed. Export growth slowed, import growth accelerated. The US trade deficit rose sharply as did the US current account deficit. The trade deficit became a larger drag on economic growth. Nevertheless, the US economy grew by more than 4 percent in 1997, 1998 and 1999, an excellent performance in the face of the continuing global financial crisis. And while the American manufacturing and agricultural sectors suffered from the Asian crisis, the United States seemed to benefit from the crisis, further evidence of the rejuvenation of its economy and the strengthening of its worldwide political economic domination.

The Asian financial turmoil was precipitated by the floating of the Thai currency – the baht – on July 2, 1997. The Thai government had previously tied the value of the baht to the US dollar. Speculative attacks on the baht began in August 1996 in the face of emerging difficulties in the Thai economy. When they would occur, the Thai government would buy baht with some of its foreign exchange reserves thereby maintaining the baht's exchange rate relative to the US dollar. However, by July 1997, Thailand was running out of foreign exchange reserves and speculation against the baht was ongoing. The government ceased supporting the baht and it immediately sank in value. Yet, why should the floating of the currency of a small Asian country provoke full-fledged economic turmoil across much of Asia?

Why had Asia become vulnerable to a financial panic? With the noted exceptions of China and Japan, many Asian countries, on the advice of the International Monetary Fund (IMF), the World Bank and their national business elites, had opened up their financial systems in the first part of the 1990s. Local citizens could now open foreign bank accounts, financial institutions and private corporations could borrow abroad and foreigners could purchase shares of stock of national companies on domestic stock exchanges.

With the rapid economic growth rates of the Asian economies in the 1980s and early 1990s and the general perception of an ongoing "Asian miracle," international lenders rushed to lend money to South-east Asian and South Korean banks and firms. Substantial amounts of debt were run up to foreign lenders, payable in foreign exchange. A bevy of "emerging markets" mutual funds were set up which funneled money from the United States and Europe to Asian stock markets. The liberalization of the Asian financial system led to large amounts of global capital flowing into the Asian economies.

Yet, it would soon become apparent that global capital is footloose and financial flows can abruptly change direction. The South-east Asian economies and South Korea ran into difficulties in 1995 and

1996. They experienced falling export growth. Worldwide demand for electronics, in general, and semiconductors, in particular, slumped. In addition China, having devalued its currency by 35 percent in 1994, was becoming a more formidable competitor. The same held for Japan whose yen fell by 60 percent against the dollar between April 1995 and April 1997. The wide swing in the exchange rate of the yen partially reversed the steady appreciation of the yen from 238 yen to the dollar to 80 yen to the dollar in the period 1985 to 1995. While the yen was appreciating, the South-east Asian economies and South Korea became much more competitive sites for export-oriented production. With the depreciation of the yen, most economies of South-east Asia were priced out of world markets as their currencies rose against the yen. Thailand was particularly devastated as the Thai baht was tied to the dollar. There was substantial excess capacity in these economies as a result, with many firms facing serious difficulties. Export growth in South Korea and in the ASEAN countries (Thailand, Malaysia, Philippines and Indonesia) fell from 30 percent in early 1995 to zero by mid-1996 (Johnson, 1998, p. 658). A balance of payments crisis was on the horizon.

The Thai economy was the first to collapse. Foreigners lost confidence in the economy and the stock market fell sharply. When the Thai government ceased supporting the baht on July 2, 1997, the currency went into a free-fall eventually falling 50 percent against the dollar. With the decline in the value of the baht, many Thai borrowers were unable to raise the foreign exchange to pay back their loans provided by foreign lenders. Capital began fleeing Thailand.

However, the crisis was not contained to Thailand. With the collapse of one of the "Asia miracle" economies, faith in the other "miracles" quickly dissipated. The Malaysian ringgit and the Indonesian rupiah were the next to be battered as investors and speculators dumped these no-longer-desirable currencies. When Taiwan unexpectedly devalued its currency by 12 percent in October, the Korean won suddenly looked ripe for a catch-up devaluation, and it too was dumped on the international financial markets. A South-east Asian crisis was now a full-blown Asian crisis. All told net private capital flows to or from the five Asian economies (the ASEAN four plus South Korea) went from plus $93 billion in 1996 to minus $12 billion in 1997. Most of the capital outflow was concentrated in the last quarter of 1997. This swing in one year of $105 billion was equivalent to 11 percent of the combined GDP of the five countries (Wade, 1998, p. 695).

Such a large capital outflow would be expected to leave damaged economies in its wake. In 1998, the economies of Indonesia, South Korea, Malaysia, the Philippines and Thailand experienced output declines of 7 percent on average (*Economic Report of the President*, 2000, p. 227).

With the collapse of their currencies and their economies, many Asians were unable to repay their foreign debts. Japan proposed the creation of a new multinational financial institution, which they would lead, to provide loans to Asian countries to enable them to repay their debts. Not willing to see Japan play such a leading role in Asia, the United States squashed this idea and successfully argued that the IMF should be given the responsibility of cleaning up the situation. And it would be the United States who would shape the overall strategy toward Asia, both directly and indirectly through the IMF. Thailand, Indonesia, South Korea and the Philippines would receive IMF assistance. The price the IMF would demand from the recipient countries would be austerity budgets, high interest rates and a willingness to sell local businesses to foreign buyers. In short order the Asian economies had gone from being seen as "miracles" in the eyes of the international financial community to being viewed as dysfunctional economies beset by "crony capitalism," needing to be restructured along IMF lines.

There would be bargains to be had throughout Asia. The crash of many Asian stock markets combined with the sharp fall in the exchange rates of many local currencies meant that Americans, as well as Europeans, could pick up Asian assets for a "song." From June 2, 1997 to March 24, 1998, in US dollar terms the Indonesian stock market lost 96 percent of its value, the South Korean 70 percent, the Malaysian 65 percent and the Thai 53 percent. Hong Kong, whose currency was not devalued, and Japan were less hard hit seeing their stock markets lose 22 percent and 28 percent respectively (Wade, 1998, p. 694).

Thus, the United States reaped several benefits from the Asian economic turmoil. First, by pushing aside Japan, it emerged with much greater power in the region than it had before. Second, Americans were able to purchase Asian assets much more cheaply than before the crisis. Third, a further benefit accrued to the United States, though not without some cost. The Asian economies would try to export their way out of the crisis. Given the decline in the value of their currencies, their exports would be relatively cheap.

The increased supply of cheap imports from Asia would be anti-inflationary for the United States. However, US manufacturing industries, in particular, suffered from increased import competition from Asia. In addition, the recession in Japan together with the out-right crisis in other parts of Asia led to the loss of export markets for the United States, hurting agriculture and manufacturing in particular. Employment fell sharply in manufacturing. Between the first quarter of 1993 and the fourth quarter of 1997, employment in the US manufacturing firms rose by about 700 000 workers. However, between the fourth quarter of 1997 and the fourth quarter of 1999, manufacturing employment fell by about 440 000 workers (*Economic Report of the President*, 2000, p. 235).

Overall, there was a sharp increase in the US balance of trade deficit. From the end of 1997, the US trade deficit rose from about 1 percent of GDP (its average throughout the mid-1990s) to about 3 percent (*Economic Report of the President*, 2000, p. 232). In 1997, imports of goods and services exceeded exports of goods and services by $110 billion. By 1999, the trade deficit had risen to $325 billion (*Economic Report of the President*, 2000, p. 309).

Not only was strong investment and consumer demand needed to offset the drag caused by a growing trade deficit if the expansion was to continue, they were also needed to offset the contractionary effects of slowing federal governmental expenditures on goods and services, particularly in the early stages of the expansion. The Omnibus Budget Reconciliation Act of 1993 and the Balanced Budget Act of 1997 placed limits on the growth of federal spending. Federal expenditures on goods and services did not even rise in step with inflation from 1993 to 1998. Not since the Nixon administration had there been such a steady decline in real federal expenditures. At that time, restrictive fiscal policy was part of a strategy to slow the economy and fight inflation. Yet, the economic context was quite different during the first Clinton administration when the declines in real federal spending were the largest. Inflation was not a problem and the economy was not growing particularly rapidly. Here the real spending declines were mainly in national defense areas, a reaction to the collapse of the Soviet Union and the end of the Cold War as well as an attempt to reverse the spending priorities of the Reagan administration. However, nondefense spending, as well, did not even keep up with inflation from 1993 to 1996.

Overall, the Clinton administration would do what the Reagan administration espoused but did not particularly accomplish.

They would diminish the role of the federal government in the economy and would eventually balance the federal budget. In 1991, federal outlays equaled 22.3 percent of GDP. By 1999, this ratio had fallen to 18.7 percent due to explicit restraints on spending and the decline in transfer payments which typically accompanies a strong economy. This decline in spending of 3.6 percentage points of GDP was much greater than the 1.3 percentage point decline which occurred during the 1982 to 1990 expansion. And this decline in federal outlays took place even as federal tax revenues were rising (*Economic Report of the President*, 2000, p. 32).

The federal budget deficit shrank rapidly as federal spending was being restrained even while federal tax revenues were rising. In 1992, the last year of the Bush administration, the federal budget deficit was $290.4 billion, a number equivalent to 4.7 percent of GDP. With the focus of the Clinton administration on deficit reduction and the growing economy, the federal budget deficit steadily declined after that. By 1998, there was a federal budget surplus of $69.2 billion, the first time the federal budget had been in surplus since 1969. The federal budget surplus grew to $124.4 billion in 1999, a number equivalent to 1.4 percent of GDP. Not since 1951 had there been as large a federal budget surplus relative to the GDP (*Economic Report of the President*, 2000, p. 397).

The Clinton administration placed the restrictive fiscal policy and the achievement of a balanced budget at the center of its explanation for the length and strength of the economic expansion. Restrictive fiscal policy enabled the Federal Reserve to pursue a more expansionary monetary policy than it otherwise would have for it had less of a fear of igniting inflation. The more expansionary monetary policy along with the shrinking federal budget deficit and eventual federal budget surplus led to interest rates lower than they would have otherwise been. Lower interest rates stimulated investment spending which led to rising productivity and a growth in the capacity to produce goods and services. Increased capacity and rising productivity help to keep inflation low enabling more rapid economic growth and a lengthy economic expansion (*Economic Report of the President*, 2000, p. 34).

While there is some truth in this story, it is only part of the explanation for the strong and lengthy economic expansion. Low interest rates do foster investment in new plant and equipment. Furthermore, the push for and the achievement of a balanced budget together with a strong concern for inflation is consistent with the Big Business and

Wall Street view of appropriate economic policy, likely fostering business confidence. Business confidence itself is a prerequisite for strong investment behavior. Nevertheless, low interest rates are only one element influencing investment behavior and likely not the most important factor. Firms will only undertake new investment projects if their expected profitability is high. More important than interest rates in determining expected profitability is the expected demand for the products or services made possible by the potential new investment. Without a sufficient expected demand, the investment will not be undertaken regardless of the interest rates.

Furthermore, the concentration of the increased investment in information processing equipment and software suggests that the ongoing revolution in information technology was more important than low interest rates in driving the investment boom. The crucial importance of increased investment spending in fostering the economic expansion and the crucial role of information technology in this increased investment raises the question of whether the US economy has entered a new stage, a "New Economy" if you will.

A "NEW ECONOMY?"

As the economic expansion continued and the rate of economic growth accelerated in the second half of the 1990s, a belief emerged, initially in the US business publications such as *Business Week* and later in the more popular press, that the US economy was in the throes of a fundamental transformation. A "New Economy" was being born, one which its most enthusiastic proponents argued would lead to a new, possibly endless, era of prosperity. When asked, in 1997, how long the good times would roll, Jack Welch, chief executive of General Electric Co. and perhaps Wall Street's most revered corporate executive, answered "What's to stop it?" (Mandel *et al.*, 1997, p. 32).

Technological innovation supported by easy access to venture capital, along with the growth of global markets are said to be the driving forces of the "New Economy." Two major technological breakthroughs are the computer and the Internet. They enable companies to boost productivity by reducing costs and help firms raise product quality by developing new products or improving existing products in terms of convenience, timeliness, quality and variety. A new information system at Hughes Electronics Corporation let engineers interact throughout the world reducing the time it took to build a satellite from 30 to 18 months. Handling most of its customer support calls via the Worldwide Web allowed Cisco Systems Inc. to eliminate 1000 staff positions and save $125 million dollars a year (Mandel *et al.*, 1997). Working over the Internet, Royal Dutch Shell employees in Houston and the Netherlands developed new methods for discovering oil which helped locate 30 million barrels of oil reserves in Gabon in 1999. Ford Motor Company created an online trading system enabling it to deal almost instantly with its 30 000 suppliers, thereby lowering the cost of auto parts and increasing the productivity of auto supplier (Reingold *et al.*, 2000). The list of companies innovating with new technologies could go on and on.

Not only do existing companies benefit from new information technology but new companies are created to develop, implement and sell new technologies. The US venture capital market is crucial for supporting "start-ups." In 1999, venture capitalists provided $45 billion to fledgling companies, compared with $3.7 billion in 1990. With the help of venture capital, half-formed ideas have the potential to be transformed into world-class products and services. A successful initial public offering of company stock or a private capital placement can create young millionaires almost overnight.

Technological advances benefiting labor productivity are taking place in the context of a globalization of economic activity. Improved labor productivity lowers costs of production. Growing global markets do the same. While expanding global markets provide opportunities for US-based firms to increase sales, worldwide competition places further pressure on costs of production and prices.

Put it all together, proponents argue, computers, well-functioning venture capital markets and globalization have brought faster productivity growth which permits rising profits, rising wages, falling unemployment and falling inflation at the same time. A "New Economy" is being born.

The notion of a "New Economy" spread rapidly among corporate executives, political and economic pundits and politicians. *The Economist*, a British business magazine, while treating the "New Economy" notion sarcastically, explained its appeal:

It flatters chief executives by implying that the cost-cutting and corporate restructuring of the early 1990s have yielded permanent

productivity gains. It appeals to investors by providing a rosy scenario to justify today's robust stock market valuations. And it suits
politicians of all stripes. The Clinton administration can claim that
the New Economy hinges largely on its fiscal rectitude and trade
openness. Republicans can look further back; Jim Saxton, who
chairs the Joint Economic Committee of Congress, claims the
New Economy began in the 1980s and derives, in part, from
lower-income tax rates introduced during Ronald Reagan's
Presidency. (*The Economist*, 1997)

For *The Economist*, the "New Economy" was a fad feeding off its own
hyperbole. It bore similarities to the early 1980s fad of "supply-side"
economics whose most enthusiastic supporters claimed that deep
tax-cuts would pay for themselves. They did not and federal budget
deficits unprecedented in the post Second World War period
emerged.

Yet, is there a "New Economy?" The evidence is mixed. First, the
3 percent annual growth rate of the 1990s is no different than the
3 percent annual growth rate of the 1980s and is below the 3.25 percent annual growth rate of the 1970s and the 4.4 percent annual
growth rate of the 1960s. Yet "New Economy" proponents point to
the second half of the 1990s when economic growth accelerated in
line with increases in investment in information technology. The
4.1 percent growth rate from 1996 to 1999 does exceed the growth
rates of the 1980s and 1970s and is close to the 1960s growth rate.
However, is four years a long enough period of time to proclaim a
"New Economy?" Furthermore, it is possible to find four consecutive
years in the 1970s (1976–79) and the 1980s (1983–86) when the
economy grew more rapidly than in 1996–99. Granted, these time
periods were at the beginning of economic expansions when rapid
economic growth would be expected and "New Economy" advocates
point out that what is new about the expansion of the 1990s is that
the economy grew more rapidly as the expansion proceeded.

Second, the 2.6 percent annual rate of growth of labor productivity from 1996 to 1999 does represent a significant improvement over
productivity performance from 1973 to 1995 and is just below the
productivity growth rate of the 1960s. Yet, to what degree were
improvements in productivity driven by information technology?
Oliner and Sichel (2000) find that two-thirds of the 1 percentage
point acceleration in labor productivity growth from the first half of

the 1990s to the second half of the 1990s was due to the growing use of information technology throughout the nonfarm business sector and rapidly improving technology for producing semiconductors and computers. These findings are consistent with a "New Economy" interpretation. On the other hand, Gordon (2000) believes that skepticism is the proper approach to take to assertions of a "New Economy." He argues that the productivity revival has occurred primarily within the production of computer hardware, peripherals and telecommunications equipment with substantial spillover to the 12 percent of the economy involved in the manufacture of durable goods. However, he does not find any evidence of a "New Economy" effect on productivity growth in the other 88 percent of the economy. The "jury is still out" on the "New Economy" and its long-term impact on the US economy.

THE PEOPLE LEFT BEHIND

As the twentieth century drew to a close, the US economy was the strongest it had been in several decades. Since March 1991, the end of the last recession, the economy had grown continuously for 106 months, and it was still growing. Profits were strong, unemployment was low, inflation was negligible, investment was high, labor productivity was improving and the economy was expanding at a rapid rate.

Some Americans benefited handily from the economic boom. Income inequality continued increasing in the 1990s, though more slowly than in the 1980s. The wealthiest 5 percent of families saw their real incomes rise by 1 percent annually, a more rapid rate of improvement than the 0.7 percent annual real income growth experienced by families in the top fifth of the income distribution.

On the other hand, for many Americans it would take approximately a decade for their real income to return to the level at the end of the 1980s. It was not until 1998 that real median family income exceeded its 1989 level. Thus, over a nine-year period, real median family income essentially stagnated (Mishel *et al.*, 1999; Jones Jr. and Weinberg, 2000).

The proportion of people living below the poverty line remained relatively stable since the late 1980s despite the long, continuous economic expansion. The plight of poor Americans steadily improved in the second half of the 1990s. The poverty rate steadily declined from 15.1 percent in 1993 to 11.8 percent in 1999. While the poverty rate in 1999 was the lowest since 1979, it was still only slightly below the 12.8 percent level of 1989. Similarly, the economic boom by-passed an important group of working Americans, the "working poor." The poverty rate for people in full-time working families with children did not change since the late 1980s (Dalaker and Proctor, 2000, p. B-2; Iceland, 2000).

While women still confronted discrimination in the labor market, they continued making gains during the economic expansion of the 1990s. However, gender-based occupational segregation declined at a slower rate in the 1990s than in the 1980s and 1970s. Similarly, the rate of improvement in the female to male earnings ratio slowed as well in the 1990s in contrast to the 1980s. Among full-time, year-round workers, the median annual income of women was 73 percent of that of men in 1998, just slightly above the 71 percent level in 1992 (Blau and Kahn, 2000; US Bureau of the Census, Current Population Reports, Series P60-206, 1999).

While African–Americans gained from the strong labor market accompanying the economic boom, serious problems remained. Most positively, black male annual income rose sharply relative to white male annual income. In 1992, the black male to white male median income ratio was 61 percent. It rose to approximately 70 percent by 1998. A part of the relative improvement was certainly due to the gains made by African–Americans as a result of sustained economic growth. However, more than half of the relative gain occurred from 1992 to 1993, and it is difficult to relate this sharp jump to overall conditions in the economy (*Economic Report of the President*, 2000, p. 344). Also, in a positive vein, occupational differentiation by race continued to decrease as African–American men increased their relative presence in professional, executive and skilled craft positions.

On the other hand, African–American men were dropping out of the labor force at a faster rate than white men. The labor force participation rate for African–American men fell from 70.7 percent in 1992 to 68.7 percent in 1999 while for white men it just dropped from 76.5 percent to 75.6 percent (*Economic Report of the President*, 2000, p. 352). And while the unemployment rates of both white and African–American men fell to levels quite low by historical standards in 1999 – 3.6 percent and 8.2 percent respectively, black men were still more than twice as likely than white men to be unemployed. (*Economic Report of the President*, 2000, p. 354). Thus, while labor markets were tight, employers were still reluctant to hire African–American men, even for low-paying positions.

The long economic expansion also provided opportunities for African–American women. Just as with African–American men, their annual income rose more rapidly than the annual income of white women. In 1992, the black female to white female median annual income ratio was 81 percent. By 1994, it had risen to approximately 90 percent and it remained at this level through 1998. However, the narrowing racial income gap was not due to gains in the relative earnings of African–American year-round, full-time workers. Of those who worked year-round, full-time in 1998, black women earned 87 percent as much as their white counterparts, below the 91 percent figure of 1992 (*Economic Report of the President*, 2000, p. 344).

African–American women entered the labor force in increasing numbers. Their labor force participation rate jumped from 58.5 percent in 1992 to 63.5 percent in 1999. White women also were more likely to be in the labor force. However, their labor force participation rate only grew from 57.7 percent to 59.6 percent over the same time period (*Economic Report of the President*, 2000, p. 352). The welfare reforms requiring many public assistance recipients to actively seek work were one factor in the increased presence of women in the labor force. And many did find jobs, albeit low-paying ones, given the increased availability of work due to the growing economy.

Not only did their labor force participation rates rise, the unemployment rate of African–American women fell to 7.8 percent by 1999, quite low by historical standards. However, African–American women were still more than twice as likely to be unemployed as were white women (*Economic Report of the President*, 2000, p. 354). There continued to be a reduction in the overall level of racial segregation among women workers. From 1992 to 1999, African–American women increased their relative presence in executive and professional positions. And they continued moving into clerical jobs.

CONCLUSION

Experiencing an economic boom as the twentieth century came to a close, the United States was prosperous and smug. Just a decade before, in 1989, it was Japan that was prosperous and smug. The "Japanese model" appeared invincible. Japanese products seemed so superior and their corporate practices so effective. However, in 1999, it was Japan that was mired in a stagnating economy, still feeling the effects of a stock market crash and a real estate collapse.

The European economies were also facing difficulties. They were growing more slowly and had higher rates of unemployment than the United States. Their common currency, the Euro, was quite weak relative to the dollar. At the close of the twentieth century, the dollar was still the main international reserve currency.

This was the case even though the United States was running large balance of trade deficits. While in the 1980s, the balance of trade deficits were interpreted as a sign of US weakness, an indication of declining international competitiveness, now they were viewed as crucial for reviving the world economy. The United States was functioning as a "buyer of last resort," providing a source of demand, for example, for countries immersed in the Asian financial crisis.

The United States was still borrowing from abroad to finance the trade deficit, essentially by selling US Treasury bonds to non-Americans. At the start of the 1990s, borrowing foreign cash to pay for imports was criticized as evidence of national weakness. By the end of the decade, the large amount of US Treasury securities held abroad was viewed as a sign of global confidence in the United States. The United States had the dominant economy in the world. And as long as foreigners were willing to hold US securities or dollars, the United States would be able to pursue its political–economic goals without worrying that the large balance of trade and balance of payments deficits would eventually lead to a crisis of confidence in the dollar and a sharp fall in the value of the currency.

At the end of the twentieth century, there was no longer any talk of copying a Japanese or a German economic model. The Communist model died with the break up of the Soviet Union. Throughout the world, the US economy seemed to be looked on with a measure of envy and fear. There did not seem to be any end in sight to the US economic expansion. Yet, all economic booms eventually come to an end.

Bibliography

BOOKS (including books not referenced
in the chapters)

Aaron, Henry J., *Politics and the Professors: The Great Society in Perspective* (Washington, DC: The Brookings Institution, 1978)
AFL–CIO Committee on the Evolution of Work, *The Changing Situation of Workers and Their Unions* (Washington, DC: AFL–CIO, 1985)
America's New Beginning: A Program for Economic Recovery (Washington, DC: US Government Printing Office, 1981)
Anderson, Karen, *Wartime Women: Sex Roles, Family Relations, and the Status of Women During World War II* (Westport, CT: Greenwood Press, 1981)
Armstrong, Philip, Glyn, Andrew and Harrison, John, *Capitalism Since World War II: The Making and Breakup of the Great Boom* (London: Fontana, 1984)
Armstrong, Philip, Glyn, Andrew and Harrison, John, *Capitalism Since 1945* (Oxford: Blackwell, 1991)
Aronowitz, Stanley, *False Promises: The Shaping of American Working Class Consciousness* (New York: McGraw-Hill, 1973)
Bailey, Stephen K., *Congress Makes a Law: The Story Behind the Employment Act of 1946* (New York: Columbia University Press, 1950)
Bancroft, Gertrude, *The American Labor Force: Its Growth and Changing Composition* (New York: John Wiley, 1958)
Barnet, Richard J. and Muller, Ronald E., *Global Reach: The Power of Multinational Corporations* (New York: Simon and Schuster, 1974)
Blau, Francine D. and Ferber, Marianne A., *The Economics of Women, Men, and Work*, Second Edition (Englewood Cliffs, NJ: Prentice-Hall, 1992)
Block, Fred L., *The Origins of International Economic Disorder: A Study of United States International Monetary Policy from World War II to the Present* (Berkeley: University of California Press, 1977)
Bluestone, Barry and Bluestone, Irving, *Negotiating the Future: A Labor Perspective on American Business* (New York: Basic Books, 1992)
Bluestone, Barry and Harrison, Bennett, *The Deindustrialization of America: Plant Closings, Community Abandonment, and the Dismantling of Basic Industry* (New York: Basic Books, 1982)
Bluestone, Barry and Harrison, Bennett, *Growing Prosperity: The Battle for Growth with Equity in the 21st Century* (Boston: Houghton Mifflin Company, 2000)
Blyth C.A., *American Business Cycles 1945–50* (New York: Praeger, 1969)
Bowles, Samuel, Gordon, David M. and Weisskopf, Thomas E., *Beyond the Waste Land: A Democratic Alternative to Economic Decline* (Garden City, NY: Anchor Press/Doubleday, 1983)
Bowles, Samuel, Gordon, David M. and Weisskopf, Thomas E., *After the Wasteland: A Democratic Economics for the Year 2000* (Armonk, NY: M.E. Sharpe, 1990)
Brody, David, *Workers in Industrial America: Essays on the 20th Century Struggle* (New York: Oxford University Press, 1980)

Brooks, Thomas R., *Toil and Trouble: A History of American Labor* (New York: Dell, 1971)

Browning, Robert X., *Politics and Social Welfare Policy in the United States* (Knoxville, TN: University of Tennessee Press, 1986)

The *Business Week* Team, *The Decline of U.S. Power (and what we do about it)* (Boston: Houghton Mifflin, 1980)

Calleo, David P., *The Imperious Economy* (Cambridge, MA: Harvard University Press, 1982)

Calleo, David P. and Rowland, Benjamin M., *America and the World Political Economy: Atlantic Dreams and National Realities* (Bloomington, IN: Indiana University Press, 1973)

Campagna, Anthony S., *U.S. National Economic Policy 1917–1985* (New York: Praeger, 1987)

Chafe, William H., *The American Woman: Her Changing Social, Economic and Political Roles, 1920–1970* (New York: Oxford University Press, 1972)

Chafe, William H., *The Unfinished Journey: America Since World War II* (New York: Oxford University Press, 1986)

Chamberlain, Neil W., *The Union Challenge to Management Control* (New York: Harper, 1948)

Chandler, Lester V., *Inflation in the United States, 1940–1948* (New York: Harper, 1951)

Cherry, Robert, *Discrimination: Its Economic Impact on Blacks, Women, and Jews* (Lexington, MA: D.C. Heath, 1989)

Clinton, Bill, *Putting People First: A National Economic Strategy for America* (Little Rock, AK: The Clinton for President Committee, 1992)

Collins, Robert M., *The Business Response to Keynes 1929–64* (New York: Columbia University Press, 1981)

Collins, Robert M., *More: The Politics of Economic Growth in Postwar America* (New York: Oxford University Press, 2000)

Craver, Charles B., *Can Unions Survive? The Rejuvenation of the American Labor Movement* (New York: New York University Press, 1993)

Crozier, Michel J., Huntington, Samuel P. and Watanuki, Joji, *The Crisis of Democracy: Report of the Governability of Democracies to the Trilateral Commission* (New York: New York University Press, 1975)

Dam, Kenneth W., *The Rules of the Game* (Chicago: University of Chicago Press, 1982)

Dalaker, Joseph, US Census Bureau, Current Population Reports, Series P60-207, *Poverty in the United States: 1998* (Washington, DC: US Government Printing Office, 1999)

Dalaker, Joseph and Proctor, Bernadette D., US Census Bureau, Current Population Reports, Series P60-210, *Poverty in the United States: 1999* (Washington, DC: US Government Printing Office, 2000)

Davies, Gareth, *From Opportunity to Entitlement: The Transformation and Decline of Great Society Liberalism* (Lawrence, KS: University Press of Kansas, 1996)

Davis, Mike, *Prisoners of the American Dream* (London: Verso, 1986)

Dertouzos, Michael L., Lester, Richard K. and Solow, Robert M., *Made in America: Regaining the Productive Edge* (Cambridge, MA: MIT Press, 1989)

DuBoff, Richard B., *Accumulation & Power: An Economic History of the United States* (Armonk, NY: M.E. Sharpe, 1989)

Dulles, Foster R. and Dubofsky, Melvyn, *Labor in America: A History, Fourth Edition* (Arlington Heights, IL: Harlan Davidson, 1984)

Eckes, Alfred E., *A Search for Solvency: Bretton Woods and the International Monetary System, 1941–1971* (Austin, TX: University of Texas Press, 1975)

Economic Report of the President, 1979 (Washington, DC: US Government Printing Office, 1979)

Economic Report of the President, 1982 (Washington, DC: US Government Printing Office, 1982)

Economic Report of the President, 1983 (Washington, DC: US Government Printing Office, 1983)

Economic Report of the President, 1985 (Washington, DC: US Government Printing Office, 1985)

Economic Report of the President, 1986 (Washington, DC: US Government Printing Office, 1986)

Economic Report of the President, 1988 (Washington, DC: US Government Printing Office, 1988)

Economic Report of the President, 1990 (Washington, DC: US Government Printing Office, 1990)

Economic Report of the President, 1991 (Washington, DC: US Government Printing Office, 1991)

Economic Report of the President, 1992 (Washington, DC: US Government Printing Office, 1992)

Economic Report of the President, 1993 (Washington, DC: US Government Printing Office, 1993)

Economic Report of the President, 1994 (Washington, DC: US Government Printing Office, 1994)

Economic Report of the President, 1995 (Washington, DC: US Government Printing Office, 1995)

Economic Report of the President, 1997 (Washington, DC: US Government Printing Office, 1997)

Economic Report of the President, 1998 (Washington, DC: US Government Printing Office, 1998)

Economic Report of the President, 1999 (Washington, DC: US Government Printing Office, 1999)

Economic Report of the President, 2000 (Washington, DC: US Government Printing Office, 2000)

Economic Report of the President, 2001 (Washington, DC: US Government Printing Office, 2001)

Edwards, Richard, *Rights At Work: Employment Relations in the Post-Union Era* (Washington, DC: The Brookings Institution, 1993)

Edwards, Richard C., Reich, Michael and Weisskopf, Thomas E., *The Capitalist System*, Second Edition (Englewood Cliffs, NJ: Prentice Hall, 1978)

Eichengreen, Barry, *Golden Fetters: The Gold Standard and the Great Depression, 1919–1939* (New York: Oxford University Press, 1995)

Ellwood, David T., *Poor Support: Poverty in the American Family* (New York: Basic Books, 1988)

Employment and Earnings, XL, I (January 1993)

Employment and Earnings, XLVII, I (January 2000)

Employment and Training Report of the President (Washington, DC: US Government Printing Office, 1977)

Employment and Training Report of the President (Washington, DC: US Government Printing Office, 1981)

Foner, Philip S., *Organized Labor and the Black Worker 1619–1981* (New York: International Publishers, 1982)

Fones-Wolf, Elizabeth A., *Selling Free Enterprise: The Business Assault on Labor and Liberalism, 1945–60* (Urbana, IL: University of Illinois Press, 1994)

Freeman, Richard B. and Medoff, James L., *What Do Unions Do?* (New York: Basic Books, 1984)

Friedman, Benjamin M., *Day of Reckoning: The Consequences of American Economic Policy* (New York: Vintage Books, 1989)

Gabarino, Joseph W., *Wage Policy and Long-Term Contracts* (Washington, DC: The Brookings Institution, 1962)

Galbraith, John K., *The Great Crash 1929* (Boston: Houghton Mifflin, 1997)

Galenson, Walter, *The American Labor Movement, 1955–1995* (Westport, CT: Greenwood Press, 1996)

Gardner, Richard N., *Sterling–Dollar Diplomacy in Current Perspective: The Origins and the Prospects of Our International Economic Order* (New York: Columbia University Press, 1980)

Gatlin, Rochelle, *American Women Since 1945* (London: Macmillan, 1987)

Gilpin, Robert, *The Political Economy of International Relations* (Princeton: Princeton University Press, 1987)

Goldfield, Michael, *The Decline of Organized Labor in the United States* (Chicago: University of Chicago Press, 1987)

Goodwin, Craufurd (ed.), *Exhortation and Controls: The Search for a Wage–Price Policy, 1945–71* (Washington, DC: The Brookings Institution, 1975)

Gordon, Robert A., *Economic Instability and Growth: The American Record* (New York: Harper and Row, 1974)

Gould, William B. IV, *A Primer on American Labor Law*, Second Edition (Cambridge, MA: MIT Press, 1986)

Gowa, Joanne, *Closing the Gold Window: Domestic Politics and the End of Bretton Woods* (Ithaca: Cornell University Press, 1983)

Greider, William, *Secrets of the Temple: How the Federal Reserve Runs the Country* (New York: Simon and Schuster, 1987)

Gropman, Alan L., *Mobilizing U.S. Industry in World War II* (Washington, DC: National Defense University Press, 1996)

Gueron, Judith M. and Pauly, Edward, *From Welfare to Work* (New York: Russell Sage Foundation, 1991)

Guttmann, Robert, *How Credit-Money Shapes the Economy* (Armonk, NY: M.E. Sharpe, 1994)

Hargrove, Erwin C. and Morley, Samuel A. (eds), *The President and the Council of Economic Advisers: Interviews with CEA Chairmen* (Boulder, CO: Westview, 1984)

Harris, Howell, J., *The Right to Manage: Industrial Relations Policies of American Business in the 1940s* (Madison, WI: University of Wisconsin Press, 1982)

Harris, William H., *The Harder We Run: Black Workers Since the Civil War* (New York: Oxford University Press, 1982)

Harris, Seymour F., *Economics of the Kennedy Years* (New York: Harper & Row, 1964)

Harrison, Bennett and Bluestone, Barry, *The Great U-Turn: Corporate Restructuring and the Polarizing of America* (NewYork: Basic Books, 1988)

Haveman, Robert H., *A Decade of Federal Antipoverty Programs: Achievements, Failures, and Lessons* (New York: Academic Press, 1977)

Heath, Jim F., *John F. Kennedy and the Business Community* (Chicago: University of Chicago Press, 1969)

Heller, Walter W., *New Dimensions of Political Economy* (New York: W.W. Norton, 1967)

Hickman, Bert G., *Growth and Stability of the Postwar Economy* (Washington, DC: The Brookings Institution, 1960)

Hodgson, Godfrey, *America in Our Time: From World War II to Nixon What Happened and Why* (New York: Vintage, 1976)

Hogan, Michael J., *The Marshall Plan: America, Britain, and the Reconstruction of Europe, 1947–52* (Cambridge: Cambridge University Press, 1987)

Hogan, Michael J., *A Cross of Iron: Harry S. Truman and the Origins of the National Security State, 1945–1954* (Cambridge: Cambridge University Press, 1998)

Holmans A.E., *United States Fiscal Policy, 1945–1959: Its Contribution to Economic Stability* (London: Oxford University Press, 1961)

Jaynes, Gerald D. and Williams, Robin M. Jr., *A Common Destiny: Blacks and American Society* (Washington, DC: National Academy Press, 1989)

Jacobs, Eva E. (ed.), *Handbook of U.S. Labor Statistics: Employment, Earnings, Prices, Productivity and Other Labor Data*, First Edition (Lanham, MD: Bernan Press, 1997)

Kaldor, Mary, *The Disintegrating West* (Middlesex, England: Penguin Books, 1979)

Kaplan, Edward, *American Trade Policy, 1923–1995* (Westport, CT: Greenwood Press, 1996)

Katz, Harry C., *Shifting Gears: Changing Labor Relations in the U.S. Automobile Industry* (Cambridge, MA: MIT Press, 1987)

Katz, Michael B., *The Undeserving Poor: From the War on Poverty to the War on Welfare* (New York: Pantheon Books, 1989)

Kessler-Harris, Alice, *Out to Work: A History of Wage-Earning Women in the United States* (New York: Oxford University Press, 1982)

Kissinger, Henry, *Years of Upheaval* (Boston: Little, Brown, 1982)

Kochan, Thomas A., *Collective Bargaining and Industrial Relations* (Homewood, IL: Richard D. Irwin, 1980)

Kochan, Thomas A., Katz, Harry C. and McKersie, Robert B., *The Transformation of American Industrial Relations* (New York: Basic Books, 1986)

Koistinen, Paul A.C., *The Military–Industrial Complex: A Historical Perspective* (New York: Praeger, 1980)

Kolko, Joyce and Kolko, Gabriel, *The Limits of Power: The World and United States Foreign Policy, 1945–1954* (New York: Harper and Row, 1972)

Krugman, Paul, *The Return of Depression Economics* (New York: W.W. Norton, 1999)

Kryder, Daniel, *Divided Arsenal: Race and the American State During World War II* (Cambridge: Cambridge University Press, 2000)

Kunz, Diane B., *Butter and Guns: America's Cold War Economic Diplomacy* (New York: Free Press, 1997)

Kuttner, Robert, *The End of Laissez-Faire: National Purpose and the Global Economy After the Cold War* (New York: Alfred A. Knopf, 1991)

Levitan, Sar A., Carlson, Peter E. and Shapiro, Isaac, *Protecting American Workers: An Assessment of Government Programs* (Washington, DC: Bureau of National Affairs, 1986)

Levitan, Sar A., Johnston, William B. and Taggart, Robert, *Still A Dream: The Changing Status of Blacks Since 1960* (Cambridge, MA: Harvard University Press, 1975)

Lewis, Wilfred Jr., *Federal Fiscal Policy in the Postwar Recessions* (Washington, DC: The Brookings Institution, 1962)

Lipsitz, George, *Class and Culture in Cold War America: "Rainbow at Midnight"* (South Hadley, MA: J.F. Bergin, 1982)

MacEwan, Arthur, *Debt and Disorder: International Economic Instability and U.S. Imperial Decline* (New York: Monthly Review Press, 1990)

Marmor, Theodore, R., Mashaw, Jerry L. and Harvey, Philip L., *America's Misunderstood Welfare State: Persistent Myths, Enduring Realities* (New York: Basic Books, 1990)

Matusow, Allen J., *The Unraveling of America: A History of Liberalism in the 1960s* (New York: Harper and Row, 1984)

Meeropol, Michael, *Surrender: How the Clinton Administration Completed the Reagan Revolution* (Ann Arbor, MI: University of Michigan Press, 1998)

Meier, Gerald M., *Problems of a World Monetary Order* (New York: Oxford University Press, 1974)

Millis, Harry A. and Brown, Emily C., *From the Wagner Act to Taft–Hartley: A Study of National Labor Policy and Labor Relations* (Chicago: University of Chicago Press, 1950)

Milward, Alan S., *The Reconstruction of Western Europe, 1945–51* (Berkeley: University of California Press, 1984)

Mishel, Lawrence, Bernstein, Jared and Schmitt, John, *The State of Working America, 1996–97* (Armonk, NY: M.E. Sharpe, 1997)

Mishel, Lawrence, Bernstein, Jared and Schmitt, John, *The State of Working America, 1998–99* (Ithaca, NY: ILR Press, 1999)

Mishel, Lawrence and Frankel, David M., *The State of Working America: 1990–91* (Armonk, NY: M.E. Sharpe, 1991)

Mitchell, Daniel J.B., *Unions, Wages, and Inflation* (Washington, DC: The Brookings Institution, 1980)

Moody, Kim, *An Injury to All: The Decline of American Unionism* (New York: Verso, 1988)

Moody, Kim and Sagovac, Kim, *Time Out! The Case for a Shorter Work Week* (Detroit: Labor Education and Research Project, 1995)

Mort, Jo-Ann (ed.), *Not Your Father's Union Movement: Inside the AFL–CIO* (London: Verso, 1998)

Moynihan, Daniel P., *The Politics of a Guaranteed Income: The Nixon Administration and the Family Assistance Plan* (New York: Vintage Press, 1973)

Murphy, Henry C., *The National Debt in War and Transition* (New York: McGraw-Hill, 1950)

New York Times, *The Downsizing of America* (New York: Times Books, 1996)

Northrup, Herbert R., *Organized Labor and the Negro* (New York: Harper, 1944)

Okun, Arthur M., *The Political Economy of Prosperity* (New York: W.W. Norton, 1970)

Parboni, Ricardo, *The Dollar and its Rivals* (London, England: Verso, 1981)

Peterson, Wallace C., *Our Overloaded Economy: Inflation, Unemployment, and the Crisis in American Capitalism* (Armonk, NY: M.E. Sharpe, 1982)

Pierson, Paul, *Dismantling the Welfare State? Reagan, Thatcher and the Politics of Retrenchment* (Cambridge: Cambridge University Press, 1994)

Piven, Frances F. and Cloward, Richard A., *Regulating the Poor: The Functions of Public Welfare* (New York: Vintage Books, 1971)

Polenberg, Richard, *War and Society: The United States, 1941–45* (Philadelphia: J.B. Lippincott, 1972)

Quadagno, Jill S., *The Color of Welfare* (New York: Oxford University Press, 1994)

Ratner, Sidney, Soltow, James H. and Sylla, Richard, *The Evolution of the American Economy: Growth, Welfare, and Decisionmaking* (New York: Macmillan, 1993)

Reich, Michael, *Racial Inequality: A Political–Economic Analysis* (Princeton, NJ: Princeton University Press, 1981)

Renshaw, Patrick, *American Labour and Consensus Capitalism, 1935–1990* (London: Macmillan, 1991)

Rockoff, Hugh, *Drastic Measures: A History of Wage and Price Controls in the United States* (New York: Cambridge University Press, 1984)

Rukstad, Michael G., *Macroeconomic Decision Making in the World Economy: Text and Cases* (Chicago: Dryden Press, 1986)

Rukstad, Michael G., *Macroeconomic Decision Making in the World Economy: Text and Cases*, Third Edition (Orlando, FL: Dryden Press, 1992)

Scammell W.M., *The International Economy Since 1945* (New York: St Martin's Press, 1980)

Schatz, Ronald W., *The Electrical Workers: A History of Labor at General Electric and Westinghouse 1923–60* (Urbana, IL: University of Illinois Press, 1983)

Schiller, Bradley R., *The Economics of Poverty and Discrimination*, Sixth Edition (Englewood Cliffs, NJ: Prentice Hall, 1995)

Schwarz, John E., *America's Hidden Success: A Reassessment of Twenty Years of Public Policy* (New York: W.W. Norton, 1983)

Seidman, Joel, *American Labor From Defense to Reconversion* (Chicago: University of Chicago Press, 1953)

Sheahan, John, *The Wage–Price Guideposts* (Washington, DC: The Brookings Institution, 1967)

Shultz, George P. and Dam, Kenneth W., *Economic Policy Beyond the Headlines* (New York: W.W. Norton, 1977)

Slaughter, Jane, *Concessions and How to Beat Them* (Detroit: Labor Education and Research Project, 1983)

Slichter, Sumner, Healy, James J. and Livernash, E. Robert, *The Impact of Collective Bargaining on Management* (Washington, DC: The Brookings Institution, 1960)

Solomon, Robert, *The International Monetary System, 1945–1981* (New York: Harper and Row, 1982)

Spain, Daphne and Bianchi, Suzanne M., *Balancing Act: Motherhood, Marriage, and Employment Among American Women* (New York: Russell Sage Foundation, 1996)

Spero, Joan E. and Hart, Jeffrey A., *The Politics of International Relations*, Fifth Edition (New York: St Martins Press, 1997)

Stein, Herbert, *The Fiscal Revolution in America* (Chicago: University of Chicago Press, 1969)

Stein, Herbert, *Presidential Economics: The Making of Economic Policy from Roosevelt to Reagan and Beyond* (New York: Simon and Schuster, 1984)

Stevens, Robert W., *Vain Hopes, Grim Realities: The Economic Consequences of the Vietnam War* (New York: Franklin Watts, 1976)

Stockman, David A., *The Triumph of Politics: How the Reagan Revolution Failed* (New York: Harper and Row, 1986)

Taub, Edward and Needleman, Ruth, *Introduction to Labor Law Update* (Gary, IN: Division of Labor Studies, Indiana University, Northwest, 1984)

Taylor, George W., *Government Regulation of Industrial Relations* (New York: Prentice-Hall, 1948)

US Bureau of the Census, Current Population Reports, Series P60-178, *Workers with Low Earnings: 1964 to 1990* (Washington, DC: US Government Printing Office, 1992)

US Bureau of the Census, Current Population Reports, Series P60-206, *Money Income in the United States: 1998* (Washington, DC: US Government Printing Office, 1999)

US Bureau of the Census, Special Demographic Analyses, *American Women: Three Decades of Change* (Washington, DC: US Government Printing Office, 1983)

US Bureau of the Census, *Statistical Abstract of the United States: 1993* (Washington, DC: US Government Printing Office, 1993)

US Bureau of the Census, *Statistical Abstract of the United States: 1996* (Washington, DC: US Government Printing Office, 1996)

US Bureau of the Census, *Statistical Abstract of the United States: 1998* (Washington, DC: US Government Printing Office, 1998)

US Bureau of the Census, *Statistical Abstract of the United States: 1999* (Washington, DC: US Government Printing Office, 1999)

US Department of Health, Education and Welfare, *Work in America* (Cambridge, MA: MIT Press, 1973)

US Department of Labor, Bureau of Labor Statistics, *Handbook of Labor Statistics, 1978* (Washington, DC: US Government Printing Office, 1979)

US Department of Labor, Bureau of Labor Statistics, *Handbook of Labor Statistics, 1983* (Washington, DC: US Government Printing Office, 1983)

US Department of Labor, Bureau of Labor Statistics, *Labor Force Statistics Derived from the Current Population Survey, 1948–87* (Washington, DC: US Government Printing Office, 1988)

Vatter, Harold G., *The U.S. Economy in the 1950s: An Economic History* (Chicago: University of Chicago Press, 1963)

Vatter, Harold G., *The U.S. Economy in World War II* (New York: Columbia University Press, 1985)

Vogel, David, *Fluctuating Fortunes: The Political Power of Business in America* (New York: Basic Books, 1989)

Volcker, Paul A. and Gyohten, Toyoo, *Changing Fortunes: The World's Money and the Threat to American Leadership* (New York: Times Books, 1992)

Wachtel, Howard M., *The Money Mandarins: The Making of a Supranational Economic Order* (New York: Pantheon Books, 1986)

Weaver, Robert C., *Negro Labor: A National Problem* (New York: Harcourt Brace, 1946)

Weber, Arnold R. and Mitchell, Daniel J.B., *The Pay Board's Progress: Wage Controls in Phase II* (Washington, DC: The Brookings Institution, 1978)

Williams, William A., *The Tragedy of American Diplomacy* (New York: Dell, 1962)

Wolfson, Martin H., *Financial Crises: Understanding the Postwar U.S. Experience* (Armonk, NY: M.E. Sharpe, 1986)

Wolfson, Martin H., *Financial Crises: Understanding the Postwar U.S. Experience*, Second Edition (Armonk, NY: M.E. Sharpe, 1994)

Women's Work Project, *Separated and Unequal: Discrimination Against Women Workers After World War II (The U.A.W. 1944–54)* (New York: Union for Radical Political Economics, n.d.)

Wood, Robert E., *From Marshall Plan to Debt Crisis: Foreign Aid and Development Choices in the World Economy* (Berkeley: University of California Press, 1986)

Zieger, Robert H., *The CIO 1935–1955* (Chapel Hill, NC: University of North Carolina Press, 1995)

ARTICLES (including chapters from edited books)

Abraham, Katherine G., "Restructuring the Employment Relationship: The Growth of Market-mediated Work Arrangements," in Katherine G. Abraham and Robert W. McKersie (eds), *New Developments in the Labor Market: Toward a New Institutional Paradigm* (Cambridge, MA: MIT Press, 1990), 85–120

Abraham, Katherine G. and Taylor S.K., "Firms' Use of Outside Contractors: Theory and Evidence," *Journal of Labor Economics*, XIV, 3 (July, 1996), 394–424

Ackerman, Frank and MacEwan, Arthur, "Inflation, Recession and Crisis, Or Would You Buy a New Car from this Man?" *Review of Radical Political Economics*, IV, 2 (August 1972), 4–37

Arsen, David D., "International and Domestic Forces in the Postwar Golden Age," *Review of Radical Political Economics*, XXIII, 1 & 2 (Spring and Summer 1991), 1–11

Baldwin, Marc and McHugh, Richard, "Unprepared for Recession: The Erosion of State Unemployment Insurance Coverage Fostered by Policy in the 1980s," Economic Policy Institute Briefing Paper (1992)

Barbash, Jack, "Union Response to the 'Hard Line,'" *Industrial Relations*, I, 1 (October 1961), 25–38

Barbash, Jack, "The Causes of Rank-And-File Unrest," in Joel Seidman (ed.), *Trade Union Government and Collective Bargaining: Some Critical Issues* (New York: Praeger, 1970), 39–79

Baron, Harold M., "The Demand for Black Labor," *Radical America*, V, 2 (March–April 1971) (reprinted by New England Free Press, Somerville, MA)

Bernanke, Ben S., "Nonmonetary Effects of the Financial Crisis in the Propagation of the Great Depression," *American Economic Review*, LXXIII, 3 (June 1983), 257–276

Bernstein, Barton J., "The Removal of War Production Board Controls on Business, 1944–1946," *Business History Review*, XXXIX (Summer 1965), 243–260

Bernstein, Barton J. "America in War and Peace: The Test of Liberalism," in Barton J. Bernstein (ed.), *Towards A New Past: Dissenting Essays in American History* (New York: Pantheon, 1968), 289–321

Blau, Francine D., "The Data on Women Workers, Past, Present, and Future," in Ann H. Stromberg and Shirley Harkness (eds), *Women Working: Theories and Facts in Perspective* (Palo Alto, CA: Mayfield, 1978), 29–62

Blau, Francine D. and Ferber, Marianne A., "Occupations and Earnings of Women Workers," in Karen S. Koziara, Michael H. Moskow and Lucretia D. Tanner (eds), *Working Women: Past, Present, Future* (Washington, DC: Bureau of National Affairs, 1987), 37–68

Blau, Francine D. and Hendricks, Wallace E., "Occupational Segregation by Sex: Trends and Prospects," *Journal of Human Resources*, XIV, 2 (Spring 1979), 197–210

Blau, Francine D. and Kahn, Lawrence M., "Gender Differences in Pay," *Journal of Economic Perspectives*, XIV, 4 (Fall 2000), 75–99

Blecker, Robert A., "The Trade Deficit and U.S. Competitiveness," in Robert A. Blecker (ed.), *U.S. Trade Policy and Global Growth* (Armonk, NY: M.E. Sharpe, 1996), 179–214

Block, Fred L., "Economic Instability and Military Strength: The Paradoxes of the 1950 Rearmament Decision," *Politics and Society*, X, 1 (1980), 35–58

Bluestone, Barry and Rose, Stephen, "The Macroeconomics of Work Time," *Review of Social Economy*, LVI, 4 (Winter, 1998), 425–441

Blum, Albert A., "Why Unions Grow," *Labor History*, IX, 1 (Winter 1968), 39–72

Boddy, Raford and Crotty, James, "Food Prices: Planned Crisis in Defense of the Empire," *Socialist Revolution*, V (April 1975), 101–109

Borden, William S., "Defending Hegemony: American Foreign Economic Policy," in Thomas G. Patterson (ed.), *Kennedy's Quest for Victory: American Foreign Policy, 1961–1963* (New York: Oxford University Press, 1989), 57–85

Borum, Joan D., Conley, James R. and Wasilewski, Edward J., "The Outlook for Collective Bargaining in 1988," *Monthly Labor Review*, CXI, 1 (January 1988), 10–23

Bosworth, Barry, "Phase II: The U.S. Experiment with an Incomes Policy," *Brookings Papers on Economic Activity*, 2 (1972), 343–383

Bowles, Samuel, Gordon, David M. and Weisskopf, Thomas E., "Power and Profits: The Social Structure of Accumulation and the Profitability of the Postwar Economy," *Review of Radical Political Economics*, XVIII, 1 & 2 (Spring & Summer 1986), 132–167

Branson, William H., "Trends in United States International Trade and Investment Since World War II," in Martin Feldstein (ed.), *The American Economy in Transition* (Chicago: University of Chicago Press, 1980), 183–257

Brown, Clair, "Unemployment Theory and Policy," *Industrial Relations*, XXII, 2 (Spring 1983), 164–185

Brown, Douglass V. and Myers, Charles A., "The Changing Industrial Relations Philosophy of American Management," *Proceedings of the Ninth Annual Meeting of the Industrial Relations Research Association*, December 28–29, 1956 (Madison, WI: Industrial Relations Research Association, 1957), 84–99

Buchele, Robert and Christiansen, Jens, "Industrial Relations and Relative Income Shares in the United States," *Industrial Relations*, XXXII, 1 (Winter 1993), 49–71

Buchele, Robert and Christiansen, Jens, "Employment and Productivity Growth in Europe and North America: The Impact of Labor Market Institutions," *International Review of Applied Economics*, XIII, 3 (September 1999), 313–332

Business Week, "NLRB Rulings that are Inflaming Labor Relations," June 11 (1984) 122–130

Capelli, Peter, "Comment on 'Is Pattern Bargaining Dead?'" *Industrial and Labor Relations Review*, XLIV, 1 (October 1990), 152–155

Carter, Robert L. and Marcus, Maria L., "Trade Union Racial Practices and the Law," in Julius Jacobson (ed.), *The Negro and the American Labor Movement* (Garden City, NY: Anchor Press/Doubleday, 1968), 380–400

Clarke, Stephen V.O., "Perspectives on the United States External Position Since World War II," *Federal Reserve Bulletin of New York Quarterly Review* (Summer 1980), 21–38

Crotty, James R. and Rapping, Leonard A., "The 1975 Report of the President's Council of Economic Advisers: A Radical Critique," *American Economic Review*, LXV, 5 (December 1975), 791–811

Crowther, Don Q., "Work Stoppages Caused by Labor–Management Disputes in 1945," *Monthly Labor Review*, LXII, 5 (May 1946), 718–735

Crowther, Don Q., "Work Stoppages Caused by Labor–Management Disputes in 1946," *Monthly Labor Review*, LXIV, 5 (May 1947), 780–800

Crowther, Don Q. and Cole, Ruth S., "Strikes in 1943," *Monthly Labor Review*, LVIII, 5 (May 1944), 927–947

Crowther, Don Q. and Cole, Ruth S., "Strikes and Lockouts in 1944," *Monthly Labor Review*, LX, 5 (May 1945), 957–973

Cummings, Laurie D., "The Employed Poor: Their Characteristics and Occupations," *Monthly Labor Review*, LXXXVII, 7 (July 1965), 828–835

Currie, Elliott, "The Politics of Jobs: Humphrey–Hawkins and the Dilemmas of Full Employment," *Socialist Review*, VII, 2 (March–April 1977), 93–114

Cutcher-Gershenfeld, Joel, Kochan, Thomas A. and Wells, John C., "How do Labor and Management View Collective Bargaining?" *Monthly Labor Review*, CXXI, 10 (October 1998), 23–31

Danziger, Sheldon and Haveman, Robert, "The Reagan Budget: A Sharp Break with the Past," *Challenge*, XXIV, 2 (May/June 1981), 5–13

Derber, Milton and Netreba, Sidney, "Money and Real Weekly Earnings During Defense, War and Reconversion Periods," *Monthly Labor Review*, LXIV, 6 (June 1947), 983–996

Devine, James N., "Underconsumption, Over-Investment, and the Origins of the Great Depression," *Review of Radical Political Economics*, XV, 2 (Summer 1983), 1–28

Dwyer, Paula, "The Blow to Affirmative Action May Not Hurt that Much," *Business Week*, July 3 (1989), 61–62

Eakins, David W., "Business Planners and America's Postwar Expansion," in David Horowitz (ed.), *Corporations and the Cold War* (New York: Monthly Review Press, 1969), 143–171

Eastwood, Mary, "Legal Protection Against Sex Discrimination," in Ann H. Stromberg and Shirley Harkness (eds), *Women Working: Theories and Facts in Perspective* (Palo Alto, CA: Mayfield, 1978), 108–123

Edelman, Peter, "The Worst Thing Bill Clinton Has Done," *The Atlantic Monthly*, March 1997, 43–58

Eisenhower, Dwight D., "The Military–Industrial Complex," in Roger E. Bolton (ed.), *Defense and Disarmament: The Economics of Transition* (Englewood Cliffs, NJ: Prentice-Hall, 1966), 173–175

Fairris, David, "Appearance and Reality in Postwar Shopfloor Relations," *Review of Radical Political Economics*, XXII, 4 (Winter 1990), 17–43

Fairris, David, "The Crisis in US Shopfloor Relations," *International Contributions to Labour Studies*, 1 (1991), 133–156

Flaherty, Sean, "Strike Activity, Worker Militancy, and Productivity Change in Manufacturing, 1961–1981," *Industrial and Labor Relations Review*, XL, 4 (July 1987), 585–600

Focus, VIII, I (Spring, 1985), Institute for Research on Poverty, University of Wisconsin, Madison

Flanagan, Robert J., "Wage Concessions and Long-Term Union Wage Flexibility," *Brookings Papers on Economic Activity*, 1 (1984), 183–216

Freeman, Ralph E., "Postwar Monetary Policy," in Ralph E. Freeman (ed.), *Postwar Economic Trends in the United States* (New York: Harper, 1960), 51–90

Freeman, Richard B., "Why are Unions Faring Poorly in NLRB Representation Elections," in Thomas A. Kochan (ed.), *Challenges and Choices Facing American Labor* (Cambridge, MA: MIT Press, 1985), 45–64

Freeman, Richard B., "Unionism Comes to the Public Sector," *Journal of Economic Literature*, XXIV, 1 (March 1986), 41–86

Freeman, Richard B., "Contraction and Expansion: The Divergence of Private Sector and Public Sector Unionism in the United States," *Journal of Economic Perspectives*, II, 2 (Spring 1988), 63–88

Freeman, Richard B. and Medoff, James L., "New Estimates of Private Sector Unionism in the United States," *Industrial and Labor Relations Review*, XXXII, 2 (January 1979), 143–174

Friedman, Sheldon, "Trade Adjustment Assistance: Time for Action, Not False Promises," *AFL–CIO Reviews the Issues*, Report No. 53 (September 1991)

Friedman, Sheldon and Prosten, Richard, "How Come One Team Still Has to Play with Its Shoelaces Tied Together?," *Proceedings of the 1993 Spring Meeting* (Madison, WI: Industrial Relations Research Association, 1993), 477–485

Fullerton, Don, "Inputs to Tax Policy-Making: The Supply-Side, the Deficit, and the Level Playing Field," in Martin Feldstein (ed.), *American Economic Policy in the 1980s* (Chicago: University of Chicago Press, 1994), 165–208

Garfinkle, Stuart H., "Occupations of Women and Black Workers, 1962–74," *Monthly Labor Review*, XCVIII, 11 (November 1975), 25–35

Gold, David A., "The Rise and Decline of the Keynesian Coalition," *Kapitalistate*, 6 (Fall 1977), 129–161

Golden, Lonnie and Appelbaum, Eileen, "What was Driving the 1982–88 Boom in Temporary Employment? Preferences of Workers or Decisions and Power of Employers," *American Journal of Economics and Sociology*, LI, 4 (1992), 473–493

Goldfield, Michael, "Labor in American Politics – Its Current Weakness," *Journal of Politics*, XLVIII, 1 (February 1986), 2–29

Gordon, Robert J., "Does the 'New Economy' Measure Up to the Great Inventions of the Past?" *Journal of Economic Perspectives*, XIV, 4 (Fall 2000), 49–74

Gramlich, Edward M., Kasten, Richard and Sammartino, Frank, "Growing Inequality in the 1980s: The Role of Federal Taxes and Cash Transfers," in Sheldon Danziger and Peter Gottschalk (eds), *Uneven Tides: Rising Inequality in America* (New York: Russell Sage Foundation, 1993), 225–249

Grodin, Joseph, "The Kennedy Labor Board," *Industrial Relations*, III, 2 (February 1964), 33–45

Haber, William, "Manpower," in Colston E. Warne (ed.), *Yearbook of American Labor: Vol. 1, War Labor Policies* (New York: Philosophical Library, 1945), 225–232

Hathaway, Dale E., "Food Prices and Inflation," *Brookings Papers on Economic Activity*, 1 (1974), 63–109

Henle, Peter, "Economic Effects: Reviewing the Evidence," in Jerome M. Rosow (ed.), *The Worker and the Job* (Englewood Cliffs, NJ: Prentice-Hall, 1974), 119–144

Hermansen, Svend O., "An Analysis of the Recent Tax Cut," *National Tax Journal*, XVIII, 4 (December 1965), 425–429

Hill, Herbert, "The AFL–CIO and the Black Worker: Twenty-Five Years After the Merger," *Journal of Intergroup Relations*, X, 1 (Spring 1982), 5–78

Iceland, John, US Census Bureau, Current Population Reports, Series P23-203, *Poverty Among Working Families: Findings from Experimental Poverty Measures* (Washington, DC: US Government Printing Office, 2000)

Jeszeck, Charles, "Structural Change in CB: The U.S. Tire Industry," *Industrial Relations*, XXV, 3 (Fall 1986), 229–247

Johnson, Chalmers, "Economic Crisis in East Asia: The Clash of Capitalisms," *Cambridge Journal of Economics*, XXII, 6 (November 1998), 653–661

Jones Jr., Arthur F. and Weinberg, Daniel H., US Census Bureau, Current Population Reports, Series P60-204, *The Changing Shape of the Nation's Income Distribution, 1947–1998* (Washington, DC: US Government Printing Office, 2000)

Karper, Mark D., "Tires," in David B. Lipsky and Clifford B. Donn (eds), *Collective Bargaining in American Industry: Contemporary Prospects and Future Directions* (Lexington, MA: D.C. Heath, 1987), 79–101

Katz, Harry C., "The Decentralization of Collective Bargaining: A Literature Review and Comparative Analysis," *Industrial and Labor Relations Review*, XLVII, 1 (October 1993), 3–22

Kaufman, Bruce E. "The Propensity to Strike in American Manufacturing," *Proceedings of the Thirtieth Annual Meeting of the Industrial Relations Research Association*, December 28–30, 1977 (Madison, WI: Industrial Relations Research Association, 1978), 419–426

Kerr, Clark, "Employer Policies in Industrial Relations, 1945 to 1947," in Colton E. Warne (ed.), *Labor in Postwar America* (New York: Remsen Press, 1949), 43–76

Kilborn, Peter T., "The Daily News Strike Tests the Will of Weakened Labor," *New York Times*, January 27 (1991), Section I, p. 1

King, Mary C., "Occupational Segregation by Race and Sex, 1940–88," *Monthly Labor Review*, CXV, 4 (April 1992), 30–37

Klein, Janice A. and Wanger E.D., "The Legal Setting for the Emergence of the Union Avoidance Strategy," in Thomas A. Kochan (ed.), *Challenges and Choices Facing American Labor* (Cambridge, MA: MIT Press, 1985), 75–89

Kotlowitz, Alex, "Work Rules Shape Up as Major Battleground in U.S. Labor Disputes," *Wall Street Journal*, June 4 (1986), 1, 19

Kuhn, James, "Electrical Products," in Gerald Somers (ed.), *Collective Bargaining: Contemporary American Experience* (Madison, WI: Industrial Relations Research Association, 1980), 209–262

Lawrence, Robert Z., "An Analysis of the 1977 U.S. Trade Deficit," *Brookings Papers on Economic Activity*, 1 (1978), 159–186

Leonard, Jonathan S., "The Impact of Affirmative Action on Employment," *Journal of Labor Economics*, II, 4 (1984), 439–463

Leonard, Jonathan S., "Women and Affirmative Action," *Journal of Economic Perspectives*, III, 1 (Winter 1989), 61–75

Leonard, Jonathan S., "The Impact of Affirmative Action Regulation and Equal Employment Law on Black Employment," *Journal of Economic Perspectives*, IV, 4 (Fall 1990), 47–63

Leonard, Jonathan S., "The Specter of Affirmative Action," in Clark Kerr and Paul Staudohar (eds), *Labor Economics and Labor Relations: Markets and Institutions* (Cambridge, MA: Harvard University Press, 1994), 574–600

Lichtenstein, Nelson, "UAW Bargaining Strategy and Shop-Floor Conflict: 1946–1970," *Industrial Relations*, XXIV, 3 (Fall 1985), 360–381

Livernash, E.R., "Special and Local Negotiations," in John T. Dunlop and Neil W. Chamberlain (eds), *Frontiers of Collective Bargaining* (New York: Harper and Row, 1967), 27–49

Lo, Clarence Y.H., "Theories of the State and Business Opposition to Increased Military Spending," *Social Problems*, XXIX, 4 (April 1982), 424–438

Lynn, Laurence E., "A Decade of Policy Developments in the Income–Maintenance System," in Robert H. Haveman (ed.), *A Decade of Federal Antipoverty Programs: Achievements, Failures, and Lessons* (New York: Academic Press, 1977), 55–117

MacEwan, Arthur, "International Economic Crisis and the Limits of Macropolicy," *Socialist Review*, XI, 5 (September–October 1981), 113–138

Mandel, Michael S. "The Next Downturn," *Business Week*, October 9 (2000), 173–180

Mandel, Michael, Naughton, Keith, Burns, Greg and Baker, Stephen, "How Long Can This Last?" *Business Week*, May 19, 1997, 29–34

Michl, Thomas R., "The Two-Stage Decline in U.S. Nonfinancial Corporate Profitability," *Review of Radical Political Economics*, XX, 4 (Winter 1988), 1–22

Milkman, Ruth, "Organizing the Sexual Division of Labor: Historical Perspectives in 'Women's Work' and the American Labor Movement," *Socialist Review*, X, 1 (January–February 1980), 95–150

Mills D.Q., "Construction Wage Stabilization: A Historic Perspective," *Industrial Relations*, XI, 3 (October 1972), 350–365

Mills D.Q., "Construction," in Gerald Somers (ed.), *Collective Bargaining: Contemporary American Experience* (Madison, WI: Industrial Relations Research Association, 1980), 49–97

Mitchell, Daniel J.B., "Shifting Wage Norms in Wage Determination," *Brookings Papers on Economic Activity*, 2 (1985), 575–599

Mitchell, Daniel J.B., "A Decade of Concession Bargaining," in Clark Kerr and Paul D. Staudohar (eds), *Labor Economics and Labor Relations: Markets and Institutions* (Cambridge, MA: Harvard University Press, 1994), 435–474

Moran, Donald W., "Human Resource Implications of the Budget Cuts," in *Proceedings of the Thirty-Fourth Annual Meeting* (Madison, WI: Industrial Relations Research Association, 1982), 400–405

Naples, Michele I., "Cyclical and Secular Productivity Slowdowns," in Robert Cherry, Christine D'Onofrio, Cigdem Kurdas, Thomas R. Michl, Fred Moseley, Michele I. Naples (eds), *The Imperiled Economy: Macroeconomics from a Left Perspective* (New York: Union for Radical Political Economics, 1987), 159–170

Norton, Eleanor H., "Quota Scare Must Not Destroy Civil Rights Bill," *Wall Street Journal*, May 16, 1991, A17

Oliner, Stephen D. and Sichel, Daniel E., "The Resurgence of Growth in the Late 1990s: Is Information Technology the Story?" *Journal of Economic Perspectives*, XIV, 4 (Fall 2000), 3–22

Owens, Patrick, "Unionbuster at the N.L.R.B.," *The Nation*, July 23–30 (1983), 71–74

Pechman, Joseph A., "Individual Income Tax Provisions of the Revenue Act of 1964," *Journal of Finance*, XX, 2 (May 1965), 247–272

Pidgeon, Mary E., "Women Workers and Recent Economic Change," *Monthly Labor Review*, LXV, 6 (December 1947), 666–671

Pollock, Michael A. and Bernstein, Aaron, "A Work Revolution in U.S. Industry: More Flexible Rules on the Job are Boosting Productivity," *Business Week*, May 16 (1983), 100–110

Power, Marilyn, "The Reagan Administration and the Regulation of Labor: The Curious Case of Affirmative Action," in Samuel Rosenberg (ed.), *The State and the Labor Market* (New York: Plenum Press, 1989), 197–206

Prosten, Richard, "The Longest Season: Union Organizing in the Last Decade, a/k/a How Come One Team Has to Play with Its Shoelaces Tied Together?" *Proceedings of the Thirty-First Annual Meeting of the Industrial Relations Research Association*, August 29–31, 1978 (Madison, WI: Industrial Relations Research Association, 1979), 240–249

Reich, Michael, "Postwar Racial Income Differences: Trends and Theories," in Garth Mangum and Peter Philips (eds), *Three Worlds of Labor Economics* (Armonk, NY: M.E. Sharpe, 1988), 144–167

Reingold, Jennifer, Stepanek, Marcia and Brady, Diane, "Why the Productivity Revolution Will Spread," *Business Week*, February 14 (2000), 112–118

Rosen, Sumner M., "The CIO Era, 1935–55," in Julius Jacobson (ed.), *The Negro and the American Labor Movement* (Garden City, NY: Anchor Press/Doubleday, 1968), 188–208

Rosenberg, Sam, "Reagan Social Policy and Labour Force Restructuring," *Cambridge Journal of Economics*, VII, 2 (June 1983), 179–196

Rosenberg, Sam, "Restructuring the Labor Force: The Role of Government Policies," in Robert Cherry, Christine D'Onofrio, Cigdem Kurdas, Thomas R. Michl, Fred Mosely and Michele I. Naples (eds), *The Imperiled Economy: Through the Safety Net* (New York: Union for Radical Political Economics, 1988), 27–38

Rosenberg, Samuel, "The Restructuring of the Labor Market, the Labor Force, and the Nature of Employment Relations in the United States in the 1980s," in Samuel Rosenberg (ed.), *The State and the Labor Market* (New York: Plenum Press, 1989), 63–85

Rosenberg, Sam, "The Workweek of Capital and the Workweek of Labor: The United States Experience," *Economies et Societes*, XVII, 9-10 (September–October 1991), 155–173

Rosenberg, Sam, "More Work for Some, Less Work for Others: Working Hours in the USA," *Futures*, XXV, 5 (June 1993), 551–560

Rosenberg, Sam, "The More Decentralized Mode of Labor Market Regulation in the United States," *Economies et Societes*, XVIII, 8 (August 1994), 35–58

Rosenberg, Sam and Lapidus, June, "Contingent and Non-Standard Work in the United States: Towards a More Poorly Compensated, Insecure Workforce," in Alan Felstead and Nick Jewson (eds), *Global Trends in Flexible Labour* (London: Macmillan, 1999), 62–83

Rosenberg, Sam and Weisskopf, Thomas E., "A Conflict Theory Approach to Inflation in the Postwar U.S. Economy," *American Economic Review*, LXXXI, 2 (May 1981), 42–47

Rosenthal, Steve, "Building to Win, Building to Last: The AFL–CIO Political Program," in Jo-Ann Mort (ed.), *Not Your Father's Union Movement: Inside the AFL–CIO* (London: Verso, 1998), 99–111

Ruggles, P., "Measuring Poverty," *Focus*, XIV, 1 (Spring 1992), University of Wisconsin, Madison, Institute for Research on Poverty, 1–9

Schloss, Clara F., "Employment in Government-Owned, Privately Operated, New War Plants," *Monthly Labor Review*, LIX, 1 (July 1944), 39–46

Schnittker, John A., "The 1972–73 Food Price Spiral," *Brookings Papers on Economic Activity*, 2 (1973), 498–507

Seeber, Ronald L. and Cooke, William N., "The Decline in Union Success in NLRB Representation Elections," *Industrial Relations*, XXII, 1 (Winter 1983), 34–44

Simkin, William E., "Refusals to Ratify Contracts," in Joel Seidman (ed.), *Trade Union Government and Collective Bargaining: Some Critical Issues* (New York: Praeger, 1970), 107–145

Sleemi, F.R. and Brown, P.I., "Collective Bargaining Agreements in 1992," *Monthly Labor Review*, CXVI, 5 (May 1993), 22–33

Smith, R.E. and Vavrichek, B., "The Minimum Wage: Its Relation to Incomes and Poverty," *Monthly Labor Review*, CX, 6 (June 1987), 24–30

Staines, Graham L., "Is Worker Dissatisfaction Rising?" *Challenge*, XXII, 2 (May/June 1979), 38–45

St. Antoine, Theodore J., "The Role of Law," in Jack Stieber, Robert B. McKersie and D. Quinn Mills (eds), *U.S. Industrial Relations 1950–1980: A Critical Assessment* (Madison, WI: Industrial Relations Research Association, 1981), 159–197

Stern, James, "The Kennedy Policy: A Favorable View," *Industrial Relations*, III, 2 (February 1964), 21–32

Stevenson, Mary, "Women's Wages and Job Segregation," in Richard C. Edwards, Michael Reich and David M. Gordon (eds), *Labor Market Segmentation* (Lexington, MA: D.C. Heath, 1975), 243–255

Stockman, David A., "How to Avoid an Economic Dunkirk," *Challenge*, XXIV, 1 (March/April 1981), 17–21

Sweezy, Paul M. and Magdoff, Harry, "The End of U.S. Hegemony," *Monthly Review*, XXIII, 5 (October 1971), 1–16

Tasini, Jonathan, "Why Labor is at Odds with the NLRB," *New York Times*, October 30 (1988), Section III, p. 4

Teixeira, Ruy A. and Rogers, Joel, "Who Deserted the Democrats in 1994?" *American Prospect*, No. 23 (Fall 1995), 73–77

The *Economist*, "Assembling the New Economy: A New Economic Paradigm is Sweeping America. It Could Have Dangerous Consequences," September 12 (1997)

Troy, Leo, "The Growth of Union Membership in the South, 1939–1953," *Southern Economic Journal*, XXIV, 4 (April 1958), 407–420

Tsuru, Tsuyoshi, "The Reserve Army Effect, Unions, and Nominal Wage Growth," *Industrial Relations*, XXX, 2 (Spring 1991), 251–270

Ulman, Lloyd, "The Development of Trades and Labor Unions," in Seymour E. Harris (ed.), *American Economic History* (New York: McGraw Hill, 1961), 366–482

Ulman, Lloyd, "The Labor Policy of the Kennedy Administration," *Proceedings of the Fifteenth Annual Meeting of the Industrial Relations Research Association*, December 27–28, 1962 (Madison, WI: Industrial Relations Research Association, 1963), 248–262

US Department of Labor, Bureau of Labor Statistics, "Postwar Work Stoppages Caused by Labor–Management Disputes," *Monthly Labor Review*, LXIII, 12 (December 1946), 872–892

US Department of Labor, Bureau of Labor Statistics, "News Release: Work experience survey shows that 116.3 million workers worked at some time in 1982, and 26.5 million encountered some unemployment," (Washington, DC: US Government Printing Office, August 9, 1983)

US Department of Labor, Bureau of Labor Statistics, "Employment in Perspective: Women in the Labor Force," Report 872 (Washington, DC: US Government Printing Office, First Quarter, 1994)

Vroman, Wayne and Abowd, John M., "Disaggregated Wage Developments," *Brookings Papers on Economic Activity*, 1 (1988), 313–338

Wachter, Michael and Carter, William H., "Norm Shifts in Union Wages: Will 1989 Be a Replay of 1969?" *Brookings Papers on Economic Activity*, 2 (1989), 233–264

Wade, Robert, "From 'Miracle' to 'Cronyism': Explaining the Great Asian Slump," *Cambridge Journal of Economics*, XXII, 6 (November 1998), 693–706

Wall Street Journal, "Some Seniority that Arose from Bias is Exempted by Justices from Sanctions," June 1, 1977

Webb, Laura B., "Wartime Changes in Consumer Goods in American Markets," *Monthly Labor Review*, LV, 5 (November 1942), 891–902

Webb, Laura B., "Recent Changes in the Character of Civilian Textiles and Apparel," *Monthly Labor Review*, LVII, 3 (September 1943), 421–434

Weisskopf, Thomas E., Bowles, Samuel and Gordon, David M., "Hearts and Minds: A Social Model of U.S. Productivity Growth," *Brookings Papers on Economic Activity*, 2 (1983), 381–441

Westcott, Diane N., "Blacks in the 1970s: Did they Scale the Job Ladder?" *Monthly Labor Review*, CV, 6 (June 1982), 29–38

Winter, Ralph E., "New Givebacks: Even Profitable Firms Press Workers to Take Permanent Pay Cuts," *Wall Street Journal*, March 6 (1984), 1, 24

Wolfbein, Seymour L., "War and Post-War Trends in Employment of Negroes," *Monthly Labor Review*, LX, 1 (January 1945), 1–5

Wool, Harold, "Recent Trends in the Labor Force," *Monthly Labor Review*, LXV, 6 (December 1947), 638–644

Wrenn, Rob, "The Decline of American Labor," *Socialist Review*, XV, 4–5 (July–October 1985), 89–117

Index

Supplemental Security Income (SSI)
program   220, 288–9
supply-side economics   190, 192,
277, 308
and monetarism   235–43
Sweeney, J. J.   292
Switzerland   167
sympathy strikes   67, 72

Taft-Hartley Act   64, 70–81
Taggart, R.   160
Taiwan   259
tariff reductions   177
tax cuts   108, 110, 113
"tax expenditures", use of   219
tax
plan   54
politics   190
rates   8, 54, 56, 109, 240
Tax Reduction and Simplification Act
of 1977   190
Tax Reform Act of 1986   241–2
tax revenues   61
Teamsters   293
technological innovation   306
telecommunications market   261
Temporary Assistance for
Needy Families
(TANF)   287–8
Thailand   301–3
Third Multifiber Arrangement
260
Third World nations   250
Trade Act of 1974   220
Trade Adjustment Assistance
(TAA)   220
cutbacks   245, 276
trade
deficit   162, 252–3, 260, 300–1
with Japan   258–9
Trade Expansion Act   164–5
trade
free   280
liberalization   177
surpluses   83, 170, 174

trade unions   71, 135–40, 213–18,
266–8
transfer payments   186, 277
Treaty of Rome   164
Truman administration   44, 48,
53–5, 57–8, 60, 67, 104
Truman Doctrine   92
Truman, President, H. S.   49, 53–4,
65, 67, 69,
Twentieth Century Fund   90

unemployment   7, 15, 44, 56, 61–2,
119–20, 123, 183–4, 189, 309
benefits   78, 126
Unemployment Insurance (UI)   11,
189, 239, 245
cutbacks   244, 276
unemployment
rate   6, 20, 52, 104, 112, 115,
132, 159, 187, 190, 236, 245,
254, 265, 297
unfair trade enforcement   206
union-management relations   31, 145
union-nonunion wage differential
213, 262
unions see also trade unions
busting   247
legitimacy of   136
membership   3, 12, 38, 74, 135,
266
security   29, 31
shop   72
United Aircraft Corporation   81
United Auto Workers (UAW)   26,
66, 68–9, 79–80, 126, 213, 215,
262, 264–5
United Electrical Workers   76, 133,
139
United Kingdom   258
United Mine Workers and Railroad
Brotherhoods   65, 70
United Rubber Workers (URW)   294
United States see also America
Bureau of Labor Statistics   66, 264
Department of Agriculture   150